Canary Islands

Lanzarote
p110

La Palma
p200

La Gomera
p180

Tenerife
p138

El Hierro
p224

Gran
Canaria

Fuerteventura
p86

Isabella Noble

Contents

PARQUE NACIONAL DE
GARAJONAY P186

STIAN KLO/LONELY PLANET ©

LA LAGUNA, TENERIFE P149

ALEKSANDAR TODOROVIC/SHUTTERSTOCK ©

LOVETHIEF PHOTOGRAPHY/GETTY IMAGES ©

LA PALMA P200

Contents

Welcome to the Canary Islands

Scented pine forests, haunting volcanoes, lunar-like landscapes, sandy coves, miles of Sahara-style dunes, beach-hugging resorts – the beautiful, unique Canary Islands wear many tantalising hats.

Otherworldly Landscapes

Marvel at the pine-forested peaks of Gran Canaria's mountainous interior, the tumbling waterfalls of La Palma or the subtropical greenery of Parque Nacional de Garajonay. Then contrast all this lushness with the extraordinary bare flatlands flanking Tenerife's El Teide, the surreal party of colours glittering across Lanzarote's lava fields, the gentle flower-filled hillsides of El Hierro, and Fuerteventura's endless cacti-sprinkled plains. The Canary Islands' near-perfect temperatures mean that, year-round, you can soak up fantastical, varied landscapes otherwise only found by crossing continents.

The Great Outdoors

It's this very diversity that makes outdoor pursuits such an easily accessible pleasure of the Canaries. Hike the many footpaths criss-crossing the islands, from meandering coastal trails to challenging mountain treks to tranquil forest walks; go diving or snorkelling in blissfully warm waters inhabited by more than 350 species of fish (and the odd shipwreck); or pump up the adrenaline by riding the wind and the waves – kitesurfing, windsurfing, surfing and paragliding are all big here. Then slow things down with horse rides, boat trips, kayaking and paddleboarding jaunts or beachfront yoga.

Art & Architecture

Contrary to expectations, the Canary Islands are immensely rich in both original art and architecture – you just need to know where to look. The spectacular surrealist canvases of acclaimed painter Óscar Domínguez grace his Tenerife homeland; the enormous abstract sculptures of Martín Chirino are impossible to miss on Gran Canaria; and César Manrique's inspired 'interventions' pop up all over Lanzarote (and beyond). Everywhere, seek out the emblematic wooden balconies, leafy internal patios and painted facades that typify vernacular Canarian architecture, and pop into palm-shaded churches, many of which date back centuries.

Or Just Relax...

If your perfect trip is all about that enticing combo of R&R, the Canaries are the ultimate destination. The most obvious spot to kick back on is the beach, and you'll be spoilt for choice – from Fuerteventura's rolling dunes to Tenerife's sandy golden arcs to Isla Graciosa's wild strands. Yoga, meditation, massages and a world of other self-care therapies abound across the archipelago, and thalassotherapy is something of a local speciality. Alternatively, nothing soothes the soul like relaxing over a tropical cocktail or a glass of local wine as the sun sinks into the Atlantic.

MARQUES/SHUTTERSTOCK ©

Why I Love the Canary Islands

By Isabella Noble, Writer

Those who love Las Canarias are in on a sunny secret: there's a whole lot more to these sparkling, far-flung islands than their much-maligned reputation. Having grown up in Andalucía, I've always been fascinated by the Canaries, with their Latin American–influenced accents, cultural riches and glorious volcanoscapes. This is an entrancing, wonderfully varied pocket of Spain – intimately interwoven with the mainland, yet also worlds apart. I can't help but smile when landing on Lanzarote's volcanic shores; hiking through La Gomera's magical laurel forests; or escaping into natural pools on distant El Hierro.

For more about our writers, see p288

Above: Jardín de Cactus (p123), Lanzarote

Canary Islands

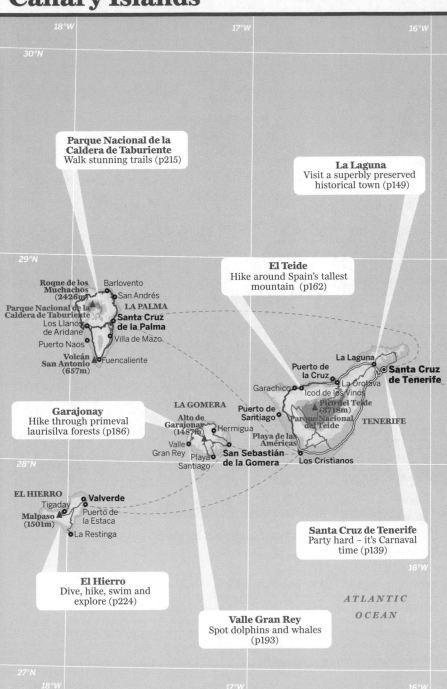

Parque Nacional de la Caldera de Taburiente
Walk stunning trails (p215)

La Laguna
Visit a superbly preserved historical town (p149)

El Teide
Hike around Spain's tallest mountain (p162)

Garajonay
Hike through primeval laurisilva forests (p186)

Santa Cruz de Tenerife
Party hard – it's Carnaval time (p139)

El Hierro
Dive, hike, swim and explore (p224)

Valle Gran Rey
Spot dolphins and whales (p193)

Roque de los Muchachos (2426m)
Barlovento
San Andrés
LA PALMA
Parque Nacional de la Caldera de Taburiente
Los Llanos de Aridane
Santa Cruz de la Palma
Puerto Naos
Villa de Mazo
Volcán San Antonio (657m)
Fuencaliente

La Laguna
Puerto de la Cruz
La Orotava
Santa Cruz de Tenerife
Garachico
Icod de los Vinos
Pico del Teide (3718m)
Parque Nacional del Teide
TENERIFE

LA GOMERA
Puerto de Santiago
Alto de Garajonay (1487m)
Hermigua
Valle Gran Rey
Playa Santiago
Playa de las Américas
San Sebastián de la Gomera
Los Cristianos

EL HIERRO
Tigaday
Valverde
Malpaso (1501m)
Puerto de la Estaca
La Restinga

ATLANTIC OCEAN

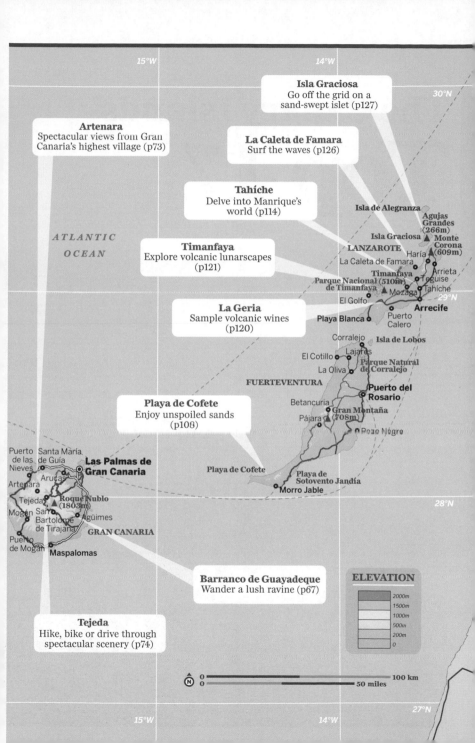

Isla Graciosa
Go off the grid on a
sand-swept islet (p127)

Artenara
Spectacular views from Gran
Canaria's highest village (p73)

La Caleta de Famara
Surf the waves (p126)

Tahíche
Delve into Manrique's
world (p114)

Timanfaya
Explore volcanic lunarscapes
(p121)

La Geria
Sample volcanic wines
(p120)

Playa de Cofete
Enjoy unspoiled sands
(p108)

Barranco de Guayadeque
Wander a lush ravine (p67)

Tejeda
Hike, bike or drive through
spectacular scenery (p74)

*ATLANTIC
OCEAN*

30°N

Isla de Alegranza

Agujas
Grandes
(266m)
Isla Graciosa
Monte
Corona
(609m)
LANZAROTE   Haría
La Caleta de Famara   Arrieta
Timanfaya   Teguise
Parque Nacional (510m)   Tahíche
de Timanfaya ▲ Mozaga
El Golfo   29°N
Arrecife
Playa Blanca   Puerto
Calero

Corralejo   Isla de Lobos
El Cotillo   Lajares
La Oliva Parque Natural
de Corralejo
FUERTEVENTURA
**Puerto del
Rosario**
Betancuria
Gran Montaña
Pájara (708m)
Pozo Negro

Puerto Santa María
de las de Guía
Nieves **Las Palmas de
Aruca Gran Canaria**
Artenara
Tejeda Roque Nublo
Mogán San (1803m)
Bartolomé Agüimes
de Tirajana
Puerto **GRAN CANARIA**
de Mogán **Maspalomas**

Playa de Cofete   Playa de
Sotovento Jandía
Morro Jable

28°N

ELEVATION

	2000m
	1500m
	1000m
	500m
	200m
	0

Ⓝ 0 ————————— 100 km
0 ————————— 50 miles

15°W   14°W   27°N

The Canary Islands'
Top 17

El Teide

1 Start with a gentle hike around the base of Tenerife's El Teide (p162), kidding yourself that you're enjoying a stroll on the surface of the moon; it really is that extraordinary. Trails take you deep into an alien landscape with red, yellow and brown craters resembling giant prehistoric molehills, bizarre volcanic rock formations and pebble-like lapilli. If you've booked a permit you can hike to the summit; otherwise, take it easy on the cable car to the top. Wrap up warm: it gets chilly up in the clouds (especially in winter).

Carnaval!

2 The *canarios* love a good party and, in Santa Cruz de Tenerife, the fiesta spirit reaches its sequin-clad crescendo during the annual Carnaval (p27). Festivities generally high-kick off with a flourish in early February and last for around three weeks, featuring gala performances, fancy dress competitions, fireworks and Rio-style parades. All of the Canary Islands celebrate Carnaval with dawn-to-dusk frivolity and distinctive customs, so book your accommodation way ahead of time (unless you aren't planning on sleeping at all, of course).

SANTIAGO URQUIJO/GETTY IMAGES ©

LUCIANO DE LA ROSA/SHUTTERSTOCK ©

ALEXANDER FRIEDRICH/500PX ©

TANE MAHUTA/GETTY IMAGES ©

5

Driving Gran Canaria's Rugged Heart

3 While most people stick to Gran Canaria's coast, it's in the mountains that you'll be wowed. Around every bend – and there are a lot of bends – you'll discover another stand of towering pines, or another dramatic view that will have you desperate for a spot to pull over. Luckily, there are also plenty of pretty villages, such as Tejeda (p74), dotted around where you can take a break to sample hearty soups and sugary cakes without ever tearing your eyes away from it all.

Hiking the Caldera de Taburiente

4 Put your best hiking boot forward and discover La Palma's spectacular Parque Nacional de la Caldera de Taburiente (p215) by trekking one of its numerous trails. For many, the pine forests and curtains of clouds slipping over the side of the sheer caldera walls add up to the finest walking experience in the archipelago. Walks here range from simple hour-long strolls to demanding day-long feats of endurance. Waterfall in the Parque Nacional de la Caldera de Taburiente

Fuerteventura's Stunning Beaches

5 Some of the Canary Islands' most glorious beaches are on Fuerteventura and possibly the finest of them all is remote southern Playa de Cofete (p108). To escape the rows of sunbeds, head for the northwest of the island and the wild beaches and thundering surf around El Cotillo. Windsurfers can catch waves at Playa de Sotavento de Jandía. For paddling tots and kids' activities, check out family-friendly beaches like Costa Calma and Caleta de Fuste.

César Manrique Art & Architecture

6 The late César Manrique's influence on Lanzarote is special in many ways. Forest-greens and sky-blues are the colours of door and window frames everywhere here. Then there are the steel sculptures decorating many roundabouts – classic examples of Manrique's fusion of natural phenomena and architectural wizardry. Wander Manrique's former home (p125), and don't miss his other sights: the Cueva de los Verdes, Jameos del Agua, Mirador del Río and Casa-Museo César Manrique.

La Laguna's Historic Old Quarter

7 Visit Tenerife's La Laguna (p149) for a stroll around one of the best-preserved historical quarters on the island: all cobbled alleys, spruced-up merchants' houses and pine-balconied mansions. The unique architecture and layout was originally provided as a model for many colonial towns in the Americas. La Laguna may have an air of old-fashioned history about it, but it's far from dull; there's a tangible youthful energy here. There's some vigorous nightlife too, plus plenty of terrace bars and cafes where you can kick back.

ROSHELEN/SHUTTERSTOCK ©

JESUS SIERRA/GETTY IMAGES ©

Parque Nacional de Garajonay

8 Peeking above the clouds that drift across La Gomera for much of the year, the 1487m Alto de Garajonay crowns both the small circular island and its magical Parque Nacional de Garajonay (p186). The eerily beautiful *laurisilva* (laurel) forests that carpet the top of the island date back beyond the last ice age, and wandering their shady trails is among the most serene experiences in the Canaries. The climb to the Alto is easy and the views from the summit, which take in snow-dusted El Teide on Tenerife, are outstanding.

El Hierro

9 From blissfully quiet electric-green pine forests and wind-sculpted juniper trees to shimmering natural saltwater pools and gentle hiking trails, the joys of far-flung El Hierro (p224) creep up on you slowly and before you know it the Canaries' little westernmost isle has your heart. Under the waves in the island's south, a hidden wonderland of weird and wonderful aquatic creatures awaits, which combined with warm waters and reliable diving conditions make this one of the most exciting diving locations in all of the North Atlantic.
Natural swimming pool, El Hierro

Artenara

10 On and up into the central peaks beyond Tejeda sits Artenara (p73), the highest village in Gran Canaria, gazing out on enough extensive views and plunging panoramas to make you feel on top of the world. Choose your lookout, then turn to Artenara's astonishing caves, one serving as the cutest little chapel you'll ever see, and others converted into small homes with domestic paraphernalia. When all is almost said and done, dine in a cave restaurant, with even more views sprawling from your table.
Santuario de la Cuevita, Artenara (p74)

Farmers Markets

11 Glossy blue-black aubergines, blood-red tomatoes, garlicky sausages, buttery almond biscuits, gigantic garlic bulbs, freshly baked bread, pungent cheeses... Who can resist a farmers market? The Canary Islands do them very well – across all islands, weekly markets are fuelled by local produce, plenty of it organic and/or sustainably grown. Look for regional specialities such as creamy *queso de flor* from Gran Canaria (p63), sweet Malmsey wine from La Palma or La Gomera's goat's cheese (famously so delicious that Columbus packed stashes of it for his trip to the Americas).

Wine Tasting in Lanzarote

12 La Geria (p120) is not your standard bucolic viticulture postcard of lush green vineyards, rows of vines and verdant rolling hills. On Lanzarote, wine cultivation is, well, extraordinary, with vines grown in dimpled craters within volcanic-stone semicircles called *zocos*. Wine tasting is really made easy here: you can visit most of the main bodegas on the same stretch of road in La Geria, tasting, among others, the island's famous *malvasía* sweet wine, once the tipple of choice of the European aristocracy.

ELOI_OMELLA/GETTY IMAGES ©

Lanzarote Water Sports

13 Known to surfers as the 'Hawaii of Europe', the Canary Islands are full of world-class surf spots, but none comes with a bigger rep than Lanzarote's radical left reef break, El Quemao. For those not quite up to El Quemao standards, La Caleta de Famara (p126) suits surfers of all levels and offers ideal conditions for learners to hop on a board. All across the island, other delicious watery pursuits run from kayaking, snorkelling and diving to sailing and stand-up paddleboarding yoga.

Surfers on Lanzarote

ORBON ALIJA/GETTY IMAGES ©

Barranco de Guayadeque

14 The best time to visit this lush ravine (p67) in Gran Canaria is springtime, when the almond trees are in brilliant pink-and-white bloom. Year-round, however, it is leafy and lovely, flanked by steep mountains where caves have been dug out for restaurants, bars and even a chapel. Time your visit for a mealtime, when you can dine deep within the rock. Walk off your lunch by following one of the trails, which reward with sprawling views stretching right to the sea.

Parque Nacional de Timanfaya

15 Without a doubt one of the most unworldly landscapes you'll lay eyes on, Lanzarote's Parque Nacional de Timanfaya (p121) is a natural canvas of shimmery greys, earthy reds and pine-green clashing against the brilliant-blue sky. Formed in the 18th century by a volcanic eruption, this beautiful, fiercely protected land can only be explored by bus tour or, if you're organised, by guided walk. Head out hiking in the surrounding Parque Natural de los Volcanes for a soul-stirring taster. Park landscape behind sign

Spotting Cetaceans

16 Human tourists aren't the only creatures who enjoy swimming and cavorting in the Atlantic Ocean off the Canary Islands. Year-round (but especially from March to June), pods of whales and dolphins also love a good splash around in the warm waters. The channel between Tenerife and La Gomera (p194) is their favourite holiday destination, and if you're staying on either of these islands, a whale- and dolphin-watching boat tour – with an environmentally responsible operator – will almost certainly be a highlight of your time in the Canaries.

Isla Graciosa

17 There aren't many places in Europe with traffic-free roads, but beautiful, diminutive Isla Graciosa (p127) goes one better – the eighth Canary Island doesn't even have roads. Well, not paved ones anyway. Jump on the ferry from Órzola on Lanzarote and within half an hour you're indulging in some of life's simplest pleasures: cycling on sandy tracks, sunbathing on wild, empty beaches, enjoying a plate of freshly caught fish alongside the amiable islanders, and wandering the near-deserted sand-lashed streets of Caleta de Sebo.

Need to Know

For more information, see Survival Guide (p261).

Currency
Euro (€)

Language
Spanish

Visas
Generally not required for stays of up to 90 days; some nationalities will need a Schengen visa.

Money
Debit or credit cards are the easiest way to handle money; bring some extra cash in case of an emergency.

Mobile Phones
Buy a pay-as-you-go mobile with credit from €30. Local SIM cards are widely available and can be used in unlocked GSM phones.

Time
Greenwich Mean Time (UTC+0); daylight savings time in summer

When to Go

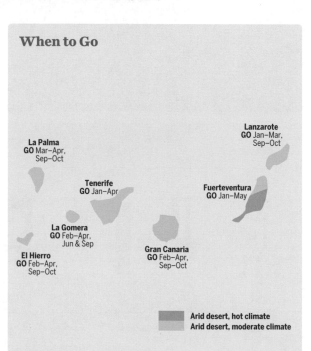

Lanzarote
GO Jan–Mar, Sep–Oct

La Palma
GO Mar–Apr, Sep–Oct

Tenerife
GO Jan–Apr

Fuerteventura
GO Jan–May

La Gomera
GO Feb–Apr, Jun & Sep

El Hierro
GO Feb–Apr, Sep–Oct

Gran Canaria
GO Feb–Apr, Sep–Oct

Arid desert, hot climate
Arid desert, moderate climate

High Season
(Dec–Apr & Jul–Aug)

➡ Coincides with Christmas, Carnaval season and Easter.

➡ Accommodation prices are highest in January and February.

➡ Midsummer, especially August, is holiday time on the Spanish mainland, so expect more visitors.

➡ July and August are the hottest months of the year, but temperatures rarely climb higher than 38°C.

➡ Rain is possible from January to March, especially in the mountains.

Shoulder (May–Jun & Sep–Nov)

➡ Temperatures average around 28°C, nights are cooler.

➡ Fewer tourists visit in the autumn overall.

➡ Higher altitudes, particularly in Gran Canaria, Tenerife and El Hierro, can be far cooler with some fog.

Useful Websites

Lonely Planet (www.lonely
planet.com/canary-islands)
Destination information, hotel
bookings, traveller forum and
more.

Canary Islands Government
(www.gobiernodecanarias.org)
Local government informa-
tion with plenty of details for
tourists.

Official Tourism Office
(www.holaislascanarias.com)
Region-wide and island-specific
information.

Daily Connections (www.
islandconnections.eu) Daily news.

Turismo Tenerife (www.
webtenerife.com) Helpful local
tourism board.

Turismo Gran Canaria (www.
grancanaria.com) Gran Canaria's
handy tourism body.

Important Numbers

If you're calling within the
Canaries, all numbers will have
a total of nine digits beginning
with 9 for landlines and 6 for
mobile phones.

Country code	34
International access code	00
Ambulance	061
Police	112

Exchange Rates

Australia	A$1	€0.63
Canada	C$1	€0.67
Japan	¥100	€0.80
New Zealand	NZ$1	€0.60
UK	£1	€1.15
US	US$1	€0.89

For current exchange rates see
www.xe.com.

Daily Costs
Budget: Less than €60

➡ Budget hotel room with
shared bathroom: €25–50

➡ Self-catering market/
supermarket meal: €6

➡ Bus ticket: €3

➡ Parks, churches, walks and
some museums: free

Midrange: €60–150

➡ Room in midrange hotel or
private apartment: €65–100

➡ Three-course meal with wine
in midrange restaurant: €30

➡ Admission to top museums,
galleries and sights: around €6

➡ Car hire per day: from €20

Top end: More than €150

➡ Boutique hotel or resort
room: from €100

➡ Fine-dining meal with wine:
from €50

➡ Taxi trip: €20

➡ Activities (diving, surfing,
boat tours): €60

Opening Hours

The following standard opening
hours are for high season only;
hours tend to decrease outside
that time:

Banks 8.30am to 2pm Monday
to Friday

Bars 7pm to midnight

Post offices 8.30am to 8.30pm
Monday to Friday, 9.30am to
1pm Saturday (large cities);
8.30am to 2.30pm Monday to
Friday, 9.30am to 1pm Saturday
(elsewhere)

Restaurants meals served 1pm
to 4pm and 7pm to late

Shops 10am to 2pm and 5pm to
9pm Monday to Friday, 10am to
2pm Saturday

Supermarkets 9am to 9pm
Monday to Saturday

Arriving in the Canary Islands

Aeropuerto de Gran Canaria
Regular buses to Las Palmas.
Taxis €30; around 25 minutes.

**Aeropuerto César Manrique–
Lanzarote** Regular buses to
Arrecife. Taxis €12; around 15
minutes.

Aeropuerto Tenerife Sur Regular buses to Los Cristianos. Taxis
€20; around 30 minutes.

Aeropuerto de Fuerteventura
Regular buses to Puerto del
Rosario. Taxis €10; around 15
minutes.

Etiquette

Greetings Spaniards almost
always greet friends and
strangers alike with a kiss on
each cheek, although two males
only do this if they're close
friends.

Church visits It is considered
rather disrespectful to visit
churches for the purposes of
tourism during Mass and other
worship services.

Punctuality As with mainland
Spain, timeliness is not held in
such high regard as it may be in
other European nations, so try
to go with the flow.

For much more on
getting around,
see p269.

Accommodation

Find more accommodation reviews throughout the On the Road chapters (from p51).

Accommodation Types

Apartments & Villas Self-catering and often the best-value option; much more common in the Canaries than hotels. *Aparthotels* blend the two, with kitchenettes and hotel services.

Casas Rurales Reimagined farmsteads or village houses; usually self-catering, and the perfect choice for those seeking to escape the bustle of the resorts. Book ahead to ensure someone is around to receive you.

Hostels Contemporary backpacker-style spots featuring dorms, wi-fi and shared kitchens, in Santa Cruz de Tenerife, Las Palmas de Gran Canaria and some of the surf towns.

Pensiones & Hostales Good-value budget operations, often family-owned; some of them are simple shared-bathroom operations, while others are charming gems full of stylish touches.

Hotels From no-frills guesthouses to boutique beauties to luxurious five-stars with complimentary bathrobes, spa treatments and superior restaurants.

Paradores A Spanish state-run chain of high-class hotels; five *paradores* in the Canary Islands.

Camping There isn't much camping in the Canaries, though some national parks have official campsites; you'll need to reserve online well ahead.

PRICE RANGES

The following price ranges refer to a double room with private bathroom. Unless otherwise stated, breakfast is not included in the price.

€ less than €65

€€ €65–140

€€€ more than €140

Best Places to Stay

Best for Families

The big resort-style hotels in the Canaries' major tourist destinations (Gran Canaria's Maspalomas, Tenerife's Los Cristianos etc) offer the most obvious and extensive family-friendly set-ups, while private self-catering apartments and villas are ideal for travellers with tots in tow. But there are some more one-of-a-kind options sprinkled around the islands too.

Finca de Arrieta (p124) Arrieta, Lanzarote

Barceló Castillo Beach Resort (p94) Caleta de Fuste, Fuerteventura

Lopesan Villa del Conde (p58) Maspalomas, Gran Canaria

Apartamentos Playa Delphin (p215) Puerto Naos, La Palma

Best on a Budget

The Canary Islands are absolutely doable on a shoestring – in fact, there's some wonderfully characterful budget accommodation to be found here. Urban centres like Santa Cruz de Tenerife and Las Palmas de Gran Canaria, as well as some of the surf towns, have excellent backpacker hostels. Self-catering apartments and wallet-friendly *hostales* and *pensiones* are popular across the archipelago.

El Sitio (p235) La Frontera, El Hierro

Laif Hotel (p94) El Cotillo, Fuerteventura

Downtown House (p58) Las Palmas de Gran Canaria, Gran Canaria

El Jostel (p165) Santa Cruz de Tenerife, Tenerife

Los Telares (p189), Hermigua, La Gomera

La Fuente (p215) Santa Cruz de la Palma, La Palma

ALEX POLO/SHUTTERSTOCK ©

Anaga Mountains, Tenerife (p153)

Best Boutique Bliss

Look beyond the resorts and you'll find the Canaries host some exquisite independent properties with boutique flair, many of them inspired by local art and architecture, inhabiting beautiful historical buildings and/or hidden away amid utterly spectacular landscapes.

Buenavista Lanzarote (p124) Wine Country, Lanzarote

Hotel La Quinta Roja (p165) Garachico, Tenerife

Finca Malvasía (p124) Wine Country, Lanzarote

Hotel San Telmo (p215) Santa Cruz de la Palma, La Palma

Hotel Palacio Ico (p124) Teguise, Lanzarote

Best Rustic Stays

Gracing every island in the archipelago, the Canaries' rural hotels and self-catering *casas rurales* represent excellent value for the charm of their setting and facilities, and can be a great base for hiking and escaping the world. Note that many of them are distant from public transport and advance bookings are usually essential.

Casa Isaítas (p94) Pájara, Fuerteventura

El Sitio (p235) La Frontera, El Hierro

Caserío de Mozaga (p124) Mozaga, Lanzarote

Los Telares (p189) Hermigua, La Gomera

Booking

Book well ahead year-round. During busy periods, some hotels (especially big resorts) impose multinight stays and/or compulsory half- or full-board arrangements, and prices skyrocket. There are sometimes good deals in autumn (October/November).

Lonely Planet (lonelyplanet.com/hotels) Find independent reviews, as well as recommendations on the best places – and then book them online.

Airbnb (www.airbnb.com) From city apartments with sea views to enormous houses in the mountains.

Canari Rural (www.canarirural.com) Over 200 rural cottages and country hotels.

Casas Rurales (www.ecoturismocanarias.com) An extensive selection of rural accommodation, but doesn't cover La Gomera or Lanzarote.

Getting Around

For more information, see Transport (p268).

Travelling by Car

Having your own wheels is the best way to explore the Canary Islands in depth, and driving here is generally safe and very enjoyable. There are some spectacular drives, from coastal expeditions to mountain-tastic loops. Many of the most exciting beaches, hikes and other attractions can only be reached by private vehicle (especially if you're looking for off-beat destinations), and the wealth of car-hire operations on the islands keeps prices competitive (taxi prices can quickly add up). Most roads are well kept and signposted, though speeding and tailgating are common, and drivers unfamiliar with the local terrain occasionally cause jams and disturbances. Many of the most beautiful drives track along winding mountain roads – awe-inspiring for drivers, but sometimes challenging for new arrivals. Driving in the cities and major towns can be hectic, with traffic jams common and parking limited (and expensive!), especially during peak periods; it's better to use public transport in such cases. Remember that Spain drives on the right.

Car Hire

Renting a car in the Canaries is strongly recommended. Cars can be hired at airports and in resorts and larger towns. Be sure to book in advance for smaller islands such as El Hierro and La Gomera, which have a limited number of vehicles that can get snapped up quickly. Some operators now hire out electrical vehicles, too. Cicar (p271) is a reliable Canaries-wide operator, and all the big international car-hire firms have outlets across the islands. Local agencies often have slightly lower rates than better-known brands. Note that most car-hire firms won't allow you to transport your car from one island to another by ferry, so if you're visiting more than one island it's easiest to pick up a new car on each one.

Driving Conditions

All major roads are sealed and well maintained, and driving in the Canaries is *mostly* a joy. Some roads fade into dusty or rocky tracks in remote regions, most notably around Fuerteventura's Jandía region and Isla Graciosa; driving on sand can be challenging and sand-dusted routes should be avoided at night. Note that most rental insurance agreements won't cover vehicles for use on unsealed roads, so it's usually best to tackle these with help from a local tour/transport operator with a fleet of 4WDs.

DRIVING FAST FACTS

➡ Drive on the right.

➡ All vehicle occupants must wear a seatbelt.

➡ Minimum age for a full licence is 18 years.

➡ Carry your licence at all times.

➡ Maximum speed 120km/h on motorways, 50km/h in built-up areas.

➡ Blood alcohol limit 50mg per 100ml (0.05%).

No Car?

Air

The seven main islands have airports (Tenerife has two), which means flying is the most efficient means of hopping between them. Distances are short and prices are usually very reasonable. Binter Canarias (p269), Canary Fly (p269) and Air Europa Express (www.aireuropa.com) are the major inter-island operators.

RESOURCES

The islands are connected by ferries, 'fast ferries' and jetfoils.

Schedules and prices – and even routes – can and do change. This isn't so important on major routes, where there's plenty of choice, but it can mean a big delay if you're planning to travel a route that has only a couple of boats running per day, or even per week. If time is tight, flying is a much faster alternative (often with competitive prices).

The three main companies:

Trasmediterránea (p269)

Fred Olsen (p269)

Naviera Armas (p270)

Bicycle

Cycling is an increasingly popular way to explore the islands, with majestic volcanic scenery making for spectacular rides. Las Palmas de Gran Canaria now has a good bike-share scheme, Sitycleta (p269), along with cycle lanes. Bike hire is available in most major towns and resorts, from around €12 per day; many local operators also run cycling tours.

Boat

For hopping between adjacent islands, the fast ferries are superb. Many routes have frequent departures. That said, it's faster and usually equally affordable to fly between islands.

Bus

The local interurban *guaguas* (buses) will get you to most important places on all islands, but advance planning is essential as there are often only a few services a day and buses tend to peter out at weekends. Local tourist offices can help with bus schedules, or check online. Chargeable bus cards are usually available, which offer slight discounts.

Caleta de Sebo, Isla Graciosa (p127)

If You Like...

Scenic Landscapes

Gran Canaria The fabulous interior feels a little like the Rockies, especially around the Cruz de Tejeda and Artenara. (p52)

El Teide No hiking boots are necessary to reach Spain's highest peak, accessible by cable car and offering heady views. (p163)

Parque Nacional de Timanfaya For a moonscape of extraordinary rock formations, colours and atmosphere, explore Lanzarote's national park. (p121)

La Gomera The whole island is mountainscape heaven; one of the finest lookout spots is the national park's Alto de Garajonay. (p186)

Mirador del Río The Manrique masterpiece hanging off a Lanzarote cliff offers sweeping views of the Chinijo Archipelago. (p125)

El Hierro Viewpoints gaze out over tumbling panoramas all over the Canaries' second-smallest island. (p224)

Beaches

The southern resorts have magnificent but crowded beaches, while the black-sand gems of El Hierro, La Palma and La Gomera are often deserted.

Playa de Cofete, Fuerteventura Quite possibly the most adorable, unspoilt stretch of golden sand on the entire archipelago. (p108)

Playa de las Teresitas, Tenerife Powder-soft sands, good seafood restaurants and a reassuringly Spanish vibe. (p152)

Endless dunes, Gran Canaria Clamber across the extraordinary dunes in Maspalomas. (p77)

Playa del Papagayo, Lanzarote Drive along a dirt track to this pale-sand nature-reserve beach, then hit its neighbour Playa Mujeres. (p135)

Playa de las Conchas, Isla Graciosa You're likely to have this gorgeous stretch of blonde sand all to yourself, but take care in the water. (p127)

Natural pools, El Hierro Not *exactly* the beach, but El Hierro's seawater pools are a Canaries highlight. (p224)

Hiking

Aside from July and August, when the weather is at its hottest and dustiest, the climate is sufficiently mild to enjoy spectacular walks across all islands.

Parque Nacional del Teide, Tenerife Tackle the summit or base for some of Tenerife's top hikes, through lunar landscapes. (p162)

Ruta de los Volcanes, La Palma This 19km trek shuffles over volcanic ash towards the site of the Canaries' latest eruption. (p214)

Parque Nacional de Garajonay, La Gomera Shady walks of all difficulty levels criss-cross La Gomera's enchanting *laurisilva* forest. (p186)

Parque Nacional de Timanfaya, Lanzarote Book ahead to walk through silent lava fields, or hike the park-bordering Caldera Blanca. (p121)

Parque Nacional de la Caldera de Taburiente, La Palma Climb the path to Pico Bejenado for stunning views or opt for any other viewpoint trail. (p215)

Roque Nublo, Gran Canaria It takes just 30 minutes to reach Gran Canaria's iconic monolith from the roadside car park. (p76)

Barranco de Masca, Tenerife A demanding and dramatic descent through a ravine to the ocean (closed for maintenance at the time of research). (p166)

El Hierro Follow the 27km Camino de la Virgen pilgrimage or tackle the cliffside Camino de Jinama. (p238)

Isla de Lobos You'll feel entirely alone as you skirt the edge of this uninhabited island off Fuerteventura. (p102)

Top: Cenobio de Valerón (p71), Gran Canaria

Bottom: Goats on the Anaga Mountains (p153), Tenerife

Art & Architecture

Hotspots for art lovers include Las Palmas de Gran Canaria, Santa Cruz de Tenerife and the entire island of Lanzarote.

César Manrique's designs Sprinkled all over Lanzarote, the artist's modern sculptures and buildings blend beautifully with the island's stark landscapes. (p114)

Tenerife Espacio de las Artes A breathtakingly modern architectural marvel housing exhibitions with an emphasis on socially conscious pieces. (p144)

Santa Cruz de la Palma Probably the best-looking town in the archipelago, with a surfeit of ancient churches and heritage architecture. (p202)

Centro Atlántico de Arte Moderno, Gran Canaria Along with its two satellite museums, Las Palma's CAAM showcases superb contemporary exhibitions. (p57)

La Laguna, Tenerife Ancient town stuffed to the gills with charm and traditional architecture at every turn. (p149)

San Sebastián de la Gomera Wander pastel-hued alleys past ancient homes and churches, on an island with a boho artist scene. (p183)

Teguise Lanzarote's original capital dates back to at least the 15th century. (p117)

History

La Laguna, Tenerife A Unesco World Heritage site and veritable open-air museum of heritage architecture. (p149)

Santa Cruz de la Palma Possibly the best looking and most charming historic town centre of them all. (p202)

San Sebastián de la Gomera The colourful capital where Columbus made his final pre-Americas stop. (p183)

Betancuria Oodles of history up in the hills of Fuerteventura. (p91)

Teguise Lanzarote's long history unravels across the scenic streets of its former capital. (p117)

Teror Picturesque hill town on Gran Canaria, with history at every good-looking turn. (p68)

Water Sports

Fuerteventura and Lanzarote are known for wind and waves, while diving is best on El Hierro.

El Cotillo At the heart of Fuerteventura's surfing scene, surrounded by unspoilt wind-swept beaches. (p101)

La Caleta de Famara Lanzarote's hottest surf spot: kiteboarding, windsurfing, body-boarding, yoga... (p126)

La Restinga Warm, clear waters make this coastal El Hierro village a diver's dream. (p232)

Playa de Sotavento de Jandía Kitesurfers and windsurfers flock to this golden Fuerteventura beach that hosts the Windsurfing World Cup. (p91)

Pozo Izquierdo A quieter place to windsurf with a handful of well-trusted agencies, on Gran Canaria. (p81)

Southern resorts At Tenerife's Los Cristianos, and Gran Canaria's Puerto de Mogán, Maspalomas and Playa del Inglés. (p168)

Archaeology

The islands' pre-Hispanic culture was virtually wiped out during the Spanish conquest, but a few fascinating Guanche sites remain.

Cueva Pintada, Gran Canaria The geometric designs at this cave are thought to be some sort of calendar. (p71)

Cenobio de Valerón, Gran Canaria An impressive set of caves and grain stores clinging to a cliffside. (p71)

Cuatro Puertas, Gran Canaria A human-made cave with four entrances sits atop a hill just outside Telde. (p66)

La Zarza, La Palma A small visitor centre close to ancient swirling rock engravings. (p221)

Museo de la Naturaleza y el Hombre This Santa Cruz de Tenerife museum has superb exhibits on pre-Hispanic culture. (p143)

Museo Arqueológico de Lanzarote Arrecife's excellent 2018-opened archaeology gallery highlights the island's turbulent history. (p114)

Off the Beaten Track

In addition to these recommendations, heading out hiking will get you right off the beaten track on pretty much every island.

Cofete, Fuerteventura A vertiginous dirt road leads to a minuscule hamlet, spectacular surf beach and mysterious mansion... (p108)

Anaga Mountains, Tenerife Hike in verdant pine forests

and discover bucolic hamlets untouched by time. (p153)

Isla Graciosa, Lanzarote Camp on the beach and cycle a circuit of the tiny eighth Canary Island. (p127)

Cala de Tacorón, El Hierro Kick back at idyllic rocky coves with crystal-clear waters – though the entire island is OTBT! (p233)

Charco Azul, La Palma Dine on the day's catch then take a dip in saltwater pools carved from volcanic rock. (p220)

Fortaleza de Ansite, Gran Canaria Hike to this spectacularly positioned Guanche site, where a tunnel is hollowed out through the mountainside. (p74)

Playa del Risco, Lanzarote Trek for an hour to reach a pristine pale-gold beach in the island's northwest. (p126)

Wine & Cheese

La Geria Lanzarote's most famous volcanic-vine region, with bodegas for buying, touring and tasting (local goat's cheese included!). (p120)

Queso Majorero Buy your Fuerteventura cheese at a local *quesería* where you can taste it first. (p93)

Malvasía wine The *malvasía* grape produces a sweet dessert wine – taste at bodegas in Tenerife and La Palma. (p209)

Queso de Flor, Gran Canaria Sample creamy cheese blended with thistle flowers at the source in pretty Santa María de Guía. (p70)

El Hierro Unravel the western-most isle's slowly growing wine scene, with its unusual grapes and enterprising bodegas. (p236)

Month by Month

January

A popular month: the southern resorts are generally still warm and weather is (mostly) pleasant. Northern and Inland is cooler and rainier, while Tenerife's El Teide can be snow-capped.

☆ Día de los Reyes Magos

Spanish children receive gifts on 6 January, brought by the three kings rather than Father Christmas. There are regal parades the night before and traditional food on the day.

☆ Festival de Música de Canarias

January sees the launch of the Canaries' annual classical music festival, which has been running for over 30 years (www.gobiernodecanarias.org).

February

Southern resorts are generally sunny, while cooler weather in the islands' interiors creates ideal conditions for walking. This is also Carnaval month – book your bed early!

☆ Carnaval

Second only to Rio in terms of exuberance, Carnaval is at its best in Santa Cruz in Tenerife and Las Palmas de Gran Canaria. Santa Cruz de la Palma hosts a memorable party. (p145)

☆ Fiestas del Almendro en Flor

Numerous villages hold markets and festivities in honour of the pinky-white blossom that beautifully blotches the hillsides and valleys across several islands at this time of year; may fall in January.

March

Springtime flowers and great hiking, particularly on El Hierro, La Palma, La Gomera and Gran Canaria.

☆ Semana Santa

During Easter week, evocative and sombre parades of religious floats make their way through the islands' towns and villages. Sometimes falls in April.

☆ Opera Season

March sees the height of the Las Palmas de Gran Canaria's opera festival, attracting world-class virtuosos from across the globe. (p61)

April

The sun shines brightest on the southern beaches, though evenings are cooler and there can be showers, particularly on Tenerife. Walking remains good.

☆ Deliciously Cheesy

Celebrate Gran Canaria's wonderfully creamy *queso de flor* directly at its source – in Santa María de Guía during the annual cheese festival (www.santamariadeguia.es). Sometimes held in May.

May

Another good month with plenty of space on the sand and warmer evenings.

Gay Pride

Spain's second-largest *orgullo gay* event (after Madrid) takes over Maspalomas, Gran Canaria, mid-month, with parties, parades, performances and much, much more. (p80)

June

You're still *just* ahead of the tourist onslaught, and the weather is perfect in most places, with 10 hours of daily sunshine and temperatures in the low 20s.

July

The mercury level is rising, with the average temperature in the southern resorts in the low 30s. Tourism numbers (and hotel rates) whizz up with the summer-holiday crowd.

Bajada de la Virgen de los Reyes

Held every four years (next in 2021, 2025 etc), El Hierro's most famous fiesta sees its patron saint carried from her chapel in the island's west to the capital Valverde in early July. (p240)

International Jazz Festival

The Festival Internacional Canarias Jazz & Más Heineken attracts big names from the international jazz world. (p63)

Theatre, Music & Dance

Gran Canaria's Festival de Teatro, Musica y Danza is another world-class festival. (p61)

August

The prime holiday month for Spaniards, August is when the weather is at its hottest (though it rarely hits the 40°C common along the mainland's southern *costas*).

Rain Dance

The 4 August Fiesta de la Rama in Agaete is one of Gran Canaria's most important festivals. With origins in a pre-Hispanic rain dance, today it's part religious parade, part riotous night out. (p72)

Wine Festival

Lanzarote's biggest wine festival celebrates its volcanic drops with grape trampling, live music and plenty of tours and tastings – all part of La Geria's mid-August Fiesta de la Vendimia. (p120)

Saint's Day

Día de San Ginés, on 25 August, is a mega-celebration in Lanzarote, with the two-week celebrations taking in concerts, football matches and beauty contests. (p115)

September

Temperatures linger in the mid-20s and summer crowds ease off; nights grow a tad cooler, particularly at higher altitudes. Perfect hiking in most areas.

Columbus Festival

La Gomera's capital San Sebastián throws a week-long street party and cultural celebration, the Fiestas Colombinas, in honour of Christopher Columbus' first journey to the Americas. (p185)

October

Average temperatures hover in the low 20s, with cooler nights (especially higher up). Quieter October is ideal for hiking, including in the mountains – or just beaching.

November

While evenings can be chilly, daytime temperatures of around 20°C still lend themselves to beach time, and it's just before the winter-sun-seeking masses start to arrive.

December

Christmas sees tourists, particularly northern Europeans, in search of warmer climes. Temperatures drop into the mid-teens; the northern resorts and higher altitudes can be cloudy.

Street Party

El Hierro's Fiestas de la Concepción culminate on 8 December with religious revelry; on the previous evening, Valverde's streets are packed with people eating, drinking and making merry. (p228)

Itineraries

 The Best of Gran Canaria

A week on Gran Canaria gives you enough time to explore the capital's museums and restaurants, dine on seafood along the coast, admire the mountains and even squeeze in some beach time.

Start in **Las Palmas de Gran Canaria** with a gentle stroll on Playa de las Canteras or a dip in the ultracalm ocean – perfect for snorkelling. Spend the second day wandering the cobbles of historic Vegueta with its stellar museums. Day three head to the lovely town of **Arucas** before hitting the north coast to sample seafood in **Puerto de las Nieves**. Day four tackle the spectacular winding west-coast road, grabbing lunch in quiet **Puerto de la Aldea**, then continue the magnificent drive to pretty **Puerto de Mogán**, with its Mediterranean-style yachting harbour. Day five, swing southeast to the shimmering sands of for a stroll or a swim, then take the GC60 north to **Tejeda** for lunch with a view. Spend day six on a mountain hike or drive, drinking in the jaw-dropping scenery. To finish, meander your way down to **Agüimes** with its lovely pastel-painted buildings and historic charm, then veer back inland to the lush **Barranco de Guayadeque** for lunch in a cave.

Top: Parque Nacional de la Caldera de Taburiente (p215), La Palma

Bottom: Dining in the Barranco de Guayadeque (p67), Gran Canaria

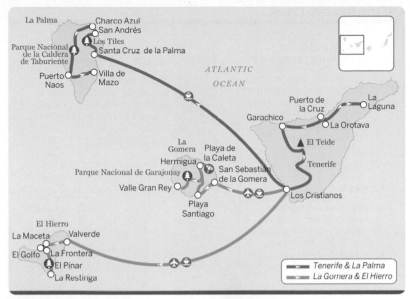

La Palma

Charco Azul
San Andrés
Los Tiles
Santa Cruz de la Palma

Parque Nacional de la Caldera de Taburiente

Puerto Naos

Villa de Mazo

ATLANTIC OCEAN

Puerto de la Cruz
La Laguna
Garachico
La Orotava
El Teide
Tenerife

La Gomera
Playa de la Caleta
Hermigua
San Sebastián de la Gomera
Parque Nacional de Garajonay
Valle Gran Rey
Playa Santiago
Los Cristianos

El Hierro
La Maceta   Valverde
El Golfo   La Frontera
El Pinar
La Restinga

Tenerife & La Palma
La Gomera & El Hierro

10 DAYS Tenerife & La Palma

It's all perfectly preserved architecture and impressive mountain backdrops on this island-hopping adventure.

On Tenerife, stay two nights in **Puerto de la Cruz**, enjoying the shops, bars and beaches. Day three visit **La Orotava**, with its grand 17th-century mansions. Still in historical mode, continue on to **La Laguna**'s traditional quarter for an overnight stay. Next day, retrace your steps to contrasting **Garachico** and its simple fisher's cottages. Day five head to extraordinary **El Teide** for a day of walking and gawping. Day six hightail it to **Los Cristianos** and catch the daily ferry to La Palma.

Spend a couple of nights in the capital **Santa Cruz de la Palma**, exploring the old town, kicking back on the beach and taking a pilgrimage to the Santuario de la Virgen de las Nieves. Continue north to explore the hilly, cobbled streets of **San Andrés**. Day eight visit the lush rainforest of **Los Tiles** before cooling off at the saltwater pools at **Charco Azul**. Day nine hike through the stunning **Parque Nacional de la Caldera de Taburiente**. Continue south to lively **Puerto Naos** before visiting the handicraft museum at **Villa de Mazo**.

1 WEEK La Gomera & El Hierro

Simple pleasures reign on these two small, western islands: traditional cuisine, forest hikes, ocean swims and plenty of winding roads.

Spend your first day on La Gomera exploring the historical backstreets in **San Sebastián de la Gomera**. The next day recover from all that urban exhaustion with a dip and lunch at **Playa Santiago**. Day three head to the verdant north, stopping at traditional **Hermigua** and sparkling volcanic **Playa de la Caleta**. Next day continue south for a hike through the **Parque Nacional de Garajonay**'s ethereal *laurisilva* forest. Drive down the stunning **Valle Gran Rey** gorge until it reaches the sea. Stay overnight before hopping over to El Hierro, via Tenerife, by ferry or plane.

Check out the low-key capital of **Valverde**, before heading south to majestic **El Golfo** and perhapsg hiking the cliff-hugging Camino de Jinama. Dine on superb Canarian food in down-to-earth **La Frontera** and stay overnight. Next day head for the natural pools at **La Maceta**, before seeking out the lush pines of **El Pinar** and the offshore scuba diving at **La Restinga**.

Off the Beaten Track

TO THE END OF TENERIFE, TENERIFE

Meander past craggy mountains and curving hairpin bends through the untouristed northwestern reaches of the Canaries' most beloved island, to finally reach wild Punta de Teno and its knockout sunsets. (p166)

EXPLORING THE EAST COAST, TENERIFE

Quiet fishing villages, bare volcanic landscapes and black-sand beaches are the stars on a journey through Tenerife's little-explored east coast. (p176)

LA PALMA

Gloriously green and deliciously unspoiled, La Isla Bonita sidesteps the crowds of neighbouring Tenerife. Its charming capital is filled with handsome historical mansions, while the hiking, especially around the Parque Nacional Caldera de Taburiente, is outstanding. (p200)

18°W

17°W

16°W

29°N

Roque de los Muchachos (2426m)
LA PALMA
Los Llanos de Aridane
Santa Cruz de la Palma

LA GOMERA
Alto de Garajonay (1487m)
Valle Gran Rey
Puerto de Santiago
San Sebastián de la Gomera

Puerto de la Cruz
La Laguna
La Orotava
Santa Cruz de Tenerife
Pico del Teide (3718m)
TENERIFE
Los Cristianos

EL HIERRO
Malpaso (1501m)
Valverde
La Frontera

28°N

GRAN CANARIA

ATLANTIC OCEAN

17°W

16°W

EL HIERRO

The westernmost Canary Island takes extra effort to get to, which means you'll often have many of its soul-stirring viewpoints, pastoral walking trails, glittering natural pools, intriguing churches and homes, and down-to-earth restaurants all to yourself. (p224)

ERMITA DE GUARÁ, LA GOMERA

Lace up your hiking boots and stride out to find this lonely little chapel, perched above a spine-tinglingly deep gorge on southern La Gomera, then visit the age-old pottery workshops in the hamlet of El Cercado. (p193)

N 0 ⌐═══════════ 100 km
0 ⌐═══════════ 50 miles

PLAYA DEL RISCO, LANZAROTE

You'll have to hike an hour down steep hillsides to find this all-natural throwback curled into northern Lanzarote's wild coastline. (p126)

ISLA GRACIOSA

Now officially the Canaries' eighth island, far-flung Graciosa is a protected dream of sand-dusted streets, blonde beaches and long-slung volcanic cones gazing out on the Famara cliffs; it's reachable only by boat from Órzola on Lanzarote. (p127)

15°W

14°W

30°N

ATLANTIC OCEAN

Isla de Alegranza
ISLA GRACIOSA

PLAYA DEL RISCO 🌀

LANZAROTE

○ ○ **Arrecife**   29°N
Playa Blanca ○ Puerto del Carmen
Corralejo ○ Isla de Lobos

FUERTEVENTURA **Puerto del**
Gran Montaña ○ **Rosario**
(708m) ▲
○ **POZO NEGRO**

Las Palmas de **PLAYA DE**
○**Gran Canaria** **COFETE**
🌀
○Telde ○ Morro Jable
▲
Roque Nublo (1803m)
○ ○ **POZO IZQUIERDO**
Maspalomas

POZO NEGRO, FUERTE-VENTURA

Palm trees, green fields and jagged peaks pave the way to a tiny east-coast fishing hamlet, home to just a smattering of boats, cottages and excellent seafood restaurants. (p99)

15°W   14°W

POZO IZQUIERDO, GRAN CANARIA

Take to the waves in the off-beat, windsurf-mad town of Pozo Izquierdo, where your only companions will be other surfy types. (p81)

PLAYA DE COFETE, FUERTEVENTURA

Despite being the island's most loved beach, honey-hued Cofete on the far southern coast remains blissfully wild and undeveloped. It is watched over by a mansion wrapped in mystery. (p108)

Plan Your Trip
Activities

Being outdoors is what the Canary Islands are all about. With year-round balmy temperatures, limited rain threatening to stymie your adventures, clear waters, wild waves and a literally breathtaking variety of landscapes, you'd be forgiven for not wanting to spend any time inside at all.

Hiking

Which island of the Canaries has the best hiking is a question guaranteed to cause heated discussions among the walking fraternity. Tenerife, La Palma, El Hierro and La Gomera will have to fight it out for the hiking crown.

Kitesurfing & Windsurfing

The Canary Islands have some of the best kite- and windsurfing conditions in the world, with Lanzarote a real contender, but it's Fuerteventura that really gets the wind up people's sails.

Surfing

The Canaries aren't called the 'Hawaii of the Atlantic' for nothing. Most of the islands have great surf, but it's La Caleta de Famara in Lanzarote that's the centre of the scene.

Diving & Snorkelling

There's diving aplenty in the waters from Lanzarote to Gran Canaria, Tenerife and La Gomera, but the Canarian diving trophy goes to tiny El Hierro.

Cycling

Lanzarote and Fuerteventura appeal for their empty and comparatively flat roads, while hardcore cyclists flock to Gran Canaria's central mountains and the steep inclines of La Gomera and La Palma.

Hiking
When to Go

You can walk in the Canary Islands any time of year, but some trails become dangerous or impossible in rainy weather (more likely between October and March), and others (like the trek up to the peak of El Teide) may be harder to do during these same months, if parts of the trail are covered in snow. Be aware that while along the coast and in the lowlands it's normally warm and sunny, as you head into higher altitudes, the wind, fog and air temperature can change drastically, so always carry warm and waterproof clothing. Don't forget to take water along with you, as there are few water sources or vendors out along the trails.

Hiking on...
Tenerife

The Parque Nacional del Teide is one of the finest walking areas in all of Spain. But there's more to Tenerife hiking than El Teide. The forested Anaga Mountains in the northeast offer hikes through a mist-drenched forest filled with birdsong; in the far northwest, the hamlet of Masca is the gateway to some stunning, and very challenging, hikes; and Adeje in the south leads to the stunning Barranco del Infierno (p169) hike.

Running along a hiking trail, La Palma (p200)

La Gomera

Thanks to a near-permanent mist (called horizontal rain), the green forest of the Parque Nacional de Garajonay is dripping with life and moss. From the park's highest point, the Alto de Garajonay, you can see Tenerife and El Teide – if the clouds don't interrupt the view. There's excellent walking in and around this park for all hiking levels.

La Palma

Regarded by many as the finest island of all to walk on, La Palma's Parque Nacional de la Caldera de Taburiente offers a landscape somewhere between the verdant Garajonay and the stark Teide. You can follow the mountainous ridge of the park, hike up to mountain peaks or head down to the Puerto de Tazacorte. Numerous other trails spin off across the island and walking these can see you slipping in and out of rainforests or clambering up parched volcanic slopes. The Ruta de los Volcanes (p214) runs down the southern volcanic spine of the island to Fuencaliente.

El Hierro

The newbie on the walking scene, tiny El Hierro offers a real bonanza of trails, from family-friendly coastal hikes such

---

LOCAL MAPS

Some islands are better equipped than others when it comes to helping out hikers. La Palma and La Gomera in particular have well-signed paths and plentiful information. Elsewhere, you may find trails that are less well marked. If you're drawing a blank at the tourist office, you might have to head to the *cabildo* (island government). Hiking maps are generally available here, though having the patience and will to find the right person to help you can sometimes be as taxing as the trek itself. Alternatively, it's a good idea to use the many available hiking books (p36) for each of the islands, some of which also contain maps (eg the Discovery Walking Guides).

HIKING OFF THE BEATEN PATH

As well as the big-ticket walks there are plenty of off-the-beaten-path hikes throughout the Canary Islands. Bear in mind there is a wealth of hikes heading off from most points; the Parque Nacional de Teide, for example, covers a huge area and is home to many trails. For a truly spectacular walk, sign up for the Tremesana guided hike in the Parque Nacional de Timanfaya; you'll have to plan in advance, but the effort will be well rewarded.

Do seek local advice if you're tackling an offbeat path – some routes aren't well maintained, and overgrown vegetation or absent signage can seriously hinder your progress or present dangers. Watch out for closures too (at the time of writing, the Barranco de Masca was off-limits to allow it to regenerate and to improve safety within the gorge, and the trail up Mount Tindaya on Fuerteventura was closed to hikers).

as the easy walk between Las Puntas and La Maceta to shady ambles around the pine forests of El Pinar or the much longer Camino de Jinama (p238).

Gran Canaria

Much less hiked than the western islands, Gran Canaria nevertheless offers superlative walking opportunities. The best trails are to be found radiating away from the Cruz de Tejeda, which sits close to the highest point of Gran Canaria, or in the verdant ravines on the east of the island.

Lanzarote

Walks in the national park have to be well planned, but there are other options for hiking here. You could walk between wineries in La Geria or take a gentle wander across Isla Graciosa – as long as you don't mind getting sand in your boots.

Fuerteventura

If you want to walk but don't fancy too much of a climb, Fuerteventura has some pretty, gentle hikes. The dunes south of Corralejo offer extensive hiking opportunities; there are scenic trails along the north coast; the Isla de Lobos is a hike-worthy island; you can explore the verdant land around Betancuria; or discover the sandy extents of Playa de Cofete.

Best Hikes

Among our favourite hiking areas are walks around the Unesco-protected Los Tiles biosphere reserve on La Palma and the dunes of Maspalomas on Gran Canaria. The most rewarding individual hikes:

Pico Viejo to El Teide (p163) The most challenging – and easily the most stunning – trek in the Canary Islands is this mammoth hike that takes in not just Spain's highest peak, but its little-climbed little brother.

Ruta de los Volcanes (p214) Skip along the summits of a whole ridge of volcanoes on this long and challenging trek.

Pista de Valencia to Pico Bejenado (p216) In the Parque Nacional de la Caldera de Taburiente on La Palma.

Barranco del Infierno (p169) Beautiful ravine hike near Adeje on Tenerife.

La Laguna Grande to Alto de Garajonay (p196) Saunter through the mist-drenched forests at the summit of La Gomera on this moderately easy walk.

Camino de Jinama (p238) Hike through history, and through the best of delightful El Hierro.

Isla de Lobos (p102) Loop the loop around this desert island.

Resources

Discovery Walking Guides The best books in English for the general walker; publishes guidebooks and accompanying maps to Lanzarote, La Palma, La Gomera and Tenerife.

Sunflower Books Hiking guidebooks to all the islands.

Cicerone These walking guides are also very popular and include each of the islands (*Walking on Tenerife*, *Walking on Gran Canaria* etc).

Rother Walking Guides Highly informative guides covering Tenerife, Gran Canaria, La Palma and La Gomera.

Windsurfing, Pozo Izquierdo (p81)

Water Sports

Surfing

The Canary Islands offer a superb surfing environment. There are long hours of sunlight, a warm climate and a wide variety of waves in the islands, from heart-in-the-mouth barrels breaking over super-shallow reef ledges to gentle sandbanks ideal for learners. There's also a wide choice of schools with classes for children as well as adults; a number of surf schools also offer accommodation. The best season for surfing in the Canaries is from October through to April; at this time of year you will need a full 3mm wetsuit.

For more on surfing in the Canaries, *The Stormrider Surf Guide: Canary Islands,* published by Low Pressure, is available as an e-book and is a handy resource.

La Caleta de Famara, Lanzarote (p126) With its endless stretch of sand and plenty of surf schools, it's perfect for learners.

El Cotillo, Fuerteventura (p101) Offers perfect learner conditions.

Playa de las Américas, Tenerife (p168) Has a few mellow, learner-friendly waves and several surf schools.

Windsurfing & Kiteboarding

With constant winds, good waves and a perfect climate, the Canary Islands offer some of the best conditions in the world for windsurfing and kiteboarding.

International competitions are held here every year, and enthusiasts from all over the globe converge on the long, sandy beaches to test the waters. If you're new to the game, beginner courses are easy to come by at all the main spots. Courses last between two days and a week, and prices vary widely according to how much you're aiming to learn.

The Kite & Windsurfing Guide Europe by Stoked Publications is a superb glossy guide to the continent's best kite and windsurf spots. It includes chapters on the Canary Islands.

Playa de Sotavento de Jandía, Fuerteventura (p106) A string of soft white-sand beaches with excellent windsurfing bordering the blustery east coast.

Playa de la Barca, Fuerteventura (p106) The top windsurfing and kitesurfing choice.

Pozo Izquierdo, Gran Canaria (p81) Big winds are a constant at this windsurfing outpost.

Costa Teguise, Lanzarote (p116) Excellent conditions for windsurfers.

Corralejo, Fuerteventura (p98) Windsurfing for all levels on the northeast coast.

Playa Las Galletas, Tenerife (p175) Relaxed and easy-going town with good windsurfing in the south.

Playa El Médano, Tenerife (p175) Decent gusts on the southeast coast.

Swimming

Year-round sun and warm water (18°C to 26°C) make swimming one of the biggest attractions on the islands. From the long, golden beaches of the eastern islands to the volcanic pools of the western islands, there are plenty of splashing opportunities.

Beaches come in every shape and size – long and golden, intimate and calm, family-friendly and action-packed, rocky and picturesque, solitary and lonely, windy and wavy, black and volcanic. The natural pools of El Hierro, La Palma and Lanzarote are also excellent for swimming.

You do need to be cautious, especially when swimming in the ocean. The first rule is never, ever swim alone. There can be very strong currents and undertows in the Atlantic, and rip currents can be very strong.

The water quality around the Canary Islands is generally excellent. The only place you may find pollution is near ports (the occasional small oil spill is not unheard of) and on overcrowded tourist beaches (where smokers seem to think some beaches are a huge ashtray).

REBECA HEREDERO/GETTY IMAGES ©

Natural pool, El Hierro (p224)

Diving & Snorkelling

The variety of marine life and the warm, relatively calm waters of the Canary Islands make them a great place for diving or snorkelling. You won't experience the wild colours of Caribbean coral, but the volcanic coast is made up of beautiful rock formations and caves. As far as life underwater goes, you can spot around 350 species of fish and 600 different kinds of algae.

Diving schools and outfitters are scattered across the islands, so you won't have trouble finding someone willing to take you out. A standard single dive, with equipment rental included, costs from €30 to €55, but a 'try dive' (a first-timer diving with an instructor) can be double that price. Certification classes start from around €330 and generally last between three days and a week. Prices tend to be more competitive on El Hierro compared to the other islands. Many diving outfitters also offer snorkelling excursions for nondivers; prices tend to be about half the cost of a regular dive.

For those of you who want to explore the ocean depths on one, long breath, freediving has made inroads on several of the islands, including Tenerife, Fuerteventura, Lanzarote and El Hierro. Schools that offer freediving include Apnea Canarias (p177)

ALTERNATIVE ACTIVITIES

Ticked off diving, surfing, cycling, riding the waves, lounging on the beach and hiking those volcanoes? Here are some lesser-known ideas for great things to do in the Canaries, most of them available on every one of the islands. You can try a cooking class or a spin around the local market; join a history or architecture tour through some of the archipelago's most fascinating towns and cities (some tourist offices hand out self-guided itineraries); get to grips with the local lingo on a language course (p264); flow into yoga, Pilates, meditation and other wellness activities; or kick back with a thalassotherapy session at a swish spa.

on Tenerife and Magma Kitesurf School (p264) on Fuerteventura.

La Restinga, El Hierro (p232) A wealth of marine life and plenty of diving operators to show you the underwater wonders.

Playa Blanca, Lanzarote (p134) Especially warm waters for finding marlin, barracuda and a host of other fish.

Los Gigantes & Puerto de Santiago, Tenerife (p167) Wreck dives, cave dives and old-fashioned boat dives. Marine life ranges from eels to angel sharks and stingrays.

Puerto de Mogán, Gran Canaria (p81) Dive in and around the caves and wrecks that lie not far offshore.

Playa de las Canteras, Gran Canaria (p59) Not much of a diving spot, but this is some of the most accessible snorkelling in the archipelago, just metres from the sand.

Whale- and Dolphin-Watching & Boating

Around 30 species of whales and dolphins pass through Canarian seas; the most commonly seen are pilot whales and bottle-nosed dolphins.

The best area to see such creatures is in the waters between Tenerife and La Gomera, and a number of different operators run dolphin- and whale-spotting boat trips departing from the harbour at Los Cristianos.

Other whale-watching ports include Los Gigantes and Puerto de Santiago (Tenerife); Valle Gran Rey (La Gomera); Puerto Rico (Gran Canaria); and Playa Santiago (La Gomera).

Whichever operator you choose, it's worth taking note of their environmental credentials as it's not unknown for some boat operators to take their clients too close to the whales, which causes them undue distress and can eventually cause the whales and dolphins to completely change their behaviour or leave an area altogether.

Away from whales and dolphins, virtually every tourist beach town in the archipelago offers some form of boat trip, but maybe the most impressive boat cruises on the islands are those running from Valle Gran Rey in La Gomera to the unique organ-like rock formation of Los Órganos. (p191)

Golf

Southern Tenerife has become the Canary Islands' golf hotspot. Golfers who love the warm temperatures that let them play year-round have spawned the creation of a half-dozen courses in and around Playa de las Américas alone. The courses are aimed more at holiday golfers and are not known for being particularly challenging. In balmy winter, green fees hover around €100, but in the sweltering midsummer they could be half that cost.

You'll also find several courses around Las Palmas de Gran Canaria and Maspalomas, one on La Gomera, and even a few on the arid islands of Lanzarote and Fuerteventura.

The scarcity of water on the islands makes golf rather environmentally unfriendly and a difficult sport to sustain. Golf-course owners say the water for those lush greens is used from runoff and local water-purification plants, but environmental groups argue golf courses take water from agriculture. The truth is in there somewhere, and local politicians, golfers, environmentalists and farmers are still arguing about where the water comes from.

Cycling

If you've got strong legs, cycling may be the perfect way to see the Canary Islands. The price of renting a bike depends largely on what kind of bike you get – suspension and other extras will cost more. In general, a day's rental starts at about €15, and a guided excursion will be around €50. All the islands, including La Graciosa, are well equipped with bike-hire outlets.

BEST CYCLING AREAS

ROUTE	LEVEL
El Teide (Tenerife, p62)	Advanced
Alto de Garajonay (La Gomera, p187)	Advanced
Valle Gran Rey (La Gomera, p193)	Moderate
Los Llanos de Aridane (La Palma, p218)	Moderate
Fataga Ravine (Gran Canaria, p77)	Advanced

Plan Your Trip

Travel with Children

The Canary Islands have something for even the most demanding mini traveller. Start with the natural canvas – wide beaches edged by shallow, calm water and bordered by rocks that shelter rock pools and scuttling crabs. Add to that a submarine trip or perhaps a kids' diving class, kayaking, surfing, kitesurfing, a fun bike trip into the hills or a hike around a volcano.

Best Regions for Kids

Tenerife
Go-karting, whale-watching, beaches, theme parks, boat rides, diving and surfing should have the whole family cheering.

Fuerteventura
The sandy choice at Corralejo is superb; older kids will love striding out on the dunes south of town. Splashier options include aquaparks, boat rides, snorkelling and surfing.

Lanzarote
The Parque Nacional de Timanfaya is something to impress the most blasé whippersnapper, with natural geysers and moonscape terrain.

Gran Canaria
Las Palmas' Playa de las Canteras is magnificent and the science museum should entrance. Children will also adore the sand dunes in Maspalomas.

La Palma
Older children may find the Caldera de Taburiente hikes invigorating, while children of all ages should find the Volcán San Antonio exciting. Stargazing is another big draw.

Canary Islands for Kids

While plenty of attractions, including theme parks and zoos, have been designed specifically with children in mind, public spaces, such as town and village plazas, also morph into informal playgrounds with children kicking a ball around, riding bikes and playing, while parents enjoy a drink and tapa in one of the surrounding terrace bars. Indeed, many town squares actually have a kids' playground, something you'll stumble across with gleeful frequency. Local children tend to stay up late, and at fiestas it's common to see even tiny ones toddling the streets at midnight. Visiting children invariably warm to this idea, but can't always cope with it quite so readily.

Discounts
Discounts are available for children (usually under 12 years) on public transport and for admission to sights. Those aged under five generally go free.

Eating & Drinking
Whole families, often including several generations, sitting around a restaurant or bar table eating and chatting is a fundamental element of the lifestyle

in the Canaries and it is rare to find a restaurant where children are not made welcome. Even if restaurants do not advertise children's menus (a growing number do), they will still normally be willing to prepare a small portion for your child or suggest a suitable tapa or two. Baby-friendly extras like high chairs and changing tables are commonplace in resorts, though tend to be a little thin on the ground in more out-of-the-way spots.

Aside from the normal selection of soft drinks on offer, you might come across a *zumeria* (juice bar), where you'll find a healthy variety of fresh fruit juices. In bars, a popular choice for children is Cola Cao (chocolate drink) served hot or cold with milk.

Resources

Always make a point of asking staff at tourist offices for a list of family-friendly activities, including traditional fiestas, plus suggestions on hotels that cater for kids.

For further general information about travelling with children, see Lonely Planet's *Travel with Children*.

Children's Highlights

Theme Parks

Siam Park, Costa Adeje, Tenerife (p169) This massive water park has the works, including raft rides (on rapids), an artificial wave pool and even a white sandy stretch of beach.

Maroparque, Breña Alta, La Palma (p206) A small zoo with spacious enclosures and pleasantly landscaped gardens.

Oasis Park, La Lajita, Fuerteventura (p104) Mammals, birds, sea life, plus camel rides on offer.

Acua Water Park, Corralejo, Fuerteventura (p99) Splash-tastic fun for water-loving kids.

Water Sports & Boat Rides

Dive Academy, Arguineguín, Gran Canaria (p78) One-day bubble-maker courses for children from eight to 10 years old.

Oceanarium Explorer, Calea de Fuste, Fuerteventura (p96) Dolphin- and whale-spotting trips, kayak hire and sea lions at the harbour.

Tina, Valle Gran Rey, La Gomera (p194) Four-hour whale-watching excursions, including lunch.

Beaches

All the following beaches have shallow waters, fine sand (for sandcastles), various activities (pedalos, boat rides, volleyball or similar), plus family-friendly restaurants and ice-cream vendors within tottering distance of the sand.

Fuerteventura Corralejo Viejo, Muelle Chico (Corralejo), Caleta de Fuste, Costa Calma, Playa del Matorral (Morro Jable)

Lanzarote Playa Grande (Puerto del Carmen), Playa Blanca, Playa del Castillo (Caleta de Fuste)

Gran Canaria Playa de las Canteras, Playa del Inglés, Playa Mogán

Tenerife Los Cristianos, Playa de las Américas, Costa Adeje, Las Teresitas

La Palma, La Gomera and El Hierro have mainly black-sand beaches with, overall, fewer activities for children, aside from whale-watching cruises and the ubiquitous glass-bottom boat trips.

La Palma Puerto Naos, Puerto de Tazacorte, Charco Azul (natural pools cut out of the rock)

La Gomera Playa de las Vueltas and La Playa (Valle Gran Rey), Playa Santiago

El Hierro La Restinga

Museums

Museo de la Piratería, Teguise, Lanzarote (p118) A swashbuckling museum about the history of piracy on the island.

Casa Santa María, Betancuria, Fuerteventura (p92) Folklore and crafts, plus an excellent under-water 3D film.

Museo Elder de la Ciencia y la Tecnología, Las Palmas de Gran Canaria (p59) Fascinating science and technology museum with lots of hands-on exhibits for kids.

Casa-Museo de Colón, Las Palmas de Gran Canaria (p55) Museum recounting Columbus' voyages with an impressive replica galleon.

Museo de la Naturaleza y el Hombre, Santa Cruz de Tenerife (p143) Natural science and archaeology, including Guanche mummies.

Museo de la Ciencia y el Cosmos, La Laguna, Tenerife (p150) Great science museum for children, including a planetarium.

Cueva de los Verdes (p124), Lanzarote

La Caldera del Rey, Los Cristianos, Tenerife (p169) Horse riding, plus petting farm, climbing wall and low rope course for kids.

Planning

This is an easy-going, child-friendly destination with precious little advance planning necessary. July and August can be very busy with Spanish families from the mainland, and hotels in the main tourist resorts are often block booked by tour companies. Early spring is a good time to travel with young children as the weather is still warm enough for beach days, without being too hot, and the theme parks and attractions are not too crowded – until the Easter holidays, that is.

You can buy baby formula in powder or liquid form, as well as sterilising solutions such as Milton, at *farmacias* (pharmacies). Disposable nappies (diapers) are widely available at supermarkets and *farmacias*.

The Big Outdoors

Isla de Lobos, Fuerteventura (p102) Children should enjoy the ferry ride and *Robinson Crusoe*–style novelty of landing on a tiny, uninhabited island.

Cueva de los Verdes & Jameos del Agua, Malpaís de la Corona, Lanzarote (p124) Intriguing caves and caverns.

Parque Nacional de Timanfaya, Lanzarote (p121) Fascinating volcanic park with geyser displays and camel rides.

Lanzarote a Caballo, Puerto del Carmen, Lanzarote (p129) Horse riding and short treks.

Troglodyte caves, Artenara, Gran Canaria (p74) Fascinating Flintstone-style prehistoric caves.

Lago Martiánez, Puerto de la Cruz, Tenerife (p156) A fabulous watery playground.

Before You Go

➡ You can hire car seats for infants and children from most car-rental firms, but you should always book them in advance.

➡ Most hotels have cots for small children, but numbers may be limited so reserve one when booking your room.

➡ When selecting a hotel, check whether your hotel has a kids club, activities geared for youngsters and/or babysitting facilities.

➡ No particular health precautions are necessary, but don't forget the sun protection essentials, including sun block and sun hat, although they can also be purchased here.

➡ Avoid tears and tantrums by planning which activities, theme parks, museums and leisure pursuits you want to opt for and, more importantly, can afford early on in the holiday.

Plan Your Trip
Eat & Drink Like a Local

Canarian cuisine is all about using simple, fresh ingredients and doing as little as possible to them: grilled fish served with a zesty herb sauce, crinkly boiled potatoes with salted skin, juicy grilled goat, sliced tomatoes drizzled with olive oil, and freshly picked fruit for dessert. Feasting is year-round, but menus change with what's available.

Food Experiences
Meals of a Lifetime

Casa Efigenia (p192) Charmingly rustic introduction to La Gomera cooking.

Enriclai (p205) Only four tables at this enticing Santa Cruz de la Palma restaurant.

La Cantina (p118) One of Lanzarote's very best, adding a creative modern spin to local ingredients.

Llévame al Huerto (p62) Far-reaching and diverse flexitarian menu in Las Palmas de Gran Canaria.

Texeda Brewery & Restaurant (p75) Worth a trip to Tejeda alone.

La Cabaña (p132) Mediterranean-fusion dishes in a swish dining space at Playa del Carmen on Lanzarote.

Tas-k (p168) Winning tapas choice hidden away behind the Los Gigantes harbour.

Guannabi (p147) Sensational in all respects, this Tenerife restaurant has a focus on superb rice dishes.

Cheap Treats

Chocolate con churros Deep-fried doughnut strips, dipped into rich hot chocolate; a Canarian favourite for breakfast or an afternoon snack.

The Year in Food

The Canary Islands' warm climate means fruit and vegetables can be grown year-round. It also guarantees terrific variety in local produce, with tropical fruits and exotic vegetables.

Spring (March to May)
Almond trees are in blossom across many islands; other fruit trees are in flower.

Summer (June to September)
Mangoes are in season from the later summer, joining plums, oranges, peaches, apricots, apples, avocados and pears in filling markets.

Autumn (October to November)
Papayas are at their fullest best; bananas too. The smell of roasted *castañas* (chestnuts) is everywhere and the fiesta of San Andrés sees Tenerife wine cellars open for new wine tastings.

Winter (December to February)
Orange trees are harvested between October and May, and tomatoes spill from markets. Street stalls feed revellers during the Carnaval in Santa Cruz de Tenerife.

Papas arrugadas Canarian wrinkly potatoes are unavoidable; usually served with *mojo* (spicy sauce).

Tapas Superb snacking in a huge variety and widely available.

Bocadillos Bread rolls filled with *jamón* (cured ham) or other cured meats, goat's-milk cheese or chorizo.

Tostada con tomate Toast or bread with tomato puree, olive oil and salt.

Dare to Try

Almogrote A pungent form of cheese paste from La Gomera. Hard, mature cheese, pepper, chillies, tomatoes and olive oil are mixed into a paste in a pestle and mortar and then spread on toast.

Morcilla dulce canaria Sweet black pudding made from pig's blood, pork, lard, sweet potato, sugar, raisins, almonds, cinnamon, nutmeg and aniseed.

Chorizo de Teror Very smooth paste-like chorizo containing ample amounts of fat, paprika, salt, spices, garlic and lean meat. There's a red and a white version (the latter without paprika). The chorizo is usually spread on bread or toast or as a filling in a *bocadillo*. Best eaten at the source in Teror (Gran Canaria).

Local Specialities

Canarian cuisine owes much to the New World; it was from South America that elementary items such as potatoes, tomatoes and corn were introduced. More exotic delights such as avocados and papayas also originated from there, while sweet mangoes arrived from Asia; look out for all three in the valleys and on supermarket shelves.

Some of the classic mainland Spanish dishes are also widely available, including paella (saffron rice cooked with chicken and rabbit or with seafood), tortilla (potato omelette), gazpacho (a cold, tomato-based soup), various *sopas* (soups) and *pinchos morunos* (kebabs).

Gofio

The traditional staple or *pan de los Canarios* (bread of the Canarian people) is *gofio,* a uniquely Canario product and, it must be said, perhaps an acquired taste. A roasted mixture of wheat, barley or, more often, corn, *gofio* has long been an integral part of the traditional Canarian diet, though these days bread is just as common in the home – and far more so in restaurants. *Gofio* is mixed in varying proportions, and used as a breakfast food or combined with almonds and figs to make sweets.

Papas Arrugadas

By a long chalk, the most-often-spotted Canarian dish is *papas arrugadas* (wrinkly potatoes), cooked in an abundance of salt and always served with some variation of *mojo* (Canarian spicy sauce made from coriander, basil or red chilli peppers). *Papas arrugadas* are made by boiling potatoes in heavily salted water, which makes the salt stick to the skin. The variety used is *papas antiguas* (old potatoes), descended from the first varieties imported from the Americas in the 15th century.

Soups & Stews

Of the many soups and stews you'll find, one delicious Canarian variant is *potaje de berros* (watercress soup). You will also often find *ropa vieja* (literally 'old clothes') on the Canarian menu, a fortifying chickpea stew typically utilising whatever leftovers are lying around, and *rancho canario,* a hearty broth with thick noodles and the odd chunk of meat and potato.

Fish & Seafood

Among the cornucopia of seafood choices, look out for *sancocho canario,* a typical Canarian dish that migrated to South America. Here in the Canary Islands it is salted fish served with *papas arrugadas,* sweet potatoes and *gofio,* and often spiced up with a lively dash or two of *mojo picón* (with added spicy heat).

Meats

Meat plays an important role in Canarian cooking, and while beef and lamb dishes are often sighted on menus, these meats are usually imported. Opt instead for the island specialities: pork, chicken, rabbit and, above all, goat.

Cheese

Queso (cheese) on the Canary Islands deserves an encyclopaedia of its own. You can find superb goat's-milk cheese on all of the islands, but perhaps the most famous is Majorero (p93) from Fuerteventura. The

Traditional Spanish paella

milk comes from the Majorero goat and the cheese is so celebrated it has its own Denominación de Origen (DO; an appellation certifying high standards and regional origin) label. Canarian cheese boards are common at tapas restaurants; fried goat's-milk cheese is a popular dish.

Sweets & Desserts

Canarios have a sweet tooth. Some of the best-known desserts are *bienmesabe* (a kind of thick, sticky goo made of almonds, egg yolks, cinnamon and sugar – deadly sweet!), *frangollo* (a mix of cornmeal, dried fruit, milk and honey), *bizcochos lustrados* (sponge cake) and *truchas de batata* (sweet potato parcels).

Don't miss the *quesadillas* from El Hierro – this cheesy cinnamon pastry (sometimes also made with aniseed) has been baked since the Middle Ages. Made with raisins, almonds and spices, m*orcillas dulces* (sweet blood sausages) are not everyone's cup of tea (perhaps the closest comparison is a Christmas mince pie).

Drinks

Cafe culture is a part of life here, and the distinction between cafes and bars is negligible; coffee and alcohol are almost always available in both. Bars take several different forms, including *cervecerías* (beer bars; a vague equivalent of the pub), *tabernas* (taverns) and bodegas (old-style wine bars).

Coffee

Coffee is produced on a tiny scale in the islands, mostly in the Agaete Valley in the north of Gran Canaria.

Café con leche About half coffee, half hot milk.

Sombra The same, but heavier on the milk.

Café solo A short black coffee (or espresso).

Cortado An espresso with a splash of milk.

Cortado de leche y leche Espresso made with condensed and normal milk.

Barraquito A larger cup of *cortado* coffee.

Café con hielo Glass of ice and hot cup of coffee to be poured over the ice.

EATING PRICE RANGES

The following price ranges refer to a standard main course.

€ less than €12

€€ €12–€20

€€€ more than €20

Ask if there is a surcharge to sit on the outdoor terrace – a few places add on an extra 10% to 15%.

Wine

One of the most common wines across the islands is the *malvasía* (Malmsey wine; also produced in Madeira, Portugal). It is generally *dulce* (sweet), although you can find the odd *seco* (dry) version. It is particularly common on La Palma and Lanzarote where it is grown in the dark volcanic soils.

Tenerife is the principal source of wine, and the red Tacoronte Acentejo was the first Canarian wine to earn a DO. Other productive vineyards are in the Icod de los Vinos, Güímar and Tacoronte areas of Tenerife. In Lanzarote, the vine has come back into vogue since the early 1980s, and in late 1993 the island's *malvasías* were awarded a DO.

El Hierro's wines (p236) are gaining in popularity, made from a generally quite acidic grape, and wine tourism on the island is growing. Wine tourism on La Palma, Tenerife, Lanzarote and other islands is also flourishing.

Beer

The most common way to order a *cerveza* (beer) is to ask for a *caña,* which is a small draught beer (*cerveza de barril* or *cerveza de presión*). If you prefer a larger version, ask for a *jarra*. Dorada, brewed in Santa Cruz de Tenerife, is a smooth pilsner. Tropical, another slightly lighter pilsner produced on Gran Canaria, is a worthy runner-up and the preferred tipple of the eastern isles.

There are several microbreweries on the islands, including the excellent Cervecería Isla Verde (📞 691 44 51 53; www.cervezaisla verde.com; Calle General Plaza el Jesús 41, El Jesus; ⏱ noon-10pm Mon & Wed-Fri, 10am-10pm Sat & Sun; 🅿 📞) in El Jesús on La Palma and the Texeda Brewery & Restaurant (p75) in Tejeda, Gran Canaria. Bars (and

restaurants) serving craft beers have mushroomed over the years, so there's increasing variety; a good choice is La Buena Vida (p62) in Las Palmas de Gran Canaria or La Jaira de Demian (p90) in Puerto del Rosario, Fuerteventura.

Spirits

Apart from the mainland Spanish imports, which include *coñac* (brandy) and a whole host of *licores* (liqueurs), you could try some local firewater if you come across it. One to seek out is *mistela* from La Gomera, a mixture of wine, sugar, spices and *parra* – a local version of *aguardiente* (similar to schnapps or *grappa*). Altogether easier to swallow is the rum that is produced across the islands. Dark rum is the favourite tipple while *ron miel* (honey rum) is a sweet concoction sometimes given after meals as a complimentary *chupito* (shot).

How to Eat & Drink

When to Eat

Desayuno (breakfast) Breakfast in the Canary Islands is usually straightforward and over and done with in a few bites: expect juice, coffee or tea, cereal or *gofio,* and toast with ham or cheese. *Churrerías* serve delicious deep-fried spiral-shaped *churros* (doughnuts), often accompanied by a cup of thick hot chocolate. Otherwise it's a *café con leche* or *cortado* with a croissant or *tostada* (buttered toast), or *tostada con tomate*.

Comida or almuerzo (lunch) The big meal of the day. While lots of Canarians may eat at home with the family during the week, many working Canarians choose a tapas bar or restaurant, often with the *menú del día* for its good value and convenience. At weekends lunch is a more drawn-out affair with family and friends, at home or out. Lunch usually starts relatively late, at around 2pm (or at the earliest 1pm) through to 4pm.

Cena (dinner) Dinner is often a relaxed affair and pretty late: although you'll find restaurants serving from around 6pm or 7pm, Canarians tend to wait to dine till around 8pm or 9pm.

Where to Eat

Asador A restaurant specialising in roasted meats.

Bar de copas Gets going around midnight and serves hard drinks and cocktails.

Chocolate con churros

Cafetería Serves coffee and snacks, and often double as a bar and social hub.

Casa de comidas A simple restaurant that cooks up affordable home cooking.

Cervecería The focus is on *cerveza* on tap.

Guachinche Home-style cooking in an informal dining space on Tenerife.

Restaurante A restaurant.

Taberna Usually a rustic place serving tapas and *raciones* (large tapas).

Tasca Tapas bar.

Terraza Open-air bar, for warm-weather tippling and tapas.

Vinoteca Wine bars where you can order by the glass.

Menu Decoder

a la parrilla – grilled

asado – roasted or baked

bebidas – drinks

carne – meat

carta – menu

casera – homemade

ensalada – salad

entrada – entrée or starter

entremeses – hors d'oeuvres

frito – fried

menú – usually refers to a set menu

menú de degustación – tasting menu

pescado – fish

plato combinado – main with three veg

postre – dessert

raciones – large-/full-plate-sized serving of tapas

sopa – soup

Regions at a Glance

The Canary Islands may share the same archipelago, but in every other way they are truly diverse. If you love the outdoors, there are spectacular natural landscapes and scope for scenic strolls or more arduous hikes on all islands, but especially Tenerife, La Palma, Gran Canaria and La Gomera. Beaches abound on every island but Fuerteventura has, arguably, the best of the bunch and, like neighbouring Lanzarote, is a hot destination for water sports. Something darkly different? That has to be Lanzarote: its black volcanic lava fields form the ideal backdrop for some dramatic sculpture and architecture. History lovers have plenty to ponder here as well, particularly in Gran Canaria, which digs deep into its past with some truly extraordinary archaeological sites.

Gran Canaria

Mountains
Archaeology
Food

Diverse Terrain

The mountainous interior is ruggedly beautiful, with laurel and pine forests, volcanic craters and cool mountain reservoirs; spring sees almond trees create a blush of pink-and-white blossom and the island's few waterfalls burst into full flow.

Guanche Heritage

Gran Canaria's ancient Guanche history is vividly brought to life at the excellent Cueva Pintada (Painted Cave) museum in Gáldar and the Cenobio de Valerón, plus other fascinating museums and lesser-known cave sites around the island.

Fish to Fusion

Textures and flavours here range from splendid seafood on the coast to hearty stews in the hills, fine local cheese and traditional sweetmeats, with lengthy tapas lists, fusion bistros and international menus in Las Palmas.

p52

Fuerteventura

Beaches
Water Sports
Driving

Alluring Sands

Fuerteventura's beaches are its major draw and justifiably so: secluded golden-sand coves, wild surf-thrashing beaches or darkly volcanic pebbles against a backdrop of sublime cliffs.

Surf's Up

Surfers, windsurfers and kitesurfers do what they do best, especially on the north, east and southeast coasts. And, no need to fret, you can rent all the equipment necessary if your board doesn't fit in your baggage, or join a class if you're a newbie.

Straight Lines

Farewell to the endless hairpin bends of the western islands – try the long, straight roads of Fuerteventura. Driving here is a delight, but it's never boring: the winding dirt roads of the Jandía peninsula can be heart-in-the-mouth.

p86

Lanzarote

Art & Architecture
Volcanic Landscape
Beaches

César Manrique

Thanks to César Manrique's lingering influence, the whole island is one giant natural canvas. Open-air sculptures, art galleries and gentle whitewashed architecture combine with Manrique's visionary art-meets-nature 'interventions'.

Parque Nacional de Timanfaya

Lanzarote's dark, brooding volcanic landscape has real drama, particularly at the Timanfaya National Park's core, where undulating peaks, sweeping chasms and shifting colours unravel against blue skies.

Secluded Sands

Although it's the black-pebble beaches that are so emblematic of Lanzarote, there are plenty of gorgeous golden sands here too. Seek out the beautiful protected beaches on Punta del Papagayo, hike to Playa del Risco or hop on the ferry to reach tiny Isla Graciosa's blissfully untouched sandy strips.

p110

Tenerife

Volcanic Landscape
Festivals
Traditional Villages

El Teide

Step out into the ultimate volcanic experience to hike upon Spain's highest point and the third-largest volcano on the planet (the cable car is at hand for a less thigh-burning ascent).

Carnaval!

This island knows how to party – big time. The annual Carnaval in Santa Cruz is Rio-scale in its vivacity, vibrancy and fiesta spirit, with three weeks of exuberant, fun-loving mayhem (hotels of course fill up, so book way ahead).

Traditional Villages

Traditional villages and towns with cobbled streets and typical architecture offer an antithesis to Tenerife's busy resorts. La Laguna and La Orotava are stunners, but don't miss other pretty towns like Garachico, Masca and Vilaflor either.

p138

La Gomera

Nature
Hiking
Food

Parque Nacional de Garajonay

One of the Canary Islands' most beautiful protected spaces, La Gomera's Garajonay is carpeted with ancestral *laurisilva* forests that seem plucked straight out of a fairy tale and are criss-crossed by serene walking trails.

Beyond the Park

The Parque Nacional de Garajonay is laced with fabulous, unmissable hiking trails, but the rest of the island also deserves your time. Walking paths traverse sheer gorges in the north and south, and you can hike for hours (even days!) between quiet beaches, banana plantations and extraordinary rock formations.

Gomero Cuisine

Traditional cooking and local ingredients reign supreme: delicious *miel de palma* (honey made from the sap of palm trees), smoked or fresh goat's cheese, hearty stews, *almogrote* (pâté of goat's cheese, peppers, oil and garlic)...

p180

La Palma

Nature
Activity
Hiking

Lush Landscapes

Dense tropical forests, pine-clad mountains, rolling hills and rocky cliffs: La Palma has some sensationally verdant scenery, which contrasts beautifully with the starker, more arid south. You won't even miss the beaches.

Adventure Sports

Pump up that adrenaline and try something new. Paragliding, tandem glides, caving, sea kayaking and canoeing are all popular here, plus guided mountain biking, scuba diving and strenuous treks.

Volcanic Trails

A hiker's paradise through some of the most dramatic scenery in the Canary Islands: the staggering Parque Nacional de la Caldera de Taburiente or the Ruta de los Volcanes down to Fuencaliente and the sea. And that's just the start of it all on La Isla Bonita.

p200

El Hierro

Nature
Hiking
Diving

Southwesternmost Spain

The landscape here has a wonderfully remote feel with vast big-sky views, pine-clad hillsides and plunging basins. Head to the southwest reaches of the island (and Spain!) to find wild beaches, volcanic cliffs and eerie groves of wind-sculpted juniper trees.

Historical Trails

Walking trails fan out across El Hierro, many of them with cultural importance dating back centuries. Tackle the famous 27km Camino de la Virgen across the island's spine, or the spine-tingling Camino de Jinama zigzagging high above El Golfo.

Mar de las Calmas

While there are thrilling dive sites all around the island, the calm marine-reserve seas off La Restinga are the epicentre of El Hierro diving, with plenty of multilingual schools at hand. Water temperatures are a tad higher than off other islands, which means some different fish species.

p224

On the Road

Gran Canaria

POP 847,000

Best Places to Eat

➜ Samsara (p80)

➜ Llévame al Huerto (p62)

➜ Qué Tal by Stena (p82)

➜ Texeda Brewery & Restaurant (p75)

➜ Valle de Mogán (p83)

Best Beaches

➜ Playa de las Canteras (p59)

➜ Dunas de Maspalomas (p78)

Why Go?

Gran Canaria is the third-largest island in the Canaries' archipelago, but accounts for almost half the population. It lives up to its reputation as a continent in miniature, with dramatic variations of terrain ranging from the green and leafy north to the lush mountainous interior and the desert south. You can also run headlong into three or even four seasons in one day, with microclimates dotted around the coast and hills that can transport you from piercing sunlight into clammy fog banks at the drop of a hat. To capture a sense of Gran Canaria's breathtaking diversity, head to beautiful Artenara, where the sheer drama of the mountains reaches a crescendo.

Gran Canaria keeps the adrenaline pumping further with hiking, cycling and water sports, while culture vultures won't miss out, particularly in the historic cosmopolitan capital of Las Palmas.

When to Go

➜ Peak season here is late winter to early spring (February to Easter): the weather is warm, rain is sporadic and the island's stunning interior is green, with the occasional visual blast of almond trees in blossom.

➜ Spring is festival season, with the vivacious February Carnaval celebrations followed by the sombre ceremonies of Semana Santa (Easter).

➜ June sees one of the island's largest fiestas, San Juan, and temperatures are perfect, with an average of 24°C.

➜ July and August is a busy time, with Spaniards from the mainland and families from northern Europe on holiday.

➜ September and October are perfect: the weather is ideal and the crowds have headed home.

Map labels:

Santa Cruz de Tenerife; Santa Cruz de la Palma

Cádiz (Spain)

Punta Sardina

Santa María de Guía

Punta de la Vieja

Playa de las Canteras

La Isleta Roque Negro

Sardina

Gáldar

7

Isleta (239m)

Las Palmas de Gran Canaria

Puerto de las Nieves

Pico del Viento (837m)

Cenobio de Valerón

Moya

GC2

La Montaña de Arucas

Arucas

Morro Jable (Fuerteventura); Gran Tarajal (Fuerteventura); Puerto del Rosario (Fuerteventura); Arrecife (Lanzarote)

Bahía del Confital

2

Agaete

Barranco de Agaete

San Fernando

Firgas

GC30

Jardín Botánico Canario Viera y Clavijo

Finca La Laja

Los Berrazales

GC75

GC21

Teror

Tafira

Playa de la Laja

Tamadaba (1444m)

Valleseco

Santa Brígida

Bandama

Caldera de Bandama

GC200

GC15

Artenara

4

Cruz de Tejeda

GC42

La Atalaya

GC1

GC100

Puerto de la Aldea

Roque Bentayga (1404m)

1

Tejeda

GC15

Vega de San Mateo

GC41

Telde

Playa de Melenara

Aldea de San Nicolás

GC210

Roque Nublo (1803m)

Pozo de las Nieves (1949m)

GC130

Cuatro Puertas

GC200

Montaña de las Monjas (1468m)

Presa de las Cuevas de las Niñas

Ayacata

GC605

Barranco de Guayadeque

GC140

GC100

Los Azulejos

Mogarenes (892m)

Mirador Degollada de la Cruz Grande

San Bartolomé de Tirajana

3

Ingenio

Gran Canaria Airport

Mirador El Mulato

Santa Lucía de Tirajana

Temisas

Agüimes

6

Mogán

5

Guirre (932m)

Fataga

Fortaleza de Ansite

GC551

Las Rosas

Amurga (1131m)

GC65

GC1

Puerto de Mogán

GC200

Barranco de Tirajana

Arinaga

Taurito

GC60

Vecindario

Playa del Cura

Mundo Aborigen

El Doctoral

Playa del Tauro

Juan Grande

Puerto Rico

San Agustín

GC500

Playa de Tarajalillo (Bahía Feliz)

Arguineguín

GC1

Maspalomas

GC500

Playa Aguila

Playa de Triana

Playa del Inglés

Playa de las Burras

Pasito Bea

Dunas de Maspalomas

Costa Meloneras

Playa de Carpinteras

Playa de Maspalomas

ATLANTIC OCEAN

0 — 10 km
0 — 5 miles
N

Gran Canaria Highlights

1 Tejeda (p74) Drinking in the incredible views from a restaurant terrace at this mountaintop village.

2 Las Palmas de Gran Canaria (p54) Setting out to explore the historic Vegueta *barrio* (district) in the capital.

3 Barranco de Guayadeque (p67) Motoring up this stupendous ravine and dining in a cave restaurant at the very end of the road.

4 Artenara (p73) Looking out into the void from the highest village on the island.

5 Mogán (p82) Driving down from the hills into this delightfully located village for a Canarian dinner.

6 Agüimes (p66) Pondering the pastel-painted buildings in this handsome 15th-century village.

7 Cueva Pintada Museum & Archaeological Park (p71) Wondering at the ancient cave paintings at this pre-Hispanic site in Gáldar.

History

Gran Canaria has an intriguing mix of nationalities and ethnic cultures, particularly in the capital, Las Palmas. This is nothing new. The island has historically been home to waves of settlers who have all had a deep and lingering impact.

The first human settlers to arrive, possibly as far back as 1000 BC, were the Guanches, who were most probably migrants from North Africa and who named the island Tamarán after the date palms (*tamar*) found here. In 1478, despite some plucky resistance, the Guanches' culture was largely obliterated by the Spanish. Gran Canaria was soon colonised by a ragtag assortment of adventurers and landless hopefuls from as far away as Galicia, Andalucía, Portugal, Italy, France, the Low Countries and even Britain and Ireland.

Las Palmas subsequently became the seat of the Canary Islands' bishopric and royal court, as well as a way station en route to the Americas. The economy was further boosted by sugar exports and transatlantic trade. As demand for the Canary Islands' sugar fell and the fortunes of wine grew, however, the island declined before its main rival and superior vine-grower, Tenerife.

Many Canarians subsequently immigrated to South America, initiating a strong affinity between the two cultures that is still in evidence today. It was not until the late 19th century that Gran Canaria recovered its position; the importance of the island as a refuelling port for steamships resulted in investment from foreign merchants, including the British.

It's an investment that continues to this day, only now in the form of tourism. The package-holiday boom of the mid-20th century brought a lasting prosperity to the island. However, the fortunes of Gran Canaria are dependent on the influx of foreign visitors, and the environmental price of tourism has been costly.

❶ Getting There & Away

AIR

Gran Canaria Airport (☏ 913 21 10 00; www.aena.es; off GC-1) is 25km south of the capital. Binter Canarias (p269) has direct flights to all of the Canary Islands. Canary Fly (p269) offers direct flights to Lanzarote, Tenerife and La Palma. **Air Europa** (www.aireuropa.com) flies to Tenerife, Fuerteventura and Lanzarote. Flights service destinations throughout Europe, including Madrid, Lisbon, Paris, Brussels, London, Manchester, Edinburgh, Berlin, Zürich, Vienna, Amsterdam and Helsinki.

BOAT

There are two passenger harbours on Gran Canaria that offer inter-island ferries. Boats from Las Palmas head to Tenerife, Fuerteventura, Lanzarote and, less frequently, to La Palma. There are also regular ferries from Puerto de las Nieves to Tenerife. Three companies operate on the island.

Fred Olsen (p269) Operates a fast ferry service from Las Palmas to Morro Jable (Fuerteventura; €45, two hours, twice daily), and from Puerto de las Nieves (Agaete) to Santa Cruz de Tenerife (€45, 1½ hours, six daily) from where there are onward connections to La Gomera and La Palma.

Naviera Armas (p269) Runs direct ferry services from Las Palmas to Santa Cruz de Tenerife (€32, 2½ hours, four daily), Morro Jable (Fuerteventura; €43, three hours, daily), Puerto del Rosario (Fuerteventura; €35, 6½ hours, daily) and Arrecife (Lanzarote; €49, seven hours, Monday to Friday). There are also regular services to Santa Cruz de la Palma (La Palma) and San Sebastián (La Gomera) via Santa Cruz de Tenerife, plus a daily service to Isla Graciosa via Arrecife (Lanzarote).

Trasmediterránea (p269) A weekly ferry leaves Las Palmas on Thursday, stopping at Puerto del Rosario (Fuerteventura; €27, six hours) and Arrecife (Lanzarote; €27, 9½ hours). There is also a weekly service on Saturday to Santa Cruz de Tenerife (€22, four hours) and Santa Cruz de la Palma (La Palma; €28, 19 hours).

❶ Getting Around

BUS

There is a comprehensive network of buses around the island, with Las Palmas and, to a lesser extent, Maspalomas serving as hubs. All corners of the island are covered by **Global** (☏ 928 25 26 30; www.guaguasglobal.com), although smaller, more remote towns are often served by just one or two buses a day.

CAR & MOTORCYCLE

There are car-hire firms at Gran Canaria Airport, and at the ferry terminal and throughout the Santa Catalina district in Las Palmas.

LAS PALMAS DE GRAN CANARIA

POP 379,000

Las Palmas has a mainland-Spain feel, spiced up with an eclectic mix of other cultures, including African, Chinese and Indian, plus the presence of container-ship crews, and the flotsam and jetsam that tend to drift around port cities. It's an intriguing place, with the sunny languor and energy you would normally associate with the Mediterranean or North Africa. The hooting taxis, bustling shopping districts, chatty bars and thriving port all contribute to the energy of this city, which is Spain's ninth-largest.

Vegueta, the oldest quarter, is both atmospheric and fashionable, with a fine selection of boutiques and cool bars. At the other end of town, the sweeping arc of Playa de las Canteras provides you with the tantalising possibility of taking a plunge in between sightseeing and shopping. Las Palmas is an authentic Spanish working city, and while there are areas you wouldn't walk through at night with a camera slung round your neck, overall, you should feel perfectly safe here.

By the time Christopher Columbus passed by on his way to the Americas in 1492, the busy little historic centre had already been traced out by the Spanish. The city benefited greatly from the Spanish conquest of Latin America and subsequent transatlantic trade but, inevitably, became a favourite target for pirates and buccaneers. In 1595 Sir Francis Drake raided Las Palmas with particular gusto.

In 1822 Santa Cruz de Tenerife was declared capital of the single new Spanish province of Las Islas Canarias, which left the great and good of Las Palmas seriously disgruntled; this was redressed in 1927, when Las Palmas became capital of Gran Canaria, Fuerteventura and Lanzarote.

The fortunes of the port city continued to fluctuate until the end of the 19th century, when prosperity arrived thanks to the growing British presence in the city. In early 1936 General Franco was appointed General Commander of the Canaries – a significant demotion and a posting he considered to be a form of banishment. While staying in the city – reportedly at the Hotel Madrid in Triana – Franco planned and launched the coup that sparked the Spanish Civil War.

Since the 1960s tourism boom, Las Palmas has grown from a middling port city of 70,000 to a bustling metropolis of close to 400,000 people. And, while it shares the status of regional capital evenly with Santa Cruz de Tenerife, there is no doubt that Las Palmas packs the bigger punch in terms of influence and size.

GETTING AWAY FROM IT ALL

Hike in the mountains Pick up a tourist-office brochure of mapped walks around Tejeda (p75).

Keep driving Get behind the wheel to explore the hilly interior, and just keep on going – it's beautiful.

Pack a picnic Head for the lush and green Barranco de Guayadeque (p67) or the lakeside picnic tables at Presa de las Cuevas de las Niñas (p82).

Visit a farmers market Teror (p68) is one of the interior's most stunning small towns. Come here on a Saturday morning to join the locals at the weekly produce market.

◉ Sights

The most interesting historical sights are concentrated in the narrow, cobbled lanes of Vegueta, while the heavier, more international and diverse action is around Santa Catalina.

◉ Vegueta & Triana

This is the most historic and architecturally rich city district, with traditional colonial buildings and enticing hidden courtyards. Take the time to stroll the streets and alleys, ducking into the atmospheric bars and restaurants along the way.

★**Casa-Museo de Colón**   MUSEUM
(☑ 928 31 23 73; www.casadecolon.com; Calle Colón 1; adult/child €4/free; ⊙ 10am-6pm Mon-Sat, to 3pm Sun) This fascinating museum documents Columbus' voyages and features exhibits on the Canary Islands' historical role as a staging post for transatlantic shipping. Don't miss the large section of model galleons ('La Niña') on the ground floor, which particularly impresses children with its working detail. The crucifix is said to have come from Columbus' ship. In the next room are models of all three of Columbus' ships: *La Niña, La Pinta* and the *Santa María*.

Rooms five and six contain historical maps and facsimiles of ancient maps, many from the early 16th century. Look out for the facsimile of the 'Universalis Cosmographia' map by the German cartographer Martin Waldseemüller, which was conceived in 1507 and is staggeringly accurate for its time. Astrolabes are also on display.

Las Palmas (South)

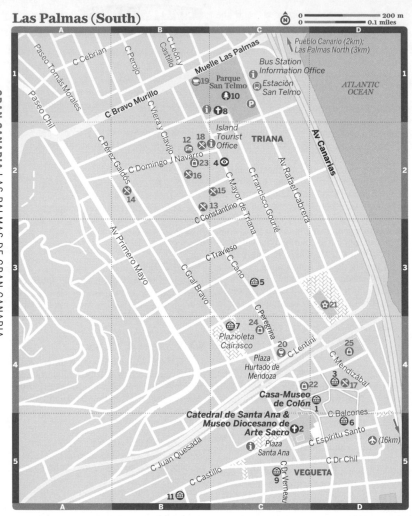

A large collection of artwork dwells upstairs, as well as a diorama of old Las Palmas with buttons for illuminating specific buildings and edifices. After descending the long stairs into the basement you are rewarded with displays on ancient South American pottery and history.

The building is a superb example of Canarian architecture, built around two lovely balconied patios, complete with fountains, palm trees and colourful macaws (the last make for excellent photo ops, but watch out, they can peck). The exterior is a work of art itself, with some showy plateresque (silversmith-like)

elements, combined with traditional heavy wooden balconies.

Although called Columbus' House (it's possible he stopped here in 1492), most of what you see dates from the time this building was the opulent residence of Las Palmas' early governors.

Check the website for details on free-entry days, including the first weekend of each month.

★**Catedral de Santa Ana &
Museo Diocesano de Arte Sacro** CATHEDRAL
(☑ 928 33 14 30; Calle Obispo Codina 13; adult/child €3/free; ⊙ 10am-4.30pm Mon-Sat) The spiritual

Las Palmas (South)

heart of the city, this brooding, grey cathedral was begun in the early 15th century, soon after the Spanish conquest, but took 350 years to complete. The neoclassical facade contrasts with the sunlight-through-stained-glass-dappled interior, which is a fine example of what some art historians have named Atlantic Gothic, with lofty columns that seem to mimic the palm trees outside. You can also admire several paintings by Juan de Miranda, the Canary Islands' most-respected 18th-century artist.

Your entry ticket also includes admission to the sacred art museum, set on two levels around the Patio de los Naranjos. The collection is a fairly standard array of religious art and memorabilia, including centuries-old manuscripts, wooden sculptures, sacred art and other ornaments, but the setting is lovely – and fragrant with the scent of orange blossom in springtime.

Once you've explored within, take the lift (€1.50; 10am to 6pm Monday to Friday and 10am to 1.30pm Saturday) to the top of the bell tower for a stunning wide-angle view of the surrounding city and coast.

Beyond the cathedral is an expansive and good-looking plaza, which provides a dramatic setting for highly photogenic images of the entirety of the church facade against the (usually) blue sky.

Museo Canario   MUSEUM
(🖊 928 33 68 00; www.elmuseocanario.com; Calle Dr Verneau 2; adult/child €5/free; ☺ 10am-8pm Mon-Fri, to 2pm Sat & Sun; 👶) This slightly old-fashioned yet still fascinating museum chronicles Gran Canaria's preconquest history. It claims the heady boast of having the largest collection of Cro-Magnon skulls in the world. There are also several mummies, plus a collection of pottery and other Guanche implements from across the island. The gift shop stocks some excellent children's educational material.

Centro Atlántico de Arte Moderno GALLERY
(CAAM, Atlantic Centre of Modern Art; 🖊 928 31 18 00; www.caam.net; Calle Balcones 11; adult/child €5/free; ☺ 10am-9pm Tue-Sat, to 2pm Sun) The city's main modern art museum is housed in a tastefully rejuvenated 18th-century building. There are no permanent collections but the galleries, flooded with natural light, host some superb temporary exhibitions. Two satellite galleries also feature rotating exhibitions: **CAAM San Antonio Abad** (Plaza San Antonio Abad; adult/child €2/free) near Casa-Museo de Colón, and the **San Martín Centro de Cultura Contemporánea** (🖊 928 32 25 35; www.sanmartincontemporaneo.com; Calle Ramon y Cajal 1; ☺ 10am-9pm Tue-Sat, 10am-2pm Sun) FREE, based in a former hospital. A combined ticket to enter all three is €8 per adult.

Gabinete Literario   HISTORIC BUILDING
(Library; www.gabineteliterario.com; Plazoleta Cairasco) Dating from 1844, this ornate historical building is a national monument. It was the island's first theatre and retains an old-world display of faded elegance, with a gracious internal patio – topped with a splendid atrium – and rooms lined with bookcases. The place now functions as a private club, although the fancy terrace restaurant is open

FOUR PERFECT GRAN CANARIA HOTELS

Lopesan Villa del Conde (☑928 56 32 00; www.lopesan.com; Mar Mediterráneo 7; s/d €200/350; [P][❄][🐕][🛜]) A sprawling, tasteful Maspalomas resort showcasing typical Canarian architecture.

Fonda de la Tea (☑928 66 64 22; www.hotelfondadelatea.com; Calle Ezequiel Sánchez 22; s/d €65/95; [❄][🛜]) This traditional stone-clad building in the heart of Tejeda has colourful, terracotta-tiled rooms around a Canarian-style courtyard.

Downtown House (☑639 62 93 35; www.houselaspalmas.com; Calle Domingo J Navarro 10; without/with bathroom s €30/40, d €40/50, f without bathroom €40-60, dm €20; [🛜]) Just off Las Palmas' Calle Mayor de Triana, this fabulous 1920s building with simply decorated rooms was designed by the same architect as the Gabinete Literario (p57).

La Ventana Azul (☑671 50 53 59; www.ventana-azul.de; Paseo de las Canteras 53; dm from €20; [🛜]) Bright, welcoming, surfy beachfront hostel in Las Palmas.

to all, with seats outside, and you can walk around the lobby area.

Calle Mayor de Triana
STREET

This pedestrianised street has long been the main shopping artery in Las Palmas. In between purchases, look skyward to enjoy some real architectural gems, including several striking examples from the modernism school of architecture, including the **Wiot Building** (1930–35) at No 106, designed by Miguel Martín. Note the surviving section of old tramway – trams used to come down here – embedded into the grey brickwork of the pavement.

Casa-Museo de Pérez Galdós
MUSEUM

(www.casamuseoperezgaldos.com; Calle Cano 6; adult/child €3/free; ⊙10am-6pm Tue-Sun) In 1843 the Canary Islands' most famous writer, Benito Pérez Galdós, was born in this house in the heart of old Las Palmas. He spent the first 19 years of his life here before moving on to Madrid and literary greatness. Guided tours (in English and Spanish) leave every hour to explore the upstairs rooms, with a reconstruction of the author's study and various personal effects transported from his mainland Spain home following his death.

Parque San Telmo
PARK

This lovely paved park shelters beneath a canopy of shade provided by a lovely group of huge, mature magnolias. The **Iglesia de San Telmo** is a charming feature on the southwestern side, as is the fascinating El Modernista kiosk (p63) in the northwest corner, which functions as a classy cafe with outdoor tables for breakfast, sandwiches or a good cup of coffee.

◉ Ciudad Jardín

This leafy, upper-class suburb is an eclectic mix of architectural styles, ranging from British colonial to whitewashed Andalucian and a fantastic seam of modernist villas from the 1930s. A tour map of the area's modernist buildings is available from the main tourist office. Also here is lovely **Parque Doramas**, with its fine *drago* (dragon) trees and superlative children's play areas. The park was designed by the British towards the end of the 19th century, when the UK dominated the economic life of Las Palmas.

Pueblo Canario
AREA

(⊙10am-8pm Tue-Sat, to 2.30pm Sun) **FREE** This mock Canarian village was designed by artist Néstor Martín Fernández de la Torre and built by his brother Miguel. It's a little unloved and the restaurant here keeps sporadic hours, but it's worth a visit on Sunday mornings, when traditional folk music is played here at 11.30am. Shut for restoration at the time of research, the *pueblo* is located on the south side of the Parque Doramas, accessed from Calle León y Castillo.

◉ Santa Catalina & Playa de las Canteras

The area between Las Canteras and Parque de Santa Catalina is an intriguing mix of city beach, multicultural melting pot, edgy port and business hub. At times you'll feel like you're in the developing world; at other times you're firmly in mainland Spain. Parque Santa Catalina is safe enough in daylight, though you can expect a fair number of down-and-outs, which increases after dark. On Saturdays at 11am, performances of traditional Canarian music and dancing take place in the park.

★ Playa de las Canteras BEACH

The fine 3km stretch of yellow sand is magnificent, and is considered by many to be one of the world's best city beaches. There's an attractive seaside promenade – the Paseo de las Canteras – which allows walkers, cyclists and joggers to enjoy the entire length of the beach free from traffic. Perhaps the most marvellous part, though, is the reef, known as La Barra, which in low tide turns the waters of Las Canteras into a giant salty swimming pool that's perfect for snorkelling.

Museo Elder de la Ciencia y la Tecnología MUSEUM

(Museum of Science & Technology; www.museoelder.org; Parque Santa Catalina; adult/child €6/3, incl 3D film €8.50/€7; ⊙10am-8pm Tue-Sun; ⊕) This 21st-century museum is full of things that whir, clank and hum. In a revamped green-painted 19th-century dockside warehouse in Parque Santa Catalina, it's a great space to spend a few hours. You can pilot a supersonic fighter plane, see how rockets send satellites into orbit or ride the Robocoaster, where a robotic arm whizzes you through a series of programmable manoeuvres. Children will be rapt – the space pod and Van de Graaff generator are particularly popular.

◉ Other Areas

Jardín Botánico Canario Viera y Clavijo GARDENS

(⏾928 21 95 80; www.jardincanario.org; Camino del Palmeral 15; ⊙9am-6pm Oct-Mar, to 7pm Apr-Sep; P) FREE About 9km southwest of Las Palmas, this vast botanical garden – Spain's largest, encompassing 27 hectares – hosts a broad range of Macaronesian flora from across the Canary Islands, including many species on the verge of extinction. The garden clings to the walls of the Guiniguada Ravine (Barranco Guiniguada), and has plenty of information boards in English and Spanish. Buses 301, 302, 303 and 323 pass by the garden's upper entrance. The lower entrance is on the GC-310.

🏃 Activities

There are 12 surf spots around Las Palmas, with the most popular being La Cicer at the southern end of Playa de las Canteras. It's a great place for beginners and there are a few surf schools, as well as some dive schools.

Vegueta Guided Walk WALKING

(⏾674 12 88 49; www.tripgrancanaria.com; adult/child €6/free; ⊙noon Mon-Sat) Get better acquainted with the pretty, narrow alleys of the old town on a walking tour of this historic quarter with these hour-long guided walks. They leave from Plaza Hurtado de Mendoza (known locally as Plaza de las Ranas), at the southern end of the Triana district. Advance bookings are essential.

7 Mares Las Canteras DIVING

(⏾928 46 79 59; www.7mares.es; Calle Tenerife 12; dive with equipment hire €25, 2hr initiation dive €60) Has English-speaking diving instructors and offers speciality and PADI courses at all levels up to instructor, plus wreck dives and equipment hire. Individual dives set out at 9.30am and 3pm.

Oceanside SURFING

(⏾928 22 04 37; www.grancanariasurf.es; Calle Numancia 47; 2hr course €30) A well-respected surf school offering a range of classes for adults and kids as well as board and wetsuit hire (from €25 per day for a basic board and wetsuit). Stand-up paddleboarding (SUP) courses are also available for the same price. Oceanside also organises bike tours (from €40) and hikes (from €55); yoga classes (€18) are also available.

📖 Courses

There are several language schools in Las Palmas where you can study Spanish.

Gran Canaria School of Languages LANGUAGE

(⏾928 26 79 71; www.grancanariaschool.com; Calle Dr Grau Bassas 27; 1-week intensive course €170) This school has been in business for more than 55 years and has an excellent reputation. Lodging can also be arranged.

🎭 Festivals & Events

Carnaval CARNIVAL

(www.laspalmascarnaval.com; ⊙2 to 3 weeks before Lent) Two to three weeks of madness and fancy dress mark the first rupture with winter in February. The bulk of the action takes place around Parque de Santa Catalina, where a giant outdoor stage goes up, along with a host of temporary bars. An extravagant fireworks display is a fitting end to the celebrations. It's held throughout Gran Canaria, but particularly in Las Palmas.

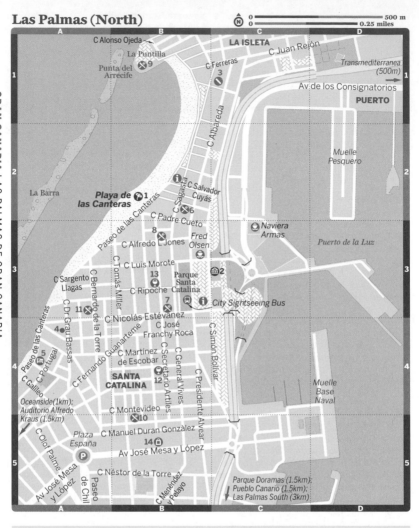

Las Palmas (North)

◎ **Top Sights**
1 Playa de las Canteras...........................B2

◎ **Sights**
2 Museo Elder de la Ciencia y la
Tecnología.......................................C3

✦ **Activities, Courses & Tours**
3 7 Mares Las Canteras.........................C1
4 Gran Canaria School of
Languages.......................................A4

🛏 **Sleeping**
5 La Ventana Azul..................................A4

✕ **Eating**
6 Bodegón El Biberón............................B2
7 El Cid Casa Pablo...............................B3
8 Kim's Pojangmacha............................B3
9 La Marinera...B1
10 Llévame al Huerto............................B5
11 Peccôu de Gôa.................................A3

🍷 **Drinking & Nightlife**
12 Bar La Tienda...................................B4
13 La Buena Vida..................................B3

🛍 **Shopping**
14 El Corte Inglés.................................B5

Opera Festival
MUSIC

(www.operalaspalmas.org; ☉ Feb-Jun) This opera festival attracts virtuoso international talent to Las Palmas, with performances held at the Teatro Pérez Galdós.

Corpus Christi
RELIGIOUS

(☉ Jun) This feast with movable dates is marked by the laying out of extraordinary floral 'carpets' in some of Las Palmas' historic streets.

Fiesta de San Juan
RELIGIOUS

(☉ 23 Jun) This Las Palmas festival honours the city's patron saint. Cultural events are staged across the city, while fireworks and concerts draw crowds to Playa de las Canteras, along with the tradition of jumping over bonfires on the beach then plunging into the ocean at midnight. The following day is usually a public holiday.

Theatre, Music & Dance Festival
PERFORMING ARTS

(www.lpatemudasfest.com; ☉ Jul-Aug) Las Palmas' Festival de Teatro, Musica y Danza is a world-class event that sees top-drawer performing talent coming to the city.

🍴 Eating

Las Palmas is teeming with restaurants. For those with the most atmosphere, head to Vegueta and Triana. At the other end of the city, with a couple of exceptions, the restaurants in the north of town on the beachfront tend to be multifarious places with multilingual menus, eat-all-you-can buffets and below-par food, but venture a street or two back and you'll find old-school Spanish restaurants and characterful tapas bars plus some excellent international choices.

🍴 Vegueta & Triana

★ Street Market Triana
MARKET €

(☑ 667 67 09 42; Calle Domingo J Navarro 4; ☉ 8am-11pm Mon-Wed, to 2am Thu & Fri, 10am-2am Sat & Sun) This super-duper indoor market is an excellent culinary addition to the town. Inside is a line of small outlets selling all manner of foods, plus a bar. Try the Mojos and the Papas for tapas or El Sibarita for wine, cheese and ham; other outlets fling together baked goodies and croquettes. There's a long communal wooden table for dining at, busy with elbows.

Panadería Miguel Díaz
BAKERY €

(☑ 928 36 29 64; Calle Viera y Clavijo 18; items from €1; ☉ 6.30am-8.30pm Mon-Fri, 7.30am-2pm Sat) Behind tall wooden doors, this *panadería* (bakery) has been serving up tasty baked goodies to the fine folk of Las Palmas since 1920.

Amaki
JAPANESE €

(☑ 928 37 22 92; www.amakisushi.com; Calle Viera y Clavijo 4; mains €2-8; ☉ 12.30-4pm & 7.30-10.30pm Mon-Wed, to 11pm Thu-Sat) With a wood interior and neat rows of bento boxes (from €8.90), this prim, petite Japanese place serves decent steamed chicken and vegetable gyoza (dumplings; €3.60), filling miso soup (€2.95) with tofu and seaweed, udon noodles as well as a wide range of *nigiri, sashimi, uramaki* and *hosomaki* choices. A bottle of sake is €8.75, a bottle of Asahi beer costs €2.90.

★ Deliciosa Marta
SPANISH €€

(☑ 928 37 08 82; Calle Pérez Galdós 33; mains €15-20; ☉ 1.30-4pm & 9-11pm Mon-Fri) This chic place with its exposed stone wall and moody lighting has become one of Las Palmas' prime dining spots over the last decade or so. Chef-owner Pol trained in Barcelona at the famous El Bulli – and it shows, with the ever-changing menu featuring scallops, pork belly and truffles. Reservations are recommended.

Restaurante Casa Montesdeoca
CANARIAN €€

(☑ 928 33 34 66; Calle Montesdeoca 10; mains €15-20; ☉ 6am-4pm Mon-Fri, 10am-4pm Sat & Sun) This romantic restaurant is set in an exquisite 16th-century house (later restored in 1757). Dine in the gorgeous, leafy patio with its traditional wooden balconies and sunny yellow walls. The steaks are recommended.

Lava
BURGERS €€

(Calle de Perdomo 7; burgers from €13; ☉ 1.30-11pm Tue-Sat, to 5pm Sun; 🛜) If you're hankering after decent burgers in a snappy environment, flash-looking Lava has a busy sense of purpose about it and some neat aesthetics too: cool, black table mats, black ceramic plates, black napkins, blood-red glasses, chilled-out jazz or ambient pop sounds, and staff togged out in red-check shirts and aprons. Special burgers include lamb, free-range chicken and veggie.

RUTA DE LAS TAPAS

On Thursday evenings, **Calle Mendizábal** in Vegueta is a top spot for meeting locals – and other travellers – and partaking in a bit of a tapas crawl. You can enjoy a small beer and a tapa for €2 in a number of bars along this strip. You will need follow-on food plans as portions are tiny; this is more about socialising than eating, but it's a great way to get a feel for the Canarian alfresco lifestyle. The fun starts at 8pm.

🍴 Santa Catalina & Playa de las Canteras

⭐Peccôu de Gôa   ITALIAN €
(📞654 19 64 66; Calle Bernardo de la Torre 63; mains from €6.50; ⊗1-5pm & 7.30-11pm Wed-Mon) This superb Italian place in the north of town is so often packed, they may have to shove you in a back room. But it's worth it. The restaurant specialises in *fainà*, a kind of unleavened flatbread made of chickpea flour – ask about it; they'll give you a sample and the *fainà* low-down. Beyond that, the pizzas and pastas are meritorious indeed.

Kim's Pojangmacha   KOREAN €
(📞628 99 35 80; www.facebook.com/kims.pojangmacha; Calle Secretario Artiles 82; mains from €8; ⊗8pm-1am Mon-Sat) Head north up Calle Secretario Artiles from Calle Alfredo L Jones and on your right you'll find this glowing, no-frills hole-in-the-wall spot. There's no English or Spanish writing outside, just the name in *hangul* (Korean). You may also notice it's packed. The reason is Mr Kim, his bibimbap rice dishes and whatever else he has up his sleeve (he decides what to cook each day).

⭐Llévame al Huerto   FUSION €€
(Calle Ruíz de Alda 26; flexitarian menu €11 Tue-Thu; ⊗1-11pm Tue-Thu, to 11.30pm Fri, 12.30-11.30pm Sat) With its blonde-wood tables, plants in baskets, outsize lampshades and colourful cushions, this superb *cocina eco fusión* place serves a to-die-for 'flexitarian' menu, delivered to your table (with mismatched chairs) by very amiable staff. The pad thai (€11.40) is superb, lightly but superbly flavoured with mushrooms, tofu and prawns, or you can flush out your insides with a quinoa falafel and vegan coriander risotto.

Bodegón El Biberón   TAPAS €€
(📞928 27 13 95; Calle Pedro Castillo Westerling 15; menú €23; ⊗5pm-1am Mon-Thu, 1pm-1.30am Fri-Sun) With a huge number of hams hanging from hooks, this popular tapas restaurant has a good-looking traditional interior and serves dependable takes on all the classics: *papas arrugadas con mojo* (wrinkly potatoes with homemade spicy sauce), Canarian cheeses, grilled fish and a great selection of sausages.

El Cid Casa Pablo   SPANISH €€
(📞928 22 46 31; Calle Nicolás Estévenez 10; mains €15-19; ⊗1pm-midnight) This grand old restaurant with a knight in armour over the front door has copious Spanish-celebrity pics adorning its walls, telling you this is *the* place for solid traditional dishes, particularly seafood and grilled meats – expect dishes like grilled stuffed salmon or suckling roast pork. The affordable *menú del día* (daily set menu; €11) takes a big sting out of the bill. Dinner reservations are recommended.

La Marinera   SEAFOOD €€
(📞928 46 15 55, 928 46 88 02; www.restaurante lamarineralaspalmas.com; Paseo de las Canteras; mains €12-18; ⊗12.30pm-late) Dine within earshot of thundering surf at this enduring and popular seafront fave. There are a few meat dishes, but the menu is predominantly and suitably fishy, with fresh fish sold by the kilo (keep an eye on the price-by-weight to avoid bill shock). Solid choices include paella, *filete de pescado a la plancha* (grilled fish fillet) and *sopa de marisco* (seafood soup).

🍸 Drinking & Nightlife

There's no shortage of watering holes in Las Palmas, though the city has few bars with much personality. The Vegueta area has a good selection, while the northern part of the city has some decent bars for craft beer and individual ambience. For live music, try the southern end of the Paseo de las Canteras, near the auditorium.

⭐La Buena Vida   BAR
(📞928 49 27 66; www.facebook.com/LaBuenaVida LasPalmas; Calle Ripoche 6; ⊗10.30am-midnight Sun-Thu, to 1am Fri & Sat; 🛜) Although it looks like a regulation Canarian bar, this place is one of the best spots in town for its crop of Viva craft beers, starting at €1.60 for a small glass or €2.90 for a pint glass. Choose between the Viva pale ale, Viva Morena, Viva Negra 'Happiness' or a Viva lager – each one is superb.

La Azotea de Benito COCKTAIL BAR
(☑928 36 74 50; Centro Comercial Monopol, 2nd fl, Plaza Hurtado de Mendoza; ◷5pm-2am Mon-Thu, 4pm-2am Fri-Sun) It's not cheap, but this relaxing cocktail bar in the historic heart of town is a pretty suave and appealing choice as the sun sets, with bamboo chairs and all-weather furniture amid the greenery on the roof of the Centro Comercial Monopol building. Head up the central stairs within the building to reach the bar.

El Modernista CAFE
(El Quiosco de San Telmo; Parque San Telmo; ◷10am-9pm Mon-Fri, 11am-11pm Sat, noon-8pm Sun) This extraordinary kiosk in lovely Parque San Telmo is a stunning art-nouveau confection from 1923, with pretty tiling and stained glass, and garlanded up on high with ceramic clusters of fruit. Sit out front with a short *cortado* (espresso with a splash of milk) and admire the premodernist lines.

Bar La Tienda BAR
(Calle Isla de Cuba 21; ◷9pm-2am Mon-Sat) This place has genuine character, with shelf upon shelf of liquor, an old black-and-white chequered floor, cabinets stuffed with books and more, a ceiling that goes on forever and a pervasive sense of seasoned personality. There's a further room at the back with wood panelling and table football.

☆ Entertainment

Auditorio Alfredo Kraus LIVE MUSIC
(☑928 49 17 70; www.auditorioteatrolaspalmasgc.es; Avenida Príncipe de Asturias) Designed by Catalan architect Óscar Tusquets, this spectacular auditorium is striking in its geometric modernity. Constructed partly of volcanic rock, with a huge window and panoramic ocean views, it's the dominant feature of the southern end of Playa de las Canteras. Most performances are of classical music, though this is one of the venues for the annual summer **Canary Islands International Jazz Festival** (www.facebook.com/canariasjazz; ◷Jul).

Guided tours (€5; 30 minutes) are held from Monday to Friday at 10.15am, 11.15am and 12.15pm.

Teatro Pérez Galdós THEATRE
(☑928 43 33 34; www.auditorioteatrolaspalmasgc.es/teatroperezgaldos; Plaza Stagno) Stages theatrical performances and music recitals. Guided tours (€5; 40 minutes) of the theatre are held from Monday to Friday at 10.15am, 11.15am and 12.15pm.

ⓘ LAS PALMAS MARKETS
····································

For the freshest and cheapest produce, including everything you might need for a picnic, check out the covered markets: the best are located between Calles Barcelona and Néstor de la Torre, and the large and excellent Mercado de Vegueta on the corner of Calles Mendizábal and Juan de Quesada in Vegueta.

🛍 Shopping

The long-time traditional shoppers' street is grand Calle Mayor de Triana (p58). Other recommended shopping strips include Calle Cano, Calle Viera y Clavijo and the surrounding streets, all in the southern part of the city.

Las Palmas' super-chic shoppers' hang-out is Avenida Mesa y López, where you can find two branches of the mammoth department store **El Corte Inglés** (www.elcorteingles.es; Avenida Mesa y López 15 & 18; ◷9.30am-10pm).

★**Mercado de Vegueta** MARKET
(☑928 33 41 29; Calle Mendizábal 1; ◷6.30am-2pm Mon-Thu, to 3pm Fri & Sat) Trading since the mid-19th century in a fabulous old building, this Vegueta market has a real abundance of aroma, and an explosion of colour from the fruit stalls, chilled fish on shaved ice, stacks of tasty cheeses, quality hams, sacks of grains, pulses and everything you might ever need. There are also cafes and *churrerías* round the perimeter.

★**Librería Moebius** BOOKS
(☑928 36 94 10; Calle Peregrina 3; ◷10am-1.30pm & 4.30-8.30pm Mon-Sat) This temple to the graphic novel has a seriously wide selection in English and Spanish in a quite riveting display.

★**Casa del Perfume Canario** PERFUME
(☑928 32 48 10; www.casadelperfumecanario.com; Calle Herrería 6; ◷9.30am-6.30pm Mon-Sat, 10am-5pm Sun) Stop by this family-run museum-shop, producing perfumes since the 1870s, and the staff will take you through the distillation and water-filtering process before arranging some of the 163 perfumes on sale for you to appreciate. Some of the aromas are simply exquisite, utilising fragrances from seasonally chosen oils, including sources such as melon, lemon, lavender and other natural aromas.

DISCOUNT CARDS

Las Palmas de Gran Canaria has issued a **Live bus pass** (www.guaguas.com/tarifas-carnets/tarjeta-turistica) for use on city transport lines; one-/three-day unlimited travel cards cost €5/12. The cards are available from tourist offices and bus stations in the city.

Fedac ARTS & CRAFTS

(Foundation for Ethnography & the Development of Canarian Handicrafts; 928 36 96 61; www.fedac.org; Calle Domingo J Navarro 7; ⊗10am-2pm & 5-9pm Mon-Fri, 10am-2pm Sat) Head to this government-sponsored, nonprofit store for handicrafts and modern designs, including exquisite hand-painted silk scarves, woven shawls and jewellery, pottery, glazed tiles, paintings, glassware, aluminium bowls and basketware.

Information

Bus Station Information Office (Estación San Telmo, Parque San Telmo; ⊗6.30am-8.30pm Mon-Fri, 7.30am-1pm Sat & Sun)

Island Tourist Office (928 21 96 00; www.grancanaria.com; Calle Triana 93; ⊗9am-6pm Mon-Fri, 10am-2pm Sat & Sun) Ask for hiking maps.

Main Tourist Office (928 44 68 24; www.lpavisit.com; Parque Santa Catalina; ⊗9am-6pm Mon-Fri, 10am-2pm Sat & Sun) Architecture fans should collect the Modernist Architecture route map, which guides you along two straightforward routes, one in the vicinity of Parque San Telmo.

Tourist Information Kiosk (Plaza de Santa Ana; ⊗9am-6pm Mon-Fri, 10am-2pm Sat) At Plaza de Santa Ana. Other kiosks are located at **Parque San Telmo** (www.lpavisit.com; Parque San Telmo; ⊗9am-2pm & 3-6pm Mon-Fri, to 3pm Sat) and **Playa de las Canteras** (Paseo de las Canteras; ⊗10am-7pm Mon-Sat).

ℹ Getting There & Away

BUS

Global (p54) operates buses to all points around the island, leaving from **Estación San Telmo** (Parque San Telmo), at the northern end of the Triana district.

Frequent main bus routes:

➡ Buses 30 and 50 express to Maspalomas (€6.15, one hour)

➡ Bus 1 to Puerto de Mogán (€8.75, 1½ hours)

➡ Buses 12 and 80 to Telde (€1.65 to €2.30, about 20 minutes)

➡ Bus 105 to Gáldar (€3.10, one hour)

The night-owl bus 5 links the capital and Maspalomas. It leaves on the hour from 8pm to 3am from Estación San Telmo in Las Palmas, and on the half-hour from 9.30pm to 4.30am from Maspalomas.

CAR & MOTORCYCLE

There are car-hire firms at Gran Canaria Airport, the ferry terminal and throughout the city's Santa Catalina district. **Avis** (928 09 23 30; www.avis.es; Muelle Santa Catalina; ⊗8am-4pm Mon-Fri, 9am-noon Sat) has a branch at the ferry terminal.

FERRY

Ferries link Las Palmas with Fuerteventura (Morro Jable, Puerto del Rosario, Gran Tarajal), Tenerife (Santa Cruz de Tenerife), La Palma (Santa Cruz de la Palma), Lanzarote (Arrecife) and the Spanish mainland (Huelva and Cádiz). Vessels are operated by **Naviera Armas** (928 30 06 00; www.navieraarmas.com; Edificio Fundación Puertos; ⊗8am-8pm Mon-Fri, to 1pm Sat), **Fred Olsen** (922 29 60 69; www.fredolsen.es; Calle Luis Morote 4) and **Trasmediterránea** (928 47 44 44; www.trasmediterranea.es; Muelle de León y Castillo; ⊗8.30am-4.45pm Mon-Fri).

ℹ Getting Around

TO/FROM THE AIRPORT

Gran Canaria Airport Bus 60 runs between the airport and Estación San Telmo twice-hourly between 6am and 7pm, and hourly thereafter (€2.30, 25 minutes), continuing on to Santa Catalina (€2.95, 35 minutes). A taxi from the airport to central Las Palmas costs about €30.

BICYCLE

The bike-hire scheme Sitycleta (p269) has stations dotted around the city.

BUS

Yellow buses (*guaguas municipales;* www.guaguas.com) serve the metropolitan area. Pick up a route map from tourist offices, kiosks or the bus station. Individual journeys are all €1.40 but if you plan to take the bus more than a few times, it's worth investing in a 10-trip *bono de guagua* (€8.50), on sale at bus stations and newsagents. One *bono de guagua* can be shared between a number of users.

Yellow buses 1, 12, 13 and 17 all run from Triana northwards as far as the port and the northern end of Playa de las Canteras, calling by the bus station and Parque Santa Catalina.

The hop-on, hop-off **City Sightseeing Bus** (902 70 20 71; www.city-sightseeing.com/en/22/las-palmas-de-gran-canaria; adult/child €15/7.50; ⊗9.30am-6pm) is a good way of getting an initial overview of the city. The main departure point is Parque Santa Catalina, but you can jump on at any of the 10 stops between there and Vegueta.

CAR & MOTORCYCLE

Driving in Las Palmas is a pain, with the normal big-city rush-hour traffic jams and a baffling one-way-street system. Most of the centre operates meter parking (coins only), but finding a space is challenging. Otherwise, there are several underground car parks, where you pay around €2 per hour. The most central are at Parque Santa Catalina, Plaza España and at Parque San Telmo, opposite the main bus station.

TAXI

If you need a **taxi** (⊡ 928 15 47 77, 928 46 90 00, 928 46 00 00), you can call, flag one down or head for one of the plentiful taxi stands across the city.

EASTERN GRAN CANARIA

Just a short drive south of Las Palmas you'll find picturesque historic towns, misty mountain villages and the sublime vistas of the gorgeously verdant Barranco de Guayadeque, a magnificent ravine that's rightly popular with both locals and tourists. The fine-looking town of Agüimes is similarly a picture when approached from afar. Dominating much of the region is the imposing Caldera de Bandama, one of the largest extinct volcanic craters on the island, while the drive from Agüimes through Temisas takes you on to San Bartolomé de Tirajana and the astonishing panoramas high up in the hills of central Gran Canaria.

Caldera de Bandama & Santa Brígida

Caldera de Bandama   VOLCANO
South of Tafira Alta is the impressive Caldera de Bandama, at 200m deep and 1km in diameter. You can drive to the top for superb views into the crater and beyond. If you're fairly fit, you can walk down to the crater floor. The hike leaves from the cluster of buildings on the GC-802, where you'll find a cosy local restaurant and a winery.

Close by is **La Atalaya**, the prime pottery-producing village on the island, where you can buy lovely ceramics...then stress about transporting them home.

Bus 311 (€1.55, 30 minutes) leaves hourly from Las Palmas to Santa Brígida, stopping at Bandama and La Atalaya en route.

Casa Museo del Vino   MUSEUM
(⊡ 928 64 44 84; Calle Calvo Sotelo 26, Santa Brígida; ⊙1-4pm & 8-11pm Tue & Thu, to midnight Fri & Sat, 1-5pm Sun, 1-4pm Wed) **FREE** This museum in the village of Santa Brígida has a modest display of wine-making implements; you can also sample wines and there's a good Canarian restaurant here too (mains €10-18).

Telde

POP 102,000
The name given to the surrounding municipality in the east of the island, Telde is Gran Canaria's second-largest city. Although relatively devoid of notable museums and sights, the historic centre is well worth exploring.

The town dates back prior to the Spanish conquest and is known for its production of stringed instruments, above all the *timple* (a kind of ukulele) – the islands' musical emblem.

◎ Sights

Skip the city's drab industrial shell and head for the historic core that comprises three distinct neighbourhoods: San Juan, San Francisco and, a little further afield, San Gregorio. Start with San Juan, where it's fairly easy to park the car and wander the narrow cobbled streets towards San Francisco, stopping for photographs of simple whitewashed houses punctuated by crimson bougainvillea, before reaching San Gregorio, which is centred around its namesake plaza and church.

Iglesia de San Francisco   CHURCH
(Plaza San Francisco; ⊙hours vary) In this church dedicated to St Francis, note the three polychrome stone altars on the northernmost of the twin naves, and the fine *artesonado* (coffered) ceiling. To reach the church from the central Plaza San Juan Bautista, take cobbled Calle Ynes Chimida due west (this tranquil street runs alongside an old aqueduct, with orange and banana groves below).

Basílica de San Juan Bautista   CHURCH
(Plaza San Juan Bautista; ⊙9.30am-12.30pm & 5-8pm) Among the grand old buildings of the San Juan area is this neo-Gothic church. You can't miss the gloriously kitsch 16th-century altarpiece, all gilt and gold, with a crucifixion at its heart. The Christ figure was made by the Tarasco Indians in Mexico.

Museo León y Castillo MUSEUM
(www.fernandoleonycastillo.com; Calle León y Castillo 43; adult/child €2/free; ☺10am-6pm Tue-Sun) This museum is devoted to the city's most famous resident, the late-19th-century politician Fernando León y Castillo. The lovely building, his former home, has galleried wooden balconies; in contrast, the exhibits (ambassadorial credentials and the like) are less engaging.

Cuatro Puertas ARCHAEOLOGICAL SITE
FREE Although it's only 5km south of Telde, this impressive pre-Hispanic site is seldom visited, even by locals. 'Cuatro Puertas' means 'four doors' and takes its name from the multiple entrances carved into the rock face of this human-made cave complex. There are information panels here but no visitors centre, meaning you can visit whenever you like. It's just off the GC-100 in the minute hamlet of Cuatro Puertas. Bus 36 from Telde (€1.40, 10 minutes) passes by hourly en route to Maspalomas.

Playa de Melenara BEACH
This decent beach is 5km from Telde and frequented by townsfolk rather than tourists. The wide arc of dark sand is fronted by apartments and several good, inexpensive seafood restaurants. A footpath follows the rocky coast to Playa de la Garita, another popular local beach, located 3km to the north. There are some good surf spots en route.

ℹ Information

Tourist Office (www.telde.es; Calle Conde de la Vega Grande 9; ☺8am-3pm Mon-Fri) Centrally located one street north of the Basílica de San Juan Bautista.

ℹ Getting There & Away

Buses 12 and 80 run to/from Las Palmas (€1.65 to €2.30, about 20 minutes, every 20 minutes).

Agüimes

POP 30,740

A short bus ride (or drive) south of Telde brings you to lovely Agüimes, with its perfectly restored historic centre. Agüimes is sometimes overlooked by tourists, but it's one of the prettiest towns on Gran Canaria, and a couple of manageable museums offer excellent insights into the history of the settlement.

◉ Sights

The pedestrian streets of Agüimes are lined with lovely buildings that reflect vernacular Canarian architecture, especially those surrounding shady Plaza del Rosario.

Iglesia de San Sebastián CHURCH
(Calle de San Sebastián; ☺9.30am-12.30pm & 5-7pm Tue, Thu, Sat & Sun) This vast church, with its dome of 12 large windows (symbolising the 12 apostles) and rounded arches, is considered one of the best examples of Canarian neoclassicism. Construction started in the late 18th century, but the church wasn't completed until the 1940s.

Museo de Historia de Agüimes MUSEUM
(☑928 78 54 53; Calle Juan Alvarado y Saz 42; adult/child €3/2.50; ☺9am-5pm Tue-Sun) Covering more than just the history of the town, the well-presented exhibits here give a good insight into Canarian history, covering everything from pre-Hispanic customs to agriculture, folklore, poverty, rebellion, emigration and witchcraft. Captions are detailed and very informative.

Centro de Interpretación del Casco Histórico MUSEUM
(Old Town Interpretation Centre; Plaza San Antón 1; ☺8.30am-4pm Mon, to 6pm Tue-Fri, 9am-1pm Sat) FREE There are some well-documented and absorbing exhibits here on the evolution of Agüimes' urban structure through the centuries. You can find it in the same building as the tourist office. Don't forget to peep into the old chapel.

✕ Eating & Drinking

El Populacho CANARIAN €
(☑928 78 45 14; Plaza del Rosario 17; tapas €2.50-6; ☺10am-11pm Sun-Thu, to midnight Fri & Sat) On the corner of Agüimes' main square, this welcoming tapas joint, with its green-painted bar and art-deco lights, is housed in a former grocer's shop (dating to 1933), as depicted in the murals covering the walls. Rumbling tummies should opt for a portion of *ropa vieja* (chickpea stew).

★Almogaren CAFE
(☑628 87 99 27; Calle el Progreso 14; ☺9am-5pm Wed-Mon) Run by welcoming Carmen and Roberto, this delightful place is a very tasteful choice with a small courtyard, shafts of sunlight, a handful of tables, a sofa, a wind chime or two and a scattering of secondhand books. Grab a chilled beer (€1.50 to €2.30) from the fridge or line up a coffee. It acts as a crafts shop too.

🔒 Shopping

Aragüeme FOOD & DRINKS
(📞 645 31 39 25; Calle el Progreso 22; ⊘ 10.15am-6pm Wed-Mon) There's an enticing collection of deli items at this good-looking shop, from a wonderfully whiffy selection of cheeses to locally made olive oil, *mojo*, sweet potato jam, wines, *gofio* (ground, roasted grain), honey and handmade ice cream, as well as jewellery and more.

ℹ️ Information

Tourist Office (www.aguimes.es; Plaza San Antón 1; ⊘ 8.30am-4pm Mon, to 6pm Tue-Fri, 9am-1pm Sat) In the same building as the Centro de Interpretación del Casco Histórico.

ℹ️ Getting There & Away

Buses 11 and 21 connect Las Palmas with Agüimes (€3.40, 45 minutes, hourly). Bus 22 heads southeast to Arinaga (€1.40, 20 minutes, hourly), a popular coastal swimming spot even though it lacks a real beach.

There is a paying car park on Calle Acebuche, just outside the historic centre.

Barranco de Guayadeque

One of the island's most captivating experiences and popular destinations, the sublime Barranco de Guayadeque (Guayadeque Ravine) rises up into central Gran Canaria in a majestic sweep of crumpled ridges. For most of the year the vegetation here is lush and green; if you can, visit in early spring when the almond trees are in blossom and the landscape is remarkably verdant and beautiful.

Start your visit at the extensive **Centro de Interpretación** (📞 928 17 20 26; adult/child €3/2.50; ⊘ 9am-5pm Tue-Sat, 10am-3pm Sun; 🅿️), occupying a cave at the entrance of the *barranco* (ravine). Exhibits explain the geology of the ravine and cover its fascinating history, from the pre-Hispanic inhabitants to the troglodytes of today.

Around 4km from here, stretch your legs at **Cueva Bermejas** (GC-103), a small settlement of cave homes carved out of the mountainside. Be sure to peek into the tiny chapel next to the Bar Guayadeque, where the pulpit, altar and confessional are all hewn from rock.

The road continues to wind upwards until you reach **Montaña de las Tierras**, with its cave restaurants and smattering of homes. If you want to continue from here you'll need sturdy hiking boots. There are a couple of trails with stunning views that stretch right to the sea; ask at the interpretation centre for information.

The ravine is really at its best once the lunchtime crowd has left.

Bar Guayadeque TAPAS €
(https://barrestauranteguayadeque.negocio.site; Cueva Bermejas 23; tapas €4-9; ⊘ 9am-11pm Mon-Thu, to midnight Fri-Sun) With a photogenic line of hams hanging from the ceiling and an appealing tapas menu, this place attracts a large number of visitors but somehow maintains its poise. You can find it next door to the chapel (Ermita de Guayadeque), with parking opposite.

⭐ Restaurant Tagoror CANARIAN €€
(📞 928 17 20 13; www.restaurantetagoror.com; Montaña de las Tierras 21; mains €8-16; ⊘ 1-4pm & 7pm-late) There's not much to choose between the numerous cave restaurants in Barranco de Guayadeque, but Tagoror is a welcoming, long-standing and labyrinthine choice with consistently good reviews and good-natured staff. Hearty stews are the order of the day and there's no shortage of *gofio*, Canarian *potaje* (stew) and *papas arrugadas* with spicy *mojo*. The *menú del día* (€11) is excellent and superb value.

ℹ️ Getting There & Away

The sensible approach is to explore the ravine with your own car. Bus 27 ($1.40, 25 minutes) departs once daily (at 8.15am) from Agüimes to Montaña de las Tierras.

WORTH A TRIP

MARKET TIME

The towns and villages are the scene of some interesting small markets, most of which sell local cheeses, cold meats and bakery goods, as well as souvenirs and trinkets. Markets generally run from 9am to 2pm.

Puerto de Mogán (Friday) One of the most touristy.

San Fernando (Wednesday and Saturday)

Arguineguín (Tuesday and Thursday)

Santa Brígida (Saturday)

Teror (Saturday and Sunday)

Vega de San Mateo (Saturday and Sunday)

GRAN CANARIA FOR CHILDREN

Gran Canaria is a kiddie wonderland with plenty of natural, manufactured and theme-parked stuff to do. The beaches are the most obvious attraction and those in the southern resorts come complete with all manner of boat rides. In southern Puerto Rico you can go dolphin-spotting with Spirit of the Sea (☑928 56 22 29; www.dolphin-whale.com; Calle Puerto Base, Puerto Rico; adult/child €33/20). Further west is Taurito, which resembles a family-themed park with several pools (and pool tables) plus an abundance of amusements geared towards children. Theme parks are prolific in these parts, particularly around Playa del Inglés (p78), including Maspalomas' enormous Aqualand (www.aqualand.es; Carretera Palmitos Park; adult/child €27/18; ⊗10am-6pm Jul & Aug, to 5pm Sep-Jun;). Cocodrilo Park (www.cocodriloparkzoo.com; adult/child €9.90/6.90; ⊗10am-5pm Sun-Fri), near Agüimes, is part zoo, part sanctuary, with the majority of its animals being abandoned exotic pets. On a more highbrow note, even the most museum-jaded tot cannot fail to be impressed by the model galleons at the Casa-Museo de Colón (p55) in Las Palmas. Or tag after the school trips at the superb Museo Elder de la Ciencia y la Tecnología (p59) in the island's capital.

Temisas

The impressive setting for Temisas, with its backdrop of impenetrable cliffs, provides views across a ravine that falls away down to the sea, while the village itself is sleepy and atmospheric, with original stone houses and cottages. To get here by car, take the GC-550 weaving around the mountains from Agüimes to Santa Lucía de Tirajana. As the road approaches Temisas, set on a natural balcony, note the terracing up each side of the centre and incised into the valleys below.

Observatorio Astronómico
de Temisas   OBSERVATORY
(www.astrotemisas.probooking.es; GC-550, Montaña de Arriba; tour adult/child €35/30; ⊗9-11pm Mon-Sat) Located 850m about sea level on the edge of the Caldera de Tirajana, this observatory has guided stargazing visits from Monday to Thursday from 8.30pm to 10.30pm. A free bus also runs to the observatory, for those with tickets; contact the observatory for details. If driving from Temisas, look out for the sign at the side of the road that leads to an unpaved track going up to the observatory. Book online for discounted tickets.

NORTHERN GRAN CANARIA

Gran Canaria's fertile north presents a gently shifting picture from its rugged, mountainous interior and the southern beach resorts and dunes. Dramatic ravines, intensively tilled fields and terraces, and forests of pine trees, covered with mossy lichen fed by mist and rainfall, typify the changing landscape as you wind along twisting roads, passing myriad villages and hamlets. Only as you reach the west does the green give way to a more austere, although no less captivating, landscape.

Teror

POP 6650 / ELEV 543M

Despite its name, Teror does anything but inspire fear: the central Plaza Nuestra Señora del Pino and Calle Real, near the stupendous Basílica Nuestra Señora del Pino, are lined with picturesque old houses – painted in bright colours and all with leaning walls and wooden balconies. The centre of town is a vignette of historical charm and, despite the popularity of this picturesque hamlet in the hills, locals extend an inviting welcome to visitors.

There's a small farmers market (Plaza Nuestra Señora del Pino; ⊗8am-2pm Sun) in the plaza on Saturday mornings, with stalls selling local goodies such as the deliciously garlic-laden chorizo de Teror (Teror sausage). The Sunday market is larger and more commercial.

The only building that entirely jars with the town's manifest historical sensibilities is the modern Auditorio de Teror (Plaza de Sintes), just west of the basilica.

Teror is located up in the hills 20km southwest of Las Palmas.

◉ Sights

★Basílica Nuestra
Señora del Pino   CHURCH
(Plaza Nuestra Señora del Pino 3; ⊗8am-noon & 2-6pm) Dominating the square is this

neoclassical 18th-century church, home to Gran Canaria's patron saint. According to legend, the Virgin was spied atop a pine tree in the nearby forest in the 15th century, which converted Teror into a pilgrimage site. The church interior, a lavishly gilt-laden affair, sees the enthroned Virgin illuminated at the heart of an ornate altarpiece, surrounded by angels. For a splendid close-up of the Virgin, visit the museum, also called the 'treasure house'.

★ **Museum of the Basílica Nuestra Señora del Pino**　MUSEUM
(Plaza Nuestra Señora del Pino 3; admission €1; ⊙noon-3pm Mon-Fri, 11am 2.30pm Sat & Sun) Don't miss this museum (also called the 'treasure house'), accessed upstairs from the rear of the basilica, where you can get a real close-up view of the Virgin and see the armfuls of unusual items gifted by the devout. There's also a room displaying the outfits she's worn through the ages (a new dress is premiered each year during the fiesta held in her honour) – however, the standout image is of the Virgin herself, with child, set upon a brilliantly burnished silver throne.

Casa de los Patronos de la Virgen　MUSEUM
(Calle Real de la Plaza 1; admission €3; ⊙11am-4pm Mon-Fri, 10am-2pm Sun) One of the loveliest buildings in Teror houses this modest museum. Pleasantly musty, it's devoted to preserving 18th-century life and is stuffed with intriguing odds and ends, mostly from the Las Palmas family, who used it as a second home. The museum was shut at the time of research and was due to reopen later in 2019.

🎉 Festivals & Events

Fiesta de la Virgen del Pino　RELIGIOUS
(⊙1st week of Sep) Teror is the religious capital of Gran Canaria and the Virgen del Pino is the patron of the island, so this festival is not only a big event in town, it's the most important religious feast day on the island's calendar, with processions, a livestock fair and plenty of music, dancing and celebration.

🍴 Eating

El Encuentro　CANARIAN €€
(Plaza Nuestra Señora del Pino 7; mains €8-16; ⊙10am-5pm Tue-Thu & Sun, to 11pm Fri & Sat) This cheery place, right on the square, has a fine selection of steaks as well as a traditional *potaje* of the day – perfect in winter when Teror can be bitterly cold.

🛍 Shopping

Cistercian Convent　FOOD
(Calle del Castaño 24; ⊙10am-1pm & 3-6pm) A divine aura of sorts hangs over Teror, a fitting place to find snacks handmade by nuns. Climb up steep Calle Herrería, next to the museum, until you reach Calle del Castaño and this Cistercian convent, where the nuns produce some tasty biscuits. If no one's around, ring the bell and have your cash ready – transactions are carried out by a speedy, unseen sister.

ℹ️ Information

Tourist Office (Calle Real de la Plaza 2; ⊙9.30am-5.30pm Tue-Sat) Opposite the church.

ℹ️ Getting There & Away

Buses 216, 220 and 229 connect with Las Palmas (€2.30, 30 minutes, hourly); bus 215 runs to/from Arucas (€1.40, 20 minutes, hourly).

Arucas

POP 10,400

A visit to Arucas makes a great day trip from Las Palmas. It is a handsome, easily manageable and compact town, with pedestrian streets lined with elegant historic buildings, a superb flower-filled garden and a noteworthy church.

👁 Sights

From the church, walk down Calle Gourié to Calle León y Castillo, flanked by colourful colonial-style buildings. Turn right into Plaza Constitución, situated across from the gorgeous Parque Municipal de Arucas de las Flores (p70) and home to the late-19th-century modernist *ayuntamiento* (town hall) and a couple of pleasant terrace bars.

If you have your own wheels, take the steep, well-signposted route to La Montaña de Arucas, 2.5km north of town. From here there's a splendid panorama of Las Palmas, the northern coast of the island, orchards and banana groves (with the less-photogenic sight of hectare upon hectare of plastic greenhouses).

★ **Iglesia de San Juan Bautista**　CHURCH
(Calle Párroco Cárdenes 3; ⊙9.30am-12.30pm & 4.30-7.15pm) The extraordinary, neo-Gothic church stands sullen watch over the bright, white houses of Arucas in a striking display of disproportion and contrast. The church has a Sagrada Familia (Gaudí) look with

elaborate pointed spires and was, fittingly, designed by a Catalan architect. Construction started in 1909 on the site of a former *ermita* (chapel) and was completed 70 years later. Treasures within include a nude, a reclining image of Christ carved by local sculptor Manolo Ramos and three magnificent rose windows.

★ Parque Municipal de Arucas de las Flores
GARDENS

(Carretera Arucas-Bañaderos; ⊙ 9am-10pm) **FREE** These terraced municipal gardens are laid out in French style with fountains, pavilions, sculptures and tropical trees, including the rare evergreen soap bark tree *(Quillaja saponaria)* and several magnificent dragon palm trees, as well as some astonishing flowering plants and groves of gentle bamboo. Note the elaborate system of irrigation channels and water courses built into the park.

Jardín de la Marquesa
GARDENS

(📞 928 60 44 86; www.jardindelamarquesa.com; Carretera Arucas-Bañaderos; adult/child €6/3; ⊙ 9am-6pm Mon-Sat; 🅿) This lovely botanical garden, located northwest of town on the road to Bañaderos, is owned by the Marquesa de Arucas (along with the Hacienda del Buen Suceso). It's lushly planted with more than 2500 different perennials, trees and cacti, and there are ponds, places to sit and a greenhouse with banana trees amid the verdant foliage.

Destilerías Arehucas
DISTILLERY

(📞 928 62 49 00; www.arehucas.com; adult/child €3.50/free; ⊙ 9am-2pm Mon-Fri; 🅿) The 45-minute guided tour of this rum distillery, its ancient cellar (one of the oldest rum cellars in Europe) and the fermentation and distillation rooms culminates in a rum and liqueur tasting.

Municipal Museum
MUSEUM

(📞 928 62 81 65; Plaza de la Constitución; ⊙ 10am-6pm Mon-Fri, to 1pm Sat) **FREE** The municipal gardens house the town's main museum, which has a permanent exhibition by Canarian painters and sculptors, including the masterful Guillermo Sureda (1912–2006) and Manolo Ramos (1899–1971) – both Arucas natives – as well as large sculptural works by Abraham Cárdenes (1907–71), who was born in Tejeda. Temporary art shows are also held here.

✗ Eating

Tasca Jamón Jamón
TAPAS €

(📞 928 60 34 97; Calle Gourié 5; tapas €4-8; ⊙ 1-4pm & 7pm-late Tue-Sun) This place boasts an ace position on a narrow pedestrian street, with views of the church from the outside tables. Enjoy good basic tapas such as wedges of crumbly Manchego cheese with crusty white bread.

❶ Information

Tourist Office (Calle León y Castillo 10; ⊙ 10am-4pm Mon-Sat)

❶ Getting There & Away

Buses 205 and 210 connect the **bus station** (Calle Bruno Pérez Medina) in Arucas with Las Palmas (€2.10, 25 minutes) every 30 minutes. Bus 215 runs hourly to Teror (€1.40, 20 minutes).

Moya

POP 1320 / ELEV 490M

The spectacular 20km drive between Arucas and Moya hugs the flank of the mountain, providing gee-whiz views of the northern coast. The town of Moya itself is an unpretentious working place with a sprinkling of traditional Canarian architecture, including the lovely **Casa-Museo Tomás Morales** (www.tomasmorales.com; Plaza Tomás Morales; adult/child €2/free; ⊙ 10am-6pm Tue-Sun), once home to the namesake Canarian poet, who died in 1922 aged just 37. A more immediate and impressive sight, however, is the vista across the *barranco* from the back of the 16th-century church, bettered only by the view of the church itself from the other side of the ravine, clinging precariously to the mountainside.

Buses 116 and 117 run hourly to/from Las Palmas (€2.95, one hour).

Santa María de Guía

Just off the main GC-2 highway southeast of Gáldar, Santa María de Guía (or just Guía) is an atmospheric small town that was temporarily home to the French composer Camille Saint-Saëns (1835–1921), who used to tickle the ivories in the town's 17th-century neoclassical church. The church overlooks a spacious square, which is a pleasant place to stretch your legs.

In the 18th century, the town and surrounding area were devastated by a plague of locusts. To rid themselves of this blight, the locals implored the Virgin Mary for help. This remains a tradition and on the third Sunday of September the townsfolk celebrate La Rama de las Marías by dancing their way to the doors of the church to make offerings of fruit. The town is also known for its *queso de flor* (flower cheese).

Buses 103, 105 and 150 (€2.85, 50 minutes) pass by roughly every half-hour on their way from Las Palmas.

Cenobio de Valerón   ARCHAEOLOGICAL SITE
(www.arqueologiacanaria.com; Cuesta Silva; adult/child €3/free; ⊙10am-6pm Tue-Sun Apr-Sep, 10am-5pm Tue-Sun Oct-Mar; P) This a fascinating ancient site consisting of over 350 caves, silos and cavities of varied size, which were used to store grain in pre-Hispanic times. They're located on deep slopes and separated by steps and walkways, with informative plaques throughout explaining the history and archaeology of the site, as well as the volcanic geology of the area.

Gáldar

POP 10,780 / ELEV 124M

This historic town was the capital of the *guanartemato* (kingdom) in pre-Hispanic times and is most famous for the extraordinary cave paintings on display in the Cueva Pintada Museum and Archaeological Park. The town has a small, bustling and attractive historic core, centred around the gracious Plaza de Santiago with its neoclassical **Iglesia de Santiago** (Plaza de Santiago; ⊙9am-8pm, Sacred Art Museum 10am-1pm Tue-Thu & Sun, 10am-1pm & 4-7pm Fri & Sat), which also contains a sacred art museum. Also alongside the square is 19th-century **Casas Consistoriales**, where one of the oldest *drago* trees on the island, dating from 1718, rises up to the sky from within a patio.

◉ Sights

★ **Cueva Pintada Museum & Archaeological Park**   ARCHAEOLOGICAL SITE
(☑928 89 54 89, 902 40 55 04; www.cueva pintada.com; Calle Audiencia 2; adult/child €6/free; ⊙10am-6pm Tue-Sat & 11am-6pm Sun Oct-May, 10.30am-7.30pm Tue-Sat & 11am-7pm Sun Jun-Sep) Discovered by a local farmer in the late 19th century, this is one of Gran Canaria's most important pre-Hispanic archaeological sites: a cave adorned with geometric shapes, possibly thought to relate to the lunar and solar calendars (though this is debated). It's also the most accessible of the island's archaeological sites, situated not halfway up a cliff but right in the heart of town (it is wheelchair-friendly also). The highlight is the cave itself, fully explained on the tour.

The museum complex features videos and reconstructions shedding light onto local life before the conquistadors arrived, and showcases the 5000-sq-metre excavated site where the remains of cave houses have been dug out from the volcanic rock (around which you can walk). Videos in various languages offer pointers about the history of the site, but you will need to tag along on the 90-minute tour (in Spanish, English, French and German) to see the painted cave itself from within the confines of a glass room and to be in a position to ask questions. The colours and triangular shapes and patterns on the wall have deteriorated considerably but are still clear enough to admire. Try to book in advance via the website or over the phone – there is a limit of 20 people on each tour so you might be disappointed if you just show up.

In order to prevent further deterioration to the paintings, the cave is open at numerous set times and viewing periods can be brief. In the decade after 1972 the colours of the pigments were reduced by a shocking 50% due to the constant stream of visitors (just the effects of human breath were enough to do considerable damage, hence the enclosed viewing experience).

After seeing the wall paintings, you can explore the interiors of some recreated dwellings, strewn with animal skins.

A combination €6 ticket is available that includes the Casa Museo Antonio Padrón, and the Casa-Museo Tomás Morales in Moya.

Casa Museo Antonio Padrón   MUSEUM
(Calle Capitán Quesada 3; adult/child €2/free; ⊙10am-6pm Tue-Sun Oct-Jun, to 7pm Tue-Sun Jul-Sep) Locals are justifiably proud of native son Antonio Padrón who, in the 1960s, was just starting to gain serious recognition in the European art world when he tragically died of an allergic reaction to penicillin at just 48 years old. The museum is located at the artist's former studio. His paintings are wonderfully colourful and distinctive, many inspired by the geometric motifs of the Guanches. A combination €6 ticket is available that includes the Cueva Pintada Museum, and the Casa-Museo Tomás Morales in Moya.

WORTH A TRIP

AGAETE TO ALDEA DE SAN NICOLÁS

Sometimes referred to as San Nicolás de Tolentino, but more often known simply as La Aldea ('the hamlet'), this rather scruffy town has little to excite the senses – it's the sort of place you might only hang around if your car has broken down. The lure here is the travelling, not the arriving.

The GC-200 road between Agaete and San Nicolás takes you on a magnificent cliff-side journey. If you head southwest in the late afternoon, the setting sun provides a soft-light display, marking out each successive ridge in an ever-darker shadowy mantle. There aren't many places to stop, so pull over at every opportunity, but you can certainly stop towards the end at Puerto de la Aldea, with its small harbour and smattering of seafood restaurants – the local speciality is *ropa vieja de pulpo* (chickpea stew with octopus).

Vertigo sufferers might want to tackle the 40km journey, which can take anything up to two hours, in the opposite direction: if you drive from south to north, you can hug the mountain rather than tackling the countless curves with the steep drop directly beneath you.

The approach from Mogán and the south, though lacking the seascapes, is almost as awesome.

ℹ Information

Tourist Office (www.ciudaddegaldar.com; Plaza de Santiago 1; ◷8am-3.30pm Mon-Fri, 10am-2pm Sat) This helpful office provides town maps; it's right alongside one of the oldest *drago* trees in Gran Canaria.

ℹ Getting There & Away

Bus 105 (€3.10, one hour) heads east for Las Palmas roughly every half-hour. Southbound, bus 103 (€1.40, 20 minutes, hourly) links Gáldar with Agaete and Puerto de las Nieves. Buses all arrive at and depart from the **Estación de Guaguas Gáldar** (Carretera General), a walk of five to 10 minutes east of the historic centre of town.

There are two free car parks on Calle Real de San Sebastián as you approach town from Las Palmas.

Agaete & Puerto de las Nieves

POP 5600

The pretty main street of the leafy town of Agaete, Calle de la Concepción, is flanked by typical Canarian buildings, some with traditional wooden balconies, while in the centre of town stands its handsome main church. Agaete is also home to the sole coffee-producing plantation in Europe.

Situated just 1km away is Puerto de las Nieves, the island's principal port until the 19th century but now better known as the terminal for fast ferries linking Gran Canaria with Tenerife. It's a small place with black pebbly beaches, but the mountainous setting is lovely, with stunning views south along the Andén Verde. The port has a tangible fishing-village feel and the buildings, with their brilliant blue trim against dazzling white stucco, look as though they've been transplanted from some Greek island. The port is well known for its excellent seafood restaurants and fills up with locals on weekends.

◉ Sights

Iglesia de Nuestra Señora de la Concepción   CHURCH
(Plaza Constitución, Agaete; ◷hours vary) Built in 1874, this handsome church is strikingly Mediterranean in style.

Huerto de las Flores   GARDENS
(Calle Huertas, Agaete; adult/child €1.50/1; ◷10am-4pm Tue-Sat; P) A leafy retreat on a sweltering day, this charming 19th-century garden has more than 300 tropical plants and a cafe that serves coffee produced in the nearby Valle de Agaete.

Ermita Nuestra Señora de las Nieves   CHURCH
(Carretera al Puerto de las Nieves, Puerto de las Nieves; ◷11am-1pm Mon-Sat, 9-11am Sun) This beautiful, whitewashed chapel in Puerto de las Nieves sits just back from the water, a tiny and exceptionally rewarding haven of peace. The small chapel contains a renowned 16th-century Flemish triptych painted by Joos van Cleve and dedicated to the Virgen de las Nieves (Virgin of the Snows).

★✦ Festivals & Events

Fiesta de la Rama   CULTURAL
(◷4 Aug) This extraordinary festival in Agaete has origins that lie in an obscure Guanche rain dance. Nowadays, locals accompanied

by marching bands parade into town brandishing tree branches and then get down to the serious business of having a good time.

Eating

Finding a table in Puerto de las Nieves can be hard at weekend mealtimes: arrive early.

Terraza Angor SEAFOOD €
(☑ 928 55 41 09; Avenida de los Poetas 2, Puerto de las Nieves; mains €8-12; ☺ 7am-10pm Sun-Tue & Thu, to 11pm Fri & Sat) Based in a pretty blue-and-white building by the harbour, Angor is popular with locals and visitors, largely for its excellent-value three-course *menú del día* (€10).

Restaurante Las Nasas SEAFOOD €
(Calle Nuestra Señora Nieves 7, Puerto de las Nieves; mains €8-10; ☺ 9am-9pm Fri-Wed) There's a great atmosphere in this former warehouse with an old-fashioned black-and-white interior, jolly model boats and high ceilings. In the small open-air terrace overlooking the ocean, diners feast on grilled fish, seafood paella and calamari.

★**Ragu** SEAFOOD €€
(☑ 605 45 39 65; Paseo de los Poetas 10, Puerto de las Nieves; mains €13-15; ☺ 12.30-4pm & 6.30-9pm Wed-Sun) With views over the water, this Italian seafood restaurant never fails to deliver, with delicious homemade pasta finding its way into delectable dishes such as the spaghetti with Atlantic scallops and king prawns. Line up a Jaira craft beer for full enjoyment and don't overlook the *postres* (desserts), such as the moreish chocolate brownies and cheesecakes. Reserve ahead.

ℹ Information

Tourist Office (☑ 928 55 43 82; www.agaete.es; Calle Nuestra Señora Nieves 1, Puerto de las Nieves; ☺ 9am-5pm Tue-Fri, 9am-2.30pm Sat)

ℹ Getting There & Away

BUS
Bus 103 links the town and port with Las Palmas (€4.30, 1¼ hours) at least hourly. Bus 101 heads south for Aldea de San Nicolás (€3.95, one hour, four daily).

BOAT
From Puerto de las Nieves, Fred Olsen (p269) operates six fast ferries daily (adult/child €42/25) for the hour-long trip to Santa Cruz de Tenerife. There is a free bus connection to Las Palmas (Parque Santa Catalina). Returning, the

---

WORTH A TRIP

CANARIAN COFFEE

A pretty and reasonably straight 6km drive takes you from the town of Agaete into the fertile valley of the same name, where you can seek out one of several coffee plantations. **Finca La Laja** (www.bodegalosberrazales.com; Calle de los Romeros, Valle de Agaete; ☺ 10am-5pm) cultivates tropical fruit and grapes alongside coffee beans and a tour includes wine tastings and a cup of the fine, rich coffee. High above the valley, the Tamadaba pine forest is also a prime hiking area.

---

bus leaves Las Palmas an hour before the ferry is due to depart.

CAR & MOTORCYCLE
There's a free car park in Agaete, opposite the gardens on Calle Huertas. It's fairly easy to find street parking in Puerto de las Nieves, especially on weekdays.

CENTRAL GRAN CANARIA

Best explored behind the wheel, the winding roads looping up and into the island's lofty central terrain allow you to fully appreciate the topographical and climatic diversity of Gran Canaria. A world away from the undulating, arid dunes and resorts of the south, the high-altitude centre of the island can have you turning a bend in sharp sunlight into a deep and impenetrable fog bank. Go back round the corner and the sunlight will still be there. A huge and vastly varied region, this is what Gran Canaria is all about.

Artenara
POP 1200 / ELEV 1270M

Dramatically positioned as the highest village in Gran Canaria, Artenara offers stunning views, including an astonishing perspective over the huge volcanic crater from Mirador de Unamuno (near Iglesia de San Matías; p74), one of several signposted miradors.

In Artenara, it's also all about caves. People live in caves, the restaurants are in caves, the town museum occupies a series of caves and if you want to spend the night in the area, you can even sleep in a *casa rural*

FORTALEZA DE ANSITE

The huge rocks of **Fortaleza de Ansite** (GC-651) form a natural fortress and constitute one of Gran Canaria's most important pre-Hispanic sites. It was here that the Guanches' last stand took place, with many opting to hurl themselves into the ravine rather than face a life of slavery. An interpretive centre fills you in on the history. Break out the hiking boots to explore the 'fortress', with its caves and tunnel cutting through 34m of mountain.

(village accommodation) that's based – you guessed it – in a cave.

The sleepy town is overlooked by the Corazón de Jesus, a Rio-style statue of Christ (albeit much smaller), with arms outstretched.

◎ Sights

★**Mirador de Unamuno**　　　　VIEWPOINT
One of several viewpoints in town, the Mirador de Unamuno looks out onto a sweeping panorama of the vast volcanic caldera beyond – it is a stupefying sight.

★**Museo Etnográfico
Casas Cuevas**　　　　　　　　　MUSEUM
(Calle Pàrroco Domingo Bàez; by donation; ⊙11.30am-4.30pm) Once inhabited by locals, this cave complex is now home to the village museum, a fascinating place that focuses on village life in times gone by. You could see why someone would want to live here: the cave homes, now decorated with period furniture and all manner of religious iconography, are surprisingly roomy and have killer views. There's even a toilet here, in a cave, of course.

Mirador de la Atalaya　　　　VIEWPOINT
Mirador de la Atalaya overlooks several troglodyte caves, some still inhabited, as well as the distant peak of El Teide in Tenerife.

Santuario de la Cuevita　　　　CHURCH
(Calle Camino de la Cuevita) Dating back to the early 19th century, this is one of Gran Canaria's smallest and most endearing chapels. Everything here – the altar, confessional, pulpit – has been carved straight from the rock; it's like a small-scale version of a Lalibela church. It houses the Virgen de la Cuevita, the patron saint, bizarrely, of both Canarian folklore and cycling. The ceiling of the chapel

is all moss and scraps of vegetation, feeding off the sunlight that penetrates the cave.

Iglesia de San Matías　　　　CHURCH
(Plaza San Matías) A delightful late-18th-century church with a carved wooden ceiling, frescoed altar and art-nouveau stained-glass windows.

✖ Eating

★**Biocreperia RiscoCaido**　VEGETARIAN €€
(⌨617 50 92 57; Avenida Matías Vega 13; set menu €15; ⊙1-5pm & 7.30-9.30pm Thu, to 10pm Fri & Sat, 1-5pm Sun; ✎) ✿ With a sound organic, culinary philosophy that oversees the creation of its much-loved and delicious crepes, this enterprising restaurant is always busy. Everything, from the vegetable soups, vegan pâté, savoury and sweet crepes, and cornucopia of daily vegetable delights, conspires to fashion a wholesome and flavourful feast.

Restaurante Mirador La Cilla　BARBECUE €€
(⌨609 16 39 44; Camino de la Cilla 9; mains €8-16; ⊙1-4pm & 7pm-late) A long tunnel carved through the mountainside serves as the *entrada* to this long-standing restaurant. Book ahead to guarantee a table on the expansive terrace with stupendous views of Roque Nublo in the distance (and plenty more in the foreground). The menu is meaty, with steaks cooked over an open fire on weekends.

❶ Getting There & Away

Bus 220 runs hourly to/from Teror (€2.95, 1¼ hours), from where you can easily connect to Las Palmas.

There's a spectacularly vertiginous road (GC-210) connecting Artenara with Aldea de San Nicolás, but no buses brave this route.

Tejeda

POP 1485 / ELEV 1050M
Sitting in the centre of the island, gorgeous Tejeda is a charming hill village with a handsome church and steep, winding streets lined with balconied houses. Whichever route you take to get here by car, you'll drive through a splendidly rugged landscape of looming cliffs and deep gorges. Although pretty at any time of year, the town pulls out all the stops in February when the almond trees are blossoming. A fiesta celebrates all things almondy once the trees have bloomed. The village is scenically situated on the eastern edge of the Caldera de Tejeda, a huge volcanic basin at the heart of Gran Canaria.

◉ Sights & Activities

This region is ideal for both hardcore hiking and less arduous walks. The tourist offices have detailed brochures of surrounding trails.

Centro de Plantas Medicinales   GARDENS
(☑ 928 66 60 96; Calle Párroco Rodriguez Vega 10; adult/child €3/free; ⊙ 10am-4pm Mon-Fri, 10am-3pm Sat & Sun) An appealing garden that showcases medicinal plants, with explanations in English. There's a small interpretation centre, and a cafe where you can fittingly end your visit with a cup of curative herbal tea.

Museo de las Tradiciones   MUSEUM
(Calle Párroco Rodríguez Vega; adult/child €3/free; ⊙ 10am-4pm Mon-Fri, 10am-3pm Sat & Sun) Based in one of Tejeda's most charming buildings, this museum gives a good overview of local life, starting with the Guanche era and covering the Spanish conquest, plus some interesting exhibits on agriculture in the mountains.

✖ Eating

★ Dulcería Nublo Tejeda   BAKERY €
(Calle Hernández Guerra 15; pastries from €1; ⊙ 9am-8pm Mon-Fri, 9.30am-8pm Sat, 9.30am-6pm Sun) Everyone from sweaty German cyclists to gentle, retired British couples joins the queue at this sublime pastry shop, in business for over 70 years. The delicious treats are freshly baked on the premises: try the almond cakes coated in chocolate and take home a jar of delicious *bienmesabe* (a sickly sweet almond spread) or half a kilo of almonds (€7.50).

★ Texeda Brewery & Restaurant   FUSION €€
(☑ 928 66 66 77; www.cervezatexeda.es; Calle Los Almendros 25; mains from €6; ⊙ noon-5.30pm Tue-Sun) With a restaurant supplied with food from its own farm, and its own artisan beers (three of them), Texeda is a terrific addition to Tejeda. We went for the Burger Nublo, served on a traditional roof tile (yes, it's as tricky as it sounds), preceded by the delicious cheese soup. Service is excellent. Sit inside or out, your choice, but reserve ahead.

ℹ Information

Tourist Office (www.tejeda.es; Avenida de los Almendros; ⊙ 10am-5pm Mon-Fri) At the southern entrance to Tejeda.

ℹ Getting There & Away

Bus 305 (€2.55, one hour, six daily) connects Tejeda to San Mateo, from where there are frequent connections to Las Palmas. Bus 18 (€6.15) connects Tejeda with Maspalomas.

Around Tejeda

Cruz de Tejeda

The greenish-grey stone cross from which this spot takes its name marks the centre of Gran Canaria and its historic *caminos reales* (king's highways), along which it is still possible to cross the entire island. The site is one of the most popular coach-tour destinations with the resorts, so is usually swarming with tourists (hence the souvenir stalls and donkey rides).

From the lookouts here you can survey and contemplate the island's greatest natural wonders: to the west is the sacred mountain Roque Bentayga and, in clear weather, the towering volcanic pyramid of Teide on neighbouring Tenerife is visible; to the southeast rises the island's highest peak, Pozo de las Nieves, and the extraordinary emblem of the island, Roque Nublo (often enveloped in cloud). Dropping away to the northeast is Vega de San Mateo.

Walks of all levels extend from here, from half-hour strolls on paved paths to five-hour

---

BIRDS, MUTTS OR BERBERS?

How did the Canary Islands get their name? From the trilling native canary birds perhaps? Or maybe they were named after the Latin word for dog (*canus*), because members of an early expedition discovered what they considered unusually large dogs? Still others held that the natives of the island were dog eaters.

A more plausible theory claims that the people of Canaria, who arrived several hundred years before the time of Christ, were in fact Berbers of the Canarii tribe living in Morocco. The tribal name was simply applied to the island and later accepted by Pliny. How Canaria came to be Gran (Big) is perhaps because the island was thought to be the biggest in the archipelago, even though Tenerife and Fuerteventura are actually larger.

STRESS-BUSTING TREATMENTS

Thalassotherapy has long been a fashionable health treatment. Based on warmed-up sea water, it's designed to relieve stress and physical aches and pains. Whether or not it works (some of its claims for cellulite control could be considered dubious), this is still a sensual experience in its own right and often does wonders for skin ailments. There are centres throughout the island, including at the Hotel Puerto de las Nieves, the Centro de Talasoterapia (p79) and at Lopesan Villa del Conde (p58).

treks through the mountains. The 12.5km circular route from Cruz de Tejeda to Roque Nublo is especially recommended. Allow about 3½ hours and take warm clothing, no matter how hot the day might seem. You can get information and tips from the **Hotel Rural El Refugio** (⊘928 66 65 13; www.hotelruralel refugio.com; s/d €65/80; Ⓟ✸🛏) or the **tourist office** (⊘10am-5pm).

Bus 305 (€1.45, one hour, six daily) from San Mateo passes by on its way to Tejeda.

Roque Bentayga

A few kilometres west of Tejeda village rises Roque Bentayga (1404m); it's signposted, but you'll need your own transport to get here. Various reminders of the Guanche presence include rock inscriptions, granaries and a sacred ritual site. Don't miss the **Centro de Interpretación** (⊘10am-4pm Mon-Fri, to 5pm Sat & Sun) FREE, at the base of the rock, for excellent insights on the area's Guanche history and heritage. Ask there about walking trails to visit the caves that would've once housed the Guanches.

Pozo de las Nieves

Those with their own vehicle can drive 15km southeast of Tejeda to the highest peak on the island (1949m), which offers breathtaking views on a clear day. Follow the signs for Los Pechos.

Roque Nublo

Roque Nublo is an icon of Gran Canaria, an impressive monolith (1803m) jutting 80m skywards from the surrounding volcanic landscape. It sneaks into the background of virtually every photo you'll take in the area, but it's worth approaching to get an up-close shot as well. The half-hour walk from the roadside has a few steep sections, but isn't too challenging, and the views are wonderful.

San Bartolomé de Tirajana

POP 5800 / ELEV 890M

San Bartolomé is a handsome town with a number of lookout points offering awesome views over the Tirajana Valley. The 17th-century **Iglesia de San Bartolomé** (Plaza de Santiago) at the centre of town has striking stained-glass windows and a very peaceful complexion. The area is a grape-growing region and in the upper part of town, near the hotel, you'll find the winery **Bodega Las Tirajanas** (⊘628 21 66 83; www.bodegaslas tirajanas.com; Calle Las Lagunas; tastings per wine €1; guided tours from €6; ⊘10am-4pm Mon-Fri, to 2pm Sat & Sun) at the centre of town. You can drop by for a casual tasting, but book ahead for a tour and a sampler of local cheese, olives and *mojo* with your wine. San Bartolomé makes a good base for hiking and exploring the surrounding mountainous countryside; there are several signposted trails.

If you're planning a visit, make it on a Sunday when a lively farmers market is in swing.

★ Mirador Degollada de la Cruz Grande

VIEWPOINT

Located by the roadside between San Bartolomé de Tirajana and Tejeda, this superb viewpoint gives you vistas, in two directions, of the Caldera de Tirajana, as well as the Cuenca de Chira and the Pinar de Pilancones. Also visible is Pico de las Nieves, Risco Blanco and, in the distance, Santa Lucia.

La Panera de Tunte

BAKERY €

(⊘928 12 74 28; Calle Reyes Católicos; snacks from €2; ⊘6.30am-8.30pm Mon-Sat, 7am-3pm Sun) The mountains surrounding San Bartolomé are definitely picnic-worthy, whether you're hiking or driving. Stop at this long-running (since 1948) cafe-bakery and put together an alfresco lunch of cured meat, fresh bread and local cheese. With tables out across the road, it's also a nice spot to stop for coffee and a slice of cake.

❶ Getting There & Away

Bus 18 (€3.50, 30 minutes) runs from Maspalomas to San Bartolomé de Tirajana, en route to Tejeda.

There is a small free car park on Calle Fernando Guanarteme, just as you round the main road past the church heading north.

Fataga

POP 400 / ELEV 600M

The 7km drive from San Bartolomé south to small Fataga (607m) is as drop-dead gorgeous as the picturesque hamlet itself, sitting squat on a small knoll humbled by vast cliffs to the west. The drive up the GC-60 from the resorts of Maspalomas (a world away, both physically and existentially) is almost as astonishing, especially as you turn at the Degollada de la Yegua viewpoint, which gazes down onto the vast valley below.

The lanes of Fataga are an exquisite joy to roam, with the mountains an ever-present backdrop to the attractive white walls and terracotta roofs. There are at least three bodegas in this vine-growing centre – all are well signposted but, less happily, all have sporadic opening hours.

The small white church at the hub of the village, near which village elders sit to take stock of the day, was built in 1880.

Several restaurants are on the main road near Fataga's church, including Bar Restaurante El Albaricoque (Calle Nestor Álamo 4; mains €7-12; ☺10am-5pm Sat-Thu; 🛜), with its popular terrace at the rear, looking out onto sublime views of the mountains and valley.

Bus 18 (€2.65, 50 minutes, four times daily) from Maspalomas to San Bartolomé stops here.

Mogán, by its namesake *barranco*, where you really should spend the night to allow its magic to fully seep in. Or, for glorious seafood and a fun port atmosphere, head on down to Puerto de Mogán. Windsurfers may pay little attention to all of these attractions, however, and storm over to Pozo Izquierdo to ride the fine waves.

Maspalomas

POP APPROX 30,000

Gran Canaria's most famous holiday resort is a sun-splashed party place for a largely northern European crowd. That said, during the day (and out of season) it has a more upmarket appearance than you might expect. It's not Benidorm, nor even Los Cristianos in Tenerife. You're more likely to stumble across expensive hotels or smart apartment blocks in the centre than pubs serving full English breakfasts. On the downside, there is barely anything remotely Spanish here and the only languages you'll need are German or English. Moreover, town planning is soulless, with all the neatly traced boulevards and roundabouts suggestive of a five-year plan.

The only sights of real interest are the astonishing dunes of Maspalomas, which are also home to some of Gran Canaria's most luxurious hotels and the island's largest golf course.

◎ Sights & Activities

To enjoy an exhilarating (and free) 5km walk, simply follow the promenade that extends eastwards from Playa del Inglés. The path follows a track that is sometimes at shore level and sometimes above it.

SOUTHERN GRAN CANARIA

Although best known for Maspalomas and the resort landscape running west along the shore, the south also offers some highly picturesque pockets and breathtaking natural wonders. The most obvious example of the latter, ironically perhaps, is back in Maspalomas, with its astonishing dunes: a nature reserve of huge sand hillocks in a vast dune field that recalls the Sahara Desert. It's here that you can understand why the island is so often called a 'continent in miniature'. But there's also the delightful village of

---

JUST A SPOONFUL OF RUM

Generally associated with dancing barefoot on a Caribbean beach, rum has long been produced here, dating back to the days of the sugar plantations. The local product has a superb international reputation, being famed for both its heart-warming flavour and, yes, even the supposed medicinal properties. Feeling a tad feverish? Then have a glug of *ron miel* (a honey-infused white rum) – it sure beats an aspirin.

Beaches

★ Dunas de Maspalomas   NATURE RESERVE

These fabulous dunes cover 400 hectares and were designated a nature reserve in the 1990s, ensuring that the rapidly multiplying hotels would never encroach on their golden grains. The best view of the dunes is from the bottom of Avenida Tirajana: stroll through the arches of the Hotel Riu Palace Maspalomas to the balcony, which is surrounded by a botanical garden displaying shrubs and plants native to the Canaries. There's a small information office here too (open 10am to 1pm Monday to Friday).

Playa del Inglés   BEACH

Aside from the rolling Maspalomas dunes, the main attraction for the thousands of annual visitors to the island's quintessential package-tour destination is Maspalomas' beach, a magnificent and vast sandy stretch some 2.7km long. The individual beaches, from east to west, are **Playa de las Burras** (San Agustín), **Playa del Corralillo, Playa del Inglés** and **Playa de Maspalomas.** They all link up to form one long, spectacular length of sand.

Water Sports

Although surfing is possible here (the best waves tend to break off the western end of Maspalomas by the lighthouse), this is not mind-blowing-waves territory. Windsurfers are better off heading east, beyond the resorts to Bahía Feliz, Playa Aguila and, best of all, Pozo Izquierdo (p81), 25km along the coast.

Prosurfing Company   SURFING

(☑ 628 10 40 25; www.prosurfing.es; Avenida de Moya 6, CC Eurocenter; 1-day surf course €55, board hire per day €25) A well-regarded company offering surfing, kitesurfing, windsurfing and stand-up paddleboarding lessons, as well as board and wetsuit hire and jet-ski rental. Courses are considerably cheaper if booked online.

Canarias Extreme   KAYAKING

(☑ 675 91 19 23; www.canariasextreme.com; Varadero Shopping Centre, Calle Mar Mediterráneo; 3hr kayak tour €52) If you are looking for a watery pursuit more adrenaline-boosting than a glass-bottom boat, this outfit organises single- and double-kayak tours along the coast of Gran Canaria, as well as buggy and 4WD excursions and tours.

Dive Academy Gran Canaria   DIVING

(☑ 928 73 61 96; www.diveacademy-grancanaria. com; Calle La Lajilla, Arguineguín; 4hr discover scuba diving €60, advanced open-water course €290) Offering a professional standard of service and excellent teachers, this dive school has a free minibus to pick up plungers from their hotels. It takes them to the dive academy in Arguineguín, west along the coast, and from there on to a choice of dive sites, including various wrecks. Both boat and shore dives are available.

FROM PARROTFISH TO PIGS' TAILS

Local cuisine is renowned for making use of every part of the *cochino* (pig). That cute, curly tail *(templero)* was traditionally hung from the kitchen doorway to be periodically dipped into the cooking pot for stock. A typical tapa here, generally accompanied by the traditional rum aperitif, is *caracajas* (pieces of fried pork liver doused in a spicy sauce). Goat is also popular, along with rabbit, while seafood is, naturally enough, always a good bet – this is an island, after all. Try the much-prized *vieja* (parrotfish), a member of the sea-bream family.

Goat's cheese is produced on several islands, though one of the best-known soft cheeses, Gran Canaria's *queso de flor,* is made from a combination of cow's and sheep's milk. The cheese, which is produced exclusively in the northern Guía area, is then infused with the aroma of flowers from the *cardo alcausí* thistle. Another scrumptious winner is the similar-tasting *pastor* cheese, produced in the Arucas region. Pick up the booklet *La Ruta de los Quesos* (in English) at larger tourist offices for more cheesy information.

Almonds are a favourite ingredient of many traditional desserts, including the must-try *bienmesabe* (literally translated as 'it tastes good to me'), made from ground almonds, lemon rind, sugar and eggs.

Among the outstanding Gran Canaria wines is the fruity Del Monte, a perfect, if tiddly, accompaniment to meat dishes, with an alcohol content over 11.5%. Aside from *ron miel* (honey rum), which is more liqueur than rum, the island produces a decent drop of golden rum – head to the distillery in Arucas to taste the full range. *¡Salud!*

SCENIC DRIVE: BEACH DETOUR

If you want more space on the sand, there are several choice beaches on the coast-hugging GC-500 road, west of Playa del Inglés. Follow the signs to the town hospital and Puerto de Mogán from the centre (at the top of Avenida Tirajana), passing Holiday World on your left. The road climbs past palm plantations and the golf course, Meloneras Golf. At Km 7 watch for the **Pasito Bea** sign, turning left on the rough approach that leads to a small black sandy cove secluded by rocks, which is mixed nude and clothed.

After a quick dip continue along the road, which winds around arid hills and, after 1.2km, comes to **Playa de Carpinteras**. Follow the track east of the main beach here, park on the cliffs and you will discover an idyllic, little-known broad arc of sand with shallow water backed by sloping dunes. It's known as the **Playa de Montaña Arenas**; here you can clamber around the rocks due east to reach the beach, which, again, is mixed nude and clothed. The third beach worth recommending is at Km 9.2. **Playa de Triana** is a black pebbly beach, with parking on the main road; note that you will be expected to wear your clothes here!

Follow the road a further 4km to a roundabout, where it rejoins the GC-1, heading towards the vastly more commercial beaches of Puerto Rico and beyond.

Theme Parks & Zoos

Families may find these interesting, but note that zoos and parks may create stressful conditions for their animals through live performances or cramped living compounds.

Mundo Aborigen AMUSEMENT PARK
(GC-60; adult/child €10/5; ⊙9am-6pm; ⊕) Situated 6km along the road north to Fataga, around 100 model Guanches stand in various ancient poses, designed to give you an idea of what life was like before the conquistadors arrived.

Camel Safari Park La Baranda OUTDOORS
(⊒928 79 86 80; www.camelsafarigrancanaria. com; Carretera Playa del Inglés-Fataga; 1hr camel ride €25; ⊙9am-5pm Mon-Sat; ⊕) This place has 70 camels and is located in a lush property with palm, avocado and citrus trees 13km north of Playa del Inglés. There's also a restaurant, bar and small zoo. Mountain horse treks (€36), donkey rides (€36) and bike rides (€36) of the Fataga Valley are also available.

Other Activities

★ **Free Motion** CYCLING
(⊒928 77 74 79; www.free-motion.com; Hotel Sandy Beach, Avenida Alféreces Provisionales; bike hire per day from €15, tours from €22; ⊙8.30am-7pm Mon-Sat, 9am-5pm Sun) This slickly run company offers a range of tours for small groups, and has mountain, road and city bikes, as well as e-bikes, for hire. For a small fee they will arrange transport to/from various places on the coast, including Puerto Rico and Puerto de Mogán. E-bike hire starts at €18 per day.

Happy Horse HORSE RIDING
(⊒658 92 52 86; Calle Islas Malvinas; ⊙9am-10pm) Organises one-, two- and three-hour horse treks in the area. Pick-up from your hotel is included in the price.

Centro de Talasoterapia SPA
(Thalassotherapy Centre; ⊒928 776404; www.gloria palaceth.com; Hotel Gloria Palace, Calle Las Margaritas, San Agustín; 2hr circuit €24; ⊙10am-9pm) Massive and luxurious, this is Europe's largest centre for thalassotherapy – a relaxing spa therapy that uses heated seawater. The standard treatment at the 7000-sq-metre complex is a circuit featuring a variety of Jacuzzi-type treatments, saunas and an ice cave. Massages, facials, reflexology, pressure therapy, body wraps, acupuncture and other therapies are also available.

🍴 Eating

Maspalomas is predictably swarming with restaurants, with the normal mix of Chinese buffets, Argentinean grills, bland international platters and that increasingly rare breed – authentic Spanish cuisine.

El Salsete CANARIAN €€
(⊒928 77 82 55; Calle Secundino Delgado, edificio Jovimar Bloque 1; mains €12-18; ⊙6-11pm Mon-Fri, 1-4pm & 6-11pm Sat) Located off the beaten tourist path in the north of the San Fernando district, El Salsete has an unassuming facade concealing a welcoming dining room that offers food that wouldn't be out of place at a cutting-edge restaurant in Barcelona. Dishes are creative in taste and presentation, and

LGBT+ GRAN CANARIA

Gran Canaria is the gay honeypot of the Canaries, and Playa del Inglés is Europe's winter escape playground. There are several hotels and apartment blocks that cater for LGBT+ guests. A seemingly endless string of bars, discos and clubs are crammed into the Yumbo Centrum, which is predominantly a gay scene, although this doesn't stop small numbers of lesbians and straights from wading in. Little happens before midnight. From then until about 3am the bars on the 4th level of the Yumbo Centrum bear the brunt of the fun, after which the nightclubs on the 2nd level take over.

At dawn, people stagger out for some rest. Some make for the beach at Maspalomas, across the dunes, which are themselves a busy gay cruising area.

First celebrated in 2001, Maspalomas Pride (www.gaypridemaspalomas.com; ☺May) consists of 10 days of parades, concerts, excursions and parties.

For more information about LGBT+ clubs, events, accommodation and personal classifieds, check www.gaymap.info and www.travelgay.com.

use only market-fresh ingredients. Reservations are recommended.

Mundo FUSION €€
(☑928 93 78 50; Apartamentos Tenesor, Avenida Tirajana 9; mains €10-18, menú €10; ☺1-4pm & 7-11pm Mon-Fri, 7-11pm Sat; ☑) Mundo is an excellent choice for fusion, Canarian and European dishes, with an excellent-value *menú del día* with crowd-pleasing dishes such as *pollo al horno* (baked chicken) or tuna salad. Reservations are recommended.

Restaurante Etiopico Afrika ETHIOPIAN €€
(☑648 76 04 98; www.restauranteafrika.es; Centro Comercial Ronda, Calle La Palma 9; mains €9-20; ☺7-11pm Tue-Thu, noon-3.30pm & 7-11pm Fri & Sat; ☑) The first Ethiopian restaurant on Gran Canaria, Restaurante Etiopico Afrika has received great fanfare for its menu. There's also a huge amount of choice for vegans.

Casa Vieja CANARIAN €€
(☑928 76 90 10; www.restaurantegrilllacasavieja. es; Calle El Lomo 139, Carretera de Fataga; mains €8-17; ☺noon-11.30pm Sun-Thu, to midnight Fri & Sat; ☑) Just north of the GC-1 motorway along the road to Fataga, the 'Old House' bursts with a *campo* (countryside) feel. Plants festoon the low roof, canaries trill and the menu is pretty authentic. Try the grilled meats (such as garlic chicken or *ropa vieja*) or fish; there's a kids' menu too. Diners are serenaded with live traditional music from 8pm most nights.

★**Samsara** FUSION €€€
(☑928 14 27 36; www.samsara-gc.com; Avenida Oasis 30; mains €18-25; ☺7.30pm-late Tue-Sun) Samsara is located across from the Palm Beach hotel, with a giant Buddha statue setting an appropriate tone. Dishes blend Canarian and Spanish ingredients with Asian flavours, such as smoked goat's cheese with wasabi or black pasta with prawns and shellfish in lemon sauce and lemongrass. Reservations are recommended.

 Drinking & Nightlife

The Yumbo Centrum transforms into a pulsating clubbers' scene at night, with both straight and gay places.

Pacha CLUB
(☑928 72 01 14; www.pachagrancanaria.com; Avenida Sargentos Provisionales 10; ☺11pm-5am) A vast nightclub with big-name DJs. Admission is €15.

Shopping

The main shopping centres are north of the centre, in San Fernando and Bellavista.

Fedac ARTS & CRAFTS
(Centro Insular del Turismo, cnr Avenidas España & EE UU; ☺10am-2pm & 4-7.30pm Mon-Fri) If you're after local handicrafts, visit the small Fedac shop located within the main tourist office. Fedac is a government-sponsored nonprofit store, whose prices and quality are a good standard by which to measure those of products sold elsewhere. You'll also get a guarantee with your purchase.

Information

Main Tourist Office (☑928 77 15 50; www. grancanaria.com; cnr Avenidas España & EE UU; ☺9am-5pm Mon-Fri, to 1pm Sat) Just outside the Yumbo Centrum, with maps, helpful staff and public toilets.

Playa del Inglés Tourist Office (Commercial Centre Anexo 11; ☺9am-7pm Mon-Fri, to 1pm Sat)

POZO IZQUIERDO

The hugely windswept but likeable settlement of Pozo Izquierdo, 25km northeast of Playa del Inglés, has just one reason for being: windsurfing. In June and July, the town fills up with enthusiasts when it stages a leg of the Windsurfing World Cup. The rest of the year it's a quiet place (no one comes here apart from windsurfers, certainly not sunbathers), but the conditions for windsurfing are always fine.

There are a number of companies offering equipment hire and windsurfing classes (you can find kitesurfing and stand-up paddleboarding instruction too): try Cutre or Pozo Winds.

ℹ Getting There & Away

Buses link regularly with points along the coast, westwards as far as Puerto de Mogán (€4.15, 45 minutes) and eastwards to the capital: for Las Palmas (€6.15, one hour), take nonstop express lines 30 or 50. There is also a night bus (line 5) if you're seeking the *marcha* (nightlife) at the other end of the island. The main tourist office has timetables covering both the southern and northern routes.

ℹ Getting Around

TO/FROM THE AIRPORT

Gran Canaria Airport Bus 66 runs to/from the airport (€4.05, 30 minutes, hourly) until about 8pm. For a taxi, budget for about €35 for Playa del Inglés and €40 for Maspalomas.

BUS

There are bus stops all over Maspalomas, including a couple beside Yumbo Centrum. Global (p54) runs buses to many of the theme parks. A standard fare within town is €1.40.

CAR & MOTORCYCLE

If you must take your car down to the beach, there's a large paying car park beside Playa del Inglés. Street parking costs from €0.50 for 30 minutes, though you will find quite a few streets (along Avenida de Alemania leading to the dunes, for example) where the ticket machines do not work, so you should be able to park for free.

TAXI

You can call a **taxi** (📞 928 76 67 67), otherwise reliable taxi stands abound. From Playa del Inglés, no fare to a destination within the urban area should cost more than €10.

Puerto de Mogán

A tempting little crescent of sandy beach and, next to it, a busy little yacht harbour and fishing port, Puerto de Mogán may be largely given over to the tourist trade, but the port is in a different world compared to its garish cousins to the east. It may not have the unassailable charm of Mogán up the road, but there's an attractive port atmosphere still unblighted by resort architecture.

Although its nickname 'Venice of the Canaries' may be exaggerated, the architecture and bridged waterways are as pretty as a chocolate box, and Puerto de Mogán exudes an air of opulence and charm. In the heart of the port, low-rise apartments have wrought-iron balconies and brightly coloured trim, and are covered in dazzling bougainvillea.

On the downside, the place is busy with tourists from other resorts during the day, particularly on Friday morning when a street market takes over part of the town.

◉ Sights & Activities

This is a great place for scuba diving and snorkelling, with caves and wrecks just offshore.

Ermita de San Fernando   CHURCH
(Paseo de los Pescadores 5) Tucked among the restaurants and bars on Paseo de los Pescadores, the simple Ermita de San Fernando church dates back to 1936. You may well find the church open so you can take a peek at the spartan and largely unadorned interior.

Canary Diving Adventures   DIVING
(📞 610 81 06 19; www.canary-diving.com; Hotel Taurito Princess, Playa de Taurito) This enthusiastic and responsible outfit offers guided boat dives (€40 including equipment hire) and a full range of courses, including Discover Scuba Diving (€80), PADI Open Water (€339) and Rescue Dive courses (€280). There are also meditation and oneness dives.

🍴 Eating & Drinking

Culinary competition is intense, and there are plenty of cafes and restaurants offering fresh fish on pleasant *terrazas* overlooking the water.

PACK A PICNIC

Trade sand in your sandwiches, nasty jellyfish stings and parasols on the beach for a picnic with civilised tables and benches, paired with idyllic lakeside surroundings and a strong sense of the topographical variety on this beautiful island.

Head around 3km north along the GC-200 beyond Mogán to reach the GC-605, and from there onwards to immerse yourself in a bucolic scenery of sublime rock forms, lofty mountains and a growing abundance of pine trees. About 10km after the turnoff you will reach the mirador **Cruz de San Antonio**, from where dramatic views plunge to the lake and the snaking road below. There is also a lovely signposted walk to **Inagua** from here (10km). The road continues winding through the **Pinar de Pajonales** pine woods until you reach your destination: the **Presa de las Cuevas de las Niñas** lake, and the aforementioned strategically positioned picnic tables by the water. The journey from Mogán will take just under an hour. From here you could turn back or continue on to Tejeda and the highest peaks on the island, or continue along the route of the Agüimes-to-Mogán drive (p138), but in the reverse direction.

La Cucina ITALIAN €

(Calle Corriente 8; pizzas €6-10; ☺noon-4pm & 6-10pm Tue-Sun) Run by Italians, this tiny place is predominantly a takeaway spot but has a few outside tables. The pizzas are highly recommended, and there's also a good range of pasta dishes and salads, plus the obligatory creamy tiramisu. It's pleasantly set back from the main complex and drag in the old part of town.

Jack El Negro BARBECUE €€

(Paseo de los Pescadores 6; mains €12-15; ☺6pm-midnight Tue-Sun) Housed in one of precious few original fishers' cottages, this restaurant has carafe-loads of earthy atmosphere. It is named after a legendary Caribbean pirate, and run by Italian owner Claudio since 1970 (hence the Chianti-bottle candleholders). A speciality is the steaks cooked to a T on a *parilla* (open grill). The pizzas also come recommended.

★**Qué Tal by Stena** SPANISH €€€

(☎692 94 89 86; www.quetalbystena.com; Urbanización Puerto de Mogán; 5-course menu €69; ☺8pm-late) With contemporary paintings from local artists on the walls, white tablecloths and an exquisite set menu that changes regularly, Qué Tal is the place for a special dinner. Opt for the wine-pairing option (€49) to sample some special vintages from the cellar. There is one sitting daily at 7.30pm. Reservations are highly advisable.

★**Olivia Lounge** COCKTAIL BAR

(☎928 56 52 54; www.olivia-lounge.com; ☺11.30am-midnight Wed-Mon; 🛜) Set back from the marina and behind the bandstand, this is the bar to come to for ambience, chillaxing

and superb cocktails (from €8), highballs, Canarian wines, liqueurs and more, from a terrific, lengthy list (though the prices are not cheap).

❶ Getting There & Away

BUS

There is no shortage of buses heading east to Puerto Rico (€1.55, 15 minutes) and Playa del Inglés (€2, 45 minutes). Bus 1 (€8.75, two hours) departs hourly for Las Palmas. Ferries also run between the port and Puerto Rico (adult/child €6.50/3.50, 30 minutes).

CAR & MOTORCYCLE

There are two underground car parks; the cheapest is on Calle La Mina, signposted as you come into town. There is blue-zone street parking throughout the centre (€1.80 per hour); keep your distance from the waterfront.

Mogán

POP 1415

Just as Puerto de Mogán is a relief from the south coast's relentless armies of apartments, bungalows and Guinness on tap, so the GC-200 road north from the port is another leap away from the crowds. As it ascends gradually up a wide valley towards Mogán, just 8km away, you'll pass craggy mountains and orchards of avocados, the main crop in these parts.

Mogán is an entirely relaxed, tranquil and unspoiled small town in a quite beautiful mountainous setting. There may be no real attractions, but it's a lovely spot for lunch, a stroll or an overnight in pastoral silence.

Eating

Restaurante Acaymo CANARIAN €€
(☑928 56 92 63; www.restauranteacaymogan.
es; Calle los Pasitos 21; mains €11-19, menú del día
€12.50; ☺ noon-11pm Sun-Thu, to midnight Fri & Sat)
Don't let the flags fluttering outside put you
off – long-standing, rustic Acaymo is as popular with locals as it is with tourists. It's best
known for meat, with veal, rabbit and steaks,
and perhaps mainly its roasted suckling lamb
shoulder (€18), but fish is another mainstay,
including the fish soup (€7.90). You'll also
find local classics such as Canarian chickpea
stew with octopus (€8.95).

Casa Enrique CANARIAN €€
(☑634 25 14 07; Calle San José 7; mains €9-15;
☺9am-6pm Sun-Fri) This place serves sound
Canarian dishes, superb coffee and cakes.

★ Valle de Mogán CANARIAN €€€
(☑928 56 86 49; Calle los Pasitos 2; tasting menu
€56; ☺noon-4pm & 7-10.30pm) This is an outstanding choice in Mogán, with some of the
best food on Gran Canaria paired with tantalising mountain views from its terrace. If
you're looking for something special, aim for
the *menú degustación* (tasting menu), and
choose dinner for optimum ambient charm.
Reserve ahead.

❶ Getting There & Away
Bus 84 (€1.40, 11 minutes) runs regularly between Puerto de Mogán and Mogán.

Mogán to Aldea de San Nicolás

From Mogán, the GC-200 winds off to the
northwest, wending 26km through some
spectacularly craggy mountains to Aldea
de San Nicolás, though the final approach
is sadly blighted by the surrounding sea of
plastic greenhouses. Stop for a glass of fresh
papaya juice at Restaurante Las Cañadas
(☑928 94 35 90; www.restaurantelascañadas.es;
GC-200; mains €4-12; ☺9am-8.30pm Thu-Tue),
around 8km from Mogán on your left-hand
side. The winding road continues through
Los Azulejos, a colourful rock formation created by minerals of brilliant greens, yellows
and ochres. To avoid a head-on collision, take
your photos from the signposted lookout
Fuente de los Azulejos Mirador.

ROAD TRIP: AGÜIMES TO MOGÁN

This highly dramatic and winding journey from the southeast of Gran Canaria to the southwest is a stupendous voyage, setting out from the historic town of Agüimes to climb up winding roads to a mirador, before swooping down through pine trees and hairpin bends to the tranquil town of Mogán.

❶ Agüimes

The narrow and winding GC-550 road climbs meanderingly northwest from **Agüimes** (p66), offering views of the mountains and, beyond, the vast Atlantic Ocean.

❷ Temisas

Drive for 10km to reach the tiny village of Temisas, perched on a natural ledge, with its backdrop of impenetrable cliffs and views across a ravine that falls away down to the sea. The village itself, of stone houses and cottages, is sleepy and atmospheric.

❸ Observatorio Astronómico de Temisas

Leave Temisas but look down on the village from a higher perch for a different

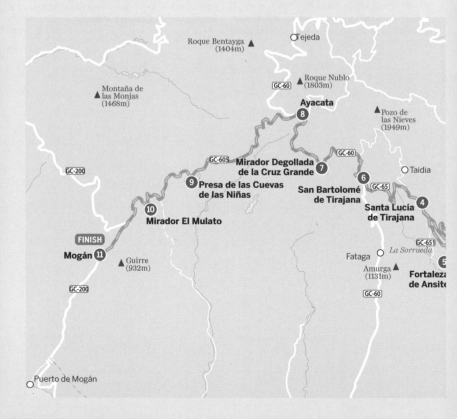

Start Agüimes
End Mogán
Length 63km, three hours

perspective. You will pass the Observatorio Astronómico de Temisas.

❹ Santa Lucía de Tirajana

Continue along the GC-550 for another 8km or so to Santa Lucía de Tirajana, to then head south along the GC-65 and shortly pass a turn-off along the GC-651 for La Sorrueda, a breathtaking reservoir backed by verdant mountains and fringed with palm trees.

❺ Fortaleza de Ansite

A little further south beyond the reservoir is the Fortaleza de Ansite, a natural fortress and one of Gran Canaria's most important pre-Hispanic sites. It was here that the Guanches' last stand took place; an interpretive centre fills you in on the history.

❻ San Bartolomé de Tirajana

Return to drive through Santa Lucia de Tirajana and up the GC-65 for 7km to the lovely town of San Bartolomé de Tirajana (where the road then becomes the GC-60). Stop here for baked goodies and a coffee at La Panera de Tunte and to admire the Iglesia de San Bartolomé.

❼ Mirador Degollada de la Cruz Grande

Continue north along the GC-60 out of town; after about 4km you will reach the jaw-dropping Mirador Degollada de la Cruz Grande. This superb viewpoint delivers vistas of the Caldera de Tirajana, the Cuenca de Chira and the Pinar de Pilancones.

❽ Ayacata

Continue driving for another 4.5km to the village of Ayacata and look for the turning to your left down the CG-605 along the Barranco de Ayacata to Mogán.

❾ Presa de las Cuevas de las Niñas

Drive down the CG-605, through the pine trees and on to the Presa de las Cuevas de las Niñas, a beautiful reservoir lake surrounded by pine-clad hills and named after the huge dam (presa) on the south side.

❿ Mirador El Mulato

Continue on through the pine trees downhill; the road becomes very windy several kilometres further on before it brings you to the Mirador El Mulato, with a long, deep and beautiful view down the valley.

⓫ Mogán

Continue down a series of hairpin bends that almost double back on themselves and head on and into the valley below. You'll pass through various small settlements before driving into the pretty town of Mogán. If you've a room booked, stop here and unload your stuff for the night. You can also have a superb Canarian dinner at either Restaurante Acaymo or Valle de Mogán. Beyond lies the Puerto de Mogán and the sea.

Fuerteventura

POP 113,000

Best Places to Eat

➡ Restaurante Avenida (p100)

➡ El Goloso de Cotillo (p103)

➡ La Jaira de Demian (p90)

➡ Restaurante La Vaca Azul (p103)

➡ Frasquita (p96)

Best Beaches

➡ Playa de Cofete (p108)

➡ Parque Natural de Corralejo (p99)

➡ Playa de la Barca (p106)

➡ Playa de la Mujer (p97)

➡ Playa del Matorral (p106)

Why Go?

Lying just 100km from the African coast, Fuerteventura recalls its neighbour Lanzarote, only with more colour. Resembling shallow piles of saffron, chilli and coriander, there are none of the mist-wreathed pines or cooling, hilly microclimates of Gran Canaria. Blown by the wind and baked by the sun, the island is truly an arresting spectacle: for the full-on, wide-angle perspective of the Martian-like landscape, climb up to the Mirador Astronómico de Sicasumbre and take it all in.

Most visitors, however, are more interested in mastering the waves and the wind than contemplating the raw aesthetics of the scenery. The second-largest island in the archipelago (after Tenerife), Fuerteventura has year-round sunshine (a blistering 3000 hours a year), and the biggest and best beaches in the Canaries.

The island was declared a Unesco Biosphere Reserve in 2009.

When to Go

➡ High season runs from December to February, with accommodation filling up well in advance; temperatures are slightly cooler with prevailing winds, but still very pleasant.

➡ Late spring (April and May) is perfect temperature-wise, although Easter can mean crowded beaches.

➡ Spanish holidaymakers favour the islands in July and August, along with families travelling with school-age children. Temperatures often surpass 30°C, though it rarely gets stiflingly hot. The Windsurfing World Cup takes place in July.

➡ Autumn is an excellent time for festivals, including Corralejo's Kite Festival and the Fiesta de la Virgen del Rosario in the capital. Average daytime temperatures hover around the agreeable 20°C mark, while nights gradually become cooler.

Map labels

Playa Blanca (Lanzarote)

Isla de Lobos ④

Majanicho

Museo de la Pesca Tradicional

Corralejo

Parque Natural de Corralejo ②

Los Lagos

El Burro

El Cotillo ①

Lajares

FV101

FV10

FV1

Montaña de Tindaya (401m)

Villaverde

La Oliva

Arrecife (Lanzarote)

Playa de la Mujer

Tindaya

La Matilla

ATLANTIC OCEAN

Los Molinos

FV211

FV207

Tefía

Tetir

FV10

Puerto del Rosario

Casillas del Ángel

FV20

Los Llanos de la Concepción

Playa Blanca

Valle de Santa Inés

La Ampuyenta

FV20

Aeropuerto de Fuerteventura

Mirador de Morro Velosa

Betancuria ⑤

Antigua

Ajuy & Puerto de la Peña

FV621

Caleta de Fuste

Gran Montaña (708m)

Vega de Río Palmas

FV30

FV2

Museo de la Sal

Las Salinas

Pájara

Tiscamanita

Tuineje

Pozo Negro

FV605

Mirador Astronómico de Sicasumbre ⑥

FV20

FV2

Poblado de La Atalayita

Las Playitas

Playa de la Pared

La Pared

FV2

El Brasero

Gran Tarajal

La Lajita

Giniginamar

Tarajalejo

Costa Calma

Pico de la Zarza (807m)

Parque Natural de Jandía

Playa de la Barca

Playa de Cofete

Cofete

Villa Winter

Playa de Sotavento de Jandía

Puerto de la Cruz

Península de Jandía

FV2

Punta de Jandía ⑦

Morro Jable

Punta de Jandía Lighthouse

Playa del Matorral

Las Palmas de Gran Canaria

Las Palmas de Gran Canaria; Santa Cruz de Tenerife

0 20 km
0 10 miles

Fuerteventura Highlights

① **El Cotillo** (p101) Surfing, windsurfing or just enjoying a sunset dinner in this laid-back coastal town.

② **Parque Natural de Corralejo** (p99) Kicking off your shoes to do cartwheels in the soft, powdery sand.

③ **Playa de Cofete** (p108) Discovering these beautifully unspoiled sands in the southwest of Fuerteventura.

④ **Isla de Lobos** (p102) Jumping on the ferry to hike around this wind-whipped island.

⑤ **Betancuria** (p91) Becoming besotted with the verdant valley location of this charming town.

⑥ **Mirador Astronómico de Sicasumbre** (p92) Taking in the gob-smacking views of Fuerteventura's astonishingly arid landscape.

⑦ **Punta de Jandía Lighthouse** (p107) Exploring the southern tip of the island before feasting locally on seafood.

History

Fuerteventura has had several names over the centuries, ranging from the Romans' matter-of-fact Planaria ('Plains', due to the island's overall flatness), to the considerably more exciting Fuerteventura (Strong Adventure), which dates from the first European conquerors. Ruled by the Norman nobleman Jean de Béthencourt, the conquerors turned up in 1405 to find the island divided into two tribal kingdoms separated by a low 6km-long wall. The Guanche kingdom of Jandía occupied the southern peninsula, as far north as La Pared; Maxorata controlled the rest of the island.

Béthencourt established a permanent base, including a chapel, in the mountainous zone of what came to be known as Betancuria, with Santa María de Betancuria evolving as the island's capital. The choice of location was determined by the natural water supply that is still in evidence: this is one of the lushest regions on the arid island. The mountainous location also created a measure of natural defence against those dastardly pirate raids.

New settlements spread slowly across the island and, in the 17th century, Europeans occupied El Cotillo, once the seat of the Guanche Maxorata kingdom. At this time, the Arias and Saavedra families took control of the *señorío* (the island government deputising for the Spanish crown). By the following century, however, officers of the island militia had established themselves as a rival power base in La Oliva. Los Coroneles (the Colonels) gradually took virtual control of the island's affairs, enriching themselves at the expense of the hard-pressed peasantry. You can learn more about their reign by visiting their extraordinary former home: Casa de los Coroneles in La Oliva.

The militia was disbanded in 1834 and, in 1912, the island, along with others in the archipelago, was granted a degree of self-administration with the installation of the *cabildo* (island government).

ℹ Getting There & Away

AIR

Fuerteventura airport (☑ 902 40 47 04; www.aena.es; El Matorral) is 6km south of Puerto del Rosario in El Matorral. **Binter Canarias** (www.binternet.com) and **CanaryFly** (www.canaryfly.es) have direct flights to Gran Canaria and Tenerife, from where you can fly on to the other islands. **Air Europa** (www.aireuropa.com) flies to Gran Canaria.

BOAT

Fred Olsen (p269) Ferries depart Corralejo for Playa Blanca (€27, 25 minutes, seven daily) in Lanzarote; you can buy tickets at the port in Corralejo. There's also a service from Morro Jable to Las Palmas de Gran Canaria (€49, two hours, twice daily).

Naviera Armas (☑ 928 30 06 00, in Corralejo & Morro Jable 902 45 65 00; www.navieraarmas.com) Ferries leave Corralejo for Playa Blanca (€27.20, 35 minutes, seven daily) in Lanzarote. From Morro Jable, daily ferries leave for Las Palmas de Gran Canaria (€48.80, three hours) and to Santa Cruz de Tenerife (€83.60, 6½ hours). From Puerto del Rosario there are ferries to Las Palmas de Gran Canaria (€35.20, six hours) and Santa Cruz de Tenerife (€62, 11 hours) at 11am from Tuesday to Saturday.

Trasmediterránea (☑ in Puerto del Rosario 902 45 46 45; www.trasmediterranea.es; León y Castillo 58) Operates a weekly Saturday service to Puerto del Rosario (€33, six hours) from Las Palmas de Gran Canaria. There are also indirect boats from Santa Cruz de Tenerife and Santa Cruz de la Palma, but journeys are long and you'd be better on a plane.

FUERTEVENTURA FOR CHILDREN

The main attraction for families is always going to be Fuerteventura's beaches, many of which have fine white sand and shallow waters that are safe for paddling tots. Playa del Castillo (p95) and Playa del Matorral (p106) are both good choices, while Playa Chica (p89) in the capital Puerto del Rosario is lovely and safe too. For an artificial water adventure, the massive Acua Water Park (p99) in Corralejo has 10-pin bowling, crazy golf and a driving range, as well as wave pools and kamikaze-style slides and rides.

There are plenty of boat trips throughout the resorts as well. At Caleta de Fuste, Oceanarium Explorer (p96) has a daily dolphin- and whale-spotting trip, while in Corralejo there are regular boats to the Isla de Lobos (p102), where there is a lovely Robinson Crusoe–style beach and the possibility to explore the island via pedal power. Alternatively, popular Oasis Park (p104) in La Lajita has all manner of mammals, birds and sea life, plus shows and camel rides. It's not cheap, but it's a hit with the kids.

ⓘ Getting Around

Tiadhe (p270) has 18 bus routes covering the main destinations across the island. A rechargeable Bono Transport card (€2) will only net you a 5% discount off the ticket price but might be worth it if you're travelling frequently by bus.

Driving is a pleasure here; the terrain is largely flat, the roads are excellent and there are some stunning drives. **Cicar** (🖉 928 82 29 00; www. cicar.com; Fuerteventura Airport) and **Avis** (🖉 928 09 23 30; www.avis.com; Fuerteventura Airport) are reliable operators.

PUERTO DEL ROSARIO

POP 37,000

Puerto del Rosario, Fuerteventura's capital, is home to almost a third of the island's population. A relatively modern little port town that only really took off in the 19th century, it can appear a confusing city with sprawling suburbs and scraps of wasteland, but head to the old town behind the promenade to find the majority of the shops, bars and restaurants.

Long-overlooked, the capital has made efforts to attract tourists, with sculptures, some terrific and very colourful murals dotted around and a growing crop of excellent restaurants as well as some reasonable accommodation choices. It's also a convenient base for reaching other towns and beaches around the island, as buses radiate to most points from here.

Puerto del Rosario, once little more than a handful of fishers' cottages, became the island's capital in 1860 as a result of its strategic position as a harbour.

Until 1956 it was known as Puerto de las Cabras, named after the goats who used to come here for water (and later becoming the main departure point for their export in the form of chops). In an early rebranding exercise, the city was renamed the more dignified Puerto del Rosario (Port of the Rosary).

When Spain pulled out of the Sahara in 1975, it sent some 5000 Legión Extranjera (Foreign Legion) troops to Fuerteventura to keep a watch on North Africa. The huge barracks in Puerto del Rosario is still in use, although troops now number less than 1000.

◎ Sights

Pick up a *Puerto on Foot* guide from the tourist office (p90); it has an easy-to-follow map showing the most centrally located

OFF THE BEATEN TRACK

GETTING AWAY FROM IT ALL

Pozo Negro (p99) Enjoy fresh seafood, a quiet black-sand beach and the surrounding craggy peaks at this tiny fishing hamlet on the east coast.

Parque Natural de Corralejo (p99) Desert-like dunes that are never crowded; don't forget the drinking water (or compass).

Playa de Cofete (p108) The antithesis of the beach resorts, with a wild, dramatic and unspoiled beauty.

Mirador Astronómico de Sicasumbre (p92) Gaze out onto the Martian landscape all about you or stare into the infinite depths of space.

modern sculptures that were fashioned to help bring some vibrancy to town. There's also a map detailing the city's very colourful street murals. The pedestrianised Avenida 1 de Mayo leads west from the main church and is lined with shops and bars.

Casa Museo Unamuno   MUSEUM
(Calle Rosario 11; ⊙9am-2pm Mon-Fri) **FREE** This small museum near the church honours the philosopher Miguel de Unamuno, who stayed here in 1924 after being exiled from Spain. His crime was criticising the dictatorship of Primo de Rivera, both verbally and in writing. He later escaped to France before returning to his position as lecturer and rector at Salamanca University in Spain when the Republicans came to power in 1931.

Centro de Arte Juan Ismael   ARTS CENTRE
(🖉 928 85 97 50; Calle Almirante Lallemand 30; ⊙10am-1pm & 5-9pm Tue-Sat) **FREE** Named for a Fuerteventura-born artist, there are rotating exhibitions on display here. None of Ismael's paintings are on show, though you can buy souvenirs and replicas of his surrealist works.

★ Playa del Pozo   BEACH
(Avenida Reyes de España) This sand and seashell beach is a picture, with its gentle curve and protected, calm turquoise waters. There are steps down into the water from the walkway along the northern side of the beach and a lifeguard is usually on duty from May to September. Often there's no one around but it can get busy during peak periods.

FUERTEVENTURA PUERTO DEL ROSARIO

STREET ART

In a bid to both prettify the buildings of the town and promote local artistic talent, several years ago Puerto del Rosario embarked on an ambitious program of mural painting across the city. These murals – some colossal and others more discreet – have made a terrific impact on the town, adding vibrant splashes of colour and imagination.

Perhaps the best known is the bold **Superheroes** mural near the main bus station – you can find it on the northwestern corner of Avenida Diego Miller and Calle Primero de Mayo. Another excellent artwork – with a white and turquoise colour-coordinated building above it – is the turtle and fish along Calle García Escámez as it nears Avenida Reyes de España. Ask at the tourist office (p90) for a map detailing all the murals.

Festivals & Events

Carnaval de Puerto del Rosario CARNIVAL
(⊘ Feb) The port town holds its own carnival celebrations over two weeks in February.

Fiesta de la Virgen del Rosario RELIGIOUS
(⊘7 Oct) Puerto del Rosario dons its party threads to honour the Virgen del Rosario, the capital's patron. Processions accompany the image of the Virgin as she is paraded around town.

Eating & Drinking

The town has experienced a culinary renaissance in recent years, so dining here could be one of the highlights of your trip.

Mercado Municipal MARKET €
(Calle Teófilo Martínez Escobar; ⊘8am-3pm) The local *mercado* is tiny but a good place to sample (and buy) some of the island's famed goat's cheese.

⭐**La Jaira de Demian** TAPAS €€
(📱928 53 37 84; www.facebook.com/lajairade demian; Calle la Cruz 26; menú €12; ⊘1-4pm & 8-11pm Tue-Thu, to 11.30pm Fri & Sat) Run by the ever-helpful and astonishingly polite Demian, this excellent restaurant enjoys a lovely setting with an outside terrace, next to a deserted plot that La Jaira has converted into a garden. Staff ferry a large wooden menu for you to read but the *menú del día* (daily set menu) is very good value at €12. Everything from the bread to the craft beers is an unalloyed joy.

Casa Toño SPANISH €€
(📱928 34 47 36; www.facebook.com/antonio.alonso chef; Calle Alcalde Alonso Patallo 8; mains €12-20; ⊘noon-4pm & 8pm-midnight Mon-Sat) Book ahead to get a table at this popular restaurant that brings a little cutting-edge cuisine to Puerto del Rosario's dining scene. The speciality is lightly seared red tuna but also expect plenty of tapas utilising fresh, local ingredients. There's an impressive gin menu with close to 50 different varieties.

La Tierra BAR
(www.facebook.com/latierrafuerteventura1; Calle Eustaquio Gopar 3; ⊘7pm-midnight) Tucked away down a narrow cobbled lane, La Tierra is a great choice for drinks at the outdoor tables. There's a jam session every Wednesday and a language exchange night kicks off on Tuesdays.

ℹ️ Information

Provincial Tourist Office (www.visitfuerte ventura.es; Almirante Lallemand 1; ⊘7am-3pm Mon-Fri)

Tourist Office (www.turismo-puertodelrosario. org; Avenida Reyes de España; ⊘9am-7pm Mon-Fri, 10am-1pm Sat) A hugely helpful office with enthusiastic staff, and maps of the street sculpture and murals in Puerto del Rosario here.

ℹ️ Getting There & Away

AIR
Fuerteventura airport (p88) is located 6km south of Puerto del Rosario in El Matorral.

BUS
Tiadhe (📱928 85 57 26; www.tiadhe.com) buses leave from the main bus stop just past the corner of Avenidas León y Castillo and Constitución. The following are some of the more popular bus services from Puerto del Rosario:
Bus 1 Morro Jable via Costa Calma (€10, two hours, at least 12 daily)
Bus 2 Vega de Río Palmas via Betancuria (€3.30, 50 minutes, three daily)
Bus 3 Caleta de Fuste via the airport (€1.50, 30 minutes, at least 18 daily)
Bus 6 Corralejo (€3.40, 40 minutes, at least 16 daily)

Bus 7 El Cotillo (€4.35, 45 minutes, three daily)

BOAT

Naviera Armas (☑ 928 85 15 42; www.naviera armas.com; Puerto del Rosario) runs daily ferries to Las Palmas de Gran Canaria (€35.20, six hours). Trasmediterránea (p88) also runs a weekly service to Las Palmas de Gran Canaria (€33, six hours) on Saturday.

ℹ Getting Around

There's a large, free car park just beyond the market heading eastwards on Avenida Marítima.

One municipal bus does the rounds of the city every hour. Otherwise you'll need to call for a **taxi** (☑ 928 85 02 16, 928 85 00 59).

Bus 3 (€1.30, 10 to 15 minutes) makes the trip to the airport. A taxi will run about €10.

CENTRAL FUERTEVENTURA

Central Fuerteventura offers the most geographically diverse landscapes on this overwhelmingly arid, desert island. The soaring mountains of the Parque Natural de Betancuria contrast in the south with the wadi-style palm-tree oasis of the Vega de Río Palmas, while the west and east coasts are characterised by rocky cliffs interspersed with small black-pebble beaches and studded with sleepy fishing hamlets.

In further contrast, the central copper-coloured plains around Antigua are dotted with old windmills that date back a couple of centuries.

This area offers you some of the most scenic drives on the island, particularly around Betancuria and Tefía.

Betancuria

POP 800

Wonderfully lush, the pretty village of Betancuria is tucked into the protective folds of the basalt hills, a patchwork of dry-stone walls, palm trees and simple, whitewashed cottages. Lording over it all is a magnificent 17th-century church and courtyard. As an escape from the predominantly arid landscape of Fuerteventura, the fine-looking settlement is one of the most popular destinations on the island and consequently attracts a large

---

GETTING ACTIVE ON FUERTEVENTURA

With its year-round sunshine, Fuerteventura is a superb destination for the sports enthusiast. Surfing the waves or sailing the breeze are the most famous sports here, but there are also more specialist activities such as freediving. Fuerteventura's peaceful but stark landscape offers some superb walking opportunities, with oases, volcanic craters, abandoned haciendas and rugged coastlines awaiting the intrepid. The Isla de Lobos nature reserve is also excellent for walkers.

Water Sports

The sea offers most of the action in Fuerteventura. From Caleta de Fuste, Morro Jable and Corralejo, you can both dive and windsurf, though the best spot for the latter is in the gusty breezes off Playa de la Barca (p106) along the beaches that make up **Playa de Sotavento de Jandía** on the southeast coast; kitesurfing is excellent here too. The coast between Corralejo and Los Molinos offers excellent surfing possibilities, as do the waters around La Pared. El Cotillo stands out as a place with excellent surfing and bundles of character too. Grab a copy of the handy *Surfer Map*, available from most tourist offices and surf shops.

Biking, Golfing & Kiting

Leaving behind those hiking trails, mountain biking in Fuerteventura is a completely different experience from the other very hilly islands of the group such as Gran Canaria. Most resorts have bicycle rental outfits. Ask at the tourist offices for a copy of the *Eco-Fuerteventura* map, which details hiking and biking routes across the island.

If you fancy swinging a golf club, Caleta de Fuste is home to the island's first PGA championship-rated golf course, the **Fuerteventura Golf Club** (www.fuerteventuragolf club.com; Carretera de Jandía; 18 holes €79). Or just make use of the blustery climate by flying a kite. If you're in Corralejo in early November you might catch the three-day international kite festival (p100) on the beach.

WORTH A TRIP

MIRADOR ASTRONÓMICO DE SICASUMBRE

If you want just one place to put the island's primordial, barren geology and Martian features into wide-angle perspective, **Mirador Astronómico de Sicasumbre** (FV-605) has breathtaking views of Fuerteventura's copper-coloured hills, valleys and ravines. At night-time, it's even more astonishing as a stargazing spot for deep views of the Milky Way. If going when dark, take a torch and check up front on the weather (usually clear, but not always). Not many people come here's so it's usually quiet.

You'll need a car to get here; the mirador is located along the FV-605 between Pájara and La Pared so is most conveniently stopped off en route between the two.

number of visitors, but Betancuria still manages to maintain a slow-moving and relaxed charm.

Jean de Béthencourt thought this the ideal spot to set up house in 1405, so he had living quarters and a chapel built. To this modest settlement he perhaps rather immodestly gave his own name, which, with time, was corrupted to Betancuria. During the course of the 15th century, Franciscan friars moved in and expanded the town. Amazingly, given its size, it remained the island's capital until 1834. Fuerteventura's proximity to the North African coast made it easy prey for Moroccan and European pirates who, on numerous occasions, managed to defy Betancuria's natural mountain defences and sack it.

◉ Sights

If you approach Betancuria from the north, look for the ruins of the island's first **monastery** on your left, built by the Franciscans.

★ **Iglesia de Santa María**   CHURCH
(Calle Alcalde Carmelo Silvera; admission €1.50; ☉10am-12.30pm & 1-5.50pm Mon-Sat, 10.30am-2.20pm Sun) This lovely church dates from 1620 and has a magnificent stone floor, carved wooden ceiling and an elaborate baroque altar. Don't miss the sacristy with its display of vestments and altar ware, and carved wooden ceiling in shades of gold and red. Pirates destroyed the church's Gothic

predecessor in 1593. The entrance ticket also covers the **Museo de Arte Sacro**, with religious paintings and statues distributed through the church.

**Museo Arqueológico
de Betancuria**   MUSEUM
(Calle Roberto Roldán; adult/child €2/free; ☉10am-6pm Tue-Sat) Archaeology buffs should check out this modest but absorbing museum that concentrates on the indigenous Guanche tribes and features a skeleton that was found in a local tomb that is thought to be between 600 and 1000 years old. Among other items on display are some artefacts from the Roman occupation. Admission includes an excellent brochure in English.

Casa Santa María   MUSEUM
(adult/child €6/3; ☉10am-4pm Mon-Sat; 🅟) This place is unabashedly tourist-orientated but nevertheless still worth visiting. The German owner, Reiner Loos, bought the original rambling building in the 1990s and spent several years collecting traditional handicrafts and ancient agricultural tools, as well as lushly landscaping the garden. Inside you can see craftspeople at work, sample local cheese and *mojo* (Canarian spicy sauce), and even visit the 'virtual goat stable'. The highlight, however, is an expertly produced 3D underwater film of the local coastal sea life, including the rare green turtle.

★☆ Festivals & Events

Día de San Buenaventura   RELIGIOUS
(☉14 Jul) Locals honour the patron saint on Día de San Buenaventura, in a fiesta dating to the 15th century.

✖ Eating

Valtarajal   CANARIAN €
(Calle Roberto Roldán 6; raciones €4.50-13; ☉1-4pm & 7pm-late Mon-Sat) This cosy place has more of an authentic and traditional local feel than other places in town, and offers a good choice of *raciones* (large portions of tapas). You can get six tapas for €13 or sit down for a slice of cake and a coffee for €4.50.

❶ Getting There & Away

Bus 2 (€2.80, 50 minutes, three daily) passes through here on its way between Puerto del Rosario and Vega de Río Palmas, a short distance south.

There's a small, free car park south of the centre.

Around Betancuria

The area around Betancuria encompasses some gorgeous scenery and superb far-reaching vistas. For a start, a couple of kilometres north of Betancuria on the FV-30, there's a handy lookout (on both sides of the road) that explains the various mountain peaks looming on the horizon. The immense statues here are of the island's two pre-Hispanic kings, Ayose and Guize. Further on, the Mirador de Morro Velosa (⊙10am-6pm Mon-Sat) FREE offers mesmerising views across the island's weird, disconsolate moonscape.

The view is almost as spectacular at the pass over which the FV-30 highway climbs before it twists its way north through Valle de Santa Inés, a hiccup of a village.

In pretty Casillas del Ángel, on the FV-20, the petite Iglesia de Santa Ana contains an 18th-century wooden carving of St Anne.

Heading south of Betancuria for Pájara, you soon hit the small oasis of Vega de Río Palmas (Fertile Plain of the Palma River). As you proceed, the reason for the name becomes clear – the road follows a near-dry watercourse still sufficiently wet below the surface to keep alive a stand of palms.

Antigua

POP 1800

In the 10th century, this sleepy little settlement shouldered the title of capital, albeit for just a year. Today it's a pleasant enough place for a wander before poking your head through the door of the church and visiting the excellent cheese museum.

★ Museo del Queso Majorero   MUSEUM
(⌐928 878 041; www.museoquesomajorero.es; Calle Virgen de Antigua; adult/child €4/2; ⊙9.30am-5.30pm; P⛟) This superb museum is one of the island's best, with lots of interactive displays including a sit-down 'virtual goat milking' activity! Kids will enjoy the touch-button exhibits with information on the island's flora and fauna, while adults can get an education on Majorero cheese production, plus tips on tasting the finished product. There's a shop selling a range of cheeses and other local produce. For an extra €3 you can sample cheese in a *degustación*.

Iglesia de Nuestra
Señora de Antigua   CHURCH
(Calle Plaza 3; ⊙10am-2pm) One of the oldest churches on the island, this large, white house of worship is built on the site of a 16th-century chapel. Set in a pleasant square, the most interesting features are the gnarled stone pillars supporting the wooden gallery, a huge oil painting depicting St Michael, and the attractive pink-and-green painted altar.

Bar El Artesano   SPANISH €
(⌐606 95 50 73; Calle Real 13; menú €9; ⊙9am-midnight Tue-Sun) This good choice has local atmosphere, friendly service and an excellent-value *menú del día*.

❶ Getting There & Away

Bus 1 (€2.15, 30 minutes) passes through Antigua en route between Puerto del Rosario and

---

FOR CHEESE LOVERS

Given that there are more goats than people on Fuerteventura (honest!), goat stew is a popular dish. But it is the goat's cheese that is the real winner. In fact, so renowned is the Majorero cheese that, just like a fine wine, it bears a Denominación de Origen (proof of origin) label, certifying that it is indeed from the island and the genuine product. It's the first Canary Island cheese to receive this accolade, and the first goat's cheese in Spain to bear the label.

At the heart of the process is the Majorero goat, a high-yielding hybrid of goat originally imported from the Spanish mainland. The cheese is ideally purchased young and soft, with a powdery white rind that becomes yellow with age. One of Europe's top goat's cheeses, Majorero is rich and buttery with a nutty flavour that goes particularly well with fruit. The wheels are often sold with a coating of oil, corn meal (*gofio*) or paprika to preserve them.

To learn more about cheese – and goats – check out the Museo del Queso Majorero in Antigua.

FIVE FAB FUERTEVENTURA HOTELS

Casa Isaítas (☑928 16 14 02; www.casaisaitas.com; Calle Guize 7; s/d incl breakfast €66/84; ✵) One of the loveliest *casas rurales* (village accommodation) on the island, in a lovingly restored 18th-century Pájara stone house with superb restaurant.

Hotel Rural Mahoh (☑928 86 80 50; www.mahoh.com; Sitio de Juan Bello, Villaverde; s/d/tr inc breakfast from €48/68/93; P 🛜 ✵) Set in an early-19th-century stone-and-wood building, this excellent La Oliva pick is surrounded by cactus gardens and has nine romantic antique-filled rooms.

Laif Hotel (☑928 53 85 98; www.laifhotel.com; Calle San Pedro 2; s/d from €50/60; 🛜 ✵) This smart, modern boutiquey 18-room hotel makes a cheery choice in El Cotillo, with a fantastic rooftop pool terrace.

Barceló Castillo Beach Resort (☑928 16 31 00; www.barcelo.com; Avenida Castillo; bungalows from €90; P ✵ @ 🛜 ✵) A sumptuous, enormous, family-friendly Caleta de Fuste resort with bougainvillea-draped bungalows and lush gardens fronting onto the wide arc of a beach.

Avanti (☑928 86 75 23; www.avantihotelboutique.com; Avenida Marítima; r incl breakfast €135; ✵ 🛜) This marvellous blue-and-white, adults-only boutique hotel in Corralejo exudes chic relaxation with its minimalist design, bright white spaces, high-end furnishings and rooftop hot tub.

Morro Jable. The bus stop for the return journey is just by the bank.

Around Antigua

Ermita de San Pedro de Alcántara   CHAPEL
(La Ampuyenta) Located in tiny La Ampuyenta, the 17th-century Ermita de San Pedro de Alcántara is surrounded by a stout protective wall built by the French from the Normandy area. Inside, the walls of the nave are decorated with large, engagingly naive frescoes that date from 1760. Although the Sistine Chapel comparisons are a trifle far fetched, the murals are undeniably stunning in their pastel colours and simple execution.

The best way to visit is on a free guided walk leaving from the grand-looking **Centro de Interpretación de Las Ermitas de Fuerteventura** (FV-20, La Ampuyenta; ⊙ guided tours 10.30am, 12.30pm, 2.30pm & 4.30pm Tue-Sat) **FREE**, which you can find right alongside the chapel. As well as the chapel, the walks take in the 19th-century Casa Museo Doctor Mena and the birthplace of Fray Andresito, a Franciscan monk born in La Ampuyenta in 1800.

La Ampuyenta is located 5km to the north of Antigua; you will need your own transport to get here.

Los Molinos Centro de Interpretación   MUSEUM
(Calle de la Cruz, Tiscamanita; adult/child €4/2.50; ⊙9.30am-5.30pm Nov-Apr, 10am-6pm May-Oct) This attractive windmill has a small information centre with all you could possibly want to know about windmills; there's also a free guide in English. The mill was not operating when we visited, though you can sample or buy *gofio* (ground, roasted grain traditionally used in place of bread in Canarian cuisine). The mill is located in Tiscamanita, a small village that is also home to the simple, white Ermita de San Marcos; the settlement is 9km south of Antigua.

Pájara

POP 19,400

Pájara is a very welcome leafy oasis in the desert landscape of Fuerteventura. The town is good looking and easy-going, and basks in some gorgeous shade cast by Pájara's abundance of trees, but what really put the place on the map is its unique 17th-century Iglesia de Nuestra Señora de Regla. The rest of the town is charming to amble about and there are a number of restaurants to help make it a half-day trip with a meal thrown in.

★**Iglesia de Nuestra**
Señora de Regla CHURCH
(Calle Nuestra Señora de Regla) The unique 17th-century Iglesia de Nuestra Señora de Regla has an Aztec-inspired exterior with its animal motifs. The simple retables behind the altar also have influences that flow to Mexico and are more subdued than the baroque excesses of mainland Spain (stick a coin in the machine on the right at the entrance to light them up). Don't forget to look up towards the magnificent carved wooden ceiling.

★**Casa Isaítas** CANARIAN €€
(📱 928 16 14 02; www.casaisaitas.com; Calle Guize 7; mains €10; ⊙10am-4.30pm; 🖉) Based in the charming hotel of the same name, Casa Isaítas is the best place to eat in Pájara. The varied menu includes lots of hearty soups and stews, fish pie, some interesting tapas and a reasonable selection for vegetarians (including vegetable pie at €9), served in a traditional dining room setting (that may be a bit sombre, but you can eat outside in the courtyard too).

❶ Getting There & Away

Bus 18 (€3.40, 30 minutes, three daily) runs between Pájara and Gran Tarajal, from where you can take onward buses to Puerto del Rosario and Morro Jable.

Caleta de Fuste

This smart, well-landscaped resort exudes an opulent Southern California feel, particularly around the sprawling Barceló mini village, which fronts the main beach. Caleta is often referred to as El Castillo (particularly on road signs) for the squat 18th-century Martello tower in the harbour.

The resort is close to the airport, and if you're travelling with a young family, the wide arc of sand and shallow waters are ideal. However, if you're seeking somewhere intrinsically Canarian, look elsewhere; this is a purpose-developed tourist resort. In all fairness, though, it is a relaxing place with some good hotels and decent restaurants.

◉ Sights & Activities

Playa del Castillo BEACH
The resort is fronted by a white sandy beach, complete with volleyball net and **camel rides** (30min for 2 people €12). It is ideal for families, although perhaps not a great

---

WORTH A TRIP

FUERTEVENTURA'S SCENIC DRIVES
···

The drive between Betancuria (p91) and Pájara on the **FV30** is one of the most spectacular on the island, although possibly not for those suffering from vertigo. The narrow road twists and turns steeply between a flowing landscape of volcano peaks and lava fields, with the sea visible (at times) in the far distance. In spring, the peaks are surprisingly lush – a vivid green contrasting with the rich ochres and reds of the soil.

The journey via La Pared (p105) south towards **Península de Jandía** is almost as dramatic. Fuerteventura is relatively flat when compared to Lanzarote and the other islands to the west, but you would never know it as you wend your way through this lonely and spectacularly harsh terrain.

choice compared to the rolling dunes and endless sands of Corralejo and Jandía.

Museo de la Sal MUSEUM
(Salt Museum; Las Salinas; adult/child €5/free; ⊙10am-6pm Tue-Sat) Just south of Caleta, this museum has audiovisual displays that explain the history of salt and demonstrate how it is extracted from the sea. It's perched on the ocean right next to the still-operational salt pans, which you can wander around.

Barceló Fuerteventura Thalasso Spa SPA
(📱 928 16 09 61; www.barcelo.com; Calle Savila 2; spa circuit €25, 55min massage from €69) You can't miss the glass building behind the beach with its giant 'Thalasso' sign. There is a range of treatments on offer: volcanic stone therapy, reflexotherapy, Hawaiian massage, anti-ageing facials and a body scrub with fruit granules. Or you can just enjoy the various bubbles and jets of the spa circuit. Guests staying at the Barceló get reduced rates.

Deep Blue DIVING
(📱 606 275468; www.deep-blue-diving.com; Muelle Deportivo, Calle Tenerife; orientation dive €23, open-water course €390; 🖉) Conveniently situated right by the port, this long-running outfit offers courses, dives for the already qualified (from €30), children's courses (€45) and snorkelling trips (€20).

WORTH A TRIP

AJUY & PUERTO DE LA PEÑA

If you have your own wheels, a 9km side trip from Pájara takes you northwest to Ajuy and contiguous Puerto de la Peña. A blink-and-you'll-miss-it fishing settlement, its black-sand beach makes a change from its illustrious golden neighbours to the south on the Península de Jandía. The locals and fishing boats take pride of place here, and the strand is fronted by a couple of simple seafood eateries serving up the day's catch.

Once you've filled up on fresh fish, walk it off on a 40-minute round-trip wander along the coast. The path starts at the north end of the beach and passes an old limestone kiln before eventually leading you to some impressive caves in the cliff face.

Oceanarium Explorer   BOATING

(☑ 928 54 76 87; Puerto Castillo Yacht Harbour; ⊞) This outfit runs a range of family-friendly activities, including half-day fishing trips (from €70), jet-ski hire (from €55 for 20 minutes), swimming encounters with sea lions (€40), glass-bottom boat trips (adult/child €16/8), whale and dolphin safaris (€40), and four-hour catamaran cruises (€52).

Caleta Cycles   CYCLING

(☑ 676 60 01 90; www.caletacycles.com; Hotel Los Geranios; bike rental per day €10, tours €30-50) A British-run place that organises guided bike tours and also rents bikes.

✗ Eating & Drinking

★ Frasquita   SEAFOOD €€

(☑ 928 56 69 98; Calle Aulaga, Playa de Caleta de Fuste; mains €15; ⊙ 1-4pm & 6-10pm Tue-Sun; Ⓟ) This is one of the best restaurants on the island to come to for fresh seafood, despite its very plain appearance and plastic tables and chairs. There's no menu, just a plate of freshly caught fish and seafood to point at. Book ahead to get a seat in the glassed-in dining room overlooking the beach.

Los Caracolitos   SEAFOOD €€

(☑ 928 17 42 42; Salinas del Carmen 22; mains €10-15; ⊙ noon-10.30pm Mon-Sat; Ⓟ) On the coast overlooking the salt pans, this is a fine alternative to the resort's multifarious tourist menus. Fish and seafood feature heavily, and travellers rave about the shellfish soup and garlic prawns. It's 2km south of Caleta de Fuste; if you don't fancy the coastal walk, the restaurant offers a free shuttle service.

El Faro   BAR

(☑ 928 16 30 35; Calle Tenerife; ⊙ 7pm-midnight) On a jetty jutting out into the ocean, this swanky glass-walled bar is the top spot for a sunset cocktail. There's also a good beer menu and light snacks are served. It's part of the Barceló complex but open to all.

❶ Getting There & Away

Bus 3 (€1.45, 15 minutes) runs regularly to Caleta de Fuste from Puerto del Rosario, via the airport. Bus 10 (€1.45, 15 minutes) from Puerto del Rosario runs four times daily (only twice a day on Sunday) via the airport before stopping at Caleta de Fuste and continuing on to Morro Jable.

Gran Tarajal

This handsome port town down on the coast between Pozo Negro and La Lajita is the island's second-largest settlement. Bordered by a long, lovely black-sand beach, the east-facing town, needless to say, has gorgeous sunrises. Gran Tarajal isn't much visited by travellers, so relaxes under an easy-going and almost half-forgotten vibe, which makes it all the more appealing.

Pizza Pomodoro   PIZZA €

(☑ 928 87 10 57; Avenida Paco Hierro 1; mains from €8; ⊙ 11am-11pm Wed-Sun) The seats out front at this top pizza restaurant down on the promenade go fast, which means you may have to perch inside at a small table – it's best to book to ensure the full alfresco effect. Standout pizzas are topped with Majorero cheese and ham, and there's a line of lip-smacking desserts.

❶ Getting There & Away

Gran Tarajal lies at the end of the FV-4, which heads abruptly south off the FV-2 artery.

Bus 16 (€5.90, one hour) links Puerto del Rosario with Gran Tarajal four times a day from Monday to Friday via Antigua, and twice daily on Saturday and Sunday; bus 1 (€5.90, one hour) also runs the same route. Bus 18 (€3.40, 30 minutes) runs several times daily from Pájara to Gran Tarajal, and bus 9 (€3.40, 30 minutes) trundles once a day at 6.30am to Gran Tarajal from Pájara, en route to Morro Jable.

Ferries used to run between Gran Tarajal and Las Palmas in Gran Canaria, but at the time of writing the service had been suspended.

NORTHERN FUERTEVENTURA

The Road to Los Molinos

The FV-10 highway heading westwards away from Puerto del Rosario to the interior of the island takes you through a landscape that typifies Fuerteventura. Ochre-coloured soil and distant volcanoes forge a barren and arid landscape of shifting colours and shapes, as the sun moves around.

Before crossing the treeless ridge that forms the island's spine, the road passes through the sleepy hamlets of **Tetir** and **La Matilla**. The tiny 1902 chapel in the latter is a good example of the simple, bucolic buildings of the Canaries – functional, relatively unadorned but aesthetically pleasing.

About 7km south of La Matilla and 1km beyond the village of Tefía along the FV-207 is the **Ecomuseo la Alcogida** (FV-207; adult/child €5/free; ⊙ 10am-5.30pm Tue-Sat; 🚗), which is worth a quick look.

West on the FV-211 from Tefía leads to Los Molinos. This is another lovely drive with the road curving around low-lying hills with isolated lofty palms and herds of goats. On the way you can't miss the old windmill used to grind cereals for the production of *gofio*, sitting squat across from a distinctive white-domed observatory.

The road continues to wind its way over the crest of the hill before descending dramatically beside a gaping gorge to tiny **Los Molinos**. Cross the bridge across the Barranco de Los Molinos – you may see ducks flapping about in the water below – and make your way to the small car park. Expect just a few simple houses overlooking a small grey-stone beach with cliff trails to the east and plenty of goats, geese and stray cats. If you do stop here, make a point of having a seafood meal at beachside **Restaurante Casa Pon** (Los Molinos; mains €11-13; ⊙ 10am-7pm) while gazing over Atlantic breakers.

A couple of kilometres north of Los Molinos, along a rough track, lies the **Playa de la Mujer**, an enticing stretch of sand, particularly popular with surfers.

If you're following the FV-10 rather than the coastal route, look out for the impressively located statue of Miguel de Unamuno part way up Montaña Quemado – a place where the writer once said he would like to be buried.

There are no buses to Los Molinos, but it is a well-surfaced, scenic road if you're driving.

La Oliva

POP 1370

One-time capital of the island, in fact if not in name, La Oliva still bears traces of its grander days, including one of the most intriguing historical buildings on the island: the Casa de los Coroneles. The weighty bell tower of the 18th-century Iglesia de Nuestra Señora de la Candelaria is another major feature, with its black volcanic bulk contrasting sharply with the bleached-white walls of the church itself. Also in La Oliva is the Centro de Arte Canario – Casa Mané, an essential stop for anyone with an interest in Canarian art.

◉ Sights

Art and history enthusiasts will have plenty to keep them busy. Try to visit on Tuesday or Friday, when a food and craft **market** (Market; Calle Tercio Don Juan de Austria; ⊙ 10am-2pm Tue & Fri) is held in town and the **Ruta de los Coroneles** (€6, ⊙ 10am-2pm) pass is available – it allows access to the two museums, the art gallery and the church.

★**Casa de los Coroneles**   MUSEUM
(House of the Colonels; admission €3; ⊙ 10am-6pm Tue-Sat; 🅿) This 18th-century building has been beautifully restored, retaining its traditional centr4al patio and wooden galleries, while other buildings on the estate have collapsed around it. The ground floor houses an

exhibition on women and agriculture, while upstairs you'll find exhibits on the history of the building itself and the island. Don't miss the simple and very small chapel with its original tiled floor and minute cross above the door. In the distance, the volcano-shaped mountain is a sublime spectacle.

The house has an interesting history. Beginning in the early 1700s, the officers who presided here virtually controlled the island. Amassing power and wealth, they so exploited the peasant class that, in 1834, Madrid – faced with repeated bloody mutinies on the island – disbanded the militia.

★ Centro de Arte Canario –
Casa Mané   GALLERY
(☑ 616 53 19 30; www.centrodeartecanario.com; Calle Salvador Manrique de Lara; admission €4; ⊙10am-5pm Mon-Fri, to 2pm Sat; P) This art museum is an island highlight, with its sculpture garden and galleries containing works by such Canarian artists as César Manrique, Ruben Dario and Alberto Agullo. Two galleries are devoted to the national award-winning watercolourist Alberto Manrique (no relation to César), displaying his landscapes and more surreal, mainly interior, scenes. The gallery is located close to Casa de los Coroneles; follow the signs from the centre of town.

ℹ Getting There & Away

Bus 7 (€2.40, 35 minutes, three daily) heads from Puerto del Rosario to El Cotillo, stopping in La Oliva. Bus 8 also runs to El Cotillo and, in the other direction, to Corralejo, via La Oliva.

Corralejo
POP 16,300

Your opinion of Corralejo will entirely depend on where you stand. Despite the influx of tourist numbers, the former fishing village near the harbour and main beach at Corralejo still have charm, with narrow, uneven streets, good seafood restaurants and even a fishers' cottage or two. Venture inland a couple of blocks, however, and you find the predictable resort fare of fish and chips coupled to a grid system of streets. At least the buildings are low-rise, and some local Spanish bars and cafes survive.

Corralejo's real allure is the miles of sand dunes to the south of town, sweeping back into gentle sugar-loaf rolls from the sea and fabulous broad sandy beaches. Protected as the Parque Natural de Corralejo (p99), no one can build on or near them (though a couple of concrete eyesores from the Riu hotel chain managed to get here before the regulation was in place).

A MOUNTAIN OF CONTROVERSY

Its summit reaches just 400m above sea level, but **Mount Tindaya** is the most important – and famous – mountain on the island. The peak, 6km south of La Oliva, has a special place in local history and mythology. More than 200 Guanche rock carvings have been found on the slopes, many in the shape of footprints seemingly pointing towards Tenerife's Mount Teide. A simple hiking trail reaches the summit, taking in some of the rock etchings en route, but ask at the tourist office in Corralejo as it was closed when we last visited.

Locals insist that curious things happen near the mountain: the sick get well, wrongdoers get their comeuppance and so on. In recent years, however, the mountain has been in and out of the headlines for a different reason. Way back in 1985, Basque sculptor Eduardo Chillida picked out Mount Tindaya as the site for a gargantuan project that was meant to be his masterpiece. Involving the excavation of 64,000 cubic metres of rock to make way for a vast 40m-high cubist cave, the project met with no small amount of protest. The conception, which Chillida called his 'Monument to Tolerance', was designed to allow people to experience the sheer size of the mountain, and artists' impressions of what the immense cavern would have looked like are certainly sublime. Vertical shafts would allow sun and moonlight into the cavern, the only source of illumination.

Chillida died in 2002, but nine years later local authorities finally gave the go ahead. It stalled once more, but in 2015 Chillida's family gave the rights of the project to the Canarian government and Fuerteventura's cabildo (island government). Protests continue to rage but authorities insist that the development, which they hope will attract 'quality tourism', will go ahead. If construction on Chillida's project begins, Fuerteventura's magic mountain will certainly be off-limits for some time.

POZO NEGRO

About 20km south of Caleta de Fuste, tiny Pozo Negro is one of Fuerteventura's most pristine fishing hamlets. Expect a small cluster of cottages, some brightly painted fishing boats and a couple of popular seafood restaurants, plus a quiet black-sand beach with gorgeous views.

The 5km drive towards the coast along the FV-420 from the FV-2 is stunning and you'll probably pass a lot of walkers en route. The landscape is all palm plantations, green meadows, craggy peaks and goat herds. Along the way, look out for signs to **Poblado de La Atalayita** (adult/child €2/free; ⊙10am-6pm Tue-Sat), a pre-Hispanic settlement of volcanic-rock ruins with a small information centre.

One of two dining options with tables directly facing the beach, **Flip-Flops** (Pozo Negro; tapas from €3.50, mains €7.50-12; ⊙noon-6pm Sat-Thu) has a menu of seaside faves and Canarian tapas: paella, mussels, fried goat's cheese, fish goujons as well as some vegetarian choices too. Look for the row of flip-flops.

FUERTEVENTURA CORRALEJO

◉ Sights & Activities

★ **Parque Natural de Corralejo**   BEACH
This nature park of yellow dunes stretches along the east coast for about 10km south from Corralejo; it's also several kilometres wide, so covers a lot of territory and is excellent for hikes through sand. Breeziness also makes it popular with windsurfers and kiteboarders. The area is also known as **Grandes Playas**; sunloungers and umbrellas are available for hire in front of the two (eyesore) luxury hotels. The FV-1 runs through the park.

Playas Corralejo Viejo
& Muelle Chico   BEACH
The small beaches surrounding the town's harbour have fine sand and shallow water – and also serve as a year-round canvas for sand sculptors.

Acua Water Park   AMUSEMENT PARK
(☑928 53 70 34; www.acuawaterpark.com; Avenida Nuestra Señora del Carmen 41; adult/child €25/19; ⊙10am-6pm) Has wave pools, kamikaze-style slides, rides, Jacuzzi and other watery attractions. If you've booked your ticket up front, a free bus service runs to the park from Caleta de Fuste and Jandía in the south.

Flag Beach Windsurf Center   WINDSURFING
(☑609 02 98 04, 928 53 55 39; www.flagbeach. com; Flag Beach; windsurf hire per hour/day €40/60, 1-/3-day beginner course €70/140; ⊛) Flag Beach has bags of experience, with beginner windsurfing courses and windsurf hire. Staff are also excellent kitesurfing instructors, with an introductory one-/two-day course costing €130/230; surfboard hire (per day €12) is also

possible. Accommodation can be arranged if you need it.

Billabong Surf Camp   SURFING
(☑928 86 62 07; www.billabongsurfcamp.com; Calle La Red 11; 4hr course €45; ⊙10am-5pm) Corralejo is a justifiably popular base for surfers, with plenty of surf schools dotted around. This long-running company right on the beach offers courses, including equipment and insurance, plus transport to the waves. 'Surfari' trips to nearby surf spots and private one-to-one lessons can be arranged, and basic beachside accommodation as well as apartments and studios are available.

Easy Riders Bikecenter   CYCLING
(☑928 17 58 57; www.easyriders-bikecenter.com; Suite Hotel Atlantis Resort, Calle Las Dunas; bike hire per day from €10, 4hr trip €42; ⊙9am-1pm & 5-8pm Mon-Sat) Easy Riders organises year-round guided excursions with flexible times according to demand, including a tour around Isla de Lobos. Bikes can also be hired here, including kids' bikes (€8), and information on cycling routes provided.

Kayak Fuerteventura   KAYAKING
(☑676 97 80 99; www.kayakfuerteventura.com; day trip €70) The coastal tour is ideal for beginners, while the more experienced might prefer the two-day advanced course (€140). You can also rent kayaks (per day from €50) and snorkelling equipment (per day €10). On land, hikes are arranged for exploration of lava caves and volcanic craters (€40).

Red Shark   WATER SPORTS
(☑928 86 75 48; www.redsharkfuerteventura.com; Calle Pedro y Guy Vandaele; Isla de Lobos trip per

CYCLING THE COASTAL ROUTE

Although you can drive the rough coastal road from Corralejo to El Cotillo, it is particularly well suited to cycling (or hiking), as the land is virtually flat. Take the track north of the Corralejo bus station on Avenida Juan Carlos 1. This graded dirt road winds between volcanic lava fields, shifting to a more desert-like landscape after around 5km. At 8km you reach the tiny fishing community of **Majanicho**, its houses clustered around a small inlet complete with scenic bobbing boats and the smallest chapel you have ever seen. From here you can detour along the FV-101 asphalt road south to Lajares (p103) (7km) for a spot of light refreshment at one of the fabulous bakeries or restaurants, or continue on the coastal road on your way to El Cotillo (p101), which will take you past white sandy beaches such as Playa El Hierro and Playa Beatriz, interspersed with black rocky coves, and a couple of the most popular kite- and windsurfing beaches in these parts. Coming direct from Corralejo you arrive at El Cotillo's lighthouse, Faro de Tostón, after 20km, where you can check out the Museo de la Pesca Tradicional (p102). Alternatively, pedal (or plod) on to the centre of El Cotillo (4.5km), past the scrubby desert setting of Los Lagos.

person €65) Surfing and kitesurfing classes, plus a three-hour stand-up paddleboarding (SUP) trip to Isla de Lobos, and surfboard, kitesurfing and SUP rental.

Ventura Surf Center   WINDSURFING
(📞 928 86 62 95; www.ventura-surf.com; Avenida Marítima 54; 1½hr course from €45, gear hire per day €55) Conditions along much of the coast and in the straits between Corralejo and Lanzarote – the Estrecho de la Bocaina – are ideal for both wind- and kitesurfing. This place is on the beach at the end of Calle Fragata, south of the centre of town. Surfing classes (full day €45) and surfboard rentals (€12 per day) can be arranged here.

Dive Center Corralejo   DIVING
(📞 928 53 59 06; www.divecentercorralejo.com; Calle Nuestra Señora del Pino 22; dive with equipment from €46, open-water course €450; ⏰8am-7pm Mon-Sat) Located just back from the waterfront, this respected outfit has been operating since 1979. You can start by taking the plunge in the pool with a beginner's dive (€45) or combine a pool and sea dive for €90. Refresher courses (€65) and PADI open-water courses plus many other options are also available.

Natoural Adventure   HIKING
(📞 664 84 94 11; www.natouraladventure.com; treks from €48) Offers several different guided treks with distances ranging from 6km to 12km and varying levels of difficulty; destinations and activities include Isla de Lobos, the trail from Antigua to Betancuria and stargazing excursions.

🎊 Festivals & Events

International Kite Festival   KITE
(La Playa del Burro; ⏰Nov) Held every year on La Playa del Burro for kite enthusiasts from around the world with an amazing variety of kites in all shapes and forms.

🍴 Eating

Citrus Surf Cafe   CAFE €
(📞 928 53 54 99; www.facebook.com/citrusfuerteventura; Calle Anzuelo 1; mains €8; ⏰9am-1am Mon-Sat; 📶🍴) This chilled-out, green- and white-themed spot serves a range of cuisines for those fleeing from tapas. Inventive salads, Tex-Mex dishes, burgers, baked potatoes, chicken tikka, salads and wraps are all on the menu, and service is amiable and prompt. Wash down your lunch with a smoothie or freshly squeezed juice.

Antiguo Café del Puerto   SPANISH €
(Calle La Ballena 10; tapas from €3; ⏰11am-11.30pm) Warm and inviting with helpful and obliging staff, this waterfront spot is good for decent wines, the 50-plus tapas selection, flavoursome servings of paella or just a *cortado* (espresso with a splash of milk) to enjoy on the terrace looking out to the ocean.

⭐ **Restaurante Avenida**   SPANISH €€
(www.facebook.com/avenidarestaurantecorralejo; Calle General Prim 11; mains €8-15; ⏰1-10.30pm Tue-Sat, 1-4pm & 6-10pm Sun) Despite the location several blocks back from the beach, this place is always heaving with a cheerful, local Canarian crowd who are here for the no-nonsense food – and virtually everyone walks out satisfied. The atmosphere is rustic with beams and

chunky dark-wood furniture. Seafood dishes start at just €8 for grilled squid; roasted meats include lamb, chicken, rabbit and pork. Cash only.

La Arrocería
SPANISH €€

(☑ 653 16 90 02; www.facebook.com/la.arroceria. de.corralejo; Calle Pejin 10; mains €11-17; ⊙ 7-10.30pm Tue-Fri, 1.30-3.30pm & 7-10.30pm Sat & Sun) In the land of multilingual menus, you know you've found a local haunt in the Canaries when the menu is solely in Spanish. Tucked away down the backstreets, this friendly place has stylish, nautical decor and a minimal but excellent menu focusing on rice dishes. Alongside superb seafood paellas, there are carnivorous and vegetarian versions plus *fideuà,* which uses vermicelli-like noodles instead of rice.

Drinking & Entertainment

For something laid-back, head to Calle La Iglesia, a pedestrian strip with a number of wine bars and cool places for a chilled-out cocktail.

Mojito Beach Bar
BAR

(Avenida Marítima; ⊙ 11am-late; 🛜) A relaxed, hip and colourful place thrown together just inches from the ocean with a menu of exotic mojitos.

Zazamira
CAFE

(www.zazafuerte.com; Calle La Iglesia 7; ⊙ 10am-2am Thu-Tue; 🛜) Elbowed down a narrow street near the harbour, this is the healthy, laid-back option with fresh juices like papaya and orange, and ginseng-spiked coffee. If you fancy something stronger, sip on a cocktail while admiring the Bob Marley memorabilia adorning the walls. There's also a shop for reggae-flavoured accessories.

★ Rock Island Bar
LIVE MUSIC

(www.rockislandbar.com; Calle Crucero Baleares; ⊙ 7.30pm-late; 🛜) For almost 30 years, Mandy and musician husband Gary have made this bar one of the most popular in town. There is acoustic music nightly, playing to an enthusiastic music-loving crowd.

Shopping

No Work Team
SPORTS & OUTDOORS

(www.noworkteam.es; Calle Marítima 6; ⊙ 10am-9pm) One local surf-wear label to check out is No Work Team. You'll find good-quality, comfy threads for men, women and children, with an unmistakeable surfing feel.

ⓘ Information

Tourist Office (☑ 928 86 62 35; www.visit corralejo.com; Avenida Marítima 2; ⊙ 8am-3pm Mon-Fri, 9am-3pm Sat & Sun)

ⓘ Getting There & Away

BUS

From the **bus stop** (Avenida Juan Carlos I), bus 6 runs regularly to Puerto del Rosario (€3.40, 40 minutes). Bus 8 heads west to El Cotillo (€3.10, 40 minutes, 13 daily) via La Oliva; some No 8 buses do not go via La Oliva, in which case the ticket is €2.05.

CAR & MOTORCYCLE

Cicar (☑ 928 53 65 21; www.cicar.com; Corralejo Muelle; per day/week from €30/99; ⊙ 8am-8pm)

BOAT

Fred Olsen (☑ 902 10 01 07; www.fredolsen.es; Estacíon Marítima) Ferries leave from Corralejo for the short hop to Playa Blanca (from €28, 25 minutes, seven daily) in Lanzarote.

Naviera Armas (☑ 928 30 06 00, 902 45 65 00; www.navieraarmas.com) Operates ferries from Corralejo to Playa Blanca (€27.20, 35 minutes, seven daily) in Lanzarote.

Naviera Nortour (☑ 616 98 69 82; www.navieranortour.com; Estacíon Marítima) Runs regular ferries to Isla de Lobos (adult/child return €15/7.50, seven daily) with departures from 10am to 5.30pm. The last boat back from the island is at 6pm.

ⓘ Getting Around

You can call for a **taxi** (☑ 928 86 61 08, 928 53 74 41), or there's a convenient taxi rank near the Centro Comercial Atlántico. A trip from the town centre to the main beaches will cost about €8.

El Cotillo
POP 1300

This former fishing village has more character than anywhere else on the island, marrying the windswept nature of an offbeat coastal town with the laid-back vibe that comes from being a popular surfing destination. El Cotillo has so far managed to avoid major construction and is an excellent place for foodies, water babes or those simply seeking relaxation and superb sea views. Calle Muelle Pescadores, behind the old harbour, doubles as an open-air gallery, with paintings and sculptures dotted around. Spend a few days here, ease into a low gear and line up at least

WORTH A TRIP

ISLA DE LOBOS

The bare Isla de Lobos (4.7 sq km) takes its name from the *lobos marinos* (sea wolves) that once lived there. They were, in fact, *focas monje* (monk seals), which disappeared in the 15th century thanks to a series of hungry mariners landing on the barren island's shores. The good news is that attempts are being made to reintroduce the seals to the island.

It is well worth taking a trip to the islet from Corralejo. Once you've disembarked you can go for a short walk to explore the island, including the pleasant beach to the north of the pier, climb the island's mountain or visit the lighthouse. Hiking around the island takes around an hour – stick to the marked paths.

Take your binoculars as Isla de Lobos is a popular **birdwatching** destination, plus you may spot a shark or two. The island is also great for surfing, but don't worry, the sharks are hammerheads – a distant (harmless) relation to Jaws. The island is also popular with divers and snorkellers.

The **Faro de Martiño** lighthouse stands at the northeastern tip of the island. The mountain in the west of the island is known as **La Caldera**, while north of the ferry terminal is the lovely, sandy **Playa de la Concha**. There is also a small **interpretation centre** (☼10.30am-5.30pm).

You can order lunch at the **restaurant** (☑928 87 96 53; El Puertito; ☼11am-3pm) in the small settlement of El Puertito east of the quay, but reserve when you arrive if you intend to lunch there. Otherwise take drinks and snacks along with you.

The cheapest and fastest way to get to Isla de Lobos is on the Naviera Nortour (p101) ferry from Corralejo (15 minutes). You can also take a snorkelling mini cruise with the same company to the island in a glass-bottomed boat. The last boat back to Corralejo from the island is at 6pm.

A quirky way to see the island is on a stand-up paddleboard (SUP). Red Shark (p99) in Corralejo offers day trips that include transport on a Zodiac, equipment rental and a brief lesson.

---

one seafood dinner to bask in the glow of a glorious Fuerteventura sunset.

Once the seat of power of the tribal chiefs of Maxorata (the northern kingdom of Guanche Fuerteventura), El Cotillo has been largely ignored since the conquest. The exceptions to the rule were the cut-throat pirates who occasionally landed here, plus the slowly growing invasion of less violent sunseekers who prize the area's unaffected peacefulness.

◉ Sights

Museo de la Pesca Tradicional MUSEUM
(Museum of Traditional Fishing; Faro de Tostón; adult/child €3/1.50; ☼10am-2.30pm & 3.15-6pm Tue-Sat; P) This museum dedicated to fisher folk is located next to the town's distinctive red-and-white-striped lighthouse (not open to visitors). You can climb to the top of the considerably smaller original lighthouse for panoramic sea views and then visit the various galleries. English information is available along with several insightful mini videos about traditional fishing methods.

Castillo de Tostón CASTLE
(adult/child €1.50/free; ☼10am-3pm Mon-Fri, 9am-2pm Sat & Sun) Tubby Castillo de Tostón is not really a castle, more a Martello tower. The art and history displays within are interesting, but the star attraction here is the sweeping view of the surf beach to the south. You may find the *castillo* shut, however – when we visited there was rather old-looking tape across the entrance. Note the two ancient lime kilns, a stone's throw away.

Molino de el Roque WINDMILL
(P) This charming windmill is named after El Roque, the next village along from El Cotillo, and with its white paint and black sails, it's really quite a picture. The windmill is close enough to reach on foot or you can drive your car all the way there.

🏃 Activities

Water sports are the main activity in El Cotillo. Only experienced surfers should make for a wave known as **the Bubble** north of the centre. Happily, there are plenty of options for the less experienced as well.

Shock Wave   SURFING
(☑ 928 53 87 49; www.shockwavesurfschool.com;
Calle Pintor Néstor de la Torre 1; 3hr course €50;
⊙ 9am-8pm Apr-Oct, to 6.30pm Nov-Mar) This
surf and windsurfing school comes highly
recommended. Surfing courses range from
four hours to five days (€200) or you can
rent a board and wetsuit (from €15 per day).
Windsurfing starts at €65 for a three-hour
course; bike rental is also available from €10
per day, or €47.50 per week.

Riders Surf 'n' Bike   SURFING
(☑ 629 25 88 61; www.riders-surfnbike.com; Calle
3 de Abril 1979; board hire per day from €10, surf
lessons per day from €50) A friendly set-up at
the entrance to the town. In addition to
courses you can rent surfboards, boogie
boards, stand-up paddleboards and, if you
prefer to stay on land, bikes (€10 per day).

✖ Eating

El Cotillo has some of the north coast's finest
restaurants, with the catch of the day reign-
ing supreme. Fresh fish dinners with sunset
is the ultimate pairing, so get a table booked.
Check out the pavement cafes on the pedestrian Calle Muelle Pescadores.

★ El Goloso de Cotillo   CAFE €
(Calle Pedro Cabrera Saavedra 1; sandwiches €3,
tarts €2; ⊙ 7.30am-7.30pm; 🐾) Enjoy decadent
tarts, cakes and pastries in this quiet spot
at the northern end of the town. There are
fresh juices and shakes, and excellent coffee.
For dessert, try the lemon meringue – it's
simply divine.

El Mentidero   CAFE €
(Calle Punta Aguda 1; sandwiches €3-8; ⊙ 8am-
5pm Wed-Sun; 🐾) Tucked away, this small and
popular blue-and-white cafe has bucketloads
of personality and an easy-going temper-
ament. It's just what the doctor ordered for
either a small or more substantial breakfast,
a glass of freshly squeezed juice, a bowl of
crema de verduras (creamy vegetable soup;
€6), a light lunch or a slice of cake with a
superb cup of coffee.

La Marisma   SEAFOOD €€
(Calle Mariquita Hierro; mains €14-20; ⊙ 1-4pm
& 7pm-late) A suitably nautical interior and
a menu that includes superbly prepared
fried squid, lobster, grilled sole, paella and
other tasty seafood. In a town stuffed with
magnificent views, this place has one of
the best with full-frontal, supreme vistas

through plate glass. There's a kids' menu
(€5.50) for the young ones. It's popular and
often busy, so reserve ahead.

Restaurante La Vaca Azul   SPANISH €€
(☑ 928 53 86 85; www.vacaazul.es; Calle Reque-
na 9, Old Harbour; mains €14-20; ⊙ 12.30pm-late
Wed-Mon) La Vaca Azul enjoys prime position overlooking the pebbly beach, with a
rooftop terrace for extensive views; dinner
is especially atmospheric, with sunset and
lit lanterns. It's mostly about the location,
though you can't go far wrong with a plate
of fresh fish or the mixed seafood platter
served with three types of *mojo*. There are
a few vegetarian options too.

Azzurro   MEDITERRANEAN €€
(☑ 928 17 53 60; www.azzurro.es; Avenida los Lagos
1; mains €10-15; ⊙ 12.30-10pm Tue-Sun, open daily
Aug) Overlooking the beach north of town at
Los Lagos, Azzurro offers quality pasta and
seafood, and a decent line of cocktails when
sunset beckons.

🛍 Shopping

Clean Ocean Project   CLOTHING
(www.cleanoceanproject.org; Calle del Muelle de
Pescadores 11; ⊙ 10am-10pm Tue-Sun, 5-10pm
Mon) 🌿 Stop by this ecologically aware
and very neat-looking place that stocks
cool surf wear in soft greens and blues. The
business donates a percentage of all profits
to beach-cleaning days and antipollution
awareness. There are also branches in Lajares and Corralejo.

ℹ Getting There & Away

Bus 7 for Puerto del Rosario (€4.35, 45 minutes)
leaves daily at 6.30am, noon and 5pm. Bus
8 leaves for Corralejo (€3.10, 40 minutes, 13
daily).

There is plenty of car parking on the streets
of the town, although the one-way system is
slightly confusing. There is also plenty of parking
near the *castillo*.

Lajares

Just 13km southwest of Corralejo via the FV-
101 and the FV-109, Lajares has a laid-back
feel but its modest main street has turned
into quite a colourful experience with several foreigners opening up an enticing combination of restaurants, shops, surf bars
and outstanding bakeries. One of the better

craft markets is also held here on Saturday mornings.

🏃 Activities

Magma Kitesurf School KITESURFING
(☑626 200345; www.magma-kiteschool.com; Calle Central 1; 1-day surfing course €50, 2-day kitesurfing course €255) This popular and efficient surf school and shop has a range of kitesurfing courses, freediving, stand-up paddleboarding, mountain biking and yoga. Accommodation can be provided plus Spanish courses for language learners.

🍴 Eating

Canela Café CAFE €
(☑928 86 17 12; www.canela-cafe.es; Calle Coronel Latherta González Hierro; mains from €8; ⊙8am-2am Fri-Wed) For something substantial, stop in at super-cool Canela Café, with its diverse menu that includes creamy pumpkin curry and the surf-and-turf choice of steak and prawns with garlic butter. There's live acoustic music here on weekends.

Pastelo BAKERY €
(Calle Coronel Latherta González Hierro; ⊙8.30am-6pm; 🕿) Stop by Pastelo for a slice of dense chocolate torte, a wicked brownie, some creamy cheesecake topped with berries or homemade cake, and sit in or take a table in the large space out front.

★722 MEDITERRANEAN €€
(☑693 01 32 10; www.facebook.com/722gradi; Calle Majanicho 11; mains from €15; ⊙5-11pm Wed-Sat, 1-10.30pm Sun) The menu isn't huge and the location isn't at the heart of Lajares, but there's a creative frisson going on in the kitchen at this excellent, elegant, appealing and neatly designed choice. Excellent service, lovely terrace and great cocktails too. The Sunday-morning brunch (€12) is highly popular.

🛍 Shopping

Cabracadabra CLOTHING
(Calle la Cancela 8; ⊙10am-2pm & 3.30-8pm Tue-Fri, 10am-2pm Sat) Try this vivacious shop for silk-screen-printed fashions or a pair of absolutely stunning Pisaverde shoes – each pair is unique (so they say).

Mandarin CLOTHING
(https://mandarin-store.negocio.site; Calle Coronel Gonzalez 22A; ⊙10am-2pm & 4.30-7pm Mon-Fri, 10.30am-2pm Sat) Gorgeous, cool and very stylish jewellery, scarves, blouses, jackets, shirts and bags.

ℹ Getting There & Away

Bus 8 runs from Lajares west to El Cotillo (10 minutes, hourly) and east to Corralejo (30 minutes, frequent); most (but not all) buses to Corralejo go via La Oliva (10 minutes).

PENÍNSULA DE JANDÍA

The southwest of Fuerteventura is a remarkable canvas of craggy hills and bald plains leading to cliffs west of Morro Jable, while much of the rest of the peninsula is composed of dunes, scrub and beaches. The highlight is the journey to the Punta de Jandía Lighthouse with its wind-buffeted perch on the tip of the island, and also over the hills and down to the stunning and golden castaway beach at Cofete, perhaps the highlight of this stark island, if not the entire archipelago.

Most of the peninsula is protected by its status as the Parque Natural de Jandía. The roads are a combination of surfaced and dirt track, but a normal car is generally fine for getting to Cofete. There is one bus that dips into the depths of the peninsula and the white-knuckle trip on this 4WD bus is a worthy enough reason to venture here in itself.

La Lajita

This pretty little fishing village presents yet another black-sand and pebble cove with colourful fishing boats and an unspoiled waterfront with its imposing cliffs. However, a sprawl of unimaginative apartment blocks stretches all the way to the highway, so keep to the sands. On the northern side of the FV-2 is the island's largest theme park: **Oasis Park** (www.fuerteventuraoasispark.com; Carretera General de Jandía; adult/child €35/20.50; ⊙9am-6pm; 👪).

Bus 1 from Puerto del Rosario (€6, 1½ hours, hourly) stops at the highway exit to town, from where it's a short walk south to the zoo.

Costa Calma

Costa Calma, about 25km northeast of Morro Jable, is a confusing muddle of one-way streets interspersed with apartments, shopping centres (at least eight!) and the

THE CLIMATE OF FUERTEVENTURA

The island's volcanic mass is over 20 million years old, eroding over this period to result in its current form of rounded hills and flattened peaks. The land on Fuerteventura is essentially desert, without the topographical diversity associated with changes of altitude seen on other islands such as Gran Canaria or La Palma.

Low precipitation (with rainfall of less than 200mm a year) helps contribute to the extreme aridity of Fuerteventura and its vegetation-free hills, a disposition exacerbated by a high degree of sunshine (over 3000 hours per year) and high winds that whip across the island, increasing evaporation and stripping moisture from the soil. All of these effects contribute to the island's Martian-like landscape, which varies little from one season to the next.

Trees find it hard to prosper or find good purchase on the island and much of the vegetation is scrub, which goats feed on. You will see lines of palms that have been planted by hand, but these are watered artificially through irrigation and would not survive without human intervention.

Fertile and lusher areas such as Betancuria display a richer degree of plant cover, but much of the island is sun-baked, stark and raw.

occasional hotel. The long and sandy beach is certainly magnificent, but the whole place lacks soul or anything historic, its lifeline being the (mostly) German tourists.

Ion Club
WINDSURFING
(☑ 661 349 689; www.ionclubfuerte.com; Club Mistral Fuerteventura; 3hr lesson €80; ⊙ 10am-7pm) This professional and popular windsurfing outfit also offers kitesurfing courses (two hours €125, including equipment). Book online.

Acuarios Jandia
DIVING
(☑ 616 27 46 81; www.acuarios-jandia.com; Sotavento Beach Club; ⊙ 9am-5.15pm Sun-Fri; ☞) This well-established company runs a wide range of courses, from pool dives for tots (€32) to advanced open-water dive courses (€300), rescue diver courses (€330) and a good range of specialist dive courses.

Rapa Nui
CAFE €
(www.rapanui-surfschool.com; Calle Punta de los Molinillos, Commercial Centre Bahia Calma; sandwiches €3-6; ⊙ 9am-midnight; ☞) This is a good choice on a sunny day (and there aren't few), with its lovely terrace and sea views. It runs the adjacent surf shop and serves sandwiches, snacks, ice cream (made on the premises), ace cocktails, coffee and full-on weekly barbecues to a primarily young and tanned surfing crowd. Daily surfing lessons are also on offer.

❶ Getting There & Away

Bus 1 connects Puerto del Rosario (€7.55, 1½ hours, frequent) with Costa Calma en route to

Morro Jable. Bus 5 connects Costa Calma with Morro Jable (€2.70, 40 minutes, frequent).

La Pared

Located on the west coast, La Pared is only a small settlement but it's a hotspot for surfers, excellent hiking is possible and there are terrific views over coastal rock formations, including absolutely killer sunsets. If driving, take your car down to the end of the road on the cliffs overlooking the sea, park it and wander along the clifftop for some astonishing panoramas to Punta Guadelupe, a long and huge shelf of rock that pokes into the sea just to the north at the end of the beach.

Waveguru
SURFING
(☑ 619 80 44 47; www.waveguru.de; 2hr board rental from €10, 10/20/30hr surfing beginners course €135/240/325; ⊙ 10am-6pm) This long-running surf school at the heart of La Pared offers beginner courses, including wetsuit and board rental, as well as classes for more advanced surfers. Accommodation packages (studios, apartments or houses) as well as the on-site surf camp (☑ 619 804447; www.waveguru.de; Avenida del Istmo 17; camping per week €130) are at hand for surfers keen on staying.

Restaurante Bahía La Pared
SEAFOOD €€
(☑ 928 54 90 30; mains €12-15; ⊙ 1-4pm & 7pm-late) With a commodious outdoor patio overlooking the mottled black basalt and sandy beach, the specialities here are fresh fish and seafood paella, though staff are rather jaded and harassed. The restaurant also runs an

CANARIES CONSERVATION

The Península de Jandía is home to an important turtle conservation project, which sees loggerhead turtles being reintroduced after an absence of some 100 years. The program dates back to 2007 when 145 loggerhead turtles were successfully hatched on the west-coast beach of Cofete in the Parque Natural de Jandía.

The beaches here are only the second site in the world selected for such a translocation of eggs; the first is in Mexico. The eggs came from a turtle colony in the southern islands of Cape Verde, which has similarities to the beaches and environment here, namely the quality of the water, the sand and, above all, the consistently warm climate. The turtle eggs are hatched in artificial nests and, before they can crawl away to an uncertain future, the baby turtles are transferred to special tanks at the 'turtle nursery' in Morro Jable until they are strong enough to swim without water wings. At this stage they are microchipped and released into the sea.

The hope is that when they are all grown up they will return to their Cofete home to lay eggs themselves so the species will once again spontaneously breed on the island. The project organisers hope to repeat the hatching at least every five years in an attempt to reverse the depletion of this species of marine turtle.

You can visit the **nursery** (📞 928 53 36 02; Puerto del Morro Jable; ⏱10am-1pm Mon-Fri) **FREE**, which also takes in injured turtles found around the island, though it is periodically not open. You can find it in Morro Jable's harbour, behind a metal fence that allows you to see the turtles occasionally poking their legs from their tubs.

adjacent swimming pool, free for diners (as long as they spend more than €6 each).

🛈 Getting There & Away

Bus 4 from Pájara connects La Pared with Morro Jable (€2.80, 45 minutes, twice daily).

Playa de Sotavento de Jandía

The name is a catch-all for the series of truly stunning beaches that stretch along the east coast of the peninsula. For swimming, sunbathing and windsurfing, this is a coastal paradise, with kilometre after kilometre of fine white sand that creeps its way almost imperceptibly into the turquoise expanse of the Atlantic. The principal beach here – in particular for windsurfers and kitesurfers – is Playa de la Barca (p106).

For 10 hyperactive days each July (and sometimes into early August), the drowsy Fuerteventura calm is shattered as Playa de la Barca hosts a leg of the **Windsurfing World Championship** (www.fuerteventura-worldcup.org; ⏱Jul).

Playa de la Barca　　　　BEACH
The beach that most people visualise when they think of Sotavento is Playa de la Barca. Signposted from the FV-2, 2.5km south of Costa Calma, this is the wind- and kitesurfers' beach par excellence, an expansive length of sand with superb facilities for both beginners and pros. At low tide, the powdery white beach is almost 200m wide; when the tide comes in it creates a shallow, turquoise lagoon ideal for children – and newbie windsurfers.

Bus 5 drops off at the Melia Fuerteventura Hotel, just above Playa de la Barca, on its run between Costa Calma (€1.40, 20 minutes) and Morro Jable (€1.70, 30 minutes) seven times daily.

René Egli　　　　WINDSURFING
(📞 928 54 74 83; www.rene-egli.com; board rental per day/week from €70/350, trial course from €65; ⏱10am-5pm) This long-established, well-advertised operator has a windsurfing centre at the northern end of Playa de la Barca and a kitesurfing centre at the south. The latter has a small bar-restaurant and emits a Caribbean feel, with its palm grove and sunloungers at the water's edge. Courses and rental are cheaper if you prebook; accommodation can also be arranged.

Morro Jable

POP 16,700

More staid than its northern counterpart Corralejo, Morro Jable is almost exclusively German. The magnificent beach, **Playa del Matorral**, is the main attraction, with pale golden sand stretching for around 4km from the older part of town. It's fronted by low-rise, immaculately landscaped apartments and hotels. Back from the beach, the charm palls somewhat with a dual carriageway lined with commercial centres and hotels. The older town centre, up the hill, provides a glimpse of what the town must have once looked like. For true solitude head for the beaches 7km further east.

🏃 Activities

Surfers Island
SURFING

(www.surfers-island.es; Calle Melindraga 2; 4hr course €49, board rental per hour €12) On top of surfing, this well-respected surf school also offers kiteboarding, stand-up paddle-boarding, windsurfing and catamaran sailing courses. A three-day surfing beginners course costs €147; all surfing courses include wetsuit, board and hotel transfer.

Ocean World
DIVING

(✆928 54 40 11; www.tauchen-fuerteventura.com; dive with equipment €48, open-water diver course €350) This reputable place organises daily dives at 9am and 2pm, and offers a variety of dive courses as well as snorkelling trips. Note that medical certificates are required for all dives except the introductory dive.

Volcano Bike
CYCLING

(✆639 73 87 43; www.volcano-bike.com; Calle Melindraga, Club Hotel Aldiana Jandia; bike rental per day from €20, e-bike rental €30; ⊗8.30-11am & 4.30-6.30pm) As well as a full range of mountain and road bikes, this outfit also offers a variety of cycling tours around the island.

🍴 Eating

If you make for the older part of town you can discover seafood and more authentic, traditional choices.

Bar La Parada
TAPAS €

(Calle Nuestra Señora del Carmen 6; tapas €2.80-9; ⊗12.30-4pm & 6.30-11pm; 🕏) The small menu here may be translated into several languages, but the voices around you are almost all Canarian and so is the entirely uncontrived feel. Local *señores* come for the hearty goat, rabbit or chickpea stews or filling servings of fried goat's cheese with jam. Sunday is paella day, when you can get a generous portion for just €7.50 (from 1pm).

La Bodega de Jandía
TAPAS €

(✆663 41 79 73; www.facebook.com/labodegade jandia; Calle Diputado Manuel Velazquez Cabrera 4; tapas €4-9; ⊗1-10pm Sun & Mon, 6-10pm Tue-Thu, 6-9.30pm Fri; 🕏) With legs of ham hanging from the ceiling and vocal locals shouting out their orders, this atmospheric place has much more charm than the tourist restaurants along the seafront. Canarian specialities like *ropa vieja* (chickpea stew), *mousse de gofio* and goat stew feature, or on Sunday you can enjoy a plate of paella at a table in the cobbled, pedestrian street.

ℹ Information

Tourist Office (✆928 54 00 77; Avenida Saladar; ⊗9am-1pm Mon-Fri)

ℹ Getting There & Away

BUS

Bus 10 (€8.20, 1½ hours, three daily) connects the town with the airport, on the way to Puerto del Rosario; a taxi costs around €70 to €80.

Bus 1 runs to Puerto del Rosario (€10, two hours, at least 12 daily) between 5.45am (weekdays) and 10.30pm; bus 10 (€9.70, 1¾ hours, three to four daily), via the airport, is faster. Bus 5 goes to Costa Calma (€2.70, 40 minutes, frequent).

BOAT

Puerto de Morro Jable is located 3km by road from the centre of town. **Fred Olsen** (www.fred olsen.es; Puerto de Morro Jable) runs a service from the port to Las Palmas de Gran Canaria (€49, two hours, two daily). **Naviera Armas** (✆928 54 21 13; www.navieraarmas.com; Puerto de Morro Jable) also runs daily ferries to Las Palmas de Gran Canaria (€41, three hours) and to Santa Cruz de Tenerife (€70, 6½ hours).

ℹ Getting Around

There is a large, free car park next to the tourist office (p107) in the Cosmo Centro Comercial. Call if you need a **taxi** (✆928 54 12 57).

Around Morro Jable

Punta de Jandía Lighthouse
LIGHTHOUSE

(⊗Tue-Sat 10am-6pm) FREE At the end of the dirt road from Morro Jable, the asphalt returns for a smooth ride to this lighthouse positioned over thundering Atlantic waves. The setting is dramatic and the journey here is, of course, half the experience. There's a small information centre within the lighthouse with information on the flora, fauna and geology of the Parque Natural de Jandía, while hikes along the coast reward visitors with stupendous, full-on views.

Just before you reach the lighthouse, you get to Puerto de la Cruz, a tiny fishing

DON'T MISS

VILLA WINTER: THE MYSTERIOUS MANSION

When you finally arrive in Cofete, you can't fail to notice the elaborate mansion perched above the coast. You also can't fail to be intrigued – and you won't be the first. The impressive structure, with its castle-like turret, was built by German engineer Gustav Winter in the 1930s. Rumours linking Winter to the Nazi party have never been confirmed, but conspiracy theories regarding **Villa Winter** (Casa de los Winter; Villa Winter Access) abound. Winter supposedly wanted to establish agriculture in the area, but little evidence of this has been found and, back then, it was unlikely there were any roads leading to the eerie mansion. Some think the house was built as a secret hideout for high-ranking Nazis, including Hitler himself. Others have suggested that Cofete was the location of a secret U-boat base, that there are secret tunnels through the mountain or that it was in fact built as a clinic to specialise in plastic surgery for German generals requiring a new look.

You can drive your car up to the mansion and then walk the last 100m or so. A caretaker lives here and for a small tip he may show you around the house, though when we last visited there was just a donation box left out at the entrance and a sign stuck to the door explaining that donations are important but only the ground-level courtyard was open. However some rather unsettling groaning was audible from one of the rooms marked 'Private'. Make of that what you will. Some visitors have said that they've been allowed into the basement, where they've seen shackles, cells and bullet holes, but like pretty much everything about the Villa Winter, you can't be too sure. Gustav Winter also built the Jandía Airstrip, possibly to fly in the top brass. What looks like a helipad can be observed just downhill from the villa.

Amid all the stories, there's really only one thing that you can be absolutely certain of: Villa Winter is a fascinating place that will have you digging deeper for the truth. Or at least for a few more yarns...

settlement with a solitary wind turbine, caravan park and beach. There are three restaurants here, all specialising in fresh fish. Each has an outdoor terraces, but only **El Caletón** (mains €8-12; ☺9am-10pm) has ocean views. Fish stew is the local speciality. The lighthouse is a superb spot for sunset, but you have to hightail it back afterwards, unless you want to be caught driving on dirt tracks after dark.

Cofete

Along the same road to Punta de Jandía from Morro Jable is the turn-off for Cofete, another 8.2km away. The road winds northeast over a pass and plunges on down to Cofete, a tiny peninsula hamlet at the southern extreme of the Playas de Barlovento de Jandía. With tight corners, steep drops and no barriers, driving the dirt road to get here is a bit hair-raising but totally worth it. Continue and you will be rewarded with one of the most remote and spectacular beaches in the archipelago (and the top sight on Fuerteventura). Get here early in the day, before everyone else turns up – you could find the beach deserted.

★ **Playa de Cofete**   BEACH

This is the main beach in far-flung Cofete, near the southern tip of the island and the main draw on the island for many. It's huge, quite beautiful and entirely undeveloped, with fine honey-coloured sand and a rumbling backdrop of relentless Atlantic rollers and the turquoise ocean. Think twice about swimming here: the waves and currents are more formidable than the generally calmer waters on the other side of the island. If you know what you're doing and have your own gear, it's a good spot for surfers.

Note the signs asking you to report any evidence of turtle activity on the sands (p106). If you see signs of turtle tracks, nesting turtles or even injured turtles, then report this by calling 112. Do not touch turtles or turtle eggs (unless you discover an injured turtle, then the advice is given to move the animal into the shade).

Look out for the ancient, sand-engulfed **Cemetery** (Cementerio del Cofete) near the beach, which is quite a picture. The simple graves are marked with small wooden crosses and piles of stones; the cemetery is bordered by a low wall that is also engulfed in sand, while the main door is similarly swamped by a huge dune (so climb over the wall). The cemetery is signposted.

Get here early in the morning to have the beach entirely to yourself. Sunsets are lovely, but weigh up the danger of returning along the treacherous mountain road at night.

Restaurante Cofete   CANARIAN €€

(☑ 928 17 42 43; mains €8-14; ☺ 10am-7pm; Ⓟ) This place powered by a wind turbine and decked out with football memorabilia has the market cornered, but it still manages a slightly more sophisticated menu than you'd expect from a restaurant that's literally at the end of the road. It serves fresh fish as well as *carne de cabra en salsa* (goat in sauce). There's outside seating and lots of parking.

❶ Getting There & Away

To drive here, take the road Carretera Punta de Jandía off the FV-2 in Morro Jable towards the Punta de Jandía Lighthouse. Much of the road is a dirt track, but you shouldn't need a 4WD. Around 10km before you reach the lighthouse, another dirt track road is signposted to Cofete. All of this road can be traversed in a normal car, though you will need to drive carefully and be extra vigilant, especially at tight bends in the road (which has no barrier).

If you're not driving, take the neat little 4WD bus (€2.70, 1½ hours) that makes the trip from Morro Jable at 10am and 2pm daily, returning at 12.30pm and 4.30pm. The bus also stops at Puerto de la Cruz and the Punta de Jandía Lighthouse.

Lanzarote

POP 148,470

Best Places to Eat

➡ La Cantina (p118)

➡ La Cabaña (p132)

➡ El Navarro (p117)

➡ Lilium (p115)

➡ Casa de la Playa (p123)

➡ El Fondeadero (p117)

Best Beaches

➡ Isla Graciosa (p127)

➡ Playa del Papagayo (p135)

➡ Playa del Risco (p126)

➡ La Caleta de Famara (p126)

➡ Playas Caletones (p125)

➡ Playa de la Garita (p123)

Why Go?

Intimately intertwined with the legacy of 20th-century *lanzaroteño* artist and environmentalist César Manrique, Lanzarote is an intriguing island with an utterly extraordinary geology of 300 volcanic cones, eerie blackened lava fields and the occasional bucolic, palm-filled valley.

A Unesco Geopark since 2015, the island also ticks all the good-time boxes. There are beautiful beaches (both blonde-sand and black-rock), fascinating sights, glittering natural pools and excellent hiking, cycling, surfing and diving, not to mention a wealth of restaurants and accommodation. Though long associated with package tourism, Lanzarote is now pulling in an ever-growing number of independent travellers.

The main holiday resorts hug the southern coastline, northeast of which rise the surreal volcanic badlands of the Parque Nacional de Timanfaya and the island's wine region. Among the wilder northern reaches, surf flourishes at Famara, former capital Teguise surprises, Haría charms with its history and, beyond, Isla Graciosa (the Canaries' eighth island) beckons.

When to Go

➡ Lanzarote's Carnaval in February or March pales slightly compared to Tenerife or Gran Canaria, but is still celebrated with great gusto.

➡ Peak periods are Easter, July, August (20°C to 28°C), December and, to a *slightly* lesser extent, January/February (20°C to 24°C). Book well ahead and expect increased hotel rates, car-hire queues and crowds at the main sights and national park.

➡ March and May (excluding Easter) are quieter months, while late-September and October are perfect for warm weather with fewer crowds.

➡ Hiking is great almost year-round, apart from hot July, August and September.

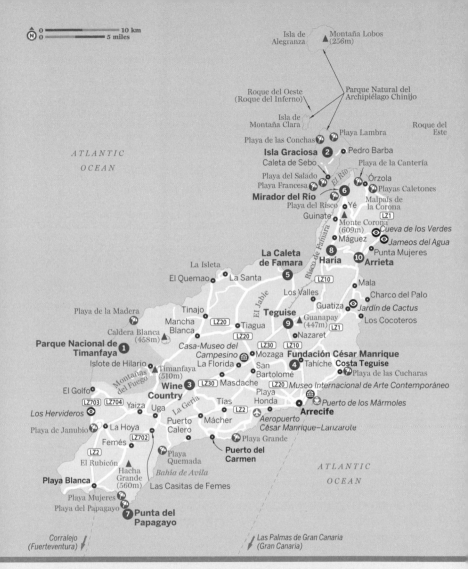

Lanzarote Highlights

1 Parque Nacional de Timanfaya (p121) Marvelling at the otherworldly lavascapes.

2 Isla Graciosa (p127) Escaping to the empty beaches.

3 Wine Country (p120) Tasting the fruits of volcanic vines.

4 Fundación César Manrique (p114) Meeting the artist amid the lava fields.

5 La Caleta de Famara (p126) Jumping into the surf scene or lazing on the beach.

6 Mirador del Río (p125) Enjoying heady sweeping views from this mountaintop lookout.

7 Punta del Papagayo (p135) Kicking back on the beaches of the south coast.

8 Haría (p125) Wandering the market in an oasis of green.

9 Teguise (p117) Strolling the history-rich streets.

10 Arrieta (p123) Sampling sensational seafood and swimming in natural pools.

History

Lanzarote's first inhabitants, the Majos, are thought to have arrived on the island from North Africa in around 1000 BC. Lanzarote was the first of the Canaries to fall to Jean de Béthencourt in 1402 and was subsequently made the unneighbourly base for conquering the rest of the archipelago. Many Majos were sold into slavery, and those remaining had to endure waves of marauding pirates from the northwest African coast. British buccaneers, such as Walter Raleigh, also got in on the plundering act, and by the mid-17th century the population here had dwindled to a mere 300.

Just as the human assault seemed to be abating, nature elbowed in – big time. During the 1730s, massive volcanic eruptions destroyed at least a dozen towns and some of the island's most fertile land. But the volcanic soil proved a highly fertile bedrock for farming (particularly wine grapes), which brought relative prosperity to the island.

In 1852 the capital was moved from Teguise to Arrecife. Today, with tourism flourishing alongside the healthy, if small, agricultural sector, the island's population of 148,470 can more than double with all the holiday blow-ins. Thankfully, the legacy of superstar 20th-century artist César Manrique (p116) has ensured that development is, to a certain extent, sensibly controlled.

ⓘ Getting There & Away

AIR

The Aeropuerto César Manrique–Lanzarote (p268) is 6km west of Arrecife, with an array of flights to/from Europe. Binter Canarias (p269) flies to/from Gran Canaria, Tenerife and La Palma; Canary Fly (p269) goes to Gran Canaria.

BOAT

From Arrecife's Puerto de los Mármoles, 4km northeast of town, ferries connect with Gran Canaria and on to Tenerife and La Palma. From Playa Blanca there are regular ferries to Corralejo on Fuerteventura.

Fred Olsen (p269) Ferries link Playa Blanca with Corralejo on Fuerteventura (€28, 25 minutes, four to seven daily), and Arrecife with Las Palmas de Gran Canaria (€54, 3¾ hours, one to two daily).

Naviera Armas (Map p113; ☑ 928 82 49 30; www.navieraarmas.com; Calle Manolo Millares 90; ☺ 8.10am-2.30pm Mon & Fri, 8.10am-2.30pm & 4.30-6.30pm Tue-Thu, 8.30am-10.30am Sat) Ferries between Arrecife and Las Palmas de Gran Canaria (€63, 5½ hours, one

daily), as well as between Playa Blanca and Corralejo on Fuerteventura (€27, 35 minutes, seven daily).

Trasmediterránea (Map p113; ☑ 928 82 49 30; www.trasmediterranea.es; Calle Manolo Millares 90; ☺ 8.10am-2.30pm Mon & Fri, 8.10am-2.30pm & 4.30-6.30pm Tue-Thu, 8.30am-10.30am Sat) Ferries between Arrecife and Las Palmas de Gran Canaria (€33, eight hours, one weekly), plus Santa Cruz de Tenerife (via Las Palmas de Gran Canaria; €35, 17 hours, one weekly).

ⓘ Getting Around

TO/FROM THE AIRPORT

Buses 22 and 23 run between the airport and Arrecife (€1.40, 15 minutes, at least every 25 minutes). Bus 161 runs between the airport and Playa Blanca (€3.30, one hour, eight to 22 daily) via Puerto del Carmen (€1.70, 15 minutes).

Taxis charge €15 to Arrecife, €20 to Puerto del Carmen and €45 to Playa Blanca.

BICYCLE

Cycling is an ever-more popular way of exploring Lanzarote, and you'll find bike-hire shops in all major towns, charging from around €10 per day.

BUS

Intercity Bus Lanzarote (☑ 928 81 15 22; www.arrecifebus.com) operates a fairly comprehensive network of buses around the island.

CAR & MOTORCYCLE

Driving on Lanzarote is the best way to see the island. You'll find plenty of car rental agencies at the airport, in Arrecife and in the main tourist resorts. Cicar (☑ 928 82 29 00; www.cicar.com; Calle Dr Ruperto González Negrín 8, Arrecife; ☺ 8am-1pm & 4.30-7pm Mon-Fri, 8am-1pm Sat) is a reliable local rental company.

CENTRAL LANZAROTE

Arrecife

POP 45,630

Lanzarote's capital is a small, agreeable, south-coast city with a pleasant Mediterranean-style promenade, an inviting sandy beach washed by the sparkling Atlantic, and a disarming backstreet hotchpotch of sun-bleached buildings, unpretentious bars, buzzy shopping streets and restaurants of all kinds. Though a little thin on the ground for a Canarian capital, Arrecife's sights are well worth exploring, including a couple of castles, a pretty saltwater lagoon, an important

Arrecife

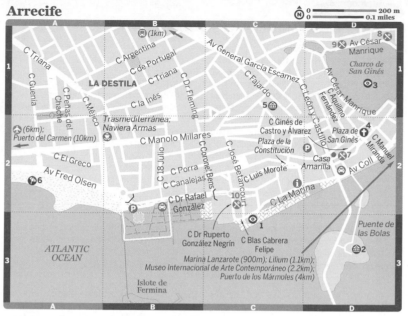

art gallery and several César Manrique creations; you'll find the most historical charm in the narrow backstreets around the church and lagoon. All that said, Arrecife's most notable quality is that it's a no-nonsense working town that earns its living from something other than tourism.

History

The single biggest factor behind Arrecife's lack of pizzazz is that, despite being a port since at least the 15th century (its two castles date from 1574 and 1799), it only became the island's capital in 1852. Until then, Teguise

ruled supreme, though the Arrecife area was lived in from the 16th century – initially mostly by fishers and merchants who inhabited local caves. By the close of the 18th century, a semblance of Arrecife town had taken uncertain shape around the harbour. As commerce grew and the threat of sea raids dropped off in the 19th century, the city thrived and the move of the island's administration to Arrecife became inevitable.

◉ Sights & Activities

From Arrecife, you can stroll southwest along the seafront promenade to Puerto del Carmen (9km, two hours) via Playa Honda.

★ Museo Internacional de Arte Contemporáneo   GALLERY

(MIAC; www.cactlanzarote.com; Castillo de San José, Carretera de Puerto Naos; adult/child €4/2; ⊙ 10am-8pm; Ⓟ) Converted into an art gallery in 1976, on César Manrique's wish, the well-preserved 18th-century Castillo de San José houses one of the Canaries' major contemporary art collections. Aside from a couple of early works by Manrique himself, its thoughtfully presented rooms spanning the 1950s to 1970s star works by such greats as Miró, Millares, Tàpies and Lanzarote-born Pancho Lasso. It's a walkable 2km northwest of central Arrecife.

DON'T MISS

TAHÍCHE & THE FUNDACIÓN CÉSAR MANRIQUE

Upon returning definitively to Lanzarote, César Manrique built his spectacular house and creative centre, Taro de Tahíche, into the lava fields just outside Tahíche, and lived here from 1968 to 1988. Now the **Fundación César Manrique** (☑ 928 84 31 38; www. fcmanrique.org; Calle Jorge Luis Borges 16, Tahíche; adult/child €8/1, combined ticket with Casa-Museo César Manrique €15; ☺ 10am-6pm), it's a real James Bond-style hideaway, with whitewashed walls, a sunken pool, bursts of bougainvillea and cacti, and white- and red-leather seats slotted into cavelike dens; upper levels are inspired by traditional Lanzarote architecture, while subterranean rooms are crafted from five huge air bubbles left by flowing lava. Beyond the lava bubbles, there's an entire gallery devoted to Manrique, plus a tiny garden cafe next to a vibrant 1992 mural. Minor works by some of Manrique's contemporaries, including Picasso, Chillida, Miró, Sempere and Tàpies, are also on show.

The Fundación is 200m west of the roundabout at the southern end of town; Tahíche is 5km north of Arrecife. Buses 7, 9 and 10 (€1.40, 15 minutes), among others, stop here between Arrecife and Teguise.

On the east side of Tahíche, Lanzarote's first microbrewery **Los Aljibes** (☑ 639 656007, 610 454294; Calle Bravo Murillo 6, Tahíche; ☺ 1-10pm Tue-Sun; 🔊) is spread across a jazzy palm-sprinkled terrace and a sunken whitewashed home in which Manrique had a hand. It concocts five artisan beers on-site, served alongside island wines and good, honest food blending Canarian and Argentine flavours (mains €14 to €19).

The castle was built to deal with pirates and provide unemployed locals with a public-works job scheme, and today also hosts a smart **restaurant** (☑ 928 81 23 21; www.cact lanzarote.com; mains €10-18; ☺ noon-4pm Tue-Thu, noon-4pm & 7-11pm Fri & Sat).

Museo Arqueológico de Lanzarote   MUSEUM
(Map p113; www.cactlanzarote.com; Calle Fajardo 5; €3; ☺ 10am-6pm Tue-Fri, to 2pm Sat) Tucked into the repurposed mansion of 20th-century *lanzaroteño* doctor and architect Fermín Rodríguez Bethencourt and his wife Manuela García Parrilla, Lanzarote's 2018-opened archaeology museum romps through the island's long history with excellent multilanguage, multimedia displays ranging from 16th-century ceramic vessels from Seville to an augmented-reality archaeological dig.

Iglesia de San Ginés   CHURCH
(Map p113; Plaza de San Ginés; ☺ hours vary) Dating from 1665 and featuring Tuscan-style columns, a neoclassical tower and a 17th-century statue of the island's patron saint, this triple-nave church looms over Arrecife's prettiest plaza.

Castillo de San Gabriel   MUSEUM
(Map p113; €3; ☺ 10am-5pm Mon-Fri, to 2pm Sat) On a little islet just off the seafront promenade, reached via the 18th-century Puente de las Bolas or a more recent Franco-era bridge,

the 16th-century Castillo de San Gabriel was originally built to fend off pirate attacks. Today it holds the **Museo de Historia de Arrecife**, with Spanish-language exhibits on the island's geology, flora and fauna as well as pre-Hispanic life, the Spanish conquest and the capital's history.

Charco de San Ginés   LAGOON
(Map p113) Fringed by homes and restaurants in a beguiling combination of mildly down at heel and freshly whitewashed (with blue trim), the attractive natural San Ginés saltwater lake just east of the city centre is one of Arrecife's main hubs.

Biblioteca Universitaria Municipal   LIBRARY
(Map p113; www.unedlanzarote.es; Calle Blas Cabrera Felipe; ☺ 9am-1pm & 5-8pm Mon-Fri) In the green-shuttered former Parador building, right on the seafront, this university library conceals four wonderful early César Manrique murals, including the stormily evocative *El viento*. Visitors are free to pop in (quietly) when classes aren't running.

Playa del Reducto   BEACH
(Map p113) If you fancy a dip, the city's main beach is lovely: an arc of pristine pale-gold sand fringed with lofty palm trees and a promenade. It's safe for children, reasonably clean and, generally, surprisingly empty, with just a few sunbeds for hire.

✦ Festivals & Events

Día de San Ginés
RELIGIOUS

(☺25 Aug) The day of the island's patron saint is celebrated with a major fiesta in even the smallest village, and celebrations build up over two weeks beforehand. In Arrecife, the streets surrounding the Iglesia de San Ginés (p114) are home to the most revelry.

Carnaval
CARNIVAL

(☺Feb/Mar) Celebrated with gusto across Lanzarote, but particularly in Arrecife, Carnaval festivities kick off the week before Ash Wednesday.

✗ Eating

The Charco de San Ginés is surrounded by breezy seafood spots.

Tabla
INTERNATIONAL €

(Map p113; ☑928 84 55 36; www.cantinateguise. com; Calle Dr Ruperto González Negrín; mains €7-12; ☺noon-10.30pm Sun-Thu, to 11.30pm Fri & Sat; ☜⚏) From the ambitious British team behind Teguise sensation La Cantina (p118), this stylishly contemporary bar-restaurant with dangling lamps and roadside tables specialises in throwing creative twists into fresh, local, often-organic produce: artisan burgers, enormous crispy salads and delicate Buddha-style bowls (try the kimchi-tofu with wholemeal rice).

Bar Andalucía
TAPAS €

(Map p113; Calle Luis Martín 5; tapas €3-8; ☺1-4pm & 7.30pm-late Tue-Sat) Bowls of glistening tomatoes and a leg of *jamón* set the scene at this side-street tapas bar, going strong since 1960 and oozing charm with its Andalusian tiles, creeping vines, artisan olive oils and authentically good, straight-from-Seville bites. Feast on uncomplicated tapas such as stuffed peppers, sherry-cooked sirloin, *tortilla de patatas* and ham-and-cheese croquettes.

★ Lilium
CANARIAN €€

(☑928 52 49 78; www.restaurantelilium.com; Avenida Olof Palme, Marina Lanzarote; mains €14-21; ☺2-4pm & 8-10.30pm Mon-Sat) In Arrecife's swish marina, minimalist-chic Lilium wows with innovative dishes like confit duck leg with fig sauce or grilled scallops with banana, coconut and lime, crafted by El Bulli–trained chef Orlando Ortega. Traditional Canarian ingredients get a creative makeover: *gofio* (roasted grain), palm syrup and *almogrote* (spicy pâté of soft cheese, pepper and tomato) all grace the menu. Bookings recommended.

Naia
CANARIAN €€

(Map p113; ☑928 80 57 97; www.restaurantenaia. es; Avenida César Manrique 33; mains €12-15; ☺11am-midnight Mon-Wed, to 2am Thu-Sat) Vases of fresh flowers and rustic-modern interiors combine with original recipes rooted in local cooking at this cheerfully informal gastrobar with terrace tables gazing out on the Charco de San Ginés. From a semi-open kitchen, Chef Mikel Otaegui works up such delights as creamy mushroom-and-asparagus rice, goat's cheese salad sprinkled with sweet-curry dressing, and potato-and-portobello tortilla dressed with truffle oil.

Cala
SEAFOOD, CANARIAN €€

(Map p113; ☑928 39 96 87; www.facebook.com/ restaurantecala2017; Avenida César Manrique 18; mains €9-20; ☺12.30-4pm & 7.30pm-late, Wed-Mon) The latest venture from prize-winning Catalan chef Luis León, elegantly relaxed Cala breathes creative flair into Canarian cuisine amid distressed-wood walls, moody lighting, circular mirrors and tables adorned with fresh flowers, overlooking the Charco de San Ginés. Expertly executed dishes swing from grilled *queso fresco* dipped in pumpkin marmalade to salmon in a *cava* sauce, and plenty of grilled meats.

❏ Drinking & Nightlife

There are a few clubs and bars clustered along central Calle Manolo Millares, open from around 10pm to 4am. The bars and restaurants strung around the Charco de San Ginés are hugely popular, while a new nightlife area is developing around Marina Lanzarote (just east of the centre).

Nao
MICROBREWERY

(☑928 84 93 16; www.naobeer.com; Calle Foque 5, Puerto Naos; ☺noon-3.30pm & 6-10pm Thu & Fri) You'll spot Nao's handful of hugely popular artisan beers all over the island – Capitán APA, Marine blonde ale, *malvasía*-grape-based Maresía. Sample them at the source in this little blue-doored brewpub tucked into a repurposed-workshop brewery by Arrecife's docks, 500m northeast of the Charco de San Ginés. Contact the team directly to enquire about one-hour brewery tours and tastings, and special events.

❶ Information

Oficina de Turismo (Map p113; ☑928 81 80 28; www.turismolanzarote.com; Calle La Marina; ☺9.30am-5pm Mon-Fri, to 1pm Sat)

LANZAROTE ARRECIFE

NATIVE SON: CÉSAR MANRIQUE

The great César Manrique, Lanzarote's most famous native son, enjoys a posthumous status on the island akin to that of a mystical hero, talked about by many *lanzaroteños* as if he were a close friend. His influence is everywhere, from the obvious, like his giant mobile sculptures adorning roundabouts all over the island, to the (thankfully) unseen: the lack of high-rise buildings and advertising billboards.

Born on 24 April 1919 in Arrecife, Manrique was initially best known as a contemporary artist. Influenced by Picasso and Matisse, he held his first major exhibition of abstract works in 1954 and, 10 years later, his art career reached its pinnacle with an exhibition at New York's Guggenheim Museum. But Manrique's birthplace remained imprinted on his imagination and he returned home in 1966, brimming with ideas for enhancing what he felt to be the incomparable beauty of Lanzarote.

He began with a campaign to preserve traditional building methods and to ban roadside hoardings. A multifaceted artist, Manrique subsequently turned his flair and vision to a broad range of projects, with the whole of Lanzarote becoming his canvas. In all, he carried out seven major projects, which he called *intervenciones* (interventions), on the island and numerous others elsewhere in the archipelago and beyond. At the time of his death – at the age of 73, in a car accident near Tahíche's Fundación César Manrique (p114) in 1992 – he had several more in the works.

It was primarily Manrique's persistent lobbying for maintaining traditional architecture and protecting the natural environment that prompted the *cabildo* (island government) to pass laws restricting urban development, fuelling a desire for sustainable tourism long before it became a hot topic. Manrique's ceaseless opposition to unchecked urban sprawl struck a chord with many locals and led to the creation of an environmental group known as El Guincho, which has had some success in revealing – and at times even reversing – abuses by developers. Manrique was posthumously made its honorary president.

As you pass through villages across the island, you'll see how traditional stylistic features remain the norm. The standard whitewashed houses are adorned with onion-shaped chimney pots and doors and shutters painted blue (by the sea) or green (inland). In such ways, Manrique's influence and spirit live on, and the centenary of his birth was joyously celebrated throughout 2019.

In the fine Casa de la Cultura building; also at the airport.

Oficina de Turismo (☑ 928 34 72 93; www. turismolanzarote.com; Avenida Olof Palme, Marina Lanzarote; ⊙8am-7pm Mon-Fri, to 5pm Sat)

ℹ Getting There & Away

Intercity Bus Lanzarote (p112) runs to all major towns and resorts, leaving from the **Intercambiador de Guaguas** (Avenida Fred Olsen) at the west end of town or the **Estación de Guaguas** (Calle Rambla Medular) 1km north of the centre. Popular routes:

Bus 1 Costa Teguise (€1.40, 20 minutes, every 20 to 60 minutes)

Bus 2 Puerto del Carmen (€1.70, 40 minutes, every 30 to 60 minutes)

Bus 60 Playa Blanca (€3.60, one hour, hourly)

Bus 7 Teguise (€1.40, 30 minutes, six daily)

Bus 9 Teguise (€1.40, 30 minutes, four to five daily) and Órzola (€3.60, 55 minutes, four to five daily)

ℹ Getting Around

Buses 22 and 23 run to/from the airport (€1.40, 15 minutes, at least every 25 minutes). Buses including 1 and 25 call in at the Puerto de los Mármoles.

There is free parking on the east side of the Charco de San Ginés and at the far west end of town near the Cabildo. Alternatively, head to the underground car park opposite the Arrecife Gran Hotel & Spa (€20 per day).

Taxis gather outside the **Arrecife Gran Hotel & Spa** (Map p113; Avenida Fred Olsen) and opposite the **Castillo de San Gabriel** (Map p113; Avenida Coll), charging around €15 to the airport and €10 to the Puerto de los Mármoles.

Costa Teguise

POP 8300

Framing pretty golden **Playa de las Cucharas**, just 8km northeast of Arrecife, the purpose-built resort of Costa Teguise is a perfectly pleasant holiday spot provided you aren't expecting cobbled streets, crumbling buildings and genuine Canarian charm. Established in the 1970s, the resort inevitably lacks real soul, but the fun here revolves around bustling shopping centres, family-geared beaches and water sports, plenty of bars and restaurants (some, admittedly, more impressive than others) and the Canarian-style *pueblo marinero*, a fishing-village-inspired plaza area on which the great César Manrique collaborated.

🏃 Activities

Three popular signed walking routes of 4.6km to 10km head out around Costa Teguise and its coastline; pick up maps at the tourist office (p117). You can also hike up the 232m Montaña Corona (5km, two hours) or walk north along the coast to/from Arrieta (20km, five hours) via Los Cocoteros and Charco del Palo, with a fair amount of up and down.

Olita Trek & Bike   HIKING
(☑ 928 59 21 48, 619 169989; www.olita-treks.com; Centro Comercial Las Maretas; walks €40) This long-running, family-owned operator offers excellent walks covering Isla Graciosa as well as Lanzarote's volcanoes, wine country and northern reaches, along with week-long Lanzarote biking tours (€680) and extended hiking trips across the Canaries.

Windsurf Club Las Cucharas   WINDSURFING
(☑ 690 674093, 928 59 07 31; www.lanzarotewindsurf.com; Calle del Marrajo, Centro Comercial Las Maretas; beginner/intermediate course from €110/125) A popular, reliable, multilingual windsurfing school that hires out kit (from €140 for three days), runs group and private classes to suit all levels, and rents kayaks and paddleboards.

Calipso Diving   DIVING
(☑ 928 59 08 79; www.calipso-diving.com; Avenida Islas Canarias, Centro Comercial Calipso; single dive €32; ⊙ 9am-6pm Mon-Sat) Long-established and reliable expat-owned school for dives and courses (PADI Open Water or BSAC Ocean Diver €415), plus equipment hire (€12) for experienced divers.

🍴 Eating & Drinking

★ El Fondeadero   SEAFOOD, CANARIAN €
(☑ 928 59 25 01; Avenida de los Corales 22, Las Caletas; mains €6-13; ⊙ 7am-midnight) Ignore the workaday facade: this gloriously down-to-earth favourite gets crammed with lunching Spaniards, who pack in for simple fruits-of-the-sea sensations including grilled *lenguado*

(sole), paella for two, fresh fish of the day and seafood stew. Tapas of tortilla, paella and *atún encebollado* (tuna with onions) are chalked up behind the bar, amid subtly nautical decor. It's 3km southwest of Costa Teguise.

★ El Navarro   CANARIAN €€
(☑ 928 59 21 45; www.facebook.com/elnavarro lanzarote; Avenida del Mar 13; mains €13-18; ⊙ 7-10.30pm Mon-Sat) Advance bookings are absolutely essential for this small, outrageously popular restaurant, considered one of the island's finest and elegantly dressed in woods and whites. With *tinerfeño* chef Jonay Morales at the helm, the menu focuses on lightly creative Canarian-inspired dishes, intricately prepared with fresh, local ingredients – prawn-mussel-and-squid stew, spinach ravioli, slow-cooked lamb shoulder, baked goat's cheese with Lanzarote black pudding.

Los Aljibes   CRAFT BEER
(off Avenida Islas Canarias; ⊙ 4.30pm-12.30am Tue-Sun) Lanzarote's original microbrewery (p115) brings its signature APA, Märzen and other star creations to this 2019-opened Costa Teguise tap room, right next to the tourist office. Beer-barrel tables, green wooden doors and local artwork set the rustic-modern tone for artisan brews, island wines and suitably beer-inspired cooking.

ℹ️ Information

Oficina de Información Turística de Costa Teguise (☑ 928 59 25 42; www.turismoteguise.com; Avenida Islas Canarias; ⊙ 9am-4pm Mon-Fri, 10am-2pm Sat & Sun)

ℹ️ Getting There & Around

Bus 1 (€1.40, 20 minutes, every 20 to 60 minutes) runs to/from Arrecife from around 7am to midnight; bus 3 runs to/from Puerto del Carmen (€2.95, one hour, hourly) via Arrecife.
Bike Station (☑ 928 82 50 14; www.tribikestation.com; Avenida Islas Canarias, Centro Comercial Las Maretas; bike rental per day from €16; ⊙ 9am-7pm Mon-Fri, 10am-2pm Sat & Sun)

Teguise
POP 1770

Lanzarote's original capital and one of the oldest towns in the Canaries, Teguise simmers with a North Africa–meets–Spanish *pueblo* feel. This intriguing mini-oasis of low-rise whitewashed buildings is set around a central plaza and restored 15th-century church, and surrounded by the bare arid

LANZAROTE TEGUISE

GETTING AWAY FROM IT ALL

Playa Quemada (p129) Enjoy a seafood lunch at a hidden-away beach, then hike up to the little village of Femés.

Explore the interior (p112) Ditch the map and drive inland, discovering unspoilt hamlets and stunning views.

Head out hiking (p117) Explore soul-stirring landscapes overlooked by most visitors.

Playa del Risco (p126) Clamber downhill for an hour to reach a wild, secluded beach.

Órzola (p125) Seek out the natural sandy white coves on the far northeastern coast.

Isla Graciosa (p127) Venture beyond the harbour to find beaches all to yourself.

plains of central Lanzarote, 12km north of Arrecife. Though firmly on the tourist trail, Teguise's old town is a delight to explore, with good restaurants, a handful of lively bars and a string of monuments testifying to the town's dominance until Arrecife took the baton in 1852. On Sunday mornings, a mammoth tourist-oriented **market** (www.mercadil lodeteguise.com; ⊙ 9am-2pm Sun) takes over.

History

Originally a Guanche settlement, Teguise prospered from 1418 onwards, after Maciot de Béthencourt (nephew of Jean de Béthencourt) moved here and married Teguise, daughter of the last local chieftain, and various convents were founded. But with prosperity came other problems, including repeated pirate attacks, which reached a violent crescendo in 1618 when 5000 Algerian raiders stormed Teguise – hence the ominously named Callejón de la Sangre (Blood Alley). The town remained the island's capital until 1852.

◉ Sights

Pick up a map of the town's historical buildings from the tourist office.

**Iglesia de Nuestra
Señora de Guadalupe**   CHURCH
(Plaza de la Constitución; ⊙ 9am-1.30pm Mon-Sat) Perched on the palm-studded main plaza, Teguise's church has its roots in the 15th century but was restored in the 20th century after a disastrous fire and an earlier series of pirate attacks.

Casa del Timple   MUSEUM
(www.casadeltimple.org; Plaza de la Constitución; adult/child €3/free; ⊙ 9am-3pm Mon-Sat, to 2pm Sun Jul-Sep, 9am-4pm Mon-Sat, to 3pm Sun Oct-May) Within the historical walls of the graceful 18th-century Palacio Spínola, this entertaining museum is dedicated to the *timple*, a

traditional Canarian stringed instrument similar to a ukulele. Spanish-language displays unveil the history of the *timple* through the ages (it was first documented in the Canaries in 1792), with *timples* on show alongside similar instruments from around the world, such as the Indian sitar.

Museo de la Piratería   MUSEUM
(Castillo de Santa Bárbara; www.museodelapirateria. com; adult/child €3/free; ⊙ 9am-3.30pm Mon-Sat, 10am-3.30pm Sun; P) Perched 396m high on the Montaña de Guanapay, 1km east of town with sweeping views across the plains, the 16th-century **Castillo de Santa Bárbara** doubles as a fascinating multilanguage pirate museum (it's hugely popular with kids). Exhibits detail the numerous attacks Lanzarote suffered at the hands of pirates from across Europe and Africa from the 15th to 18th centuries, when Teguise was its capital.

✗ Eating

La Palmera   TAPAS €
(www.facebook.com/palmeriteguise; Calle Garajonay 4; tapas €6-12; ⊙ 10am-10.30pm) Sunny terrace tables, regular live music and a cosy, cave-like red-walled interior create a buzzy setting for deliciously simple tapas and sharing platters of island cheeses, Uga salmon, potato omelette, Iberian ham and *patatas arrugadas* (wrinkly potatoes) at arty La Palmera, which gets packed on Sundays. Also perfect for coffee and crunchy *bocadillos* of, say, creamy Lanzarote cheese.

★ La Cantina   TAPAS, INTERNATIONAL €€
(☑ 928 84 55 36; www.cantinateguise.com; Calle León y Castillo 8; mains €10-20; ⊙ 10am-11pm; ⊛ ✐) Whitewashed walls, beamed ceilings and trailing greenery adorn the scattered rooms of this seductively atmospheric 500-year-old house, now reimagined as a sensational Canarian-international restaurant by

British owners Benn and Zoe. Craft beers and island wines accompany exquisite creations rooted in local produce, from vegan tacos to spicy tofu bowls to artisan burgers. Don't miss the signature sharing *tablas*.

Restaurante Hespérides   MEDITERRANEAN, CANARIAN €€

(📞928 59 31 59; www.facebook.com/restaurante hesperides; Calle León y Castillo 3; tapas €5-8, mains €17; ⊙ 2-10pm Tue-Sat, noon-4pm Sun; 🍴) A sleek marriage of visual and culinary arts, this popular and laid-back restaurant delights diners with artfully crafted Mediterranean-meets-Canarian dishes like zesty falafel, tandoori tofu rice, Lanzarote goat's cheese and smoked salmon from Uga, all washed down with local organic wines. Tables are dotted across a flower-filled courtyard and several stylish dining rooms.

❶ Information

Oficina de Información Turística (📞928 84 53 98; www.turismoteguise.com; Plaza de la Constitución; ⊙9am-4pm Mon-Fri, 10am-2pm Sat & Sun)

❶ Getting There & Away

Numerous buses, including 7 and 9 from Arrecife (€1.40, 30 minutes), stop in Teguise en route to northern destinations such as Órzola and Haría. There are also buses and organised tours to the Sunday market from Costa Teguise, Puerto del Carmen and Playa Blanca.

San Bartolomé

POP 5940

Having started life as the Guanche settlement of Ajei, San Bartolomé ended up in the 18th century as the de facto private fiefdom of a militia leader, Francisco Guerra Clavijo y Perdomo, and his descendants. These days, it's a sleepy town with a palm-dotted square and a handful of historical buildings and museums, 7km northwest of Arrecife on the fringes of Lanzarote's wine-growing region.

Casa-Museo del Campesino   MUSEUM

(📞928 52 01 36; www.cactlanzarote.com; cnr LZ20 & LZ30; ⊙10am-6pm; 🅿) FREE Just 2km north of San Bartolomé rises the modernistic **Monumento al Campesino** (Peasants' Monument), created in 1968 by (surprise, surprise) César Manrique to honour the thankless labour that most islanders had endured for generations. The attached **Casa-Museo del Campesino** – all whitewashed walls and bright-green trim – is more a scattering of craft workshops (ceramics, leatherwork, soaps, hats, natural fabrics), where you can see artisans at work and even take a quick class (€3). Most people visit for the Canarian **restaurant** (www.cactlanzarote.com; cnr LZ20 & LZ30; tapas €2-6, mains €10-17; ⊙noon-4pm; 🍴).

Museo del Tanit   MUSEUM

(www.museotanit.com; Calle Constitución 1; adult/child €6/free; ⊙10am-2pm Mon-Sat) Set in an 18th-century bodega (one of the first in the San Bartolomé area), this rambling private ethnographic collection covers just about every aspect of island life from early aboriginal Majo culture to the 20th century. Displays (with multilanguage info booklets available) range from basketry, traditional dress and a pre-Hispanic pestle-and-mortar to a chapel built from what was once a camel stable.

Caserío de Mozaga   CANARIAN €€

(📞605 076476; www.caseriodemozaga.com; Calle Malva 8, Mozaga; mains €16-19; ⊙6-10.30pm Wed-Mon; 🍴) The sophisticated contemporary-Canarian restaurant hidden away in the former stables of the tastefully converted 18th-century country house Caserío de Mozaga (p124), 2.5km northwest of San Bartolomé, is a delight. Fresh, seasonal local produce is given a few creative twists, with the likes of Lanzarote lamb chops, grilled fish of the day and handmade mushroom pasta on the tempting menu. Book ahead.

LANZAROTE SAN BARTOLOMÉ

LANZAROTE FOR CHILDREN

The main resorts of Costa Teguise, Playa Blanca and Puerto del Carmen have plenty of family-geared activities, from glass-bottom boats to snorkelling to submarine safaris. Teguise's Museo de la Piratería is a great spot for children, and several of the Manrique (p116) sights will fascinate kids just as much as their parents. Older kids will enjoy Lanzarote's excellent surfing, kitesurfing, SUP and diving scenes, and adventures across to Isla Graciosa (p127) are great for the whole family. Kids will love the eerie moonscapes of the Parque Nacional de Timanfaya (p121), while the seafront promenade along the south-central coast between Costa Teguise and Puerto del Carmen is perfect for walks.

ⓘ Getting There & Away

Buses 16, 20 and 32, among others, swing through San Bartolomé en route to/from Arrecife (€1.40, 20 minutes).

Tiagua

POP 330

Flanking the LZ20, 8km northwest of San Bartolomé, Tiagua is a whitewashed workaday town with an intriguing agricultural museum, some comfortable accommodation, a pretty 17th-century church, a couple of restaurants worth seeking out and views sweeping down to the Famara cliffs.

Museo Agrícola El Patio   MUSEUM
(www.alacenadigital.com; Calle Echeyde 18; adult/child €5/free; ⊙10am-5pm Mon-Fri, to 2pm Sat) Inhabited until the mid-20th century, this open-air museum recreates a 19th-century farmer's house (complete with wine cellar), providing good insight into traditional aspects of the island's culture. You'll see loads of old agricultural equipment, typical pottery, a windmill, a cactus garden, a tiny chapel and the odd camel, donkey or chicken. The *finca* still produces its own *malvasía* wines, which you're free to sample.

El Tenique   CANARIAN €€
(☑928 52 98 56; Avenida Guanaterme 100 (LZ20); mains €10-18; ⊙11am-11pm Mon-Wed, Fri & Sat, to 5pm Sun) At this much-loved, country-feel roadside grilled-meats specialist, you're welcomed with a splash of white wine and a nibble of *queso fresco*. Mains range from sirloin in red wine and roast kid to succulent mixed *parrilladas,* with a couple of daily-changing specials, rounded off with classic Lanzarote bites like goat's cheese with droplets of marmalade or peppers stuffed with *cherne* (cod-like fish).

ⓘ Getting There & Away

Tiagua is on the bus 16 route between Arrecife (€1.40, 30 minutes, five to eight daily) and La Santa. Bus 20 between La Caleta de Famara (€1.40, 25 minutes, five daily Monday to Friday) and Arrecife also calls in here.

Lanzarote's Wine Country

Forget any preconceived notions of what wine country should look like. On Lanzarote, you won't find neat lines of vines painting the hills with green stripes. Instead, here, sprinkled across the abstract volcanic landscape, are small crescent-shaped stone walls, behind each of which hides a low-growing vine happily sheltered from the wind. Local viticulturists have found the deep, black lava soil, enriched by Lanzarote's shaky seismic history, perfect for growing grapes, though the yield is low and the toil is high.

Most wines produced here are dry *malvasías,* though muscatel and other grapes are also cultivated. The island's two main wine-growing regions (www.dolanzarote.com) sit side by side, on the eastern side of Timanfaya: La Geria, flanking the LZ30 northeast of Uga, and the Tinajo–Masdache area.

◉ Sights & Activities

Reputable activity operator Eco Insider (p128) runs popular full-day bodega-hopping tours (€75).

Bodega La Geria   WINERY
(☑928 17 31 78; www.lageria.com; Carretera La Geria (LZ30), Km 5; tastings per half glass €1.50-4; ⊙9.30am-7pm Mon-Sat, 10am-6pm Sun; ℗) The La Geria wine cellar, established at the end of the 19th century, was the first bodega on the island to offer guided visits and sell wines to the public. You can pop in and taste by the glass in the barrel-filled warehouse, 4.5km northeast of Uga, or book ahead for a 45-minute guided visit (€9; Monday to Friday) or a three-hour walk across the vineyards (€20; 10am Tuesday). There's also a good little cafe-bar (tapas €6 to €8).

The bodega also hosts the popular summer **Fiesta de la Vendimia** (⊙mid-Aug).

Bodega Rubicón   WINERY
(☑928 17 37 08; www.bodegasrubicon.com; Carretera La Geria (LZ30), Km 5; tastings per half glass €1-3; ⊙10am-8pm; ℗) In the shade of a towering eucalyptus, Rubicón occupies part of a former 17th-century *cortijo* (farmhouse), which now also includes a good Canarian restaurant (mains €12 to €15). Wines available for tasting in the bodega include an exceptional award-winning muscatel. One-hour guided tours (€13.90), with two wines to taste, are offered Monday to Saturday; book ahead. It's 4.5km northeast of Uga.

El Grifo   WINERY
(☑928 52 40 36; www.elgrifo.com; LZ30, Km 11; admission incl glass of wine €5; ⊙10.30am-6pm; ℗) Founded in 1775, El Grifo is the oldest winery in the Canaries and also one of Spain's most ancient, its distinctive logo designed by

LAGOMAR: CELEBRITY CAVE HOUSE

Carved into the rock face, with fanciful chimneys, cupolas, lookouts and twisting stair-cases, **LagOmar** (☑ 672 461555; www.lag-o-mar.com; Calle Los Loros 2, Nazaret; adult/child €6/2; ⊙ 10am-6pm; **P**), a gallery, **restaurant** (☑ 928 84 56 65; menu €30; ⊙ noon-11.30pm Tue-Sun) and **bar** (⊙ 6pm-2am Tue-Sun) with a New Mexico–meets-Morocco look, is wrapped in legend. What is certain is that it was designed by César Manrique and prominent architect Jesús Soto, and briefly lived in by Omar Sharif (who lost it in a spectacularly unsuccessful game of bridge). Just 2km south of Teguise, it's hugely underrated and blissfully uncrowded, with regular exhibitions and a small museum.

If you arrive in the evening for dinner or a cocktail, you'll really get a feel for the wild celebrity parties that must have once taken place on the edge of sleepy Nazaret. Also here are a couple of creative apartments (per week €840).

Manrique himself. You can sample a range of wines (including *malvasía;* three/six wines with cheese €8/14) in the evocative tasting room, then stroll among the vines and explore the museum of 19th- and 20th-century winemaking equipment. Tours (€9 to €13) run throughout the day; book ahead. It's just beyond the northeastern end of Masdache.

Bodega Los Bermejos   WINERY
(☑ 627 963654, 928 52 24 63; www.losbermejos. com; Camino Los Bermejos 7; tasting per glass €2.50-3; ⊙ 8am-3pm Mon-Fri; **P**) Hidden away 3km southwest of the Monumento al Campesino, this forward-thinking bodega produces fine wines from *malvasía,* muscatel and *listán* grapes, including a dry organic *malvasía,* with minimum intervention. Visitors are welcome to drop in and taste on the terrace, but you'll need to reserve in advance for the 30-minute tours (€12), which include two wines.

Bodegas Vega de Yuco   WINERY
(☑ 928 52 43 16, 609 217014; www.vegadeyuco.es; Camino del Cabezo, Masdache; ⊙ 9am-3pm Mon-Fri; **P**) 🍷 Around 1.5km south of Masdache en route to Tías, this ecoconscious hillside bodega has a lovely terrace for admiring the landscape and stocking up on such wines as the signature blue-bottle *malvasía.* Check online for sporadic 90-minute tours of the vineyards (€10), with three wines to taste.

🍴 Eating

★ **Bodega El Chupadero**   CANARIAN €
(☑ 928 27 73 65; www.el-chupadero.com; off LZ30; tapas €5-11; ⊙ noon-10pm Wed-Sun; **P**) A wonderful wine-country surprise, this stylish bar-restaurant-bodega sits amid volcanic vines just east of the Rubicón and La Geria wineries. Enjoy elegantly presented tapas

like garlic prawns and *papas arrugadas* paired with local *malvasía* wines (€3 to €4), on a gorgeous terrace overlooking the vineyards or in the cosy whitewashed interior where vases of bougainvillea dot the tables.

ℹ Getting There & Away

Passing all the main wineries, the LZ30 between Mozaga and Yaiza is one of the island's most enjoyable drives (p140). If you don't have your own wheels, join a bodega-hopping tour (p128).

Parque Nacional de Timanfaya

Created between 1730 and 1736 by one of the greatest volcanic cataclysms in recorded history, the Montañas del Fuego (Mountains of Fire) at the heart of the eerily beautiful 51-sq-km **Parque Nacional de Timanfaya** (☑ 928 84 00 57; www.miteco.gob.es; adult/child €10/5; ⊙ 9am-5.45pm, last bus tour 4.45pm) 🍷 are appropriately named. Fine copper-hued soil slithers down volcanic cones, until it's arrested by twisted, swirling and folded mounds of solidified lava. Some robust scraps of vegetation, including 200 species of lichen, have reclaimed the earth in a few stretches of the otherwise moribund landscape of fantastical forms in shades of black, grey, maroon and red.

The main national-park reception area – a Manrique-designed lookout/restaurant on a rise known as the Islote de Hilario – is 2km west of the LZ67, signposted 8km northeast of Yaiza. By 10am there can be long queues to access the park; arrive early. Timanfaya is bordered to the north, east and south by the 102-sq-km Parque Natural de los Volcanes.

History

The eruption that began on 1 September 1730 and convulsed the southern end of the island saw a staggering 48 million cubic metres of lava flow out daily, while fusillades of molten rock were rocketed out over the countryside and into the ocean. When the eruption finally ceased to rage after six long years, around 200 sq km had been devastated, including 50 villages and hamlets, giving birth to the moonscape that became, in 1974, the Parque Nacional de Timanfaya.

◉ Sights & Activities

Access to the national park is tightly controlled. Unless you've prebooked a guided hike or are walking the Ruta del Litoral, the only way to visit is aboard the Ruta de los Volcanes bus tours, from the main park reception area.

At the Islote de Hilario, try scrabbling around in the pebbles and see just how long you can hold them in your hands. At a depth of 2m, the temperature is already 300°C; by 10m it's up to 600°C. The cause of this phenomenon is a broiling magma chamber 4km below the surface. The national-park team here runs a series of endearing volcanic-related tricks.

Ruta de los Volcanes   ECOTOUR
(Islote de Hilario; ⊙9am-5.45pm, last tour 4.45pm) The only way to explore Timanfaya (unless you've prebooked a hike), this often nail-biting 14km, 35-minute bus tour (included in park-admission tickets) weaves through some of the most spectacular volcanic country you'll ever see. Buses leave every 20 to 30 minutes from the park's reception area (2km west off the LZ67); you may have to wait unless you arrive early.

✖ Eating

Las Malvas   TAPAS €
(⌨928 84 04 75; Calle Chimanfaya 5, Mancha Blanca; tapas €3-4; ⊙9am-9pm Sun-Thu, to 11pm Fri & Sat) The perfect down-to-earth spot for a bite near Timanfaya, Las Malvas serves cracking tapas of paella, *papas arrugadas,* fried-egg-and-chorizo croquettes and Lanzarote cheese with fig jam, as well as *bocadillos* and *platos combinados,* on its tiny roadside terrace. It's 2km northeast of the park's Centro de Visitantes Mancha Blanca.

ℹ Info

Centro de Visitantes Mancha Blanca (⌨928 11 80 42; www.miteco.gob.es; LZ67, Km 11.5; ⊙9am-4pm) At the national park's official visitor centre, 2.5km southwest of Mancha Blanca village, there are excellent audiovisual and informative displays on the region's geology and history (in Spanish, English and German), including a simulation of a volcanic eruption. Also provides information about hiking in the park.

Punto de Información Echadero de Camellos (www.miteco.gob.es; LZ67, Km 5.5; 8.30am-3.30pm) Next to the camel camp, 2.5km south of the national park turnoff, this small office advises on walks in the park and hosts an exhibition on Lanzarote's camel history.

DON'T MISS

FIRE WALKS
....

It *is* possible to walk within the Parque Nacional de Timanfaya – but you'll need to plan in advance. There are only a couple of hiking routes within the national park. The demanding free-access **Ruta del Litoral** (12km, four hours one-way) heads north from El Golfo to Playa de la Madera. The 3.5km, three-hour (free) **Tremesana guided walk** (in Spanish or English) leaves from Yaiza, in a group of eight people, two to four times weekly. You'll need to book online a month ahead (www.reservasparquesnacionales.com); alternatively, call the Centro de Visitantes Mancha Blanca (p122) a day or two before to see if there's been a last-minute cancellation. There's also an abridged (free) monthly guided walk along the Ruta del Litoral (5.8km, 3½ hours), which follows the same prebooking rules.

There are also some excellent walks through the majestic volcanic landscapes surrounding the national park, including within the Parque Natural de los Volcanes, where the Caldera Blanca hike is a true Lanzarote highlight.

Beginning from a car park 2km west of Mancha Blanca village, the exceptional **Caldera Blanca Hike**, a 9km, 3½-hour loop, is one of Lanzarote's best hikes, tracking through lava fields before climbing steeply (clockwise) to the highest point of the Caldera Blanca rim, within the Parque Natural de los Volcanes. From the top, the crater sprawls below, and Isla Graciosa and Famara shimmer in the distance.

NORTHERN LANZAROTE

A refreshing, rewarding contrast to the more touristed southern reaches of the island, northern Lanzarote is a world of unspoilt towns and villages, wild natural beauty, secluded beaches and stunning panoramic views, especially in the northwest. The easy-going towns here – Arrieta, Haría, La Caleta de Famara, Órzola – are typically clusters of whitewashed buildings surrounded by a landscape of lichen and lava fields and bordered by an Atlantic coastline along which natural pools sparkle and surf waves tumble.

The key attractions here are the combined works of nature and César Manrique, as well as Famara's world-renowned surf scene.

Arrieta

POP 940

The small northern fishing village of Arrieta, 6km east of Haría, is a low-key, blink-and-you'll-miss-it beachy highlight of Lanzarote. Centred on a popular stretch of sand and backed by typical whitewashed homes and apartments, the lightly touristed village is known for its wonderful seafood restaurants and, immediately north, the glinting natural pools at Punta Mujeres.

⊙ Sights & Activities

From Arrieta, it's possible to hike south along the coastline all the way to Costa Teguise (20km, five hours).

★ **Piscinas de Punta Mujeres**   NATURAL POOL
(Punta Mujeres) One of the most magical swimming spots on Lanzarote, this cluster of glittering turquoise natural pools dots the coast in the tranquil whitewashed fishing village of Punta Mujeres, 2km northeast of Arrieta. A few ladders provide access to the pools, overlooked by sun-soaking spots.

Playa de la Garita   BEACH
Arrieta's main attraction is small, golden, sandy-rocky Playa de la Garita, home to a couple of buzzy beach restaurants where you can relax over drinks, tapas and fresh fish, and the odd swing-by surfer.

Jardín de Cactus   GARDENS
(☑928 52 93 97; www.cactlanzarote.com; Guatiza; adult/child €5.80/2.90; ☺9am-5.45pm Jul–mid-Sep, 10am-5.45pm mid-Sep–Jun) Built into

DON'T MISS

NORTHERN WALKS

There are some fantastic hikes in this region, including the steep one-hour, 4km descent to wild Playa del Risco (p126) on the northwest coast; the one-hour, 3km (unsigned) ascent to the rim of the Volcán de la Corona, starting just east of the church in Yé; and, beyond, the sandy walks criss-crossing Isla Graciosa.

an old quarry, just north of tiny Guatiza (6km south of Arrieta), the Jardín de Cactus is said to have been Manrique's favourite personal creation. Opened in 1991, it was also his final great project. It feels more like a giant work of art than a botanical garden, with gorgeous terraced slopes home to nearly 1500 different labelled varieties of cactus from all over the world (Mexico to Madagascar!). The stylish on-site bar-restaurant serves Lanzarote wines and tapas (€4 to €6).

✗ Eating

Bar La Piscina   TAPAS €
(Bar Pichón; Calle Virgen del Pino, Punta Mujeres; tapas €3-7; ☺8am-9pm Wed-Mon) Gazing out on one of Punta Mujeres' most loved natural pools, this is a blissfully down-to-earth, friendly and popular hang-out for excellent tapas of tortilla, grilled peppers, octopus and the like. At lunchtime the owner grills up fresh fish.

El Chiringuito   TAPAS €
(Playa de la Garita; tapas €3-8; ☺10.30am-8pm) Great tapas, salads, paellas, burgers and fresh grilled fish are delivered at logo-emblazoned tables with red plastic chairs on a breezy terrace overlooking Arrieta's beach. This immensely popular *chiringuito* (beach bar) gets packed out in summer and is *perfecto* for coffee, beers and mojitos, too.

★ **Casa de la Playa**   SEAFOOD €€
(☑629 525007, 928 17 33 39; Playa de la Garita; mains €9-17; ☺10am-10pm) *Lanzaroteños* and visitors alike travel from across the island to sample the gloriously fresh catch at this simple, always-busy seafood spot with tables on a delicious seaside terrace looking out on Arrieta's beach. Enormous crisp salads and gorgeous *queso frito* with strawberry marmalade pave the way for grilled king prawns, fish of the day and two-person seafood *parrilladas*.

FIVE FABULOUS LANZAROTE HOTELS

Buenavista Lanzarote (606 935753; www.buenavistalanzarote.es; Carretera Conil–Tegoyo 22; r incl breakfast €150-220; P 🛜) A soul-stirring, Manrique-inspired creativity and ecological ethos hangs in the air at this highly original, plastic-free, design-led hide-away, amid volcanic vineyards 5km northwest of Tías. Owners Gonzalo and Mayca have skilfully reimagined an old bodega warehouse into five exquisitely chic 'country suites', with homemade local-produce breakfasts.

Finca Malvasía (665 468538, 692 155981; www.fincamalvasia.com; Camino El Oratorio 14; apt/villa from €120/315; P 🛜) On a sprawling wine estate at the heart of the island, 2km south of Masdache, this British-owned, Manrique-style oasis has seven beautiful self-catering apartments and a three-room house framing a lagoon-like pool and starring thoughtful, traditional-with-a-contemporary-twist design, plus yoga and massage.

Finca de Arrieta (928 82 67 20; www.lanzaroteretreats.com; off LZ207; r €85-300; P 🛜) 🍃 Fancy sleeping in a stylish Mongolian yurt...in the Canaries? Fuelled by wind turbines and solar power, this fabulous British-owned creation hosts guests in silk-interior yurts, stone cottages, wooden cabins and an old family farmhouse, centred on a Manrique-inspired solar-heated pool. All kinds of activities, from yoga to wine tastings, are offered.

Caserío de Mozaga (928 52 00 60; www.caseriodemozaga.com; Calle Malva 8, Mozaga; r incl breakfast €83-130; P 🛜) In Mozaga, 2.5km northwest of San Bartolomé, this elegantly updated, late-18th-century family home awash in white walls and rosy bougainvillea retains its country-style charm without compromising on comfort. The eight high-ceilinged rooms are graced by antiques and original art and dotted around volcanic gardens. The restaurant (p119) has an excellent reputation.

Hotel Palacio Ico (928 59 49 42, 677 531609; www.hotelpalacioico.com; Calle El Rayo 2; r €130-190; ❄ 🛜) The former home of Swiss artist Heidi Bucher, this beauty of a 17th-century palace has been skilfully reincarnated as a stylish nine-room boutique hotel strung around a typical cactus-dotted patio with an original *aljibe* (cistern). Rooms and suites are styled with design flair.

❶ Getting There & Away

Buses 7 and 9 (€2.65, 45 minutes, five daily each) from Arrecife stop in Arrieta en route to Haría and Órzola.

Malpaís de la Corona

Lava is Lanzarote's hallmark, and the 'Badlands of the Crown' area, hugging the north-easternmost part of the island, is evidence of the volcanic upsurges that shook this area thousands of years ago courtesy of the now-extinct 609m-high Volcán de la Corona. Plant life is quietly, patiently winning its way back, and it is here that you can visit two of the island's best-known volcanic caverns on the site of an ancient lava slide into the ocean.

The gaping Cueva de los Verdes and the hollows of the Jameos del Agua are an easy 1km walk from each another, on either side of the LZ1 around 5km northeast of Arrieta.

★ Jameos del Agua   CAVE

(928 84 80 20; www.cactlanzarote.com; off LZ1; adult/child €9.50/4.75; 10am-6.30pm; P)

When molten lava seethed through this volcanic cavern around 5000 years ago, the ocean leaked in slightly, forming the startling clear azure lake that glints in the basilica-like grotto at the heart of the Jameos, one of Manrique's greatest masterpieces and the first of his *intervenciones*. The artist's idea of installing bars and a **restaurant** (901 200300; mains €12-18; 11.30am-4.30pm & 7-11pm) around the lake and adding a white-washed pool and a 600-seat concert hall (with wonderful acoustics) in the 1960s was a pure brainwave.

From July through September concerts are held on Tuesday and Saturday evenings. The Jameos' many steps mean access to the mobility impaired isn't really possible.

★ Cueva de los Verdes   CAVE

(928 17 32 20; www.cactlanzarote.com; off LZ1; adult/child €9.50/4.75; 10am-7pm Jul–mid-Sep, to 6pm mid-Sep–Jun; P) A yawning, kilometre-long chasm, the Cueva de los Verdes is the most spectacular segment of an almost 7km-long lava tube left behind by an eruption

5000 years ago. As the lava ploughed down towards the sea, the top layers cooled and formed a roof, beneath which the liquid magma continued to slither until the eruption exhausted itself. Guided 50-minute tours, in Spanish and English, run every 30 minutes; you'll wander through two chambers, one below the other.

Anyone with severe back or claustrophobia problems might think twice about entering the cave – there are a few tight passages that require you to bend at 90 degrees, although only very briefly. No advance bookings are taken, so you may have to queue for a tour; it's quietest from 3pm onwards.

Concerts are held here between November and February. It's 5km northeast of Arrieta.

🛈 Getting There & Away

Bus 9 from Arrecife (€3, 45 minutes, two to three daily) to Órzola via Arrieta stops at the Jameos del Agua.

Órzola

POP 300

Most people just zip through Lanzarote's mellow, secluded most northerly fishing village en route to and from Isla Graciosa, but it's worth lingering around. With majestic volcanic cliffs looming behind, the surrounding coastline has some stunning little coves and strips of sand, while several excellent seafood restaurants flank Órzola's port.

Playas Caletones BEACH

(P) A natural, untamed beauty graces this series of sheltered and rarely crowded sandy coves scattered around off the LZ1 east of town, with fine white sand and shallow lagoons surrounded by greenery.

Playa de la Cantería BEACH

(P) Just 1km west of Órzola, this beautiful unspoilt volcanic-stone and brown-sand beach is flanked by cliffs and famed for its big surf breaks (swimming is not recommended, though some people do).

🛈 Getting There & Away

Bus 9 connects Órzola with Arrecife (€3.60, 55 minutes, four to five daily).

Biosfera Express (p128) and Líneas Romero (p128) run between Órzola and Caleta de Sebo on Isla Graciosa (30 minutes, 16 to 19 return ferries daily).

Mirador del Río

Mirador del Río VIEWPOINT

(☑928 17 35 36; www.cactlanzarote.com; adult/child €4.75/2.40; ☉10am-6.45pm Jul–mid-Sep, to 5.45pm mid-Sep–Jun) In the late 19th century, the Spanish armed forces set up gun batteries overlooking El Río (the strait separating Lanzarote from Isla Graciosa), 2km north of Yé. César Manrique left his distinctive mark in 1973, ingeniously converting the gun emplacement into a spectacular, cave-like, 475m-high lookout point. The interior is washed in white, with spider-like iron installations adorning the ceiling. Vertiginous views sprawl across sweeping lava flows – frozen in time – falling to the ocean, and Isla Graciosa sparkles across the water.

Haría

POP 910

Eminent Canarian author Alberto Vázquez-Figueroa once described Haría as the most beautiful village in the world. Although a tad exaggerated, the village does have a pretty bucolic setting, nestled in a palm-filled valley punctuated by splashes of brilliant bougainvillea and poinsettias. In the 17th and 18th centuries, locals traditionally planted a palm tree to celebrate a birth (two for a boy, one for a girl). Later, this North African–style oasis became a popular spa for wealthy Canarians, and its modern-day streets are lined with wooden balconies, stone walls and bright-green shutters.

The central pedestrian avenue, Plaza León y Castillo, is shaded by eucalyptus trees and turns into a superb Saturday morning **craft and produce market** (Plaza León y Castillo; ☉10am-2.30pm Sat).

★**Casa-Museo César Manrique** MUSEUM

(☑928 84 31 38; www.fcmanrique.org; Calle Elvira Sánchez; adult/child €10/1, combined ticket with Fundación César Manrique €15; ☉10.30am-6pm) Frozen in time, complete with Manrique's clothes in the cupboard and personal art collection adorning the walls, the palm-shaded final home of the island's favourite son has become one of its top attractions. Manrique lived here from 1988 to 1992, transforming an old farming building into a distinctive contemporary reinterpretation of traditional architecture. The star attraction is his sunken studio, preserved exactly as it was the day he died, with unfinished works still in situ.

OFF THE BEATEN TRACK

PLAYA DEL RISCO

One of Lanzarote's wildest and most deserted beaches, sandy warm-gold Playa del Risco clings to the northwest tip of the island at the foot of the Risco de Famara, with Isla Graciosa looming across El Río. It's accessible only by boat or via a steep one-hour (around 4km) hike along the Camino de los Gracioseros, which begins immediately north of Finca La Corona (1km west of Yé).

La Tegala   CANARIAN €

(Plaza León y Castillo; tapas €4-9; ⊘ 9am-late Thu-Tue) Opposite the church on Haría's pedestrianised boulevard, this laid-back, red-walled, wood-beamed cultural centre and tapas bar gets crammed on market days. Terrific local tapas and light bites like *patatas arrugadas,* fish croquettes, grilled octopus, Canarian cheeses and pumpkin soup are guzzled down with island wines. Open early for coffee and *bocadillos,* too.

La Puerta Verde   MEDITERRANEAN €€

(☑ 928 83 53 50; www.facebook.com/puertaverde haria; Calle Fajardo 24; mains €7-18; ⊘ 1-10pm Sun-Fri, noon-10pm Sat; 🐾) Haría's most upmarket eatery, just north of the centre, makes an enticing spot for a leisurely meal or a coffee with a slice of home-baked cake. Fresh local produce fuels the creative menu, marrying Canarian, Spanish and Italian cuisines to unveil such delightful dishes as tofu moussaka, seafood risotto and slow-roasted lamb. Book ahead, especially for market Saturday.

❶ Getting There & Away

Bus 7 (€3.15, 45 minutes, six daily) connects Haría to Arrecife via Tahíche, Teguise and Arrieta.

La Caleta de Famara

POP 900

Years before he hit the big time, César Manrique whiled away many a childhood summer on the wild golden beach of La Caleta de Famara, at the foot of the rugged Risco de Famara, 8km north of Teguise. Thanks to its buzzing surf scene, this low-key seaside village – with its dramatic cliff views, romantically whitewashed homes, sky-blue windows and natural sea pool – has a youthful, bohemian vibe.

Famara is one of Lanzarote's most beautiful and undeveloped sandy spots, and the excellent waves here provide some of Europe's finest breaks, as does **El Quemao**, 12km west (one of the world's most challenging waves and only suitable for very experienced surfers).

◉ Sights & Activities

Surf schools cluster along Avenida El Marinero, offering small-group half-/full-day classes for €35/55. Private classes are also available, as are kitesurfing sessions (around €100 per day-long group class) and yoga (€15). Book a day ahead.

★ La Caleta de Famara   BEACH

One of Lanzarote's most magical beaches, wild, sandy, dark-gold Caleta de Famara is a sweeping all-natural throwback, where surfers tackle some of the Canaries' best waves, overlooked by the majestic volcanic Risco de Famara cliffs.

Calima Surf   SURFING

(☑ 626 913369; www.calimasurf.com; Avenida El Marinero 13; half-/full-day group surf class €35/55, private surf class €80; ⊘ 8.30am-2pm & 4.30-6pm) This popular, switched-on, multilingual surf school runs daily group and private surf classes, kitesurfing sessions (two days €180), yoga (€15) and SUP (one day €60), and rents out gear (surfboard per day €15).

Red Star Surf   SURFING

(☑ 928 528 808, Whatsapp 648 745447; www.red starsurf.com; Avenida El Marinero 9; half-/full-day group surf class €35/55; ⊘ 9am-7pm) Reputable surf operation with group and private lessons, kitesurfing classes (one day €100), yoga (€15), SUP (€60) and gear rental (surfboard per day €15).

ZooPark Famara   SURFING, KITESURFING

(☑ 928 52 88 46, 634 884068; www.zoopark famara.com; Avenida El Marinero 5; half-/full-day group surf course €35/55, private surf class €100; ⊘ 8.30am-8pm mid-Jul–Dec & Easter, to 3.30pm Jan-Jul) A long-running surf school organising daily group and private classes, as well as kitesurfing (group/private €100/150 per day), SUP (€55 per half-day) and yoga (€15) lessons, and renting out equipment (surf board from €15 per day).

Lanzasurf   SURFING, KITESURFING

(☑ 928 52 85 71, 697 238115; www.lanzasurf.com; Calle Chirimoya 15, Urbanización Famara; full-day surf class €55; ⊘ 10am-3pm Mon-Sat) Based on

Famara beach at **Bungalows Playa Famara**, this is a popular choice for surf training (group or private), as well as yoga (€10) and Spanish-language (€23) classes and courses.

🍴 Eating

El Rincón de la Abuela   CANARIAN €
(📱 692 338483; Avenida El Marinero 18; mains €9-13; ⊙ 10.30am-9pm Wed-Mon) Tables dot Famara's sandy main street at this relaxed, lively seafood and tapas spot, where you can dig into delicious tapas of tortilla or paella, then follow up with the day's catch (chalked up on the board) or an enormous seafood *parrillada* for two served with salad and *papas arrugadas*. Inside, it's all updated white-and-blue decor.

⭐**El Risco**   CANARIAN €€
(📱 928 52 85 50; www.restauranteelrisco.com; Calle Montaña Clara 30; mains €12-20; ⊙ noon-10pm Mon-Sat, to 5pm Sun) Famara's smartest restaurant, seafood-focused El Risco enjoys a superb seafront location, with a cliff-facing terrace gazing across the water and a nautical blue-and-white interior designed by Manrique. Elegantly prepped dishes run from grilled octopus with coriander sauce, salted La Santa prawns and fresh fish in garlic oil to seafood-packed paella and vegetable risotto topped with island cheese. Book ahead!

Restaurante Sol   SEAFOOD €€
(📱 928 52 87 88; www.restaurantesolfamara.com; Calle Montaña Clara 48; mains €12-18; ⊙ noon-10pm) Take a seat on the sun-soaked ocean-facing terrace and admire Famara's surf action and cascading cliffs while munching on grilled fish, artisan goat's cheese, steamed mussels or a shellfish *parrillada*. At weekends, popular Sol gets busy with noisy local and visiting families. Great for coffee and a slab of home-baked cake, too.

ℹ Getting There & Away

Bus 20 (€2.20, 45 minutes, five daily) connects Arrecife with La Caleta de Famara via Tiagua Monday to Friday.

ISLA GRACIOSA

POP 730

The only inhabited island of the far-flung Chinijo Archipelago, just north of Lanzarote, gorgeous sand-dusted Isla Graciosa was officially named the eighth Canary Island in 2018. Though still administered from Lanzarote, La Graciosa – with its sublime white-gold beaches, barren volcanic landscapes, world-class surfing, and low-key hiking and water sports – feels worlds away.

The island was first populated in 1867 by seven families. Today, virtually all its inhabitants live in the tranquil harbour village of Caleta de Sebo, where the Órzola boats dock,

---

FROM SALTED POTATOES TO SUBLIME WINES

Although the Lanzarote cuisine does not vary dramatically from that of its neighbours, there are some culinary stars. The addictive *papas arrugadas* (wrinkly potatoes) are generally accompanied by a choice of three *mojo* sauces (not always the Canarian case): *mojo verde* (with parsley), *mojo de cilantro* (with fresh coriander) and the classic *mojo picón* (with a spicy chilli kick). And Lanzarote's increasingly popular and recognised cheeses (mostly goat's cheeses) are arguably some of the best in the Canaries.

Latin American influences are reflected in several dishes and, for red-blooded appetites, the steaks are typically prime-cut Argentine beef. Other popular meaty choices for *lanzaroteños* include goat, baby kid and rabbit – the same options favoured by their Guanche ancestors. If you fancy a heart-warming homey stew, try the classic *puchero*, traditionally made with various cuts of meat, fresh root vegetables and chickpeas; vegetable soups are popular, too.

Seafood lovers will enjoy fresh local catch all over the island. Look for the indigenous *lapa*, a species of limpet, traditionally grilled (which releases the flesh from the shell) and accompanied by a green *mojo*. Although they do not look as appealing, black-fleshed *lapas* are tastier than the orange variety.

Volcanic wines are another Lanzarote speciality, particularly the prize-worthy dry white *malvasía* (Malmsey wine). When you buy a bottle of local wine you actively contribute to the preservation of an ancient, traditional method of viniculture in danger of dying out.

seafood restaurants cluster and streets are carpeted with silky golden sand. Behind it stretches 28 sq km of scrubland, interrupted by five minor volcanic peaks and scattered all-natural beaches. There are no sealed roads here: bicycles, walks or battered Land Rovers are the only ways to get around.

Sights & Activities

Along with Lanzarote's Famara cliffs, the five Chinijo islands (and the waters off them) form a protected nature reserve, and beyond Isla Graciosa the region is pretty much off-limits. The four other islands – Montaña Clara, Alegranza, Roque del Este and Roque del Oeste – are known for their birdlife and are generally only visited by researchers, though you can admire them up-close on boat trips organised by Eco Insider (☑650 819069; www.eco-insider.com; half-day hike €42) 🗡.

Playa del Salado   BEACH
Gazing out on the Risco de Famara, the pretty 2km-long blonde strand immediately southwest of Caleta de Sebo is the most easily accessible of Isla Graciosa's beaches, so it gets slightly busy with day trippers.

Playa Francesa   BEACH
A 3km, 30-minute walk southwest of Caleta de Sebo, little Playa Francesa is a beautiful golden-white strand lapped by turquoise Atlantic waves.

Playa de las Conchas   BEACH
Lovely, golden, wild and sandy, Playa de las Conchas sweeps across the northwest corner of the island, 5.5km north of Caleta de Sebo. It's the island's most loved beach, though swimming is dangerous.

Playa Lambra   BEACH
Curled into La Graciosa's north coast, seductively secluded, cream-sand Playa Lambra sits 8km north of Caleta de Sebo.

Buceo La Graciosa   DIVING
(☑928 84 22 13; www.buceolagraciosa.com; Avenida Virgen del Mar 119B, Caleta de Sebo; single dive €60) The waters of the Chinijo Archipelago are teeming with fascinating sealife. This company offers dive trips within the marine reserve, including off Alegranza and La Graciosa, plus diving baptisms (€65), PADI courses (Open Water €399) and dive-and-accommodation packages.

 Eating

El Veril   SEAFOOD €
(Playa del Puerto, Caleta de Sebo; raciones €9-15; ⊙10am-10pm) Lunch with your toes in the sand at this lively spot under white umbrellas right on the town beach, overlooking the harbour and the Risco de Famara. Fresh seafood platters like bream and tuna arrive with *papas arrugadas, mojo,* salad and a squeeze of lemon, topped off with *raciones* of Canarian cheese and spinach croquettes. The location is the thing.

Casa Margucha   SEAFOOD €€
(Restaurante Girasol; ☑610 768221, 928 84 21 39; Avenida Virgen del Mar 99, Caleta de Sebo; mains €8-15; ⊙8.30am-11pm) There's little to distinguish one La Graciosa restaurant from another, but Casa Margucha is a long-running place with a popular ocean-facing terrace and a good selection of fresh fish, meaty Canarian dishes, simple salads and classic snacks like *papas arrugadas* and *queso frito.*

Getting There & Away

Biosfera Express (☑928 84 25 85; www.biosferaexpress.com; adult/child return €20/11) and **Líneas Romero** (☑928 59 61 07, 638 513702; www.lineasromero.com) run between Órzola and Caleta de Sebo (adult/child return €20/11, 30 minutes), with 16 to 19 return ferries daily.

Getting Around

The best way to explore the island is on foot or by bike. Bike-hire operators gather at Caleta de Sebo's harbour, open from 10am to 6pm (last hire 2pm) and charging €10/30 for a regular/electric bike.

Taxis (4WD) gather at the harbour in Caleta de Sebo. A 1¼-hour loop around the entire island costs €50 for up to four people; one-way to Playas Francesa or de las Conchas is €20 for one to three people.

SOUTHERN LANZAROTE

The island's south is home to its most popular resorts, Playa Blanca and Puerto del Carmen, and attracts families and groups of primarily British holidaymakers looking for an easygoing, sunny trip. Over on the southwest coast though, it's a different world: one of wave-lashed cliffs and quiet, whitewashed villages. On the island's south-easternmost tip, the gorgeous Punta del Papagayo nature reserve epitomises all that's wonderful about Lanzarote.

Puerto del Carmen

POP 10,930

With sunshades four lanes deep and just 10 minutes' drive southwest from the airport, Lanzarote's original purpose-built resort is a primarily British-geared hub packed with bars, restaurants, clubs, jet skis, dive schools, banana boats, sports screens, middling hotels and apartments, and plenty of shopping. While Puerto del Carmen certainly won't be to everyone's taste, it remains Lanzarote's most popular resort, now sprawling along 7km of the island's south-central coast.

There's a glimmer of Canarian atmosphere at El Varadero harbour, at the far west end of town, which still has a faint fishing-village fee. The main street is Avenida de las Playas, a gaudy ribbon hugging the beach.

◉ Sights & Activities

Diving is deservedly popular, yoga is widely available, and there's a dedicated seafront cycle path, plus yacht trips, banana-boat rides and jet skiing. You can also walk along the coast westwards to Playa Quemada (8km, two hours) via Puerto Calero and a clifftop promenade, or eastwards along the promenade to Arrecife (9.5km, two hours).

Playa Grande   BEACH
Though it's crowded and striped neatly with sunbeds and parasols, beneath all this, Playa Grande remains a lovely, gold-hued, family-friendly 1200m-long beach with shallow waters and good amenities.

Playa Quemada   BEACH
Refreshingly secluded and unspoilt, this rocky volcanic-black beach fringed by low white buildings and superb seafood restaurants lies 12km southwest of Puerto del Carmen.

Several hiking trails weave into the hills from Playa Quemada, including the 8km, three-hour climb/descent to/from the village of Femés.'

Surf School 3S   SURFING
(☑ 630 483158, 928 51 40 34; www.school3s.es; Calle Bajamar 26, Local 4; ⊙ 10am-1pm & 5-8pm Mon-Fri, 10am-2pm Sat) A popular school that organises surfing (€40), SUP (€30), yoga (€15) and SUP yoga (€30) sessions.

Lanzarote a Caballo   HORSE RIDING
(☑ 626 593737; www.lanzaroteacaballo.com; LZ2, Km 17; ⊙ 9am-6.30pm Fri-Wed) This professional horse-riding team runs excursions of varying levels at some of the island's most beautiful spots, from easy cross-country rides to Puerto Calero (€40) to two-hour advanced jaunts around Famara (€70), as well as 45-minute classes (€45).

Manta Diving   DIVING
(☑ 928 51 68 15; www.manta-diving-lanzarote.com; Calle Juan Carlos I 6, Local 5; single dive €45; ⊙ 8.30am-5pm Mon-Sat) One of Puerto del Carmen's longest-established dive centres; offers PADI courses (Open Water €420), half-day snorkelling outings (€30) and two-dive trips at Playa Blanca's Museo Atlántico (p134) for €125.

CID Lanzarote   DIVING
(☑ 639 056797; www.cidlanzarote.com; Calle Alemania 1; single dive €45; ⊙ 8.30am-5.30pm Mon-Sat) Baptisms for beginners (€95), kids' bubble-maker courses (€60), night dives (from €55), PADI courses (Open Water €420), Museo Atlántico (p134) dives (€83) and more, with an established operator.

✗ Eating & Drinking

The slightly more traditional Spanish choices cluster around the old port.

The bulk of Puerto del Carmen's nightlife happens along waterfront Avenida de las Playas, which is crammed with British and Irish pubs, karaoke bars, clubs and the inevitable smattering of sleazier options.

Vino+ Lanzarote   TAPAS €€
(☑ 928 51 69 59; www.facebook.com/vinomaslanzarote; cnr Calle Roque del Este & Calle Cenobio, Centro Comercial Barracuda; tapas €3-15; ⊙ 1pm-midnight; ☏ ☑) Authentic Andalucian and local Lanzarote ingredients fuse on the elegantly prepared menu at this smart cordobés-owned tapas bar, hidden away towards the east end of town. Pick from platters of Iberian ham and Spanish cheeses, creative plates like couscous with king prawns, and tasty vegetarian bites including spinach-and-goat's-cheese pastry drizzled with palm honey. Excellent wines; live music on Thursdays.

Taberna de Nino   SPANISH €€
(☑ 928 51 06 58; Calle Nuestra Señora del Carmen; tapas €6-11, mains €15-19; ⊙ noon-midnight; ☑) Tempting pintxos (Basque tapas) are piled up on the bar northern-Spain-style at this easy-going old-timer with a roomy terrace overlooking the fishing port. Heartier mains include grilled meats, while tapas

LANZAROTE'S LAZY DAYS

●●●●●●●●●●●●●●●●●●●●●●●

From moodily hued volcanic coves curled into the coast to pale-blonde sandy strands open to the crashing Atlantic, there's no denying the beauty of Lanzarote's many, varied beaches – your only problem will be deciding which one to pick.

GLORIOUS BEACHES

Lanzarote's beach scene varies dramatically from one end of the island to the other. Beaches in the major resorts tend to be pretty, family-friendly strips of sand, with sunbeds, umbrellas and services on offer. The wilder, more rugged coves sprinkled around the northern coastline and the Punta del Papagayo (p135) and over on Isla Graciosa (p127) are a different story, with a blissful all-natural vibe. There can be strong currents in places, so do heed warnings. Surfers, kitesurfers and windsurfers appear when the surf is up, especially at spectacular La Caleta de Famara (p126), and you can go snorkelling, paddleboarding and even diving.

SPARKLING POOLS

It's not all about the beach, either. If you know where to look, you'll find a smattering of ridiculously pretty natural seawater pools carved into the shore, perfect for sun-soaking and cooling off. Don't miss the tantalising turquoise pools at Punta Mujeres (p123) and Famara (p126).

DINING DELIGHTS

Leisurely lunches starring sensational seafood are the natural companions to all those sunny beaches. Linger over paella, the day's catch or platters of local goat's cheese, at plastic tables on beachfront terraces: the simplest places are always the best.

UNDERWORLD/SHUTTERSTOCK ©

1. Caleta de Sebo, Isla Graciosa (p127) 2. Grilled limpets with *mojo* 3. Natural swimming pools, Punta Mujeres (p123) 4. Surfing, La Caleta de Famara (p126) 5. Punta del Papagayo (p135)

FREEARTIST/GETTY IMAGES ©

JOSE A. BERNAT BACETE/GETTY IMAGES ©

THE SCENIC LZ702 DRIVE

Lanzarote has several stunning drives (p140), particularly around wine country. Less known is the scenic LZ702, which you pick up just east of Uga if you are coming from the west (Arrecife, Puerto del Carmen etc).

Pass through the hamlet of Las Casitas de Femés (2km) and carry on to **Femés** (another 3.5km). Look for the sign to **Quesería Rubicón** (www.facebook.com/queseria rubicon; Plaza San Marcial 3; ⊙10am-7pm Mon-Fri, to 3pm Sat & Sun), one of the best places to buy and taste local goat's cheese. Afterwards, nip across the road to the **Balcón de Femés** (☑620 008874, 928 11 36 18; Calle San Marcial Rubicón 3; mains €7-15; ⊙10am-7pm Wed-Sun, to 4pm Mon) for coffee, accompanied by a magnificent view, and wander around the palm-studded plaza, with its whitewashed church. A signposted footpath leads from Femés' plaza to Playa Quemada (p129) – 8km, three hours each way.

Continue the drive winding southwest down to Playa Blanca (p134) – a further 8.5km – with the seascape opening up ahead of you. Alternatively, if you fancy, carry on all the way to spectacular Punta del Papagayo (p135).

run from fish croquettes and potatoes in Cabrales-cheese sauce to vegan-friendly bites of falafel, green-curry tofu and tempura mushroom. Great for a sunset drink with a tapa or two.

★**La Cabaña**　　　　MEDITERRANEAN €€€
(☑650 685662; www.lacabanamacher.com; LZ2, Mácher; mains €16-23; ⊙7pm-late Tue-Sat; ☑) Tucked into the village of Mácher, 4.5km northwest of Playa del Carmen, chic British-owned La Cabaña wows as one of the island's top restaurants, with a superb reputation for innovative Mediterranean-fusion dishes. Menus change regularly, starring such delicately crafted dishes as spiced Malaysian vegetable curry, pumpkin risotto, fresh fish of the day, hearty soups and roast rack of lamb.

Los Aljibes　　　　　CRAFT BEER
(Avenida de las Playas 57; ⊙9.30am-11.30pm) Savour the artisan triumphs of the island's first microbrewery over a speciality Märzen or APA (€3 to €4) and a homemade burger (mains €8 to €12), on a lively terrace at the east end of the seafront promenade.

🛈 Getting There & Around

BICYCLE

Bike Sensations (☑680 424665; www.bikesensations.com; Avenida de las Playas 49; per day from €12; ⊙9am-7pm)
Renner Bikes (☑928 51 06 12; www.mountainbike-lanzarote.com; Avenida de las Playas 47; per day from €10; ⊙9am-6pm Mon-Sat, 10am-2pm Sun)

BUS

Buses run the length of Avenida de las Playas, heading regularly for Arrecife (€1.70), 24 hours a day, including bus 2; bus 3 is the most useful, continuing to Costa Teguise (€2.95, one hour).

Bus 161 runs to/from the airport (€1.70, eight to 22 daily, 15 minutes), continuing to Playa Blanca (€2.75, 40 minutes).

CAR & MOTORCYCLE

Parking is a nightmare here, particularly in mid-summer; try the backstreets or the paying car park at the Biosfera shopping centre (Calle Juan Carlos I).

Yaiza

POP 900

Immediately south of the Parque Nacional de Timanfaya (whose volcanic eruptions it miraculously survived), Yaiza is something of a southern crossroads, so you'll probably pass through (several times) on your Lanzarote travels. The tidy whitewashed town, centred on an 18th-century **church** (Plaza Nuestra Señora de los Remedios; ⊙dawn-dusk), is the recipient of numerous awards for cleanliness, its streets adorned with twirling bougainvillea and home to some good hotels and restaurants.

Bar Stop　　　　　TAPAS €
(Plaza Nuestra Señora de los Remedios 6; tapas €3; ⊙5am-11pm) Popular with cyclists and *lanzaroteños* on lunch breaks, this back-to-basics open-all-day pitstop opposite Yaiza's church does deliciously simple tapas of tortilla, paella, Canarian potatoes and other classics, and has been in business since 1890. Sit out in the sun at roadside stools.

La Bodega de Santiago — CANARIAN €€

(☑928 83 62 04; www.labodegadesantiago.es; Calle Montañas del Fuego 27; mains €17-22; ☉12.45-10.30pm Tue-Thu, to 11pm Fri & Sat, 12.45-6pm Sun; 🖉) Fronted by a magnificent ficus tree, at the northeast end of town, this beautiful wood-beamed 19th-century manor is reason alone to stop off in Yaiza. Scattered intimate dining rooms and a background of classical music accompany the updated-Canarian menu, which tempts with hearty soups, inventive salads, meat-heavy mains and divine desserts (try the chocolate 'volcano' with mango ice cream). Reservations recommended.

Bodega de Uga — CANARIAN €€

(☑928 83 01 47; www.facebook.com/bodegade uga; Carretera Yaiza–Uga (LZ2) 6, Uga; dishes €8-15; ☉12.30-3.30pm & 7-10pm Tue-Sat, 12.30-4pm Sun) The daily-changing menu depends entirely on the local produce available at Uga's elegant roadside bodega, where colourful terrace gardens give way to a moody, rustic interior. Local cheeses, avocado salads, grilled vegetables and Canarian calamari might be the other of the day, with meat and seafood specials to follow. Uga is 2km east of Yaiza.

ℹ Getting There & Away

Bus 60, among others, links Yaiza with Arrecife (€2.20, 30 minutes, nine to 15 daily) and Playa Blanca (€1.40, 30 minutes, nine to 15 daily daily).

El Golfo

POP 200

Nuzzled into Lanzarote's southwest coast, with the Parque Nacional de Timanfaya sprawling northwards, the laid-back former fishing village of El Golfo is known for its waterfront seafood restaurants. A cluster of bars, restaurants and traditional buildings overlooking the thundering surf make it a fabulous place to come at sunset.

Tracking south from El Golfo, the LZ703 opens up one of the most dramatic and scenic drives (p140) on the island.

◎ Sights & Activities

The only free-access hike (p122) within the Parque Nacional de Timanfaya, the challenging Ruta del Litoral, heads 12km (four hours, one-way) north from El Golfo to secluded black-sand Playa de la Madera.

Charco de los Clicos — NATURAL POOL

This small emerald-green pond, just inland from the beach beyond the south end of El Golfo, was famously the backdrop for Raquel Welch and her fur bikini in the iconic publicity still for the 1960s *One Million Years BC* movie. The colour comes from algae in the water, and the visual paint palette is further enhanced by the wonderfully textured volcanic-rock surroundings. The beach isn't safe for swimming, though.

Los Hervideros — NATURAL FEATURE

(LZ703) Around 5km south of El Golfo along the LZ703, the sea glugs and froths spectacularly through this pair of caves. Arrive early to beat the tour buses.

Playa de Janubio — BEACH

(LZ703) A lengthy, surf-battered volcanic beach, 8km south of El Golfo, makes for an atmospheric stroll, but swimming here is dangerous due to strong currents. It's backed by the shimmering 19th-century **Salinas de Janubio** (LZ703).

✖ Eating

Restaurante Bogavante — SEAFOOD €€

(☑928 17 35 05; Avenida Marítima 39; mains €10-25; ☉11am-8pm) Arguably El Golfo's most popular restaurant, Bogavante has umbrella-shaded tables scattered on the sand above overlooking rocky pools and the sea beyond. Local specialities such as *vieja* (parrot fish) and *cherne* (cod-like fish) feature on the seafood-starring menu, which also offers up seafood stews and *parrilladas* and tasty paellas. Sunsets here are magical.

Casa Rafa — SEAFOOD €€

(☑625 104330; Avenida Marítima 10; mains €7-16; ☉noon-8pm Tue-Sat, to 6pm Sun) It's all about the Canarian specialities and fresh seafood (whatever that may be) at this smartish, friendly self-styled *restaurante de mar* across the road from the beach at the south end of town. Just-cooked paella, grilled *cherne*, fried *morena* (eel), octopus with *mojo*... Often open until 10pm June to September.

El Caletón — SEAFOOD €€

(☑650 064693; www.facebook.com/restaurante caleton; Avenida Marítima 5; mains €8-16; ☉11am-9pm) Slightly north of the main cluster of restaurants, El Caletón's tables spill out on to the seafront rocks from a roadside terrace and an aloe-green dining room. Expect enormous platters of the day's catch served with lemon, salad and *patatas arrugadas*, along with seafood paellas, grilled octopus and Lanzarote wines.

Playa Blanca

POP 2580

Originally a sandy-floored south-coast fishing village, happily gazing out on neighbouring Fuerteventura, Playa Blanca has become almost unrecognisable in the past decade. Though still the quieter, smaller, more upmarket cousin of Puerto del Carmen, Lanzarote's southernmost (and sunniest) resort's sprawl of dive schools, cafes, restaurants, hotels and apartment complexes now stretches almost to the tip of the Papagayo nature reserve. The activity-packed resort has a fairly upscale feel, especially around the swish Marina Rubicón at the eastern end of town, and the seafront promenade is a pleasant spot, as is pale-blonde Playa Blanca itself, though for many there's something soulless about the whole place.

🏃 Activities

Enjoyable hikes from Playa Blanca include heading east to Punta del Papagayo via Playa Mujeres (6km, 1½ hours); tracking north to the Salinas de Janubio (14km, three to four hours); walking in the hills around Femés, 8.5km northeast of Playa Blanca; or following the GR131 northeast to Yaiza (14km, four hours).

Kaboti Surf   SURFING
(☑696 85 67 89; www.kabotisurf.com; Calle Don Jaime Quesada El Maestro 12; 1-/3-day surf course €59/160; ⊗11am-2pm & 4.30-7.30pm) On-the-ball, multilingual surf school Kaboti runs classes and courses on Famara beach (with yoga on request), as well as kitesurfing training (per day €90) and three-hour SUP jaunts into the Papagayo nature reserve (€60). Also rents out equipment.

WORTH A TRIP

LANZAROTE MARKETS

➡ Mercadillo de Haría (p125)

➡ Mercadillo de Teguise (p118)

➡ Mercado Agrícola de Costa Teguise (p118)

➡ Mercadillo Marina Rubicón (www.marinarubicon.com; Marina Rubicón; ⊗9am-2pm Wed & Sat)

Rubicón Diving   DIVING
(☑928 34 93 46; www.rubicondiving.com; Marina Rubicón, Local 77B; single dive €55; ⊗8am-5.30pm) A professional, well-established SSI dive operator offering dives off Playa Blanca and Puerto del Carmen, plus courses including Open Water (€475) and freediving, and snorkelling (€40) and diving trips to the Museo Atlántico.

Museo Atlántico   DIVE SITE
(www.underwatermuseumlanzarote.com; Calle Castillo del Águila 33; €12) 🏊 Launched in 2016, off Playa Blanca at depths of 12m to 15m, Europe's first underwater sculpture 'museum' is the brainwave of British artist Jason deCaires Taylor. Consisting of 300 life-size figures, the 2500-sq-metre, pH-neutral work tackles major issues including climate change, and is evolving into a marine-life-rich artificial reef. Local diving schools run dives (€60) and snorkelling trips (€40) here.

You cannot access the museum unless it's on a trip with a dive or snorkel operator; visitors must pay a €12 'admission' charge on top of any dive-trip prices. The museum's information office is 500m east of Marina Rubicón.

🍽 Eating

There are some decent Canarian-style spots dotted around near the church, plus international offerings at Marina Rubicón. You'll find better options out of town, including in Yaiza, Uga and Punta Papagayo.

La Chalanita   CANARIAN €€
(☑928 51 70 22; Avenida Marítima 73; mains €10-19; ⊗1-11pm; 🌱) Hidden away in a charmingly homey 1st-floor dining room overlooking the seafront promenade is this busy meat-and-seafood specialist where a welcoming team tends to diners (both local and visiting). Smartly prepared dishes include smoked Uga salmon, seafood paella, fresh fish of the day, and meats flambéed at your table, plus good veggie options. The excellent wine list includes Lanzarote drops.

El Horno de la Abuela   SPANISH €€
(☑928 51 78 25; Calle La Tegala; mains €8-16; ⊗1-4pm & 6-11pm) A long-standing, rustic-style restaurant squirrelled away near Playa Blanca's church, dishing up hearty portions of Spanish cuisine, with an emphasis on goat, suckling pig and other meaty fare served with chunky chips and accompanied by island wines.

Romántica   INTERNATIONAL €€
(☑928 51 71 66; Avenida Papagayo 10; mains €11-17; ⊗6-10.30pm Mon-Sat; 🌱) With ocean views,

a warm welcome and a more imaginative menu than most around here, La Romántica gets consistently positive reviews from travellers. The world-roaming cooking dabbles in a little of everything: noodle and rice stir-fries, inventive salads, serious steaks, grilled sea bass in tomato-and-pine-nut vinaigrette. Veggie and gluten-free menus are available with advance notice.

ℹ️ Information

Oficina de Turismo (☏928 51 81 50; www.turismolanzarote.com; Calle Don Jaime Quesada El Maestro; ⊙9am-7pm)

ℹ️ Getting There & Around

BOAT

Líneas Romero (p128) runs 'waterbus' boats to/from Playa del Papagayo (adult/child return €15/8, 30 minutes, four to five daily) via Marina Rubicón, as well as a boat to Corralejo on northern Fuerteventura (adult/child one-way €15/9, 45 minutes, four daily).

Fred Olsen (p269) also has ferries to/from Corralejo (one-way €28, 25 minutes, four to seven daily), as does Naviera Armas (p112; €27, 35 minutes, seven daily).

BUS

Bus 60 runs roughly hourly between Playa Blanca and Arrecife (€3.60, one hour). Bus 161 runs to/from the airport (€3.30, one hour, eight to 22 daily) via Puerto del Carmen (€2.75). The **bus station** (Avenida de las Canarias) is just north of the centre.

BICYCLE

Papagayo Bike (☏606 109765; www.papagayobike.com; Calle La Tegala 13; per day from €12; ⊙9am-5pm) hires city, road and mountain bikes.

Punta del Papagayo

Within the bare, protected volcanoscapes of the 30-sq-km **Monumento Natural Los Ajaches**, the Punta del Papagayo promontory is one of Lanzarote's (and, dare we say, the Canaries') most beautiful natural spaces. The coastline here, leading southeast from Playa Blanca to Punta del Papagayo, is peppered with pristine golden-sand coves and beaches bathed by gentle turquoise waves, while rust-hued volcanic peaks rise to up to 560m behind. Papagayo is, understandably,

extremely popular and, sadly, there seems to be no limit on the number of cars allowed into the reserve per day. Arrive early if you hope to have the sand to yourself for a while, and tread lightly. The access road is more of a dirt track, but quite manageable in most cars; you'll pass a ticket checkpoint (€3 per vehicle) along the way.

◎ Sights & Activities

There are several lovely walks within the nature reserve, including a hike between Playa Blanca and Punta del Papagayo via Playa Mujeres (6km, 1½ hours). Playa Blanca's tourist office has hiking maps.

⭐**Playa del Papagayo**   BEACH

(Ⓟ) Hemmed in by the *punta's* craggy cliffs, deliciously unspoilt and protected Playa del Papagayo is one of Lanzarote's loveliest beaches, with pale-gold sand and aqua waters. It's popular, though, so head over early to enjoy it in peace.

Playa Mujeres   BEACH

(Ⓟ) Blessed with fine pale, blonde sand and wild dunes, and particularly popular with snorkellers and surfers, picturesque and secluded 90m-long Playa Mujeres sits 1.5km west of the *punta*.

🍴 Eating

Be Papagayo   CANARIAN €€

(☏928 17 38 33; playapapagayo@gmail.com; Playa del Papagayo; mains €12-17; ⊙10.30am-7pm) Bringing an Ibiza-chic vibe to the volcanic cliffs above Playa del Papagayo, this laid-back barefoot-style *chiringuito* (beach bar) rustles up fresh lemonades, shakes and mojitos under beach umbrellas and aqua-on-white walls. There's also an enticing, creatively contemporary menu of *papas arrugadas, huevos rotos,* grilled fish and other Macaronesian goodies. It is open into the evening for drinks during summer months.

ℹ️ Getting There & Away

If you aren't driving, the Líneas Romero (p128) 'waterbus' (adult/child return €15/8, 30 minutes) runs between Playa Blanca and Playa del Papagayo four to five times daily, via Marina Rubicón. Hiking is also a popular way to get around, including to/from Playa Blanca (6km, 1½ hours).

LANZAROTE PUNTA DEL PAPAGAYO

SOUTHWEST COAST & WINE REGION

On this scenic cross-island drive, you'll spin through some of Lanzarote's most varied landscapes, from the cliff-edged southwest coast, through the blackened volcanic wine-growing region, and on to Teguise. The route is best started early.

❶ Salinas de Janubio

Begin at the viewpoint overlooking the glassy Salinas de Janubio (p133), 6km southwest of Yaiza, before heading north along the narrow coast-hugging LZ703.

❷ Playa de Janubio

Stop at black-rock Playa de Janubio.

❸ Los Hervideros

Around 2km north of the beach you'll reach Los Hervideros, where the sea crashes around within two coastal caves – it's a particularly evocative spot first thing in the morning.

❹ Charco de los Clicos

The LZ703 runs parallel to the coast from here northwards, with rusty-hued volcanic

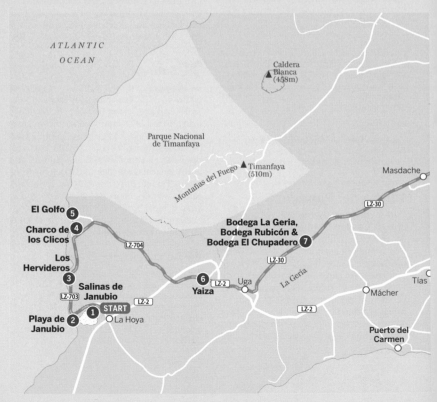

cones dotted with green lichens beginning to appear as you drive. About 3km north of Los Hervideros a track branches off to reach the Charco de los Clicos, a small beachfront pool turned emerald-green by its algae. The access road is closed to vehicles, but if you can find a spot to park you're free to walk; otherwise, there's a viewing platform accessed from a car park 2km further north.

❺ El Golfo

Next up: lunch! Welcome to the charming fishing village of El Golfo, known for its excellent seafood restaurants. Feast on paella or fresh fish of the day and stretch your legs along the shore, passing romantically

whitewashed homes overlooking the tumbling waves.

❻ Yaiza

Backtrack 2km on the LZ703 to join the LZ704 east (inland) to reach Yaiza, 6km southeast of El Golfo, where the 18th-century whitewashed church is worth a look.

❼ Bodegas

Drive 3km southeast along the LZ2 to Uga, before hopping on to the LZ30 heading northeast – one of the island's most enticing drives. There are several bodegas open to visitors for tours and tastings of the fantastic malvasía wines. Note that most tours require advance bookings.

❽ El Grifo

Back on the LZ30, spin 8km northeast to arrive at El Grifo, one of the country's oldest wineries. Check out the museum and vineyards, before pootling 3.5km along the LZ30, through the village of La Florida.

❾ Casa-Museo del Campesino

Turn off at the Casa-Museo del Campesino, where César Manrique's 1968 Monumento al Campesino looms above a roundabout. The 'museum' consists of a cluster of traditional craft shops which offer taster sessions for visitors and a chance to see artisans at work.

❿ Caserío de Mozaga

If you've had enough time behind the wheel for today, head 1km north along the LZ20 to exquisitely converted 18th-century country home Caserío de Mozaga, where hopefully you've already booked a room as well as a table for dinner at the superb restaurant.

⓫ Teguise

Whether you stop for the night or not, next you'll continue northeast up the LZ30 to arrive in Teguise, 7.5km from Mozaga. Teguise was the island's capital until 1852. Stroll its historical streets, taking in the grand ancient homes, and grab a bite at creative La Cantina, one of Lanzarote's top restaurants.

Tenerife

POP 890,000

Best Places to Eat

➡ Guaydil (p151)

➡ Kazan (p147)

➡ Guannabi (p147)

➡ Tito's Bodeguita (p157)

➡ Tas-k (p168)

Best Beaches

➡ Playa de las Teresitas (p152)

➡ Porís de Abona (p177)

➡ El Médano (p175)

➡ Los Cristianos, Playa de las Américas & Costa Adeje (p168)

➡ Los Gigantes (p167)

➡ Puerto de la Cruz (p153)

Why Go?

Tenerife is the striking grande dame in the archipelago family. Attracting over six million visitors a year, the island's most famous southern resorts offer Brit-infused revelry and clubbing, combined with white sandy beaches and all-inclusive resorts. But get your explorer's hat on and step beyond the tourist spots and you'll discover an island of extraordinary beauty and diversity, with remote mountain-ridge villages, cultured port settlements and charming ancient towns.

This potpourri of experiences continues with tropical-forest walks and designer-shop struts, dark forays into volcanic lava, a sexy and sultry Carnaval celebration that's second only to Rio's, and a stash of museums and temples to modern art. But above all else, this is an island of drama, and nothing comes more dramatic than the snow-draped Pico del Teide, Spain's tallest mountain and home to some of the most fabulous hiking in the whole country.

When to Go

➡ December to February is pleasantly warm, except on El Teide, where deep winter can result in snowfall closing the mountain.

➡ March to April is spring and is good for hiking and seeing wildflowers. Surfers are rewarded with the best waves in March.

➡ In the summer months, from May to September, expect around 11 hours of daily sunshine. The average temperature is 28°C in August; it's a few degrees cooler during the surrounding months.

➡ As autumn turns, from October to November, temperatures fall to around 21°C. There are fewer tourists, and some hotels may drop their prices slightly.

History

The original inhabitants of Tenerife were primitive cave-dwellers called Guanches, who arrived from North Africa around 200 BC. Tenerife was the last island to fall to the Spanish (in 1496) and subsequently became an important trading centre. As such, it was subject to invasions by marauding pirates and, in 1797, from the British in the battle of Santa Cruz, when Admiral Nelson famously lost his arm.

In 1821 Madrid declared Santa Cruz de Tenerife the capital of the Canaries. The great and the good of Las Palmas de Gran Canaria remained incensed about this until 1927, when Madrid finally split the archipelago into two provinces, with Santa Cruz as the provincial capital of Tenerife, La Palma, La Gomera and El Hierro. As economic links between the Canaries and the Americas strengthened, a small exodus of islanders crossed the ocean, notably to Venezuela and Cuba. In later years affluent emigrants and Latin Americans reversed the trend, bringing influences that are still evident in the food and Latino beat of the music of today's Tenerife.

ℹ Getting There & Away

AIR

Two airports serve the island. Tenerife Sur Airport (p268), about 20km east of Playa de las Américas, handles international flights, while almost all inter-island flights (plus a few international and mainland services) use the older Tenerife Norte Airport (p268), near Santa Cruz in the north of the island. Binter Canarias (p269), CanaryFly (p269) and Air Europa (p54) connect the island with the rest of the archipelago.

BOAT

Ferries from Santa Cruz

Buy tickets for all companies from travel agents or from the main Estación Marítima Muelle Ribera in Santa Cruz de Tenerife (from where the Fred Olsen boats leave). Naviera Armas has its base further to the south.

Trasmediterránea (⌨ in Madrid 902 45 46 45; www.trasmediterranea.com; 39 Calle la Marina) runs a ferry at 11.59pm every Friday from Santa Cruz that makes the following stops:

➡ Las Palmas de Gran Canaria (from €27, 8½ hours)

➡ Puerto del Rosario, Fuerteventura (from €32, 20½ hours)

➡ Arrecife, Lanzarote (from €35, 24 hours)

Naviera Armas (⌨ 902 45 65 00; www.navieraarmas.com) runs from Santa Cruz:

➡ Las Palmas de Gran Canaria, Gran Canaria (from €38, 2½ hours, 21 weekly)

➡ Morro Jable, Fuerteventura (from €70, 6½ hours, one daily)

➡ Puerto del Rosario, Fuerteventura (from €83, 11½ hours, one daily)

➡ Arrecife, Lanzarote (from €94, 11 hours, one daily Monday to Friday)

Fred Olsen (p269) has three to six daily ferries from Santa Cruz to Agaete in the northwest of Gran Canaria (€42, 1¼ hours), from where you can take its free bus onwards to Las Palmas (35 minutes).

Ferries from Los Cristianos

Routes operated by Naviera Armas from Los Cristianos include the following:

➡ San Sebastián de la Gomera, La Gomera (€32, one hour, three daily Monday to Friday, one Saturday, two Sunday)

➡ Santa Cruz de la Palma, La Palma (€46, 3½ hours, one daily Sunday to Friday)

➡ Valverde, El Hierro (€50, 3¾ hours, daily Sunday to Friday)

Routes operated by Fred Olsen from Los Cristianos include the following:

➡ San Sebastián de la Gomera (€34, 50 minutes, three daily Monday to Friday, two daily Saturday and Sunday)

➡ Santa Cruz de la Palma (from €48, two hours, one daily Sunday to Friday)

ℹ Getting Around

TITSA (p270) runs an efficient spider's web of bus services all over the island. Bus line 343 (€9.70) links Tenerife Norte Airport with Tenerife Sur Airport. Car-hire agencies are plentiful. Taxis are an expensive way to get around.

SANTA CRUZ DE TENERIFE

POP 204,000

Whatever you do, don't bypass the bustling capital, the handsome and friendly port of Santa Cruz, in your dash for the beach on Tenerife. Backing onto a superb range of undulating hills, this wholly Spanish city is home to evocative, brightly painted buildings, grand and historic architecture, sophisticated and quirky shops, riveting museums and art galleries, a showstopping auditorium, flashes of bold and vibrant street art, and a tropical oasis of birdsong, fountains and greenery in the city park. Backing all this up are friendly locals, a terrific spread of quality restaurants, as well as an excellent bus and tram system, making Santa Cruz a sensible and convenient base for exploring the sublime landscapes of the island's northeast.

Tenerife Highlights

1 Anaga Mountains (p153) Doing a Darwin and exploring the verdant expanses of the oldest geographical region on the island.

2 Parque Nacional del Teide (p162) Hiking around the staggering moonscape of Spain's most popular national park.

3 Tenerife Espacio de las Artes (TEA) (p144) Checking out the magnificent architecture and art exhibitions at this contemporary space in Santa Cruz de Tenerife.

4 La Laguna (p149) Wandering the best-preserved historical quarter on the island.

5 Masca (p166) Being overawed by the extraordinary mountain setting of this tiny village.

6 Puerto de la Cruz (p153) Enjoying the salty sea breezes at this charming and historic resort town.

7 Los Gigantes & Puerto de Santiago (p167) Watching superb sunsets from the promenade at this attractive resort area.

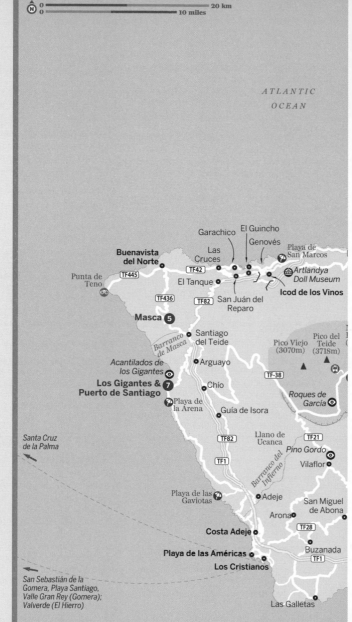

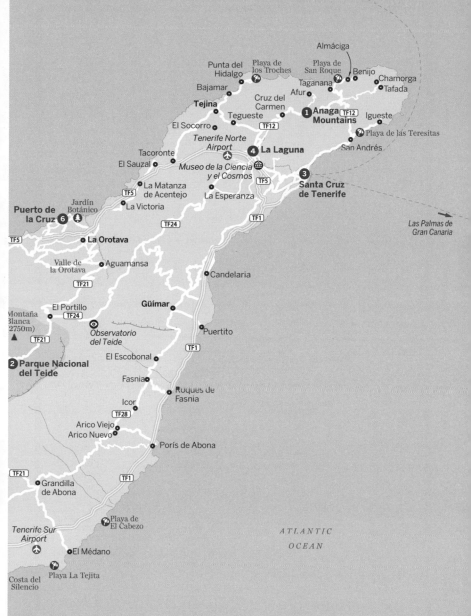

→ Santa Cruz de la Palma

Almáciga

Punta del Hidalgo
Playa de los Troches
Playa de San Roque
Benijo
Chamorga
Tafada

Bajamar
Taganana
Afur

Tejina
Cruz del Carmen
❶ **Anaga Mountains** TF12
Igueste

El Socorro
Tegueste
TF12

Tenerife Norte Airport
❹ **La Laguna**
Playa de las Teresitas

Tacoronte
San Andrés

El Sauzal
Museo de la Ciencia y el Cosmos
❸ **Santa Cruz de Tenerife**

Puerto de la Cruz ❻
Jardín Botánico
La Matanza de Acentejo
TF5
La Esperanza

TF5
La Victoria
TF1

Las Palmas de Gran Canaria

● **La Orotava**
TF24

Valle de la Orotava
Aguamansa
Candelaria

TF21

El Portillo
Güímar

Montaña Blanca (2750m)
TF24
Observatorio del Teide
Puertito

❷ **Parque Nacional del Teide**
El Escobonal
TF1

Fasnia

Icor
Roques de Fasnia
TF28

Arico Viejo
Arico Nuevo

Porís de Abona

TF21
TF1

● Grandilla de Abona

Tenerife Sur Airport
Playa de El Cabezo

ATLANTIC OCEAN

El Médano

Costa del Silencio
Playa La Tejita

Santa Cruz de Tenerife

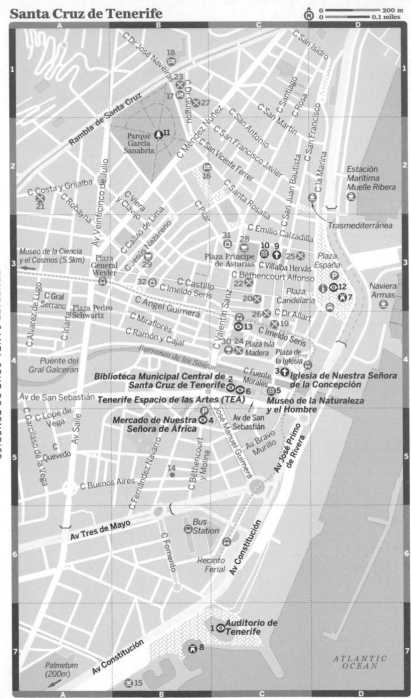

0 — 200 m
0 — 0.1 miles

C Dr-José Naveiras
18
23
17 C Dr Guigou
27
Rambla de Santa Cruz
Parque García Sanabria 11
C Méndez Núñez
C San Antonio
C San Isidro
C Santiago
C Rosa
C San Martín
C San Francisco Javier
C San Vicente Ferrer
16
Estación Marítima Muelle Ribera
C Costa y Grijalba 21
Av Veinticinco de Julio
C Viera y Clavijo
C Pilar
C Santa Rosalía
C San Juan Bautista
C la Marina
Trasmediterránea
Museo de la Ciencia y el Cosmos (5.5km)
C Robayna
C Callao de Lima
C Jesús Nazareno
Plaza General Weyler
29
32
C Emilio Calzadilla
31
28
Plaza Príncipe de Asturias
10 9
25
Plaza España
C Villalba Hervás
C Béthencourt Alfonso
22
12
7
Naviera Armas
C Castillo
C Imeldo Serís
C Ángel Guimerá
20
Plaza Candelaria
C Gral Serrano
Plaza Pedro Schwartz
C Miraflores
C Ramón y Cajal
26 C Dr Allart
19
13 C Imeldo Serís
C Valentín Sanz
30 24 Plaza Isla Madera
Plaza de la Iglesia
Barranco de los Santos
Puente del Gral Galcerán
C Álvarez de Lugo
C Iriarte
C Fuente Morales
3 Iglesia de Nuestra Señora de la Concepción
Biblioteca Municipal Central de Santa Cruz de Tenerife 2
6
5
Av de San Sebastián
Tenerife Espacio de las Artes (TEA)
Museo de la Naturaleza y el Hombre
C Lope de Vega
Mercado de Nuestra Señora de África 4
José Manuel Guimerá
Av de San Sebastián
C Garcilaso de la Vega
C Quevedo
Av Salle
14
C Béthencourt y Molina
Av Bravo Murillo
Av José Primo de Rivera
C Buenos Aires
C Fernández Navarro
Av Tres de Mayo
Bus Station
Recinto Ferial
C Formento
Av Constitución
1 Auditorio de Tenerife
Av Constitución
8
Palmetum (200m)
15
ATLANTIC OCEAN

Santa Cruz de Tenerife

History

Alonso Fernández de Lugo landed on Tenerife in 1494 to embark on the conquest of the final and most resistant island in the archipelago. La Laguna, which is a few kilometres inland, initially blossomed as the island's capital. Santa Cruz de Santiago (as Santa Cruz de Tenerife was then known) remained a backwater until its port began to flourish in the 18th and 19th centuries. Only in 1803 was Santa Cruz 'liberated' from the municipal control of La Laguna by Spanish royal decree; in 1859 it was declared a city.

Sights & Activities

Plaza España   SQUARE
The majority of Santa Cruz' sights and museums are within easy walking distance of the revamped waterfront Plaza España, with its huge circular wading pool plus fountain that spouts four times a day (indicating high and low tides). The pool makes for excellent photographs in the early morning or late afternoon, with the architecture reflected in the water.

★ **Museo de la
Naturaleza y el Hombre**   MUSEUM
(www.museosdetenerife.org; Calle Fuente Morales; €5; ⊙9am-8pm Tue-Sat, 10am-5pm Sun & Mon) This brain-bending amalgam of natural science and archaeology is an excellent museum, despite a rather confusing layout. Set inside the former civil hospital, the exhibit highlights are undoubtedly the Guanche mummies and skulls, all of which are shrivelled masses of skin, hair and bone, with faces dried into contorted and grotesque expressions. In addition, there are informative displays on wildlife, flora and geology; the audiovisual presentation about the eruption of El Teide on the ground floor is particularly powerful and mesmerising.

There's also an absorbing section on the second floor devoted to archaeological finds on each of the islands, as well as an area detailing Berber ceramics. Children will enjoy the interactive displays, with their flashing buttons and large TV screens. Most signage is only in Spanish, although most of the exhibition rooms have laminated explanatory sheets in English, and a handy online audio tour in six languages is available. There's also a cafe and gift shop.

★ Tenerife Espacio de las Artes (TEA)   ARTS CENTRE

(www.teatenerife.es; Avenida de San Sebastián 10; adult/child €7/free, films €4; ⊙10am-8pm Tue-Sun) The highlights of this dramatic contemporary building are the architecture, its three galleries and the stunning library downstairs. The galleries display temporary exhibitions of art, photography and installation works, including the creative output of up-and-coming Spanish artists reflecting edgy, contemporary themes. The building was designed by the Swiss architects and Pritzker Prize Laureates Jacques Herzog and Pierre de Meuron, famed for their innovative construction, with a prestigious portfolio that includes London's Tate Modern.

The cinema (€4) is dedicated to independent, art and experimental film and documentaries, allowing you the chance to see material that may be rarely screened. All films (shown at 7pm and 9.30pm Friday to Sunday) are in their original language, with Spanish subtitles. Guided visits of TEA are €15.

★ Biblioteca Municipal Central de Santa Cruz de Tenerife   LIBRARY

(www.bibliotecaspublicas.es/santacruztenerife/informacion.htm; Tenerife Espacio de las Artes; ⊙24hr) This library downstairs at TEA is a design classic, a vast open-plan room with overhanging globular lights, copious natural light, angular lines and a sharp contemporary feel, all fashioned with a sense of uncluttered space that all libraries should emulate. If you're footsore, there are quiet cubicles (and sofas outside) where you can sit, read or have a snooze, and books and magazines for browsing, including some in English. A kids'

OFF THE BEATEN TRACK

GETTING AWAY FROM IT ALL

Anaga Mountains (p153) Dense forest dripping with life and draped with little-trodden hiking trails.

Parque Nacional del Teide (p162) Sure, everyone wants to come here, but it's huge, so finding remote solitude isn't hard.

Punta de Teno (p164) The far-flung northwestern tip of the island still retains an alluring wildness.

---

library is downstairs, and there's a popular **cafe** (Auditorio de Tenerife, Avenida Constitucíon; snacks €3.50-6; ⊙9am-7.30pm Sun-Thu, to midnight Fri & Sat; 🛜) next door.

★ Mercado de Nuestra Señora de África   MARKET

(Avenida de San Sebastián; ⊙9am-2pm; P) Dating from 1944, this tantalising market is housed in an eye-catching building that combines a Latin American feel with Moorish-style arches and patios. A lofty clock tower helps in locating the place – or just follow the shopping baskets; the *mercado* offers fresh, competitively priced produce, and is the top choice for locals, including restaurateurs. Stalls are spread over two bustling floors and interspersed with colourful flower sellers, kiosks selling churros and lush subtropical greenery.

★ Iglesia de Nuestra Señora de la Concepción   CHURCH

(Plaza de la Iglesia; ⊙9am-9pm Sun, mass 9am & 7.30pm) It's difficult to miss the striking bell tower of the city's oldest church, which also has traditional Mudéjar (Islamic-style architecture) ceilings. The present church was built in the 17th and 18th centuries, but the original building went up in 1498, just after Tenerife was conquered. At the heart of the shimmering silver altar is the 1494 Santa Cruz de la Conquista (Holy Cross of the Conquest), which gives the city its name.

Museo de Bellas Artes   MUSEUM

(📞922 60 94 46; www.santacruzdetenerife.es; Plaza Príncipe de Asturias; ⊙10am-8pm Tue-Fri, to 3pm Sat & Sun Oct-Jun, 10am-8pm Tue-Fri, to 2pm Sat & Sun Jul-Sep) FREE Founded in 1900 and formerly part of the adjacent church (note the fabulous stained glass), this excellent museum has an eclectic collection of paintings by mainly Spanish, Canarian and Flemish artists, including Ribera, Sorolla and Bruegel. There's also sculpture, including a Rodin, and temporary exhibitions. The massive battle-scene canvases by Spanish painter Manuel Villegas Bricva are particularly sobering. Note that the galleries are accessed via several flights of stairs, and there's no elevator.

Teatro Guimerá   NOTABLE BUILDING

(www.teatroguimera.es; Plaza Isla Madera; ⊙11am-1pm & 6-8pm Tue-Fri) One of the city's architectural highlights is the rectangular, 19th-century Teatro Guimerá. The sumptuous interior is reminiscent of Madrid's Teatro Real, with semicircular balconied seating and lashings of gilt.

DON'T MISS: CARNAVAL

Channelling a true Carnaval spirit of exuberance and mayhem, Santa Cruz' own **Carnaval** (www.carnavaltenerife.com) is a nonstop, 24-hour party. Festivities generally kick off in early February and last about three weeks. Many of the gala performances and fancy-dress competitions take place in the Recinto Ferial (fairgrounds) but the streets, especially around Plaza España, become frenzied with good-natured dusk-to-dawn frivolity.

Don't be fooled into thinking this is just a sequin-bedecked excuse to party hearty, though: there is an underlying political 'message' to the whole shebang. Under the Franco dictatorship, Carnaval was banned, but still managed to continue furtively under the name 'Winter Festival'. The Catholic Church's relationship with the fascists was another source of frustration so, when Carnaval was fully relaunched after the death of General Franco, the citizens of Santa Cruz wasted no time in lampooning the perceived sexual and moral hypocrisy of the church and the fascists. Today, you will still see a lot of people dressed as naughty nuns and perverted priests, and more drag queens than bumblebees in a buttercup field. And all in the name of good, clean fun. Book accommodation ahead!

★**Auditorio de Tenerife** NOTABLE BUILDING
(📞922 56 86 25, 922 56 86 00; www.auditorio detenerife.com; Avenida Constitución; ⊘guided tours 10am, noon, 2pm, 4pm & 6pm; P) FREE This magnificent, soaring white wave of an auditorium was designed by the internationally renowned Spanish architect Santiago Calatrava, and delivers shades of the Sydney Opera House, plus superb acoustics. Guided 45-minute tours (€7.50; reserved in advance by telephone) in English, German or Spanish take you behind the scenes of the remarkable building.

Palmetum GARDENS
(www.palmetumtenerife.es, Avenida Constitución; adult/child €6/2.80, joint ticket with Parque Marítimo César Manrique adult/child €7.30/3.30; ⊘11am-1pm & 4-8pm Tue-Sun; P) Conscientiously established on a former landfill area, this excellent 12-hectare botanical garden has the most diverse collection of palm trees in Europe, with specimens imported from all over the world. A detailed map leaflet helps in identifying the trees, as does signage. It's a peaceful place for a wander, with strategically placed benches for contemplating the seamless sea views.

**Parque Marítimo
César Manrique** SWIMMING
(📞657 65 11 27; www.parquemaritimosantacruz. es; Avenida Constitución; adult/child €2.50/1.50, joint ticket with Palmetum adult/child €7.30/3.30; ⊘10am-7pm summer, to 6pm winter) Located right off the city's main *avenida* is this park, where you can have a dip in one of the wonderful designer pools or collapse on a sun-lounger and drink in the beautiful view and something refreshing. It's suitable for all ages, and great for children. Kids aged under three get in free.

🍴 Courses

Canarias Cultural LANGUAGE
(📞922 21 21 86; www.canariascultural.es; Avenida de Buenos Aires 54; 1-week intensive course €150) A range of part- and full-time Spanish courses, with an intensive course running for 20 hours a week, with three to eight students per class.

🎊 Festivals & Events

As well as Carnaval in February, Santa Cruz plays host to a number of other festivals

**Festival Internacional
de Música de Canarias** MUSIC
(www.festivaldecanarias.com; ⊘Jan & Feb) The International Music Festival of the Canary Islands is the biggest event on the music calendar, held annually in Santa Cruz de Tenerife and Las Palmas de Gran Canaria (on Gran Canaria).

Día de la Cruz RELIGIOUS
(⊘3 May) This day is observed throughout Tenerife, but particularly in Santa Cruz (and Puerto de la Cruz), where crosses and chapels are beautifully decorated with flowers in celebration of the founding of the city.

🍴 Eating

★**Café Palmelita** CAFE €
(📞922 88 89 04; www.palmelita.es; Calle Castillo 9; cakes €2.50-4; ⊘9am-9.30pm Mon-Fri, 9.30am-9.30pm Sat & Sun) This delightful cafe has a vintage exterior, a theme which continues within, and was founded in the late 1960s

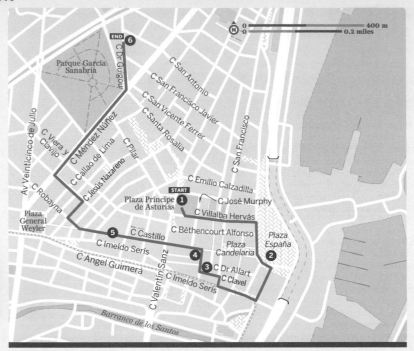

🏃 City Walk
A Taste of Traditional Santa Cruz

START PLAZA PRÍNCIPE DE ASTURIAS
END LA TASCA
LENGTH 2KM; 1½ HOURS

The traditional ❶ **Kiosco Príncipe** (p148) in the Plaza Príncipe de Asturias' subtropical park, dating from the mid-1800s, is the perfect place to sit back and enjoy the sculpture, the fountain, the trees, and the people-watching.

The emblematic ❷ **Plaza España** (p143) is at the heart of the city. Ponder the memorial to locals who died during the Spanish Civil War, take a paddle in the vast wading pool, then duck down to the tiny underground ❸ **Castillo de San Cristóbal** (☎ 922 28 56 05; Plaza España; ⊙ 10am-6pm Mon-Sat) **FREE** to see fragments of the former castle that once sat majestically here.

Weave your way through the backstreets to ❹ **La Hierbita** (☎ 922 24 46 17; www.la hierbita.es; Calle Clavel 19; mains €9-14; ⊙ noon-10.30pm) – the first restaurant to be licensed here in 1893, in the (then) heart of the red-light district. Part of the building used to be a brothel, but there's nothing seedy about the excellent contemporary-style Canarian cuisine served here now. The delightful ❺ **Café Palmelita** (p145) has a vintage exterior, a theme which continues within. The emphasis here is on serious indulgence.

The main pedestrian walkway, ❻ **Calle Castillo**, is lined with shops and boutiques and is the city's top see-and-be-seen street for locals on weekends. All the national chains are here, as well as smaller independent shops.

The nearby small grid of streets to the north of Calle Castillo is known as Soho and is home to some of the city's most fashionable cafes, tapas bars and shops. Head to nearby ❼ **La Tasca** (p147), one of the city's earthiest local restaurants. The decor is plain, the queues are long and the food is huge portions of hearty old-fashioned Canarian classics.

with German origins. The emphasis is on serious indulgence, with hot chocolate with double cream, or cold with vanilla ice cream; foamy frappés; buttery pastries; and traditional German cakes. All designed to put a contented waddle in your step. It's also a superb breakfast spot.

★ Bodeguita Canaria   CANARIAN €

(☑ 922 29 32 16; www.bodeguitacanaria.com; Calle Imeldo Serís 18; mains €8-10, set menu €19-25; ⊙ 1-4pm & 8-11.30pm Mon-Sat) This terrific local favourite has an earthy, traditional atmosphere, with chunky dark furniture and charmingly dated decor. Try local dishes such as *ropa vieja* (literally 'old clothes'), a tasty meat-based stew with chickpeas, vegetables and potatoes, or *huevos rotos con chorizo* (scrambled eggs with chorizo). The desserts are similarly heart-warmingly homely and include *torrijas,* the Spanish take on bread-and-butter pudding.

La Tasca   CANARIAN €

(☑ 922 28 07 64; Calle Dr Guigou 18; mains €7-13, menú del día €7; ⊙ noon-3.45pm & 8-11.45pm Mon-Sat Sep-Jul) The cultural and culinary opposite to the all-day English breakfasts of Tenerife's southern resorts, this neighbourhood institution makes no allowances for confused foreigners. The laughably cheap lunch menus mean there's often a queue of locals waiting for the food, which consists of huge portions of sturdy Canarian classics.

★ Guannabi   SPANISH €€

(☑ 922 87 53 75; Calle Antonio Domínguez Alfonso 34; mains €13-26; ⊙ 1-11pm Sun-Thu, to 11.45pm Fri & Sat) This excellence of this handsome restaurant is defined not just by its superb ambience and faultless service, but by its simply supreme menu. Guannabi pulls out all the stops: the focus is on rice dishes, all perfectly executed, but the entire selection is outstanding and even the aubergine starter is a feast of flavour and smooth texture.

El Lateral 27   CANARIAN €€

(Calle Bethencourt Alfonso 27; mains €10-15; ⊙ 7am-midnight Mon-Sat; 🖉) Jovial and welcoming staff, happy shoppers and a menu of tried and tested local dishes make this place a perennial favourite. Offerings like oxtail (or goat) stew, suckling lamb shoulder and seafood pie are crowd-pleasers, while a decent choice of vegetable dishes keeps vegetarians happy.

Gom   CANARIAN €€

(☑ 922 27 60 58; www.hoteltaburiente.com/gastronomia/restaurante-gom; Calle Dr Guigou 27; mains €10-15; ⊙ 1-4pm & 8-11pm; 🔊) A restaurant of the adjacent **Hotel Taburiente** (www.hoteltaburiente.com), sophisticated, seductively stylish Gom has a modern menu that applies a creative twist to otherwise typical Canarian and mainland fare. One of the more upmarket places in the city centre, it's popular with a slick and well-heeled business crowd at lunchtime.

★ Kazan   JAPANESE €€€

(☑ 922 24 55 98; www.restaurantekazan.com; Paseo Milicias de Garachico 1; tasting menu €75; ⊙ 1.30-3.30pm Mon-Sat & 8.30-11pm Tue-Sat) Kazan's Michelin star has assured it a large fanbase in town and far beyond. The setting: lightly polished wood and beige fabric chairs, muted and understated yet stylish. The food: the freshest ingredients coaxed into beautifully formed, delightful Japanese presentations. If in doubt, aim for the daily suggestions. The name Kazan and the *kanji* 火山 on the door simply mean 'Volcano'. Reserve.

El Aguarde   CANARIAN €€€

(☑ 922 28 91 42; www.restauranteelaguarde tenerife.es; Calle Costa y Grijalba 21; mains €15-25; ⊙ 1-4pm Mon, 1-4pm & 9-11pm Tue-Sat; 🔊) This special-occasion place, exuding a minimalist elegance to accompany its finely crafted dishes, gets rave reviews. The menu changes according to what is fresh and in season, but includes a good selection of meat and fish dishes (black rice and squid, crayfish croquettes) and at least one vegetarian choice. Desserts are exquisite; try the lemon mousse with *cava* and mint.

🍷 Drinking & Nightlife

The colourful cafes, restaurants and bars on Calle Antonio Domínguez Alfonso (popularly known as La Noria) – one of the oldest streets in the city – comprise the stylish hub of Santa Cruz drinking culture, while a busy contingent of bars also collects along Avenida Francisco la Roche, facing the port area.

★ La Casita   CAFE

(☑ 922 24 78 51; Calle Jesús Nazareno 14; ⊙ 10am-midnight Tue-Sat; 🔊) Managed by a fashionable young team, but themed like grandma's country cottage with cuckoo clocks and ancient bits and bobs, this enticing cafe sports original tile work and several cosy dining rooms plus a lovely terrace upstairs for sinking a beer. There are also simple lightweight mains like salads, burgers and croquettes, plus delicious cakes and pies.

TENERIFE SANTA CRUZ DE TENERIFE

★ **Cafetería del TEA** CAFE
(Tenerife Espacio de las Artes (TEA); ⊗8am-9pm Mon-Fri, 10am-9pm Sat & Sun; 🛜) Overhung by globular lights and defined by the crisp and stylishly neat lines of its stainless-steel and grey-cloth furniture, this space downstairs in Tenerife Espacio de las Artes (p144) is an excellent choice for a dose of minimalist design to go with your coffee and pastries. It's open until 9pm, making it a good choice for the evening.

★ **Kiosco Príncipe** CAFE
(Plaza Príncipe de Asturias; ⊗8am-7pm Mon-Fri, to 3pm Sat) Grab a coffee at this traditional kiosk located in the subtropical park of Plaza Príncipe de Asturias, which dates to the mid-1800s. Admire the award-winning sculpture *Courage* by Hanneke Beaumont, the traditional bandstand and fountain, and the lofty shade-providing trees, including Indian laurels imported from Cuba. It's always full of local strollers, with plenty of bench space to watch the comings and goings.

Mojos y Mojitos BAR, CLUB
(Calle Antonio Domínguez Alfonso 38; ⊗noon-midnight Mon-Thu, to 3.30am Fri & Sat, 1-11.45pm Sun; 🛜) This popular and laid-back place on La Noria serves decent food during the day, and at night morphs into a combination of cool cocktail bar and pulsating nightclub, with DJs and occasional live music. The mojitos are understandably good, with or without alcohol.

☆ **Entertainment**

Bars and clubs here often double as occasional live-music venues, particularly around La Noria (Calle Antonio Domínguez Alfonso).

★ **Auditorio de Tenerife** LIVE MUSIC
(🖉box office 902 31 73 27; www.auditoriodetenerife.com; Avenida Constitución; 🛜) One of Santa Cruz' top photo ops, Tenerife's leading entertainment option has dramatically designed curved-white concrete shells capped by a cresting, crashing wave of a roof. It covers and significantly enhances a 2-hectare oceanfront site. The auditorium hosts world-class opera, dance and classical-music performances, and there's a snazzy cafe in the lobby.

 Shopping

The main shopping area is pedestrianised Calle Castillo and its surrounding streets.

Canary Wine WINE
(🖉645 16 32 59; Patio Naciente, Mercado de Nuestra Señora de África; ⊗7.30am-3pm) The charming and helpful owner of this shop will guide you through the local wines here, including eco-wines and the famous banana wine with the peeled-back price of just €8 a bottle. Another popular choice is *viña norte*, a Lambrusco-style rosé. The owner can set you up with a tasting there and then, but book ahead if you're a group.

Mi Mundo Gourmet FOOD & DRINKS
(🖉922 09 80 57; Patio Naciente, Mercado de Nuestra Señora de África; ⊗9am-2pm Tue-Sun) Pick up your gourmet deli items at this bustling store. Look for traditional products such as jars of chilli-spiked *mojo salsa*, cactus marmalade, local honey, olive oil, herbs and spices.

Dolores Promesas FASHION & ACCESSORIES
(🖉922 28 97 46; www.dolorespromesas.com; Calle Pilar 4; ⊗10.30am-2pm & 5.30-8.30pm Mon-Fri, 10.30am-2pm Sat) This Spanish designer apparently became inspired as a child by the bolts of material, buttons and bows at her grandfather's modest haberdashery shop near Cádiz on the mainland. Her designs are aimed at various age groups and styles, ranging from casual printed T-shirts to fabulous floaty dresses in feather-light silks.

🛈 **Information**

Tourist Office (🖉922 23 95 92; www.todotenerife.es; Plaza España; ⊗9am-5pm Mon-Fri, 9.30am-2pm Sat & Sun) Enquire about the hour-long walking tour of town that sets off from here at noon and is included in the City View bus ticket.

🛈 **Getting There & Away**

BOAT
Ferries sail from the Estación Marítima Muelle Ribera (p139).

Trasmediterránea (p139) runs a ferry at 11.59pm every Friday from Santa Cruz to Las Palmas de Gran Canaria (from €27, 8½ hours); Puerto del Rosario, Fuerteventura (from €32, 20½ hours); and Arrecife, Lanzarote (from €35, 24 hours).

Naviera Armas (p139) runs an extensive ferry service around the islands from Santa Cruz, to Las Palmas de Gran Canaria (from €38, 2½ hours, 21 weekly); Morro Jable, Fuerteventura (from €70, 6½ hours, one daily); Puerto del Rosario, Fuerteventura (from €83, 11½ hours, one daily); and Arrecife, Lanzarote (from €94, 11 hours, one daily Monday to Friday).

Fred Olsen (☑ 902 10 01 07; www.fredolsen. es) has three to six daily ferries from Santa Cruz to Agaete in the northwest of Gran Canaria (€42, 1¼ hours), from where you can take its free bus onwards to Las Palmas (35 minutes).

BUS

TITSA buses radiate out from the **bus station** (www.titsa.com; Avenida Tres de Mayo) beside Avenida Constitución. Popular routes:

Buses 014 & 015 La Laguna (€1.45, 20 minutes, every 10 minutes)

Bus 102 Puerto de la Cruz via La Laguna and Tenerife Norte Airport (€5.25, 55 minutes, every 30 minutes)

Bus 103 Puerto de la Cruz (€5.25, 40 minutes, more than 15 daily)

Bus 110 Los Cristianos and Playa de las Américas (€9, one hour, every 30 minutes)

CAR & MOTORCYCLE

Car-hire companies are plentiful; for scooter rental, try **Cooltra** (☑ 663 76 81 16; www.cool tra.com; Paseo Milicias de Garachico 2; ☺ 9am-2pm & 4-7pm Mon-Fri, 9am-3pm Sat).

TRAM

A tram line (www.metrotenerife.com) links central Santa Cruz with La Laguna. Tickets cost €1.35 and the full journey takes 40 minutes.

ⓘ Getting Around

TO/FROM THE AIRPORT

Tenerife Norte Airport TITSA bus 20 (€2.65, 20 minutes) runs to Santa Cruz, as do buses 102, 107 and 108, which all go to the main Intercambiador bus station in the city. A taxi from Tenerife Norte to Santa Cruz will cost about €20.

BUS

TITSA buses provide a city service around Santa Cruz. Several buses pass regularly by the centre (Plaza General Weyler and Plaza España) from the bus station, including 910 and 914. Other local services include the circular routes 920 and 921. A local trip costs €1.25.

CAR & MOTORCYCLE

On-street parking is difficult to find in the central areas, but paid parking stations can be found underneath Plaza España and within the Mercado de Nuestra Señora de África off Avenida de San Sebastián.

TAXI

The major taxi stands in Santa Cruz include a **taxi rank** on Plaza España and another at the bus station.

NORTHEAST TENERIFE

Home to some of the island's most alluring scenery, the northeast of Tenerife is largely a verdant and wild peninsula poking into the wild waters of the Atlantic Ocean. Characterised by the huge undulations of the Anaga mountain range, this is a world of hiking trails, cliff-hugging roads and remote villages; it's also a biosphere reserve containing ancient *laurisilva* forest. This is supreme trekking and exploration territory.

La Laguna

POP 153,000

La Laguna is widely considered to be the most beautiful town in Tenerife. An easy day trip from Santa Cruz or Puerto de la Cruz, it has a gem of a historic town centre, with narrow poker-straight streets flanked by pastel-hued mansions, inviting bars and an idiosyncratic array of small shops.

La Laguna's layout provided the model for many colonial towns in the Americas and, in 1999, it was added to the list of Unesco World Heritage sites. The town has a youthful energy and possibly the island's most determined *marcha* (nightlife).

⊙ Sights

The main sights are all located in the historic centre of town. Don't worry too much if you get lost; this whole *barrio* is like an outdoor museum of historical architecture.

★**Calle San Agustín**   STREET

To see the largest number of splendid mansions standing cheek to jowl, wander along Calle San Agustín (p151). Look for the metal plaques outside the noble facades; they have fascinating historical explanations about the buildings (in Spanish and English). Several of the buildings have been turned into offices (generally located around a grand central courtyard), which you can take a peek at.

★**Museo de la Historia de Tenerife**   MUSEUM

(Casa Lercaro; www.museosdetenerife.org; Calle San Agustín 22; adult/child under 8 €5/free; ☺ 9am-8pm Tue-Sat, 10am-5pm Sun & Mon) The documents, maps, weapons and tools are interesting enough at this museum, but the 16th-century mansion – with its creaking floorboards, old window seats, elaborately carved wooden gallery and lovely patio – of Casa Lercaro is simply lovely. Don't miss the two magnificent 18th- and 19th-century carriages kept in a separate exhibition space at the rear of the museum (open noon to 3pm). The museum is free to visit on Fridays and Saturdays from 4pm.

Iglesia de Nuestra Señora de la Concepción
CHURCH

(Plaza Concepción; tower €2; ⊘ tickets sold 10am-2pm Mon, to 5pm Tue-Fri) Originally constructed in 1502, this is one of the island's earliest churches and has subsequently undergone many changes. Elements of Gothic and plateresque styles can still be distinguished, and the finely wrought wooden Mudéjar ceilings are a delight. Take a look at the font where apparently (any remaining) Guanches were traditionally baptised, then climb the five-storey tower for stunning views of the town and beyond (purchase tickets from the bell-tower office before entering the church).

★Catedral
CATHEDRAL

(www.catedraldelalaguna.blogspot.com.es; Plaza Catedral; €5; ⊘ 8am-6pm Mon-Sat, to 2pm Sun) Work on this magnificent cathedral was completed in 1915. A fine baroque retable in the chapel is dedicated to the Virgen de los Remedios and dates from the 16th century. Other highlights include some impressive paintings by Cristóbal Hernández de Quintana, one of the Canary Islands' premier 18th-century artists, and a splendid Carrara marble pulpit carved by Genovese sculptor Pasquale Bocciardo in 1762. An audio guide is included in the admission price.

★Convento de Santa Clara
CONVENT, MUSEUM

(cnr Calles Anchieta & Viana; adult/child €3/free; ⊘ 10am-5pm Tue-Fri, to 2pm Mon) Of all the convents in La Laguna, this is the most interesting, renowned for its beautiful lattice-work wooden balcony and cloister. The museum covers nine rooms and contains some of the most precious artworks and artefacts from the convent collection, including a magnificent 18th-century silver altar. A 10-minute audiovisual presentation (in English and Spanish) explains the fascinating history of the convent, from its founding in 1547 by 10 Franciscan nuns.

Fundación Cristino de Vera
GALLERY

(www.fundacioncristinodevera.com; Calle San Agustín 18; adult/child €3/free; ⊘ 11am-2pm & 5-8pm Mon-Fri,10am-2pm Sat) La Laguna's prime arts venue houses a mixture of top-calibre temporary exhibitions as well as a permanent collection of works by acclaimed contemporary artist Cristino de Vera, who was born in Santa Cruz de Tenerife in 1931. There is also a thought-provoking audiovisual presentation about the artist and his work (subtitled in English).

Santuario del Cristo
CHURCH

(Santuario del Santísimo Cristo de La Laguna; Plaza San Francisco; ⊘ 8am-1pm & 4-8.45pm Mon-Thu & Sat, to 9pm Fri & Sun) At the northern end of the old quarter, this church contains a blackened wooden sculpture of Christ – the most venerated crucifix on the island. Be as respectful as possible inside, as most of the people here are praying, not sightseeing.

Iglesia y ex-convento de San Agustín
CHURCH

(Calle San Agustín; ⊘ 10am-8pm Tue-Fri, to 3pm Sat & Sun) This church went up in flames in 1964, lost its roof and is now out of bounds and in ruins, but you can peer through the gap in the wall at the somnolent skeletal remains and the plants busy reclaiming the abandoned stonework. The cloisters, filled with tropical plants and flowers, are open to the public and are probably the prettiest in town. The rooms surrounding the cloisters contain an art gallery of frequently changing local works.

Museo de la Ciencia y el Cosmos
MUSEUM

(🗗 922 31 52 65; www.museosdetenerife.org; Avenida de los Menceyes 70; adult/child/student €5/free/€3.50, planetarium €1; ⊘ 9am-8pm Tue-Sat, 10am-5pm Sun & Mon; 🅿) If you enjoy pushing buttons and musing on the forces of nature, you'll have fun at this museum, which introduces key scientific concepts in an engaging and thought-provoking way. Located about 1.5km south of Plaza Adelantado and easily accessible by the tram to Santa Cruz (which stops right outside), it also has a *planetario* (planetarium), so you can stargaze during the day.

🎪 Festivals & Events

Corpus Christi
RELIGIOUS

Celebrated with gusto in La Laguna (and also La Orotava), where mammoth floral carpets, using tons of volcanic dirt, flower petals, leaves and branches, are used to painstakingly create intricate biblical scenes in the streets and plazas. The date changes annually, but it's always in June.

Romería de San Benito Abad
RELIGIOUS

(⊘ 1st Sun in Jul) This is one of the most important fiestas in La Laguna, held in honour of the patron saint of farmers and crops.

LA LAGUNA'S CANARIAN MANSIONS

Bright facades graced with wooden double doors, carved balconies and grey stone embellishments typify the pristinely preserved 16th- to 18th-century mansions of La Laguna, while elegant, wood-shuttered windows conceal cool, shady patios surrounded by verandas propped up by slender timber columns.

Calle San Agustín and the surrounding streets are lined with fine old houses. Take a look at the beautiful facade of **Casa del Montañés** (Calle San Agustín 16; ⊙10am-7pm Mon-Fri), with its decorative carved window frames. Destroyed by a fire in 2006, **Casa Salazar** (Calle San Agustín 28; ⊙10am-7pm Mon-Fri) has a beautiful, if austere, baroque facade and two lovely patios. The imposing **Casa de los Capitanes Generales** (Calle Obispo Rey Redondo 5; ⊙9am-8pm Mon-Fri, to 2pm Sat & Sun) beside the *ayuntamiento* (town hall) houses the tourist office. The distinctive blue facade of the mansion at **Calle Carrera 66** is the former home of surrealist painter Óscar Domínguez. Both the exterior and interior of the 19th-century **Teatro Leal** (www.teatroleal.es; Calle Obispo Rey Redondo 54; ⊙performances only) create a pleasingly over-the-top butterfly of a building that is open to the public only during performances.

Whenever you see an open door, peek inside – with luck the inner sanctum will also be open, but do remember that many are private residences or offices. To access the beauty of La Laguna hidden behind the heavy doors and walls, join a guided tour from the tourist office (p152).

🍴 Eating & Drinking

La Laguna has a splendid range of restaurants; for the best selection, head for the grid of streets surrounding the cathedral.

The bulk of the bars are concentrated in a tight rectangle northeast of the university, known as El Cuadrilátero; at its heart, pedestrianised Plaza Zurita is simply two parallel lines of bars and pubs.

⭐ Tasca 61   SPANISH €

(Calle Viana 61; mains €7-10; ⊙12.30-3.30pm & 7.30-10.30pm Wed-Fri, 7.30-10.30pm Sat & Sun) 🌿 Organic, locally sourced produce, a slow-food philosophy and *artesanal* cheeses are the hallmarks of this tiny place with its limited but delicious menu of daily specials. Even the beer is locally crafted at the only ecobrewery in Tenerife: Tierra de Perros.

La Casa de Oscar   CANARIAN €

(📞922 26 52 14; Calle Herradores 66; mains €8-10, pintxos €1.80; ⊙8am-midnight) This place always has a great buzz, particularly at weekends, when the tables are packed with exuberant local families tucking into dishes like grilled tuna in coriander-spiked sauce, spicy sausage omelettes or grilled meats with *mojo* (spicy sauce). Lighter appetites can snag a barrel table and fill up fast with the Galician-style *pintxos* (tapas) lining the front bar.

⭐ Guaydil   CANARIAN €€

(📞922 26 68 43; www.restauranteguaydil.com; Calle Deán Palahí 26; mains €10-16; ⊙1.30-4.40pm

& 8-11.30pm Mon-Thu, 1.30-4.30pm & 8.30-11.30pm Fri & Sat; 🖥) You can't go wrong at this delightful contemporary restaurant with its punchy, playful decor. Dishes are deftly executed, exquisitely presented and sensibly priced. One tip – if ordering a salad (recommended), ask for a half portion; the servings are huge and the staff won't object. Other typical dishes include couscous, prawn-stuffed crepes, chicken curry and an irresistible Cuban mojito sorbet.

NUB   FUSION €€€

(📞922 07 76 06; Calle de la Nava y Grimón 18; menú €75-95; ⊙7-9.30pm Wed & Thu, 1.30-2.30pm & 8-10pm Fri & Sat, 1-2.30pm Sun) A recent recipient of a coveted Michelin star, NUB in the La Laguna Gran Hotel works culinary wonders under the expert guidance of husband-and-wife chefs Andrea Bernadi and Fernanda Fuentes Cárdenas. Its thoughtful fusion of Canarian, Italian and Chilean flavours, perfectly presented in a set of tasting menus, are delivered in a very stylish setting.

Casa Viña   BAR

(📞922 63 37 29; www.bodegasinsulares.es; Plaza Concepción; ⊙11am-midnight Mon-Thu, to 3am Fri & Sat; 🖥) One of the best pavement settings for sipping a drink and watching La Laguna folk on the move. Within worshipping distance of the magnificent Iglesia de Nuestra Señora de la Concepción, this *vinoteca* is owned by the well-respected Viña Norte winery, based in Tacoronte. Enjoy a glass of their wine for just a couple of euros; good tapas are also available.

 Shopping

★ **Pisaverde** SHOES
(☑ 922 31 41 28; www.pisaverdestore.com; Calle Juan de Vera 7; ☉ 10am-8.30pm Mon-Fri, 11am-2.30pm Sat) The shoes at Pisaverde are quite a sight, with each pair uniquely fashioned and handcrafted with bold and brightly coloured leather and all manner of fabrics (including recycled materials too, such as car tyres). If you want some unique shoes to strut on the street, this is the place. Check out the full-length boot made for a drag queen.

ℹ Information

Tourist Office (☑ 922 63 11 94; www.web tenerife.com; Calle Obispo Rey Redondo 7; ☉ 9am-4.30pm Mon-Fri) Ask for the fascinating *San Cristóbal de La Laguna, World Heritage Site* brochure, and about the free guided tours of La Laguna's heritage sights, held from Monday to Friday at 11.30am (it's best to book in advance).

ℹ Getting There & Away

A stream of buses flows between La Laguna's **Intercambiador Laguna Bus Station** (Avenida Ángel Guimerá Jorge) and Santa Cruz. Bus 015 (€1.45, 25 minutes) is best, as it'll take you straight to Plaza España. Buses 101, 102 and 103 also offer a regular service to Puerto de la Cruz (€4.10, one hour). If La Orotava (€3.15, 1½ hours) is your next destination, take bus 62.

The very handy tram system (www.metro tenerife.com) also links La Laguna with central Santa Cruz (€1.35, 40 minutes).

San Andrés

The village of San Andrés, all narrow, shady streets lined with fishers' cottages painted in primary colours, is a short 6km drive northeast of Santa Cruz. It is distinguished by a now-crumbled 18th-century round tower, the **Castillo de San Andrés** (which played a role in the Battle of Santa Cruz de Tenerife in 1797, when Horatio Nelson lost much of his right arm), plus some good seafood restaurants and **Playa de las Teresitas**, the superb beach just north of the village. The drive from Santa Cruz takes you along the southern flank of the impressive Anaga mountains.

ℹ Getting There & Away

There are frequent 910 buses (€1.25, 20 minutes) from Santa Cruz to San Andrés, continuing on to Playa de las Teresitas.

TASTY TENERIFE

Tenerife's cuisine has moved on dramatically, and today the island's restaurant scene is home to five restaurants with six Michelin stars between them.

Don't confuse the traditional culinary fare of Tenerife with that of the Spanish mainland; there are distinctive differences, although the ubiquitous tapas of Spain are common here also. The cuisine reflects Latin American and Arabic influences, with more spices, including cumin, paprika and dried chillies, than the Spanish norm.

As on the other islands, the staple product par excellence is *gofio,* toasted grain that takes the place of bread and can be mixed with almonds and figs to make sweets. The traditional *cabra* (goat) and *cabrito* (kid) remain the staple animal protein. The rich, gamey *conejo en salmorejo* (rabbit in a marinade based on bay leaves, garlic and wine) is common, as well as stews (*potaje, rancho canario* or *puchero*). Fish is also a winner, with the renowned horse mackerel *(chicharros)* of Santa Cruz de Tenerife even lending their name to the city's residents: the *chicharreros*.

Also recommended is the *sancocho canario,* a salted-fish dish with *mojo* (a spicy salsa based on garlic and red chilli peppers). This sauce is the most obvious contribution to the Tenerife table, and is typically served with *papas arrugadas* (wrinkly potatoes; small new potatoes boiled and salted in their skins).

The wine of Tenerife is starting to earn more of a name for itself. The best-known, and first to earn the DO grade (Denominación de Origen) is the red Tacoronte Acentejo. Also worth a tipple are the wines produced in Icod de los Vinos and Güímar. Other local tipples include La Dorada lager-style beer brewed in Santa Cruz de Tenerife, and the Canary Islands' first ecological craft brewery, based in Los Realejos: Tierra de Perros (www.facebook.com/CervezaArtesanalTierraDePerros), producing pale ale and stout.

Anaga Mountains

The splendidly rugged Anaga mountains, sprawling across the far northeast corner of Tenerife, offer some of the most spectacular scenery and hiking trails on the island. If hiking isn't your idea of fun, you can still get a feel for the mountains by driving the numerous switchbacks along the TF-12 road, which links La Laguna and San Andrés. It's also worth making the short, and steep, detour to Taganana along the TF134.

Small roads connect the villages and settlements scattered among the peaks and valleys of this mountainous region. The ideal way to get around is to hire a car and take a day or two to explore Afur, Chamorga, Benijo and other hamlets, though most visitors start off by hiking the stunning trails around Cruz del Carmen.

◉ Sights & Activities

There's little to see in the small town of Taganana, but it's only a few more kilometres north to the coast and Roque de las Bodegas, which has a number of small restaurants and bars. Local surfers favour its beach – and, even more so, the rocky strand of Almáciga, 1.25km east.

Hiking

For serious exploration of these mist-shrouded peaks, you need to leave the road behind and strike out on foot. The main visitors centre is the **Centro de Visitantes** (⌨922 63 35 76; www.gaprural.com; ⊙9.30am-4pm) at Cruz del Carmen, which sits a little under halfway between La Laguna and Taganana on the TF12 road. Filled with tweeting birds you'll never actually see, the laurel forests surrounding the visitors centre are a jungle of twisted trees coated in moisture-retaining mosses. Through this forest wind several well-marked trails, including a five-minute trail suitable for wheelchairs and strollers. Another easy walk (1.8km; approximately 30 minutes return) is to the **Llano de los Loros** – a stunning viewpoint. The visitors centre can supply details of these and more taxing walks in the area.

✖️ Eating

⭐ **La Ola**   INTERNATIONAL €

(⌨922 59 03 06; Caserío Roque de las Bodegas 12; mains €9-12; ⊙11am-5.30pm Tue-Sun) This restaurant is located away from the usual tourist beach spots, and is all the better for ploughing its own furrow. Beyond the

owner's conscientious and helpful service, there's a short menu of tasty meals using locally sourced and very fresh ingredients, including Canarian roasted pork, prawns with garlic, homemade hamburgers, cod cannelloni with prawn sauce, black rice and some vegetarian offerings.

❶ Getting There & Away

Buses 76 (€1.45), 77 (€1.45), 273 (€1.45) and 275 (€1.45) run from La Laguna to the Centro de Visitantes at Cruz del Carmen. Bus 76 continues to Afur (€1.45). From Santa Cruz, bus 946 (€1.25) runs to Taganana and then on to Almáciga, past Roque de las Bodegas. For Chamorga, take bus 947 (€1.25) from Santa Cruz.

NORTH COAST TENERIFE

The north coast of Tenerife presents an entirely different complexion to the sun-baked, resort-encrusted south coast: geographically, culturally and climatically. A more cultured atmosphere reigns and a greater diversity is present in the landscape. The weather is a bit cooler and more unpredictable, with slightly more rain, though you'll get loads of sun too. Even individual towns enjoy their own micro-climates – it can be raining in one town while the sun still shines on an adjacent village.

Puerto de la Cruz

POP 29,500

Scenically and languidly spread over the slopes of north Tenerife, Puerto de la Cruz is the elder statesman of Tenerife tourism. Its history of welcoming foreign visitors dates back to the late 19th century, when the

Puerto de la Cruz

200 m
0.1 miles

ATLANTIC OCEAN

Plazoleta de Benito Pérez Galdós

Puerto Pesquero

Plaza Europa

Plaza Charco

Playa Martiánez (300m)

Playa Martiánez

Av Colón

Train to Loro Parque

Paseo San Telmo

C Obispo Pérez Cáceres

count y Molina

C la Hoya

C Iriarte

C Iriarte

Av Familia Betan

C Dr Pisaca

C Valois

Barranco Martiánez

Camino Robado

Mirador de la Paz (550m);
Hotel Botánico Spa (750m);
Jardín Botánico (1km)

Risco Belle Aquatic Gardens

Parque Taoro

Carretera de Taoro

C Zamora

C Esquivel

C Cólogan

C B Miranda

randa

C Quintana

C Lonjas

C Santo Domingo

C Agustín de Béthencourt

C San Juan

C Iriarte

Torreón de Ventoso

C Valois

C Valois

C Blanco

C Nieves Ravelo

C Cupido

C Lomo Nieve

C Canino

Tito's Bodeguita (2.7km)

C Perdomo

C de Pérez Zamora

C Mequínez

C Cruz Verde

C Lomo

C San Felipe

C Teobaldo Power

C Puerto Viejo

C Peñón

C Dr Ingram

C Mazaroco

C Pozo

Av Melchor Luz

C Peñita

C Mequínez

Av José del Campo Llarena

Paseo Luis Lavaggi

Barranco San Felipe

Loro Parque (900m)

Playa Jardín (250m)

1 ☉
2 ◎
3 ⌂
4 ◎
5 ✚
6 🏛
7 🏛
8
9 ◎
10 ●
11 ⊗
12 ✕
13 ✕
14 ✕
15 ✕
16 ✕
17 ✕
18 ✕
19 ◐
20 ✚
21 ✡

Puerto de la Cruz

cultured settlement was a spa destination popular with genteel Victorian ladies. These days the easy-going and relaxed town is a charming destination with genuine character and history. There are stylish boardwalks, beaches with safe swimming, traditional restaurants, a leafy central plaza, and lots of pretty parks, gardens and churches.

History

Until it was declared an independent town in the early 20th century, Puerto de la Cruz was merely the port of the wealthier area of La Orotava. Bananas, wine, sugar and cochineal (dye-producing insects) were exported from here, and a substantial bourgeois class developed in the 1700s. In the 1800s the English arrived, first as merchants and later as sun-seeking holidaymakers, marking the beginning of the tourist transformation that characterises the town today.

◎ Sights

The **Plaza Europa**, a balcony of sorts built in 1992, may be a modern addition, but it blends well with the historic surroundings and is a good place to start your visit. The tourist office is also conveniently here, located in the 1620-built **Casa de la Aduana** (Calle Lonjas; ⊙ 9am-8pm Mon-Fri, to 5pm Sat & Sun), the old customs house not far from the water. Just to the east is the **Ayuntamiento** (Town Hall) as well as a handful of churches and Canarian mansions.

Museo de Arte Contemporáneo   GALLERY
(Casa de la Aduana, Calle Lonjas; adult/child €1.50/ free; ⊙ 10am-2pm Mon-Sat) The first contemporary art museum to open in Spain, dating from 1953, this well-displayed collection includes outstanding foreign, Spanish and Canarian artists such as Will Faber, Óscar Domínguez and César Manrique. The setting, in the historic former customs house, is almost as inspiring as the artwork.

Museo Arqueológico   MUSEUM
(www.museosdetenerife.org; Calle Lomo 9; adult/ child €1/free; ⊙ 10am-1pm & 5-9pm Tue-Sat, 10am-1pm Sun) This small but well laid-out museum provides an insight into the Guanche way of life with its replicas of a typical cave dwelling, as well as a burial cave where pots and baked-clay adornments share the same burial area, demonstrating the Guanches' belief in an afterlife. The most interesting exhibit is a tiny clay idol – one of only a few ever found.

Plaza Charco   SQUARE
The magnificent central square of Plaza Charco (the names translates as 'Puddle Plaza' – it used to flood from the sea every time it was stormy) is shaded by Indian laurel trees and Canary palms. It's the town's meeting-and-greeting place, with kiosks, benches and a children's playground, and is flanked by relaxing bars and restaurants.

**Iglesia de Nuestra Señora
de la Peña de Francia**   CHURCH
(Calle Quintana; ⊙ 8am-6pm) This pretty 17th-century church boasts three naves, a wooden Mudéjar ceiling and a carved wood effigy of Gran Poder de Dios, one of the town's most revered saints, carved in around 1706. Side chapels include one dedicated to the Virgen del Carmen. The church is fronted by lush and attractive landscaped

TENERIFE PUERTO DE LA CRUZ

gardens, decorated with flowers, palms and *drago* (dragon) trees.

Ermita de San Juan
MONASTERY

(Calle San Juan 7) Built between 1599 and 1608, Ermita de San Juan is the oldest structure in town and is attached to the Iglesia de San Francisco (⊘10am-9.30pm).

Castillo de San Felipe
CASTLE

(☑922 37 30 39; Paseo Luis Lavagi 12; ⊘10am-1pm & 5-8pm Tue-Sat) This modest but imposing castle beside Playa Jardín plays host to a variety of temporary art exhibitions over two levels, plus regular theatre and dance performances. There is also a grand piano on the ground floor, if you fancy showing off your arpeggios.

★ Jardín Botánico
GARDENS

(☑922 92 29 81; Calle Retama 2; adult/child €3/free; ⊘9am-6pm; P) Established in 1788, this magnificent botanical garden has thousands of plant varieties from all over the world and is a delightful place to while away an afternoon smelling the roses. As well as the major collections of tropical and subtropical plants, there's a wide variety of palms, a fragrant herb garden and a giant 200-year-old Australian Moreton Bay fig. The garden is well signposted if you are driving. Alternatively, the majority of interurban buses make a stop near here on their way out of town, or a taxi will cost around €8.

★ Risco Belle Aquatic Gardens
GARDENS

(Parque Taoro; adult/child €4/free; ⊘9.30am-6pm; P) This is not just any old garden: step through the entrance and you'll be met by a sweeping lawn punctuated with tables and chairs, tropical plants (birds of paradise and poinsettias) and citrus trees. In the historic main house there's a cafe serving drinks and snacks. For a small admission fee you can also visit the magnificent aquatic gardens with herons, dragonflies, a mock lookout tower and benches for quiet contemplation.

Playa Martiánez
BEACH

(Avenida Colón) The long and sandy Playa Martiánez is at the eastern end of town, where a large jetty filters the anger of Atlantic swells and turns them into mere gentle rollers, perfect for learning to surf on. As with other beaches in town, the sand is black and volcanic, consisting of small particles of basalt.

Sitio Litre Garden
GARDENS

(www.jardindeorquideas.com; Camino Robado; adult/child €4.75/free; ⊘9.30am-5pm) This delightful garden is exquisitely laid out with walkways, fountains, tropical and subtropical plants and flowers, plus the oldest *drago* tree in town. The highlight is the orchid walk through the greenhouse, with its well-displayed and signed orchids. There's an inviting terrace cafe and a (surprisingly tacky) gift shop. The gardens have an interesting British history, which you can read about in the free leaflet.

🏃 Activities

Lago Martiánez
SWIMMING

(☑922 37 05 72; Avenida Colón; adult/child €3.50/1.20; ⊘10am-sunset) Designed by Canario César Manrique, the watery playground of Lago Martiánez has four saltwater pools and a large central 'lake'. It can get just as crowded as the surrounding small volcanic beaches. Swim, sunbathe or grab a bite at one of the many restaurants and bars.

Hotel Botánico Spa
SPA

(☑922 38 14 00; www.hotelbotanico.com; Avenida Richard J Yeoward 1) This exclusive Hotel Botánico has a spa centre offering wellness therapies and treatments, plus a pagoda surrounded by lush gardens for traditional Thai massage, and a hammam (Turkish-style steam bath).

🎓 Courses

Don Quijote
LANGUAGE

(☑922 36 88 07; www.donquijote.org; Avenida Colón 14; 1-week intensive course €185, enrolment €55, textbook €35) Nationwide organisation offering private or group classes in Spanish, including courses for over-50s (with weekend activities tailored to that age group).

🎉 Festivals & Events

Carnaval
CULTURAL

Not to be outdone by Santa Cruz, Puerto de la Cruz stages its own riotous Carnaval celebration each February.

San Juan
RELIGIOUS

(⊘23 Jun) Held on the eve of the saint's day. Bonfires light the sky and, in a throwback to Guanche times, goats (and other animals) are dragged to the sea off Playa Jardín for a ritual bathing, in a practice that some visitors may find objectionable.

Fiesta de los Cacharros
CULTURAL

(⊘29 Nov) Held in Puerto de la Cruz (as well as Taganana and Icod de los Vinos), this is a quaint festival where children rush through the streets, dragging behind them a string of old pots, kettles, pans, car spares, tin cans – just about anything that will make a racket, all in honour of San Andrés (St Andrew).

✕ Eating

Puerto de la Cruz is a serious foodie destination. Peruse the former fishers' quarter of **La Ranilla**, just a couple of streets north of Plaza Charco, for the town's most innovative restaurants.

Tapas Arcón
TAPAS €

(Calle Blanco 8; tapas €3-4.50; ⊗noon-3.30pm & 6-11pm Wed-Mon) This place is a bit of a gem. The must-have tapas are the *papas arrugadas* (wrinkly potatoes) with *mojo* (spicy salsa) and the Arcón special sauces of almond and sweet pepper or parsley and coriander, but the whole menu is solid.

Rosa Negra
TAPAS €

(📱822 10 74 08; Calle la Hoya 30; tapas from €4.50; ⊗11.30am-10pm Mon-Fri) At this small, popular tapas bar beneath Calle la Hoya's palm trees, you can take a seat under a parasol out front and watch the Puerto de la Cruz life go by while devouring some good-value, decent tapas. Partake in *papas arrugadas*, *chistorra* (Canarian sausage), *calamares a la Romana* (fried squid), *pimientos de padrón* (Padrón peppers) and more.

Bodega Julian
CANARIAN €

(📱686 556315; Calle Mequínez 20; mains €4.50-10; ⊗6-11pm Mon-Sat) If you've grown weary of voluminous multilingual menus that read like a ledger, the reassuringly snappy list here is a refreshing change. The time-tested specialties of the house that keep people coming back include a succulent roast lamb main (€10), and the live music performed by the husband and wife owners, an accomplished guitarist and singer respectively. Reservations recommended.

Malaika
VEGAN €

(📱922 19 57 14; Calle Mequínez 49; mains €4-10; ⊗10am-5pm Wed-Sun; 🖋) This bright new spark is all bare-wood tables, green cushions, spruce lines, sunny service and wholesome, vegan food. The menu is short, but sound choices include the vegan hamburger, red lentil soup with curry, and the vegan lasagna.

★ Tito's Bodeguita
CANARIAN €€

(📱922 08 94 36; www.titosbodeguita.com; Camino de Duraznol; mains €10-16; ⊗12.30-11pm Mon-Sat) Despite the mildly off-putting location off a busy roundabout a few kilometres south of the town centre, the patios, flower-filled

gardens and atmospheric interior of this 18th-century country mansion, restaurant and winery are a delight. Portions are huge and best for sharing, with dishes based on traditional Canarian cuisine with an innovative twist. It's hugely popular so book ahead.

Regulo
CANARIAN €€

(📱922 38 45 06; Calle de Pérez Zamora 16; mains €14-19; ⊗12.30-3pm & 6-10.30pm Tue-Sat) The setting is fairy-tale atmospheric: a 200-year-old building with creaky, uneven floors, rustic antiques and small dining rooms covering three floors, set around a leafy central courtyard. The Canarian cuisine attracts a reassuring mix of locals and tourists – the sophisticated yet not over-complicated dishes include salmon in champagne, Camembert-stuffed beef fillet in pepper sauce, and fish baked in salt.

Restaurante Mil Sabores
MEDITERRANEAN €€

(📱922 36 81 72; Calle Cruz Verde 5; mains €9-16; ⊗noon-11pm Fri-Wed) Styling itself as a temple to modern Mediterranean cooking, this flash, blue-fronted restaurant has the looks and the tastes down to a fine art. Expect dishes like homemade quiche with roasted vegetables, avocado with tiger prawns or Iberian ham croquettes, and a perfectly combined mix of pork, apple and bacon. It's quite dressy, without being formal. Reservations recommended.

La Cofradía de Pescadores
SEAFOOD €€

(📱922 38 34 09; Calle Lonjas 5; mains €12-20; ⊗noon-3pm) Come here for the catch of the day – or buy it at the fish stall next door and cook it yourself. Watch the cost though, as some fish dishes are priced per weight. The back terrace has appropriate fishing harbour views.

🍷 Drinking & Entertainment

Puerto de la Cruz has a steamy Latino club scene, with several bars and nightclubs on Calle Obispo Pérez Cacéres.

★ Ebano Café
CAFE

(📱922 38 86 32; Calle la Hoya 2; ⊗9am-11.30pm; 🖥) This cafe is located in a beautiful building seasoned with an age-old patina and with plenty of original features. It's equally ideal for sipping a cocktail or surfing the web with a decent cappuccino. Sit outside in one of the comfy wicker chairs (they get taken quickly so you may need to move fast), within confessional distance of the church. Tapas is also served.

Agora COCKTAIL BAR
(Plazoleta de Benito Pérez Galdós 6; ⊙10am-
12.30am Tue-Sun, 3-11pm Mon; 🐾) This easy-
going (but ever-popular) cocktail bar and
cafe exudes a chilled-out vibe, with art exhibitions, books to borrow, magazines to read
and tables overlooking one of the prettiest
squares in town. It's a lovely spot for a dose
of early morning sun while relaxing in a bamboo chair out front. To eat there's tapas, and
come evening the cocktails start from €4.

Abaco CONCERT VENUE
(📋922 37 01 07; www.abacotenerife.com; Casa
Grande, El Durazno; ⊙1-4pm & 6.30-11pm) This
sumptuous historical mansion, about 1.5km
southeast of the town centre, hosts classical-music concerts on Sunday evenings and
traditional Canarian folklore concerts on
Wednesdays. The interior, with its period
furniture, original artwork and ornate finishes, is a delight. There's also an inviting
Sky Sports–free bar, although a round of
drinks will cost a lot more than the round-
trip taxi ride back to town.

The house museum (€10) can be explored
with a guide between 10am and 1.30pm
every day except Tuesday and Sunday.

Blanco Bar LIVE MUSIC
(📋620 955197; www.blancobar.com; Calle Blanco 12; ⊙8pm-3am Sun-Thu, 9pm-5.30am Fri &
Sat; 🐾) As well as live music, there are also
comedy acts here, which may not tickle your
funny bone unless you speak Spanish (check
what's on via the website beforehand). It has
a great atmosphere, with inexpensive drinks
and free entry to many (but not all) concerts.
It also hosts art exhibitions.

ℹ Information

Tourist Office (📋922 38 60 00; www.todo
tenerife.es; Casa de la Aduana, Calle Lonjas 5;
⊙9am-8pm Mon-Fri, to 5pm Sat & Sun)

ℹ Getting There & Away

Buses leave from Calle Hermanos Fernández
Perdigón (south of the former bus station,
which now stands derelict). There are frequent
departures for Santa Cruz (€5.25, 55 minutes).
Bus 103 is direct while bus 102 calls by Tenerife
Norte Airport and La Laguna. Bus 30 (30 minutes) also runs to Tenerife Norte Airport.

Other popular routes include bus 348 to El Teide (€6.20, 1½ hours, 9.15am, returning at 4pm).
Bus 343 runs to Costa Adeje (€14.60, two hours,
six daily), via Los Cristianos. Bus 345 offers a
half-hourly service from 7.15am to 8.40pm to La
Orotava (€1.45, 20 minutes).

ℹ Getting Around

The long-distance buses starting in or passing
through Puerto de la Cruz often double up as
local buses. Otherwise, taxis are widely available
(a 15-minute ride should cost around €5).

Bike Spirit (📋822 04 42 58; www.bikespirit.
es; Calle Mequínez 49; bikes per day from €20;
⊙9.30am-2pm & 5-8pm Mon-Sat) has mountain and road bikes for hire, as well as tours.

La Orotava
POP 41,720

Along with La Laguna, La Orotava is one
of the loveliest towns on Tenerife, and one
of the most truly 'Canarian' places in the
Canary Islands: cobblestone streets, flower-filled plazas and more Castilian mansions
than the rest of the island put together. The
lush valley surrounding the town has been
one of the island's most prosperous areas
since the 16th century. Most churches and
manor houses were built in the 17th century
(with some dating back to the 16th century).
The valley is a major cultivator of bananas,
chestnuts and grapes (as in vineyards), and
is also excellent hiking country: a maze of
footpaths lead into Canarian pine woods,
with 1200m views down over the coastal
plain. The tourist office can advise on routes.

◎ Sights

Traditional mansions are flanked with ornate wooden balconies like pirate galleons
and surrounded by manicured gardens. Plaza de la Constitución, a large, shady plaza,
is a good place to start exploring. On the plaza's northeastern side is the Iglesia de San
Agustín (⊙hours vary), a simple church with
a carved wooden ceiling.

⭐ **Casa de los Balcones** HISTORIC BUILDING
(www.casa-balcones.com; Casa Fonesca, Calle San
Francisco 3; courtyard & museum €5; ⊙8.30am-
6.30pm) This ornate mansion, dating to 1632,
has a sublime setting, with balconies set
around a picturesque central courtyard and
also decorating the front of the building. An
upstairs museum is dedicated to historical
items that recreate how the house would
have looked, while another room is devoted
to lacework. Bypass the Chinese imports to
admire the fine local needlework; there may
well be a demonstration taking place.

⭐ **Jardínes del Marquesado
de la Quinta Roja** GARDENS
(Plaza de la Constitución; ⊙9am-8pm Mon-Fri,
9.30am-8.30pm Sat & Sun) FREE Also known as

La Orotava

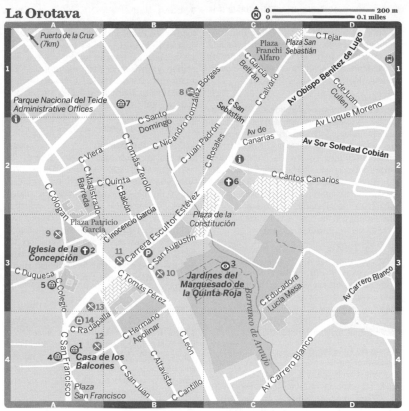

La Orotava

the Jardín Victoria, these French-influenced 18th-century gardens cascade in terraces down the hillside and are crowned by a small marble mausoleum, built as a tomb for the Marqués de la Quinta Roja. However, apparently his wife and mother disagreed about where to lay his body when he died, so the crypt was not used for its original purpose, and no one knows what (or who) lies within.

★ **Iglesia de la Concepción**　　CHURCH
(www.concepcionorotava.info; Plaza Patricia García; ◔9am-8pm) This magnificent church, located right in the centre of town, dates to 1516, although it was destroyed by earthquakes in

1704 and 1705 and rebuilt in 1768. Today it is recognised as one of the finest examples of baroque architecture in the entire Canaries archipelago, with its three-fronted facade and three 24m-high bell towers. The interior is awe-inspiring, with its carved woodwork, stonework and gorgeous stained glass.

Casa Lercaro HISTORIC BUILDING
(📞922 33 06 29; www.casalercaro.com; Calle del Colegio 5-7; ⊙restaurant 9am-7pm Mon-Thu, to 6.30pm Fri, 10am-midnight Sat) This 16th-century mansion is widely considered to be the most representative building constructed in traditional Canary Island style. Particularly noteworthy is the finely carved baroque decoration on the woodwork, including the magnificent traditional balconies. The interior plant- and palm-filled courtyard is now a restaurant, while there's a decor shop and cafe too.

Casa del Turista HISTORIC BUILDING
(Calle San Francisco 4; ⊙9am-6.30pm) The building was a 16th-century convent and today houses an art gallery, a Tenerife pearl shop and an arts-and-crafts shop that includes a permanent display of a volcanic-sand carpet, typical of those produced for the Corpus Christi celebrations.

Museo de Artesanía
Iberoamericana MUSEUM
(Iberoamerican Handicrafts Museum; Calle Tomás Zerolo 34; adult/child €2/free; ⊙9am-6pm Mon-Fri, 9.30am-2pm Sat) Housed in the former Convento de Santo Domingo, this museum explores the cultural relationship between the Canaries and the Americas. Exhibits include a huge range of musical instruments, ceramics and various artefacts, many made in the countries of South America. There's also an excellent gift shop with a splendid array of choice.

⚡ Festivals & Events

Corpus Christi RELIGIOUS
Celebrated with extravagance in La Orotava (the date changes annually, but it's always in June), when an intricately designed, colourful floral carpet (made from petals, leaves and branches) is laid on the streets. In the Plaza de Ayuntamiento, a tapestry of biblical scenes is fashioned from El Teide coloured sands.

✕ Eating

Popular with tourists on day trips, La Orotava has tons of restaurants, mainly centred around the Plaza de la Constitución and near the Casa de los Balcones.

★**Bar la Duquesa** CANARIAN €
(Plaza Patricio García 6; mains €6.50-8.50; ⊙7am-4pm Mon-Fri, 8am-3pm Sat) Cooking since 1942, this friendly and popular family-run place has a pleasing interior of old photos, decorative gourds and farming utensils. The menu includes hearty local choices such as chicken soup, lentil stew, paella, stuffed peppers, grilled pork and salmon salad. There are outside tables on the cobbled road in the shadow of the church.

★**Relieve Restaurant** BAKERY €
(www.boutiquerelieve.com; Calle Carrera Escultor; cakes €0.80-2; ⊙7am-9.30pm) With such adorable delights as blueberry tart, moist double-chocolate brownies, macaroons, pastries and a wonderful selection of breads, this small but busy corner cafe and bakery is quite simply the best place in town for cakes and baked goodies. Try the specialty *patchanga*, a deliciously creamy custard-filled doughnut. There's also an ice-cream counter opening onto the street, and a decent tea selection.

Casa Egon BAKERY €
(Calle León 5; cakes €0.80-1; ⊙cake shop 10am-8.30pm Wed-Sun, to 4pm Tue, restaurant noon-8.30pm Wed-Sun) Founded in 1916, this is the oldest *pasteleria* (cake shop) in the Canaries and has happily maintained its stuck-in-a-time-warp ambience with custard-coloured paintwork, antique weighing scales, original floor tiles and woodwork, and much of the decor. The cakes include all-time local favourites like *anís*-based *roscos* and apple-filled *cabello de angel*. There is a simple, traditional restaurant out back.

★**Restaurante Victoria** INTERNATIONAL €€
(📞922 33 16 83; www.hotelruralvictoria.com; Calle Hermano Apolinar 8; mains €9-16; menú €11; ⊙1-3.30pm & 7.30-9.30pm; 🍴) A superb restaurant in Hotel Rural Victoria's elegant atrium. There's exemplary presentation and flair in such dishes as duck confit with saffron, and the Canarian classic, rabbit in *salmorejo* (a marinade of bay leaves, garlic and wine) with *mojo* potatoes, as well as the *mus de gofio con almendras* (gofio mousse with almonds).

Sabor Canario CANARIAN €€
(www.hotelruralorotava.es; Hotel Rural Orotava, Calle Carrera Escultor 17; mains €10-15; ⊙noon-3.30pm & 6-10pm Tue-Sat; 🍴) Exercise your taste buds with soul-satisfying traditional cuisine at this fabulous restaurant located in the lovely, leafy and light-filled patio of the Hotel Rural Orotava. The building – a wonderful old

Canarian townhouse stuffed full of memorabilia – is very much part of the experience. A set vegetarian menu (€15 to €17) means non-carnivores are not excluded.

🔒 Shopping

★ **Canarias Concept** ARTS & CRAFTS
(www.canariasconcept.com; Calle Carrera Escultor 23; ☺10am-7pm Mon-Sat) As the name implies, Canarias Concept sells solely Canarian-made crafts and products. It has a large showroom packed with jewellery, ceramics, artwork, handmade toys, ornaments, glazed tiles, soap, scarves and T-shirts, plus a gourmet section with goodies like palm honey, cactus-based spreads, *tortas de almendras* (almond biscuits) and local wines.

★ **MAIT** ARTS & CRAFTS
(Museo de Artesania Iberoamericana; ☑922 32 81 60; www.artenerife.com; Calle Tomás Zerolo 34; ☺9am-6pm Mon-Fri, 9.30am-2pm Sat) Housed in a former 17th-century convent, this museum shop sells a superb range of Ibero-American art and crafts, mainly from Central and South America. Ornaments and T-shirts from Mexico, Peruvian knitwear and nativity figures, Argentinian woven rugs, Colombian woven baskets, toys, jewellery and textiles are all displayed in a dazzle of vivid colour in a spacious and well-organised showroom.

ℹ️ Information

Parque Nacional del Teide Administrative Offices (☑922 92 23 71; www.reservas parquesnacionales.es; Calle Sixto Perera González 25; ☺9am-2pm & 3.30-6pm Tue-Sun) Register here to climb the El Teide summit.

Tourist Office (☑922 32 30 41; www.todo tenerife.es; Calle Calvario 4; ☺9am-5pm Mon-Fri) A well-marked tourist route of the town's major monuments starts here.

ℹ️ Getting There & Away

Parking in La Orotava is a nightmare. If you're not staying here it's far better to come by bus from Puerto de la Cruz. which is just 9km away. Bus 345 (€1.45, 20 minutes) leaves roughly every half-hour from 5.55am to 10.10pm, running to the bus station in the east of town. Walking is also possible, as La Orotava is only around an hour from Puerto de la Cruz.

Garachico
POP 6800

A gracious and charming settlement located in a deep valley flanked by forested slopes and a rocky coastline, Garachico has successfully – and lucratively – managed to retain its Canarian identity. There are no big hotels, possibly because there is no real beach (though swimming in the natural, volcanic coves along the rocky coast is a rare delight). Handsome and historic, Garachico gets its name from the imposing rock outcrop just offshore (*gara* is Guanche for 'island', and *chico* is Spanish for 'small').

Garachico was once an important commercial port, but its unfortunate inhabitants suffered a series of disasters that all but brought ruin to the hamlet: freak storms, floods, fires, epidemics and, in 1706, a major volcanic eruption that destroyed the port and buried half the town in lava. Just outside Garachico you can hike trails that follow the path of the disastrous lava flow.

◉ Sights

Plaza Libertad SQUARE
The soul of Garachico is the main Plaza Libertad, with its towering palm trees, heritage buildings, cafe tables and lively atmosphere.

Iglesia de Santa Ana CHURCH
(Calle Julio Rosquet Garcia; church & museum €1, plus tower €2; ☺10.30am-4pm Mon-Fri) Near the Plaza Libertad is the evocative and gorgeous Iglesia de Santa Ana, with a dominating white bell tower, original 16th-century doors, a lovely wooden ceiling and a museum. You can climb the bell tower for the €2 admission fee.

Parque de la Puerta de Tierra PARK
(Calle Juan González de la Torre) Another rare remnant of Garachico's volcanic activity is in the cute and lovingly well-tended Parque de la Puerta de Tierra, just off Plaza Juan González (aka Plaza Pila), where the **Puerta de Tierra** (Land Gate) is all that's left of Garachico's once-thriving port. The gate was once right on the water but thanks to the eruption it's now in the centre of town.

Castillo de San Miguel CASTLE
(Avenida Tomé Cano; adult/child €2/free; ☺10am-4pm) This squat stone fortress by the sea was built in the 16th century and contains photos and explanations of the area's flora and fauna, as well as a chronological history of Garachico. Climb the tower for excellent views of the town and coast.

🎊 Festivals & Events

Romería de San Roque RELIGIOUS
(☺16 Aug) This is Garachico's most important annual festival, when the town fills

with pilgrims (and partygoers) from all over Tenerife. San Roque (St Roch), the town's patron, was credited with saving the town from the Black Death, which arrived in 1601.

Eating

⭐Mirador de Garachico CANARIAN €€
(📞922 83 11 98; www.miradordegarachico.com; 17 Calle Francisco Martínez de Fuentes; mains €12-19; ⏱12.30-4.30pm & 6.30-10.30pm Fri-Tue; 🛜) This pleasing combo of contemporary bar and restaurant, plus tasteful art-and-crafts store, serves creative combinations such as venison in a chocolate-and-pepper sauce, and banana, spinach and smoked-fish croquettes. Top off your meal with the delightful passion-fruit shot.

ℹ Information

Tourist Office (📞 922 13 34 61; www.todo tenerife.es; Avenida República de Venezuela; ⏱10am-5pm) By the car park in the port area; has maps of the town (€1).

ℹ Getting There & Away

Bus 107 connects the town with Santa Cruz (€8.15, two hours), La Laguna, La Orotava and Icod de los Vinos, while bus 363 comes and goes from Puerto de la Cruz (€3.75, one hour, up to 20 daily).

CENTRAL TENERIFE

Parque Nacional del Teide

Standing sentry over Tenerife, formidable El Teide (Pico del Teide) is not just the highest mountain in the Canary Islands but, at a whopping 3718m, the highest in all of Spain and is, in every sense of the word, the highlight of a trip to Tenerife. The Parque Nacional del Teide, which covers 189.9 sq km and encompasses the volcano and the surrounding hinterland, is both a Unesco World Heritage site and Spain's most popular national park, attracting some four million visitors a year. The area is truly extraordinary, comprising a haunting lunar moonscape of surreal rock formations, mystical caves and craggy peaks.

El Teide dominates the northern end of the park. If you don't want to make the very tough five-hour (one-way) climb to the top, take the cable car.

This area was declared a national park in 1954, with the goal of protecting the landscape, which includes 14 plants found nowhere else on earth. Geologically the park is fascinating: of the many different types of volcanic formations found in the world, examples of more than 80% can be found here.

The park protects nearly 1000 Guanche archaeological sites, many of which are still unexplored and all of which are unmarked, preventing curious visitors from removing 'souvenirs'. Surrounding the peak are the *cañadas,* flat depressions likely caused by a massive landslide 180,000 years ago.

The park is spectacular at any time of the year. Most people attempt to climb to the summit in the summer – and with the weather being at its most stable then this makes perfect sense – but to really see the park at its pinnacle of beauty, the best time is early spring, when the lower slopes start to bloom in flowers and, if you're lucky, the summit area may still have a hat of snow. Many visitors, having driven up from the hot coastal plains, are surprised at just how cold it can be in the national park. Deep winter in particular can see heavy snow shutting the

---

TENERIFE FOR CHILDREN

Tenerife is a favourite destination for families as there are plenty of sights and activities to keep the kiddies amused and entertained. The culture here also celebrates children, who will be made welcome just about everywhere, including restaurants and bars.

The beaches in the southern resorts (as well as Puerto de la Cruz) are superb, with sandcastle-friendly sand and shallow waters. Older children can also enjoy water sports ranging from surfing to diving; many surfing and dive schools have novice classes for kids and are experienced at looking after their young charges. Don't forget to take the kids to the high seas on an organised whale- or dolphin-watching excursion, an experience they may never forget. Older children will also find hiking on Mt Teide a unique and fascinating event, especially with the latent volcanic drama.

If watery pursuits begin to pall, the southern resorts of Los Cristianos and Playa de las Américas equal theme-park heaven. Try Siam Park (p169).

MAPS & BOOKS

Among the best maps are those by Editorial Everest. There are several good hiking guidebooks to Tenerife, although, increasingly, companies are switching to online versions. Some of the best print hiking guides include *Walk! Tenerife* (3rd edition, 2017, with GPS tracking) and the accompanying *Tenerife Hiking Map*, both by David Brawn and published by Discovery Walking Guides; *Walk this Way Tenerife*, by Andrea and Jack Montgomery, a very useful and well-written resource; *Tenerife Landscapes*, by Noel Rochford and published by Sunflower (who also publish *Southern Tenerife and La Gomera Landscapes*); *Tenerife Car Tours and Walks*, also by Noel Rochford and published by Sunflower; and Rother Walking Guides' *Tenerife: The Finest Walks on the Coast and in the Mountains*, by Klaus and Annette Wolfsperger, with GPS tracking.

main roads through the park, and access to the summit can be closed for weeks on end.

◉ Sights

★ Pico del Teide MOUNTAIN

(☑ 922 01 04 40; www.volcanoteide.com; Carretera TF21; cable car adult/child €27/13.50; ☺ 9am-5pm, to 7pm Jul-Sep, to 6pm Oct; ℗) The cable car provides the easiest way to get up to the peak of El Teide. The views are great – unless a big cloud is covering the peak, in which case you won't see a thing. On clear days the volcanic valley spreads out majestically below, and you can see the islands of La Gomera, La Palma and El Hierro peeking up from the Atlantic. It takes just eight minutes to zip up 1200m.

Each cable car holds around 35 passengers and leaves every 10 minutes, but get here early (before noon) because at peak times you could be queuing for two hours if you haven't prebooked. Booking your ticket online will indeed save you pain: you'll need to purchase a slot at a specific time (aiming for the earliest slot is advisable so you can find parking, otherwise you may find yourself stranded if you are driving; alternatively factor in time finding somewhere to park into your schedule).

Also, a few words of warning: those with heart or lung problems should stay on the ground, as oxygen is short up here in the clouds. It's chilly, too, so no matter what the weather's like below, bring a jacket. Be aware that weather conditions often force the early closure of the cable car – strong winds can whip up suddenly and the cable car can stop running with very little notice. This is normally not a huge problem for casual visitors who've caught the cable car up the mountain as a park warden based at the top cable-car station will inform everyone that it's about to stop running, but for hikers climbing all the way up the mountain

and intending to take the cable car back down it can be a very serious issue indeed.

Roques de García NATURAL FEATURE

(TF-21; ℗) A few kilometres south of El Teide peak, across from the Parador Nacional, lies this geological freak show of twisted lava pinnacles, christened with names such as Finger of God and the Cathedral. The display is a consequence of various processes: old volcanic dykes eroding or solidified vertical streams of magma. The most bizarre overture is the **Roque Cinchado**, while to the west spread out the otherworldly bald plains of the **Llano de Ucanca**.

Note that the Roque Cinchado is eroding faster at the base than above, and one of these days it is destined to topple over.

It's also the most popular spot in the park and viewed by nearly 90% of visitors, so the car park is perennially jammed.

The 1½-hour trail that circles the rocks is still pretty well travelled, but there are some excellent, photogenic views and it's a terrific hike, with quite a steep section at the end.

Pico Viejo MOUNTAIN

Calling this mountain 'Old Peak' is something of a slight misnomer considering it was actually the last of Tenerife's volcanoes to have erupted on a grand scale. In 1798 its southwestern flank tore open, leaving a 700m gash. Today you can clearly see where fragments of magma shot over 1km into the air and fell pell-mell, while torrents of lava gushed from a secondary, lower wound to congeal on the slopes.

To this day, not a blade of grass or a stain of lichen has returned to the arid slope. The ascent of this peak is overlooked by most in the hurry to stand atop Spain, but those in the know often rate this as more impressive than the climb to the summit of Teide itself, and it's certainly much less busy (you may actually find yourself alone on the mountain). Pico Viejo also has the added advantage of not requiring any special permits.

Observatorio del Teide
OBSERVATORY

(www.iac.es; P) One of the best places in the northern hemisphere to stargaze is the Observatorio del Teide, just off the TF24 highway between La Laguna and the El Portillo Visitors Centre. Scientists from all over the world come to study here and at its La Palma sister observatory. Take a free tour from December to March and add your name to the list of those who've seen through the mammoth telescopes scattered here. You'll need to make an appointment first (see the website for more information).

Volcano Teide Experience (☑ 922 01 04 44; www.volcanoteide.com; tour €30) runs tours of the observatory and also offers a number of evening stargazing packages and full-moon walking tours in Spanish, English or German.

 Activities

Most casual visitors arrive by bus or car and don't wander far off the highway that snakes through the centre of the park, but that just means that everyone else has more elbow room to explore. There are numerous walking tracks marking the way through volcanic terrain, beside unique rock formations and up to the peak of El Teide.

For a family-friendly saunter around the Roques de García you won't need anything other than comfortable shoes and some warm clothes. For more ambitious hikes, though, you'll need proper walking boots and poles, warm clothes, some food and water and a map and compass.

If you intend to climb Teide or Pico Viejo in the winter, when thick snow is common, you'll need full winter hiking gear, including thick fleeces, a waterproof jacket, gloves, a hat and sunglasses. Poles are an essential item, and on some routes crampons wouldn't go amiss either.

There are strict rules about where you can and cannot walk in the park, and you must keep to the marked trails at all times (though some of these can be very vague on the less-frequented high-altitude trails). Most importantly don't underestimate Teide: it might not be the Himalayas but it's still a serious undertaking (especially in winter) and the ocean setting means that weather conditions can change astonishingly fast, sometimes forcing the sudden closure of the cable car (a serious issue for hikers ascending the mountain and expecting a ride back down).

Self-Guided Hikes

The general park visitor guide lists 21 walks, ranging in length from 600m to 17.6km, some of which are signposted. Each walk is graded according to its level of difficulty (ranging from 'low' – the most common – to 'extreme'). You're not allowed to stray from the marked trails, a sensible restriction in an environment where every tuft of plant life has to fight for survival.

You don't have to be a masochist to enjoy the challenge of walking from road level up to **La Rambleta** at the top of the cable car, followed by a zoom down in the lift, but neither should you take this walk lightly. People unused to serious hiking will find this a very strenuous walk. Get off the bus (request

---

ⓘ **CLIMBING TO THE SUMMIT – THE PAPERWORK**

For security and conservation reasons, there's a permit scheme in force that restricts the number of visitors who can climb to the summit to 200 a day. You can reserve your place online via www.reservasparquesnacionales.es (follow the links through to the Parque Nacional del Teide). You can make a reservation up to 2pm the day before you want to climb (as long as spaces are available), but it advisable to do this as early as possible as places are often booked out several months in advance.

You can choose from several two-hour slots per day in which to make your final ascent to the summit. In addition to the permit, take your passport or ID (as well as a copy) with you on the climb, as you'll probably be asked to produce it, and don't miss your allotted time or you won't be allowed beyond the barrier. Permits for the slot between 3pm and 5pm must be used before 4.30pm, otherwise they become invalid. Only 50 people are allowed on the trail at any one time. From the cable car it's about a one-hour walk to the summit.

Note that bad weather conditions can mean the closure of the summit for weeks at a time. The website gives details of any such closures and when the summit is next expected to be open to hikers.

FOUR FAB TENERIFE HOTELS

Hotel Alhambra (☑ 922 32 04 34; www.alhambra-orotava.com; Calle Nicandro González Borges 19; incl breakfast s €76-92, d €94-120, ste €136-150; ❄ 🛜 ☎) A gorgeous 18th-century La Orotava manor house filled with period furnishings and wonderful artwork.

El Jostel (☑ 672 400922; www.eljostel.com; Calle Santa Rosalia 73; dm/d €22/45; 🛜) This adorable four-room hostel in Santa Cruz has delightful period features, plus dorms with original shutters.

Hotel La Quinta Roja (☑ 922 13 33 77; www.quintaroja.com; Glorieta de San Francisco; s/d incl breakfast €88/122; ❄ @ 🛜) With its splendid earthy-toned walls facing Garachico's main plaza, this restored 16th-century manor house is wonderfully central.

Iberostar Grand Mencey (☑ 922 60 99 00; www.iberostar.com; Calle Dr José Naveiras 38; d/ste incl breakfast from €147/215; P ❄ 🛜 ❄) Santa Cruz' sole five-star is a swish first-rate choice; it's worth paying for a garden view.

the driver to stop) or leave your car at the small road-side parking area (signposted 'Montaña Blanca' and 'Refugio de Altavista') 8km south of the El Portillo Visitors Centre and set off along the 4WD track that leads uphill. En route, you can make a short (half-hour, at the most), almost-level detour along a clear path to the rounded summit of **Montaña Blanca** (2750m) from where there are splendid views of Las Cañadas and the sierra beyond. For the full ascent to La Rambleta, allow about five hours (one-way). If you're intending on taking the cable car back down, it's vital that you allow sufficient time (and have enough food supplies) to walk back down the mountain if the cable car has to close early. Alternatively, make the Montaña Blanca your more modest goal for the day and then head back down again (about 2½ hours for the round trip).

Another long but relatively gentle route is the 16km **Las Siete Cañadas** between the two visitors centres, which, depending on your pace, will take between four and five hours (note that you'll need transport waiting for you at the end of this walk).

Maybe the most spectacular, and certainly the hardest, walk in the park is the climb to the summit of **Pico Viejo**, then along the ridge that connects this mountain to Teide and then up to the summit of Teide. Allow at least nine hours for this hike (one-way) and be prepared to walk back down Teide again if the cable car is closed. In fact, for this walk it's actually better to walk to the Refugio de Altavista at 3270m on the first day, overnight there and then continue your ascent to the summit of Teide the following morning, as this will allow you most of the second day to descend Teide on foot if required.

ℹ Information

El Portillo Visitors Centre (☑ 922 92 37 71; www.reservasparquesnacionales.es; Carretera La Orotava-Granadilla; ⏱ 9am-4pm; 🛜)
Juan Évora Ethnographic Museum (☑ 922 92 23 71; TF-21; ⏱ 9am-3.45pm)
Parque Nacional del Teide Administrative Offices (p161) In La Orotava.

ℹ Getting There & Away

Surprisingly, only two public buses arrive at the park daily: bus 348 from Puerto de la Cruz (€6.20, one hour) via La Orotava, and bus 342 from Los Cristianos (€7, 1½ hours). Bus 348 departs at 9.30am, and bus 342 at 9.30am (or 9.15am from Costa Adeje); both arrive at the Parador Nacional, and leave again at 4pm.

The best way to visit is with your own car. There are four well-marked approaches to the park; the two prettiest are the TF24 coming from La Laguna and the TF21 from La Orotava (and Puerto de la Cruz). The TF21 is the only road that runs through the park, and the Parador Nacional, the cable car and the visitors centres are all off this highway. To see anything else, you have to walk. The TF21 continues on to Vilaflor, while the TF38 highway links the park with Chío and Los Gigantes.

Vilaflor

POP 1650

This pretty and largely idyllic town, on the sunny southern flanks of Mt Teide, claims to be the highest village in Tenerife and makes a superb base for explorations of Parque Nacional del Teide. Head for the main square, where all the places of interest are located, including shops selling local lacework, and traditional bars and restaurants. Duck into the 16th-century parish church as well, which honours Tenerife's one and only saint: San

Pedro. Just outside Vilaflor, the **Pino Gordo** (TF21; P) is a fabulous 800-year-old specimen of Canarian pine tree (*Pinus canariensis*), 45m tall and with a trunk girth of 9.8m (p216).

At cosy **El Rincón de Roberto** (☑922 70 90 35; Avenida Hermano Pedro 27; mains €7.50-19; ◷noon-6pm Mon, to 10pm Wed-Sat, to 9pm Sun; ☑), a husband-and-wife team prepares typical Canarian dishes like rabbit in *salmorejo* sauce, goat meat or pork ribs.

ⓘ Getting There & Away

Bus 482 (€3.05, 40 minutes) runs three times a day here from Los Cristianos. Bus 342 (€3.50, 50 minutes) runs once a day at 9.15am from Costa Adeje to Vilaflor, via Los Cristianos.

NORTHWEST TENERIFE

Punta de Teno

When Plato mistook the Canary Islands for Atlantis, it must have been because of places like Punta de Teno. This beautiful spot, jutting into the Atlantic and the most northwestern point on Tenerife, is no secret. But it retains a wildness that visitor numbers simply can't overturn. Waves crash against a black, volcanic beach, solitary mountains rise like giants in the background, and there are some to-die-for sunsets. You can fish off the point, splash along the rocky coast or just absorb the view.

Think twice about heading out here if there have been recent heavy rains, as mud-and rockslides are common.

Take the TF445 highway towards Buenavista del Norte from Garachico and keep following the signs to the Punta, around 7km further on. Note that the access road is not open to cars on weekends or holidays. If you want to visit on the weekends, take the bus from Buenavista del Norte. Bus 369 (€1, 25 minutes) runs to Punta de Teno every hour between 10.10am and 6.05pm on Thursday, Friday, Saturday and Sunday from Buenavista del Norte's bus station.

Santiago del Teide

POP 10,750

This small town sits just to the northwest of the Parque Nacional del Teide boundary, on the road between Los Gigantes and Garachico, making it a superb base for all of these places as well as for hikers. The immediate area is littered with superb hiking trails, which reach a crescendo of colour in spring when the cherry blossoms are in bloom; ask the **tourist office** (☑922 86 03 48; www. todotenerife.es; Avenida de la Iglesia; ◷9am-4pm Tue-Sat) for details. Bus 460 (€2.45, 35 minutes) runs eight times a day between Icod de los Vinos and Santiago del Teide.

Masca

Tiny Masca must be the most spectacular village in Tenerife. It literally teeters on the very brink of a knife-edge ridge and looks as if the merest puff of wind would blow the entire village off its precipitous perch and send it tumbling hundreds of metres to the valley floor. The approach to the village, up some heart-in-your-throat switchbacks, is one of the great Tenerife driving experiences (get here early to avoid the crowds).

🏃 Activities

Barranco de Masca   HIKING

A popular but demanding trek is down Barranco de Masca to the sea. Allow six hours for the return hike, or take bus 355 from Santiago del Teide to Masca at 10.35am, walk down the gorge then catch the **Excursions Marítimas** (☑922 86 21 20; fare €15) ferry back to Los Gigantes. The barranco was shut for maintenance at the time of research, though there were tentative plans to reopen it at some point in 2019 at research time; ask for details locally.

Parque Rural de Teno   HIKING

The rugge, beautiful Parque Rural de Teno is popular for hiking – if you don't want to go it alone, El Cardón provides guides, setting out

---

TO THE END OF TENERIFE

The northwest corner of Tenerife offers some spectacular unspoiled scenery. From Garachico, head west on the TF42 highway past Buenavista del Norte and down the TF445 to the wild and remote Punta de Teno (note that the road is closed on weekends and holidays).

You'll have to return to Buenavista to then take the TF436 mountain highway to Santiago del Teide. Curve after hairpin curve obligates you to slow down and enjoy the view. Terraced valleys appear behind rugged mountains, and Masca makes the perfect pit stop. When the highway reaches Santiago, you can head either north on the TF82 back towards Garachico, or south towards Los Gigantes, where signs point the way down to Playa de la Arena, a beach that's nearly as pretty as Punta de Teno, though it's more developed.

from Garachico, Los Silos or Buenavista del Norte on Wednesday and Saturday.

El Cardón   HIKING
(☑922 12 79 38; www.elcardon.com) This long-established and highly professional outfit arranges guided hiking excursions in the northwest of Tenerife, around Masca and to Pico del Teide. Sea kayaking and whale-watching are also offered, as is bicycle hire.

✷ Festivals & Events

Fiesta de la Consolación   CULTURAL
This festival takes place in the first week of December, when villagers wearing traditional dress bring out their *timples* (similar to ukuleles) and other instruments for an evening of Canarian music.

❶ Getting There & Away

Bus 355 (€1.45, 30 minutes) runs four times each day to/from Santiago del Teide.

Los Gigantes & Puerto de Santiago

POP 5750

These two settlements have merged into one along the coastline in an attractive melange that blends, in reasonably elegant fashion, with the contours of the land. The low-rise and quite low-key nature of Los Gigantes and Puerto de Santiago creates an entirely different world from Los Cristianos and Las Américas to the south, retaining pockets of traditional street charm and some majestic views along the rocky, cove-infested coast. Welcome, indeed, to one of the most attractive resort regions on Tenerife, with superb sunsets adding golden allure to a day of sunbathing or exploration.

Just to the north of Los Gigantes rises the staggering form of Acantilados de los Gigantes. The submerged base of these cliffs is a haven for marine life, making this one of the island's supreme diving areas.

◉ Sights

If you're looking for more sunbed space, head a short distance south to **Playa de la Arena** (Avenida Marítima), a volcanic beach that is popular with families; the settlements of Alcalá and Playa de San Juan are further south again along the coast. The hilly lanes away from the resort areas between the two settlements are also lovely to explore and can get you in step with the more traditional rhythms of the region.

★Acantilados de
los Gigantes   NATURAL FEATURE
(Cliffs of the Giants) These astonishing, dark rock cliffs soar sublimely 600m from the ocean, forging a magnificent natural geological spectacle right on the edge of Los Gigantes. Try to stop by when the sun sets for added wow factor. The best views of the cliffs are from out at sea (there's no shortage of companies offering short cruises) and from Playa de los Gigantes. You can clamber up and along to the end of Calle Tabaiba to a natural lookout point for superb views.

🏊 Activities

This is the best region on the island for diving, with abundant marine life, and is excellent for spotting whales and dolphins.

Los Gigantes Diving Centre   DIVING
(☑922 86 04 31; www.divingtenerife.co.uk; Los Gigantes Harbour; dive incl equipment rental €53, introductory dive €75; ☉9.30am-5pm Mon-Sat) This large and extensive centre is one of the better places in Tenerife for diving. A range of PADI courses are offered, up to Divemaster, as well as BSAC (British Sub-Aqua Club) courses. Snorkelling costs €25. There are discounts of €10 if you pay in cash.

Katrin Whale & Dolphin Tours BOATING
(☑922 86 03 32; www.dolphinwhalewatch.com;
Calle Poblado Marinero, Los Gigantes; 90min safari
€20; ⊙11am-4.30pm) A reputable outfit that
restricts passenger numbers to just 12 and
also takes out groups with special needs.
The *Katrin* is no longer operating, but the
owners have a new, slightly larger boat
called *Carolin Sophie* (with space for sunbathing on board). There are three departures per day, at 11am, 1.15pm and 4.30pm.
Private boat charter is also available.

Eating

★**Tas-k** TAPAS €
(☑922 86 23 28; Calle Guios 16a, Los Gigantes;
tapas €2.50-8; ⊙11am-11pm Tue-Sat) Be sure to
make a reservation at this superb spot hidden away down a lane near the port. Some
27 tapas fill the menu, from fresh salmon
tartar to croutons with anchovies, Iberian
cold cuts or simple bruschetta with tomato.
New dishes also appear every day – check
the blackboard for daily offerings.

El Mesón CANARIAN €€
(☑922 86 04 76; www.mesondomingo.com; Calle
La Vigilia, Puerto de Santiago; mains €10-14; ⊙7am-
10.30pm Mon-Sat; 🐾) Don't be put off by the
nine-language menu; locals rate this place
as one of the best in town, and the owner,
who's quite a character, could talk the hind
legs off a donkey. It serves an excellent array of seafood and traditional Canarian and
mainland meat dishes, including succulent
rabbit stew, excellent lamb shoulder and
whole suckling pig (with a day's advance
notice).

★**El Rincón de Juan Carlos** CANARIAN €€€
(☑922 86 80 40; www.elrincondejuancarlos.es;
Pasaje de Jacaranda 2, Los Gigantes; mains €15-
25, menús from €29; ⊙7-10pm Mon-Sat) One
of the island's best dining choices, this superb Michelin-starred restaurant is just off
the main plaza. There's a marked leaning
towards seafood: try the sumptuous grand
menú (from €60 with wine pairing), or go
for the Gillardeau No 3 oysters with apple,
crayfish in juice and sriracha, or tuna with
bordelaise sauce. Advance reservations are
absolutely crucial.

ℹ Information

Tourist Office (☑922 86 03 48; www.todo
tenerife.es; Avenida Marítima, Playa de la
Arena; ⊙9.30am-4.30pm Mon-Fri, to 12.30pm
Sat) In a small shopping centre across from
Playa de la Arena.

Tourist Office (www.santiagodelteide.org;
Avenida José González Forte 10; ⊙8am-2pm
Mon-Fri) A very small but helpful tourist infor-
mation hut in the busy heart of Los Gigantes.

ℹ Getting There & Away

Bus 473 comes and goes from Los Cristianos to
Puerto de Santiago (€4.45, 1¼ hours) and Los
Gigantes (€4.65, 1¼ hours), and bus 325 (€7.10,
1¾ hours, six daily) travels from Puerto de la
Cruz to Los Gigantes.

For those with their own vehicle, it's a well-
marked 40km drive from Los Cristianos. Buses
477 and 473 run regularly between Los Gigantes,
Puerto de Santiago, Playa de la Arena, Alcalá and
Playa de San Juan.

SOUTH COAST TENERIFE

Tourist epicentre and kilometre zero for the
majority of beach-towel-toting holiday-goers
on Tenerife, the south coast of the island is
a breathtaking sprawl of multipool resorts,
imported sand and poured-concrete architecture. It's a shimmering realm of theme
parks, full English breakfasts, all-you-can-eat
buffets, Irish pubs, retirees in T-shirts and
shades, mobility scooters, shopping centres,
Las Vegas–style kitsch, live music and pulsing
nightlife. In other words, it's not very Canarian at all, but if you're here for the sun, it's
an excellent base for water sports, swimming,
sunbathing and reclining under a parasol.

Los Cristianos, Playa de las Américas & Costa Adeje

POP APPROX 150,000

Don't forget to don your shades when you
first hit Tenerife's southwestern tip. You'll
need them, not just for the blinding sunshine, but also the accompanying dazzle of
neon signs and shimmering sand. Large resorts with all-you-can-eat buffets have turned
what was a sleepy fishing coast into a mega-
moneymaking resort area. The sweeping,
sandy beaches are some of the most lively and
child-friendly on the island so families love it
here. The nightlife is for those with high energy and high spirits, and there is a predictably
dizzying multitude of restaurants.

That said, the old town of Los Cristianos
still retains (just) the feel of a fishing village,
while just beyond is Playa de las Américas,
with its high-rise hotels, glossy shopping
centres and Las Vegas–style fake Roman

statues and pyramids. The Costa Adeje flows seamlessly north of here and is home to luxury hotels, sophisticated clubs and restaurants, and superb beaches.

⊙ Sights

★ Puerto de Los Cristianos   HARBOUR
(Los Cristianos) Playa de Los Cristianos' grand swathe of pale golden sand is flanked to the west by Puerto de Los Cristianos, a harbour that is home to fishing boats, private yachts and commercial boats offering everything from boat rides (including live-music jaunts) to big-game-fishing trips.

La Caleta   AREA
This resort area in Costa Adeje is located north of Playa del Duque and is anchored by several hotels, including the Sheraton La Caleta Resort and Spa. The main beach is Playa de la Enramada (p173), a length of black volcanic sand; you can also find the Mirador Stone Pebble Beach here, where visitors have piled up hundreds of pebble columns, making for excellent photos at sunset.

Siam Park   AMUSEMENT PARK
(☑902 06 00 00; www.siampark.net; Autopista Sur, exit 28; adult/child €37/25; ⊙10am-6pm May-Oct, to 5pm Nov-Apr; ℗) Southern Tenerife's biggest theme park is the impressive Siam Park, which offers a chance to throw yourself down a 28m-high vertical water slide, surf in a swimming pool, get spat out of the guts of a dragon and buy tat at a Bangkok-style floating market. Entry for tots under three is free.

🏃 Activities

Hiking

Barranco del Infierno   HIKING
(☑922 78 00 78; www.barrancodelinfierno.es; Calle de los Molinos; adult/child €8.50/4.25; ⊙entrance time 8am-2.30pm) This excellent hike begins near the Restaurant Otelo in Adeje, north of the village of Fañabé, and runs along a trail for 6.5km through the ravine. The return hike takes around 3½ hours. Note that only 300 people can enter the *barranco* daily so you must book your ticket and place online, and turn up in good time for your allotted slot.

Diving
The volcanic coast and calm waters here make for some superb diving; a standard dive runs upwards of €35.

Ola Diving Center   DIVING
(☑822 66 48 76; www.ola-aventura.com; Avenida de Colón, Costa Adeje; ⊙9am-5pm) Ola Diving Center offers possibly the most extensive

choice of diving courses in the region, including recreational, technical and cave diving. It also organises diving seminars, as well as courses from beginner to instructor level. Trial dives for beginners cost €65.

Boat Trips & Whale-Watching
Companies offering two-, three- and five-hour boat cruises to view whales and dolphins operate from the end of Playa de Los Cristianos, near the port, and in Puerto Colón in Costa Adeje. Most trips include food, drink and a quick swim, with a two-hour trip costing upwards of €18. Los Cristianos' tourist office (p172) has a list of boat-trip companies.

Chartering boats is also a popular choice, especially for groups; contact **Tenerife Sailing Charters** (☑627 069912; www.tenerifesailing charters.com; Calle Colón, Puerto Colón; per person adult/child from €59/38), based in Costa Adeje.

Travelin' Lady   BOATING
(☑640 531122; www.travelinladytenerife.com; Puerto de Los Cristianos; adult/child €25/10; ⊙9.30am-5pm Mon-Sat) Organises two-hour whale-watching trips and uses an enclosed propeller to prevent any injury to the mammals. Private charters are also available

Neptuno   BOATING
(☑922 79 80 44; www.barcostenerife.com; Calle Colón, Puerto Colón; 3hr boat tour adult/child €39/19.50; ⊙9am-9pm) This reputable company organises several boat tours, including a five-hour excursion on a traditional teak-hardwood sailing ship called *Shogun* (formerly owned by a sheikh), during which you are almost guaranteed to see dolphins and whales. It also includes an option to swim in the bay of Masca and enjoy a traditional paella lunch. A complimentary hotel shuttle service is available.

Horse Riding
Note that although there are several places that offer horse riding, not all are accredited and safe.

La Caldera del Rey   HORSE RIDING
(☑648 650441; Avenida Francia, Costa Adeje; 2hr trek €50; ⊙9am-8.30pm; 🐴) Located on a traditional Canarian farm in San Eugenio Alto, this excellent riding stable also has a children's petting farm, barbecue area, climbing wall and a low rope course for children.

Surfing
The best-known surf spot in town is the creatively named La Izquierda (Spanish for 'Left'), which is found just west of Playa de Troyo. A

Playa de las Américas

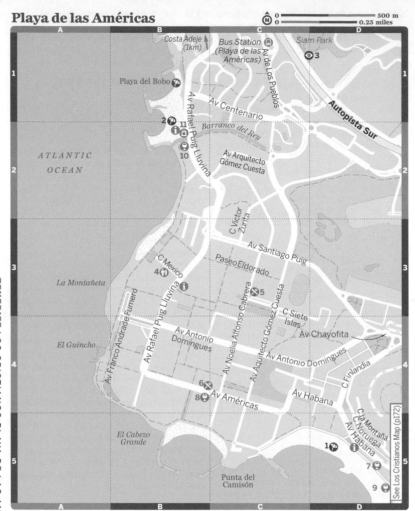

See Los Cristianos Map (p172)

long and easy left with some hollow sections, it's one of the most localised spots in Europe.

K-16 Surf
SURFING

(☑ 922 78 87 79; https://k16surf.com; Calle México 22, Playa de las Américas; surf lessons from €35, board rental per day from €15; 👶) This school hires out surfboards and provides tuition for only slightly more than the price of rental. For newbies, group surf initiation lessons are two hours (€35), a full course of five lessons is €150, and private surf lessons start at €70 for two hours. Kids and people with disabilities are also catered for. K-16 Surf sells skateboards and has two nearby surf shops.

🍴 Eating

The standard and variety of restaurants have improved over recent years. On the waterfront in Los Cristianos' port area is a row of kiosks, including **Pescadería Dominga** (fish €5-9; ⏰noon-7pm Mon-Fri, to 3pm Sat), selling fresh-off-the-boat fish.

⭐ El Cine
SEAFOOD €

(☑ 609 107758; www.grupoelcine.com/restaurante-el-cine; Calle Juan Bariajo 8, Los Cristianos; mains €7.50-13; ⏰11.30am-11pm) It's probably been said before, but El Cine deserves a medal for its inexpensive, simply prepared seafood. It's been here since the '80s, with a menu

Playa de las Américas

that's reassuringly brief; the fish of the day is always a good bet. The no-frills atmosphere and few tourists only adds to the appeal. It's tucked away in an elbow off the promenade and off the drag.

★**Sopa**   INTERNATIONAL €
(☑822 04 37 69; Calle Montaña Chica 2, Los Cristianos; salads & soups €4-7; ☺8am-8pm Mon-Sat, 8.30am-5pm Sun; ☏☑) This chilled-out space with sofas, comfy armchairs, and shelves of books and magazines provides the backdrop for a (largely vegetarian) menu of healthy soups, salads and burgers (spinach, that is). There are also delicious cakes. Try the cherry and marzipan for a real taste bud treat. The orange juice, coffee and tomato on toast (€3) is a steal for snackers.

★**La Pepa Food Market**   MARKET €
(☑922 79 48 85; Centro Comercial La Pasarela, Los Cristianos; snacks €2.50-5; ☺10am-11pm Mon-Thu, to midnight Fri-Sun; ☏) This gourmet food market has stalls including upmarket delis, a seafood counter, sushi, a pancakes and waffles stand, a wine bar and a vegetarian snack stall. There is plenty of seating on a vast terrace, with rooftop views that stretch to the sea, plus there's a children's playground.

★**Il Gelato del Mercado**   GELATO €
(Calle Dulce María Loinaz 1, Los Cristianos; gelato €1-3; ☺1-10pm Mon-Thu, noon-11pm Fri & Sat, noon-10pm Sun) This enterprising and popular hole-in-the-wall *gelateria* sells tubs and cones of superb gelato, concocted with natural and locally sourced ingredients, to help

cool off under the fierce Los Cristianos sun. Gelato comes in four sizes: *mini, piccolo, medio* and *grande*.

La Tapa   TAPAS €
(Calle Dulce María Loinaz, Los Cristianos; tapas €3.50; ☺noon-midnight Wed-Mon) Much loved by locals, buzzing La Tapa is appropriately (if unexcitingly) named, with 22 choices, including some traditional homestyle favourites such as tripe with chickpeas and chicken soup, plus fried seafood, prawns in garlic, meatballs, potatoes with aioli and much more.

★**Thai Botanico**   THAI €€
(☑922 /9 77 59; www.thaibotanicotenerife. com; Commercial Centre Safari, 1st fl, Avenida Américas, Playa de las Américas; mains €7.50-17; ☺1.30-11.30pm Mon-Sat, 6.30-11pm Sun; ☏) This enchanting choice is decorated with sumptuous decor and serves a large choice of well-crafted Thai dishes. Curries, stir-fries, salads, spring rolls, satay dishes and pad thai noodles...all the Thai favourites are here, well presented and delicately enhanced with fragrant herbs and aromatic spices. Reservations are essential.

La Torre del Mirador   CANARIAN €€
(☑922 71 22 09; www.latorredelmirador.com; Playa del Duque, Costa Adeje; mains €12-16; ☺12.30am-11.30pm Wed-Mon) This elegant bar and restaurant has a lovely terrace with flowers and palms and delightful sea views. The menu has several sound seafood choices, including king prawns in garlic and tuna cooked with onions. Or share a platter of *pimientos de padron* (small fried green peppers), the perfect accompaniment to a long cold *cerveza* after your promenade stroll.

Mesón Las Lanzas   SPANISH €€
(☑922 79 11 72; www.mesonlaslanzas.com; Avenida Noelia Alfonso Cabrera 8, Playa de las Américas; mains €7.50-18; ☺1-4pm & 7pm-midnight) Hurray. No sunbleached photos of chips-with-everything 'international' dishes on the pavement. Instead come here to enjoy traditional Spanish mains like *tigres* (deep-fried mussels), fresh fish of the day, roast shoulder of lamb or rabbit in *salmorejo*. The preparation is simplicity itself, just fresh and homely cuisine – don't miss it.

⬤ **Drinking & Entertainment**

Post-midnight, Los Cristianos' main action takes place at the Centro Comercial San Telmo, the shopping centre behind Playa de las Vistas. Look elsewhere if you're seeking somewhere classier. Many of the bars along the main Playa de las Américas strip have live music at weekends.

★**Papagayo** BAR, CLUB
(www.papagayobeachclub.com; Avenida Rafael Puig Lluvina, Playa de las Américas; ⊙10am-late; 🛜)
This neat-looking restaurant, bar and night-club oozes sophistication and good taste – it's the coolest on the strip. The decor is mostly

white, with kick-back seating facing the sun-set, shady canopies and a menu that's best for light dishes such as sushi. Come night-time the place shifts into fashionable nightclub mode, complete with slick professional DJs.

★**Bar el Pincho** BAR
(🗐922 79 77 19; Playa de las Vistas, Playa de las Américas; ⊙10.30am-9pm Mon-Sat) Come to

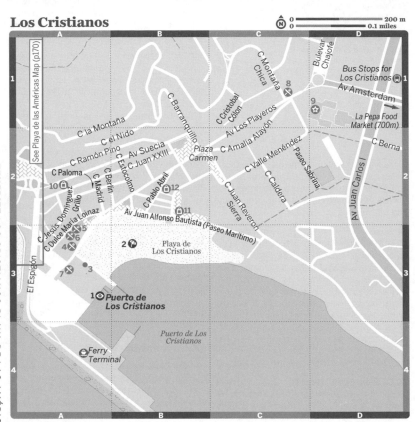

Los Cristianos

KNOW YOUR SOUTH-COAST BEACHES

Tenerife's south-coast beaches come complete with mojito-mixing beach bars and chic restaurants; for something more low-key, however, head to the beaches at the nearby towns of Las Galletas (p175) and El Médano (p175).

Playa de Los Cristianos This 1km-long taupe-coloured sandy stretch is the main beach in town and very family-friendly.

Playa de las Vistas A sublime 1.5km-long beach with fine golden sand (imported from the Sahara Desert!) and perfect swimming, linking Los Cristianos with Playa de las Américas.

Playa de Troya One of several beaches that merge seamlessly into each other in central Playa, with soft dark sand and excellent facilities.

Playa del Duque The 600m-long 'Duke's beach' is an appealing golden sandy stretch backed by restaurants.

Playa de la Enramada A dark volcanic beach with a great bar and hang-gliding.

bright-white-painted Bar el Pincho for a cocktail (€6) or gin and tonic (€6) at sunset. The mango daiquiris are the ideal accompaniment to the uninterrupted sand-and-sea views from the terrace above the boardwalk; the music's ace, too. During the day it's also an excellent choice for tapas, a coffee or a banana split (€6).

Chiringuito Coqueluche BAR
(Playa La Enramada, Costa Adeje; ⊗10am-11pm) Stroll along the promenade, past luxurious hotel gardens and around a small headland to the attractive dark-pebble beach of La Enramada, where you can sip a drink with sand between your toes at the cheerful local beach bar and watch the paragliders drift on by.

Hard Rock Cafe BAR
(☑922 05 50 22; www.hardrock.com; Avenida Américas, Playa de las Américas; ⊗noon-12.30am; 🕿) Part of the worldwide rock 'n' roll chain, with a buzzy vibe, music-themed decor and a stunning rooftop terrace with sea views beyond the palms. Regular live concerts and DJ sessions are held; check the calendar on the website.

Kiosco San Telmo BAR
(Playa de las Vistas, Playa de las Américas; ⊗9am-6pm) The antithesis of the brash drinking dens that still exist in this part of Tenerife, this simple wooden kiosk on the beach has all it needs to whip up a killer mojito. Perch on a stool for some beachside magic.

Centro Cultural THEATRE
(www.centroculturalcristiano.org; Plaza Pescador 1, Los Cristianos) Offers a variety of cultural events, such as Cine de Verano, a summer festival of open-air movies (in Spanish) that

show nightly except on Wednesdays. An auditorium acts as a concert venue.

🛍 Shopping

Librería Barbara BOOKS
(☑922 79 23 01; Calle Pablo Abril 6, Los Cristianos; ⊗10am-1.30pm & 5-8pm Mon-Fri, 10am-1.30pm Sat) A literary fixture, this bookshop was founded in 1984 and supplies avid readers with new and second-hand books in a medley of languages, plus magazines and children's titles.

Jamón y Mojo FOOD & DRINKS
(☑674 736901; Avenida Suecia 35, Los Cristianos; ⊗10am-11pm) Run by an enthusiastic young couple, this deli has a vast range of carefully sourced gourmet products, with an emphasis on Spanish delights such as wheels of crumbly Manchego cheese and several grades of chorizo and *jamón serrano*. They also make superb sandwiches using specialty breads, and carry an extensive selection of wines.

La Alpizpa ARTS & CRAFTS
(Avenida Juan Alfonso Batista, Los Cristianos; ⊗10.25am-8.15pm Tue, Thu, Fri & Sat, 11am-8.15pm Wed, 11am-4pm Sun & Mon) Right on the seafront, this shop standing all by itself sells an eye-catching range of high-quality and diverse arts and crafts created by people with disabilities, as well as local produce such as spicy *mojo* sauces and Canarian liqueurs.

Artenerife ARTS & CRAFTS
(www.artenerife.com; Avenida Rafael Puig Lluvina, Playa de las Américas; ⊗10am-5pm Tue-Fri, to 1pm Sat, to 6pm Mon) Part of an Tenerife-wide chain where quality control is very much in evidence, Artenerife carries a superb range

TENERIFE LOS CRISTIANOS, PLAYA DE LAS AMÉRICAS & COSTA ADEJE

Costa Adeje

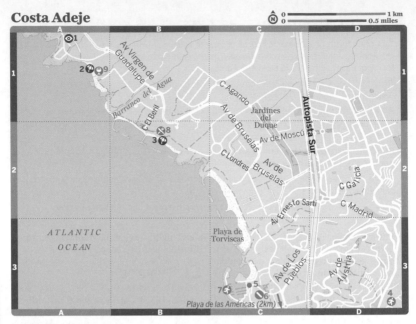

of quality handicrafts originating in the Canary Islands, including ceramics, jewellery and art, which make for excellent gifts.

❶ Information

There are tourist offices in **Playa de las Vistas** (☏ 922 78 70 11; ◷ 9am-4.30pm), **Playa de las Américas** (☏ 922 79 76 68; Avenida Rafael Puig Lluvina 15; ◷ 9am-4.30pm Mon-Sat) and **Costa Adeje** (☏ 922 71 65 39; www.costa-adeje.es; Calle Rafael Puig Lluvina 1; ◷ 8.30am-6pm) The Costa Adeje office is by the Barranco del Rey.
Orange Badge (p262) Wheelchair and mobility scooter hire, from a ground-floor office.

❶ Getting There & Away

BOAT

Ferries run by Fred Olsen depart from the **ferry terminal** (p139) for San Sebastián de la Gomera, Playa Santiago and Valle Gran Rey on the neighbouring island of La Gomera. Naviera Armas also serves La Gomera and sails to Valverde on El Hierro and Santa Cruz de la Palma on La Palma.

BUS

Plenty of Tenerife's bright-green TITSA buses come through the area. Bus 110 to Costa Adeje (direct, €9.45, one hour, every 30 minutes) passes through Los Cristianos and Playa de las Américas, and bus 111 (indirect, €9.45) comes and goes from Santa Cruz, travelling via Tenerife Sur Airport (€9.35). Bus 343 also goes from Costa Adeje to Tenerife Sur Airport (€3.70, 45 minutes). The same bus continues on to Tenerife Norte Airport (€12.40). Plenty of other buses run through the two resorts, en route to destinations such as Arona (bus 480), Los Gigantes (bus 473), Puerto de la Cruz (bus 343), El Médano (bus 470) and Las Galletas (bus 467).

The Playa de las América bus station is between central Las Américas, San Eugenio and the *autovía* (highway). In Los Cristianos, buses stop on Avenida Juan Carlos I, just beyond the crossroad with Avenida Amsterdam, opposite the Valdes Commercial Centre. For 24-hour bus information call 922 53 13 00.

❶ Getting Around

Most of the long-distance bus routes serve double duty as local routes, stopping along the major avenues of Los Cristianos and Playa de las Américas before heading elsewhere. There are taxi stands outside most shopping centres; a ride across town should cost between €6 and €8.

Las Galletas

Las Galletas is a small resort town a few kilometres south of the Las Américas strip and, in comparison, is as quiet as a Sunday afternoon in a library; for many people that is its attraction. A block back from the boardwalk, the leafy Rambla Dionisio González, with benches and playgrounds, leads to the tourist office and the sea. For simple tapas bars frequented by locals enjoying a tipple, head for the small streets leading off the central Rambla Dionisio González.

Playa Las Galletas   BEACH
Bring your own towel and parasol to this pleasant volcanic sand-and-pebble stretch. It's backed by a pleasant promenade with bars and excellent seafood restaurants.

Buceo Tenerife Diving Center   DIVING
(✉922 73 10 15; www.buceotenerife.com; Calle María del Carmen García 22; dive incl equipment rental €36; ☺9am-6pm) This well-established diving school offers discounts for multiple dives and has a good range of dive courses to suit novices to experts.

La Gaviota   SEAFOOD €€
(✉922 78 59 44; Calle La Marina 9; mains €10-15; ☺noon-10pm Thu-Tue) Continue east along the promenade and beyond to reach this atmospheric seafood restaurant set on the beach. There's a terrace out front under an awning, and at 6pm on Fridays a live Canarian guitarist and singer will accompany your *zarzuela* platter (seafood stew; €24 for two people).

Varadero Viejo   SEAFOOD €€
(✉822 14 46 52; www.restaurantevaraderoviejo. es; Calle el Varadero 26; mains from €13; ☺noon-10.30pm; ☎) This corner restaurant with a terrace is a sound choice for all manner of seafood: grilled, fried or oven-baked. The spaghetti with marinara sauce, mixed paella and fish casserole are all good options, with Tenerife wine as an accompaniment.

❶ Information

Tourist Office (✉922 73 01 33; www.todoten erife.es; Rambla Dionisio Gonzalez 1; ☺8.30am-3.30pm Mon-Fri, 9am-4pm Sat & Sun)

❶ Getting There & Away

Las Galletas is a few kilometres off the TF1, at exit 26. Bus 467 connects the town with Los Cristianos hourly (€1.50, 30 minutes).

El Médano

POP 1250

Yet to be crushed by development, El Médano is a world-class spot for kitesurfers. The laid-back atmosphere they bring with them gives the place a dab of bohemian character, and it's altogether a much more pleasant place to stay than nearby Las Américas.

◉ Sights & Activities

The sails of kitesurfers speckle the horizon here. There are several companies that offer classes and equipment hire, but novices should note that the winds are very strong and challenge even the pros.

Playa El Médano   BEACH
El Médano boasts the longest beach in Tenerife (2km), lined by a wooden boardwalk – ideal for evening strolls. The same wind that makes it good for kitesurfing and windsurfing makes it less than ideal for sunbathing.

Playa La Tejita   BEACH
Stretching for around 1km, this delightful unspoiled beach has a simple straw-roofed

GET ACTIVE ON TENERIFE

Possibly no other island in the archipelago offers so many opportunities to burn off calories than Tenerife. Windsurfing, kitesurfing, diving, hiking, fishing, golf and cycling are all not just possible here, but almost impossible to avoid. For water sports most facilities are concentrated in and around the southwestern resort areas, although the north coast has a wide variety of surf spots.

Many hiking trails criss-cross the island; some are historical paths used before the days of cars and highways. Keen walkers should avoid the peak summer heat of July and August. The best hikes:

➡ La Orotava (p158)

➡ Garachico (p161)

➡ El Teide (p163)

➡ Barranco de Masca (p166)

➡ Barranco del Infierno (p169)

➡ Anaga Mountains (p153)

bar for drinks and snacks and makes for tremendous photos as the sun rises over Montaña Roja (Red Mountain) just to the east. Find the beach just east of the main Playa El Médano; the first section is nudist.

Azul Kite School   KITESURFING

(☑922 17 83 14; www.azulkiteboarding.com; Paseo Mercedes Roja 26; 3hr course €145; ⊙11am-8pm Tue-Sat) A well-established school offering a range of courses for beginners, as well as for more advanced kitesurfers. A one-hour one-to-one lesson costs €50.

30 Nudos Kite School   KITESURFING

(☑922 17 89 05; www.30nudos.com; Paseo Nuestra Señora Mercedes de Roja 24; 3hr course €150; ⊙10am-8pm Mon-Sat) This superfriendly kitesurfing school with professional instructors has an excellent reputation.

✖ Eating

Imperio del Pintxo   TAPAS €

(☑922 17 63 04; www.imperiodelpintxo.com; 2 Paseo Marcial Garcia; raciónes €7-9.50; ⊙10am-midnight) This place is run by a young energetic team, with a view of the beach and kitesurfers. Come here for tasty tapas and *raciones* platters to share, such as vegetable tempura, goat's-cheese parcels in light flaky pastry, and prawns topped with a spicy *mojo* sauce.

★**Le Penon**   FRENCH €€

(☑922 17 97 77; Calle Tarajal 8; mains €10.50-22; ⊙1-3pm & 7-10.30pm Fri-Sun, 12.30-3.30pm & 7-10.30pm Wed, 7-10.30pm Tue & Thu; 🛜) A terrific choice with a superbly prepared menu of French seafood, meat dishes and tapas. Dishes such as the braised crispy squid cannelloni, duck breast with orange sauce or French and Basque cheeseboard are showstoppingly

---

ℹ TEN+ TRAVEL CARD

If you'll be travelling a lot by public transport then it is worth investing in a plastic Ten+ Travel Card (www.titsa.com), which can be used on all bus routes (except on Teide and Teno lines) and offers 30% off the trip fare. The travel card costs €2, with top-ups from a minimum of €5 to a maximum of €100, available at bus stations, tram-station vending machines and some newspaper kiosks. Swipe your card when you board and swipe off as you disembark (if you don't swipe your card when you get off you will be charged for the entire route). The same card can be used by several users.

---

tasty, but don't overlook the delightful *postres* (desserts). Vegetarians, the pumpkin risotto is delicious.

ℹ Information

Tourist Office (☑922 17 60 02; www.webtenerife.com; Plaza del Médano; ⊙9am-3pm Mon-Fri, to 1pm Sat) Maps covering four local walks.

ℹ Getting There & Away

El Médano is just east of Tenerife Sur Airport, off exit 22 of the TF1. Bus 470 leaves hourly to Los Cristianos (€3.60, one hour 35 minutes).

EAST COAST TENERIFE

This region is speckled with bright and colourful little villages, which bring life to the otherwise stark surroundings. The east coast of Tenerife is perhaps the forgotten coast, and at first glance that may be unsurprising as the landscape is dry and dusty. If you have the time, however, it definitely pays to uncover its pleasant low-key beach towns and the far more authentic local vibe that eludes the international resorts of the south coast.

Candelaria

POP 16,000

Just 18km south of Santa Cruz is this charming small fishing village famed for its Basílica de Nuestra Señora de Candelaria, home to a wooden statue of the Virgin of Candelaria called the Black Madonna, the patron saint of the entire Canary archipelago. The town's name comes from an effigy of the Virgin holding a candlestick that was found on a beach by two Guanche goatherds in 1392. The town is particularly worth a visit on a Sunday, when the atmosphere takes on an almost pilgrimage feel as locals throng to the church to attend mass, and the surrounding small shops sell religious artefacts, flowers, souvenirs and similar. Don't bother visiting the drab modern adjacent resort of Las Caletillas, which has little to commend it aside from a decent-size black pebble beach.

◉ Sights & Activities

★**Basílica de Nuestra Señora de Candelaria**   CHURCH

(⊙7.30am-7.30pm Tue-Sun, 3-7.30pm Mon; 🅿) This imposing domed church dates from 1959 and sits at the edge of the town centre, overlooking a rocky beach and flanked by a plaza where nine huge statues of Guanche warriors stand guard. The church has an enthralling interior as well as a palpable air of reverence, focused on the adoration of the Virgin of Candelaria. With its ornate decoration, the interior of the dome is an architectural highlight. During the official festivities for the Virgen de la Candelaria celebration on 15 August, the plaza fills with pilgrims and partygoers from all over the Canary Islands. If you visit during a Mass, you will probably find it is standing room only.

★ **Centro Alfarero de Candelaria** MUSEUM (Calle Isla de la Gomera 17; ⊗11am-5pm Tue-Sat) **FREE** Just past the basilica, steps lead up the right-hand side to the signposted Centro Alfarero de Candelaria, a small and informative pottery museum, where pots are still thrown by hand and without a wheel – the way it was most likely done by the Guanches.

★ **Apnea Canarias** DIVING (☑6075635 45, 671 845553; www.apneacanarias .com; Puerto Deportivo de Radazul, Radazul; 1-person course €80, 2 people €65 per person) This professionally run, highly reputable diving school by the marina in Radazul specialises in freediving, with instruction from experienced freedivers. It also runs From Zero to Hero instructor-level courses and caters to experienced freedivers wanting to dive deeper. Dives are in the clear waters of Radazul Bay.

✖ Eating

El Muelle SEAFOOD € (Avenida Constitución 9; mains €4-16; ⊗11am-midnight) This popular seafood restaurant with a large terrace out back with harbour views serves battered prawns, octopus vinaigrette, cuttlefish with garlic, fish of the day and tuna with *mojo*.

🔒 Shopping

★ **La Casa de las Imágenes** GIFTS & SOUVENIRS (www.facebook.com/LaCasadelasImagenes; Calle Obispo Pérez Cáceres 17; ⊗9.30am-8pm Tue-Sun, to 1.30pm Mon) Get into the soul-stirring mood in Candelaria by checking out the religious statues, shrink-wrapped Santa Ritas, photos, plaques, candles, and holograms of the Virgin Mary and every saint you can name at this amazing shop, which claims to have the largest selection of religious imagery in Spain.

ℹ Information

There's a small **tourist office** (☑922 03 22 30; www.candelaria.es; Avenida de la Constitución; ⊗9am-2pm Mon-Fri) by the car park in the port.

OFF THE BEATEN TRACK

EXPLORING THE EAST COAST
....

After visiting the pyramids at Güímar, continue on past El Escobonal to Fasnia and the tiny **Ermita de la Virgen de los Dolores**, a chapel perched on a hill at the edge of town (off the TF620 highway). It's usually closed, but is worth the short drive up for the panoramic views of the harsh, dry landscape. Keep on the TF620 to reach **Roques de Fasnia**, a little town carved into the volcanic cliff, with a tranquil black-sand beach. A bit further south is **Porís de Abona**, a charming little fishing village albeit surrounded by new housing; there's an attractive small cove here, with fishing boats and a dark sandy beach where you can take a dip, before stopping for tapas at **Café al Mar** (☑636 943820; Calle Martin Rodriguez 14; tapas from €2.50; ⊗11am-10pm Mon, Tue & Thu-Sat, 10am-10pm Sun).

ℹ Getting There & Away

If you're driving, take exit 9 off the TF1 motorway. Buses 111, 112, 115, 116, 122, 123, 124 and 131 connect the town with Santa Cruz (€2.35, 30 minutes).

Güímar

POP 16,000

Güímar is a rural east-coast town with a well-kept centre and views of a gauzy blue ocean in the distance. Most people come here to visit the six enigmatic lava-stone **Pirámides de Güímar** (☑922 51 45 10; www. piramidesdeguimar.net; adult/child €11.90/5.50; ⊗9.30am-6pm; 🅿), which pose an intriguing question: could the Canarios have had contact with America before Columbus famously sailed the ocean blue? Ponder it over the excellent, often-changing Canarian menu at charmingly rustic **Hotel Rural Finca Salamanca** (☑922 51 45 30; https://en.hotel-fincasalamanca.com; set menu €14; ⊗1.30-4pm & 7-10.30pm Mon-Thu & Sun, to 11pm Fri & Sat).

ℹ Getting There & Away

Buses 120 and 121 run roughly hourly from Santa Cruz (€3.40, 50 minutes) and stop at the Güímar bus station, a few blocks from the pyramids.

KEVIN WELLS PHOTOGRAPHY/SHUTTERSTOCK ©

LEONS/SHUTTERSTOCK ©

ALEKSANDAR TODOROVIC/SHUTTERSTOCK ©

3

1. Jardínes del Marquesado de la Quinta Roja (p158)

French-influenced 18th-century gardens crowned by a marble mausoleum.

2. Hiking through the Anaga Mountains (p153)

There are several well-marked trails through the laurel forests.

3. Auditorio de Tenerife (p145)

With superb acoustics, this magnificent auditorium was designed by Spanish architect Santiago Calatrava.

4. Playa de las Teresitas (p152)

An excellent beach just north of San Andrés.

La Gomera

POP 20,720

Best Places to Eat

Best Hikes

Why Go?

From a distance La Gomera appears as an impenetrable fortress ringed with soaring rock walls. Noodle-thin roads wiggle along cliff faces and up ravines, and the white specks that turn out to be houses seem impossibly placed on inaccessible crags. Up-close, however, that rough landscape translates into lush valleys, awe-inspiring cliffs, glittering black-pebble beaches and bold rock formations sculpted by volcanic activity and erosion.

Without the standard tourist-resort trappings of golden sands and animated nightlife, La Gomera has a tangible bohemian air; many foreign residents arrived here in the 1960s flower-power days. Pastel-painted capital San Sebastián is the low-key hub, while the laid-back southern beach towns draw sunseekers. The island is relatively laborious to reach, and, apart from those day-tripping from Tenerife, most visitors tend to be walkers heading for the hiking trails that weave across this spectacular land, which unravels around the ancient *laurisilva* (laurel) forests of Garajonay.

When to Go

➡ March and April are the best months for hiking: ideal temperatures coupled with a dazzle of subtropical flowers on the hillsides. Late autumn also offers good hiking weather.

➡ The summer months, especially August, can reach a sizzling 30°C and see the most daytrippers from Tenerife's Los Cristianos; June and September are a tad cooler and are good fiesta months, with San Juan and the week-long Fiestas Colombinas.

➡ In winter expect some rainfall in December, January and, to a lesser extent, February, with an average temperature of around 17°C. Look for wild mushrooms on local menus in February.

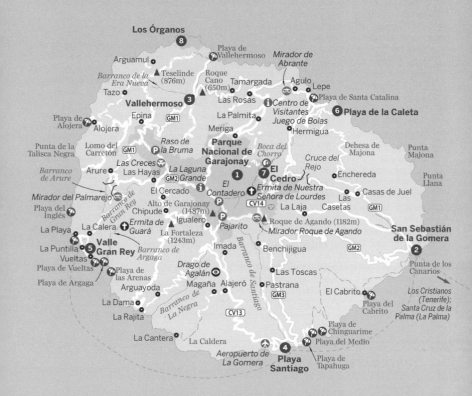

ATLANTIC OCEAN

0 ⎯⎯⎯⎯⎯ 5 km
0 ⎯⎯⎯⎯⎯ 2.5 miles

Los Órganos
8

Arguamul

Playa de
Vallehermoso

*Mirador de
Abrante*

▲ Teselinde
(876m)

*Barranco de la
Era Nueva*

Roque
Cano
(650m)

Tamargada

Agulo   Lepe

Tazo

Vallehermoso 3

Las Rosas

Playa de Santa Catalina

Epina   GM1

La Palmita

*Centro de
Visitantes
Juego de Bolas*

6 **Playa de la Caleta**

Playa de
Alojera   Alojera

Meriga

Hermigua

*Raso de
la Bruma*

**Parque
Nacional de
Garajonay**

*Boca del
Chorro*

*Cruce del
Rejo*

Dehesa de
Majona

Punta
Majona

Punta de la
Talisca Negra

Lomo del
Carretón   GM1

Las Creces
Las Hayas

La Laguna
GM2 Grande

El
Contadero

7 **El
Cedro**

Enchereda

Punta
Llana

*Barranco
de Arure*

Arure

El Cercado

1

*Ermita de Nuestra
Señora de Lourdes*

Las
Casetas

Casas de Juel

GM1

Mirador del Palmarejo

Chipude

Alto de Garajonay
(1487m) ▲

CV14

La Laja

Playa del
Inglés

Igualero

Pajarito

Roque de Agando (1182m)

**San Sebastián
de la Gomera**

La Calera

*Ermita de
Guará*

La Playa

*La Fortaleza
(1243m)* ▲

Mirador Roque de Agando

2

La Puntilla 5 **Valle
Gran Rey**

Imada

Benchijigua

GM2

Punta de los
Canarios

Vueltas

*Barranco de
Argaza*

Playa de Vueltas

Playa de
las Arenas

*Drago de
Agalán*

Las Toscas

El Cabrito

*Los Cristianos
(Tenerife);
Santa Cruz de la
Palma (La Palma)*

Playa de Argaga

Arguayoda

Magaña Alajeró

Pastrana

GM3

Playa del
Cabrito

La Dama

*Barranco de
La Negra*

CV13

Playa de
Chinguarime

La Rajita

La Cantera

La Caldera

*Aeropuerto de
La Gomera*

4 **Playa
Santiago**

Playa del Medio

Playa de
Tapahuga

ATLANTIC OCEAN

La Gomera Highlights

1 Parque Nacional de Garajonay (p186) Wandering the fairy-tale *laurisilva* forest at La Gomera's heart and climbing its tallest peak.

2 San Sebastián de la Gomera (p183) Peering into colourful backstreets and delving into the island's history in its pint-sized capital.

3 Vallehermoso (p190) Marvelling at the tropical fauna of this lush valley.

4 Playa Santiago (p191) Feasting on seafood, hiking and relaxing in a laid-back resort.

5 Valle Gran Rey (p193) Soaking up the plunging valleys and palm-sprinkled terraces.

6 Playa de la Caleta (p188) Unwinding at this black-pebble beach.

7 El Cedro (p189) Hiking to a tiny hamlet in a beautifully forested gorge.

8 Los Órganos (p189) Hopping on a boat to a rock formation resembling pipe organs.

History

From the beginning of the 15th century the Spaniards tried unsuccessfully to conquer La Gomera. When they finally managed to establish a presence on the island in the middle of the century, it was due to a slow and fairly peaceful infiltration of Christianity and European culture. Early on, the original inhabitants were permitted to retain much of their culture and self-rule, but that changed when the brutal Hernán Peraza the younger (p187) became governor. The *gomeros* rebelled against him, unleashing a bloodbath that killed hundreds of islanders.

After the activity of those first years, and the excitement that accompanied Christopher Columbus' stopovers (p184) on the island, there followed a long period of isolation. La Gomera was self-sufficient and had little contact with the outside world until the 1950s, when a small pier was built in San Sebastián, opening the way for ferry travel and trade.

Even so, it was difficult to eke out a living by farming on the island's steep slopes, and much of the population emigrated to Tenerife or South America. These days the island is the most popular in the archipelago for hiking, which has resulted in a welcome tourism boost for the economy.

Getting There & Away

AIR

The **Aeropuerto de La Gomera** (www.aena.es), 3km west of Playa Santiago, has several daily flights to/from Tenerife Norte with Binter Canarias (p269).

BOAT

Ferries arrive into San Sebastián's busy port, at the foot of the town.

Fred Olsen (p269) To/from Los Cristianos (Tenerife; €34, 50 minutes, three times daily) and Santa Cruz de la Palma (€43, two hours, one daily).

Naviera Armas (p269) To/from Los Cristianos (€40, one hour, two to three daily) and Santa Cruz de la Palma (€32, 2¾ hours, one to two daily).

Getting Around

TO/FROM THE AIRPORT

Bus 7 runs between San Sebastián and the airport (€4, 1¼ hours) via Playa Santiago, coinciding with flights. Otherwise, taxis charge €40 to/from San Sebastián.

BOAT

A faster alternative to tackling La Gomera's roads is the **Fred Olsen** Benchi Express water taxi, which links San Sebastián with Valle Gran Rey (€8, 40 minutes) via Playa Santiago (€8, 30 minutes), three times daily in each direction.

THREE DAYS ON LA GOMERA

Day One

This perfect day starts with exploring the colourful streets of San Sebastián, before heading to La Laguna Grande (p186) for hiking maps/tips and then weaving through magnificent, mist-drenched laurel forests to the summit of the island, Alto de Garajonay (p187). Then drop in for a meal at much-loved Casa Efigenia (p193) in Las Hayas and, if time allows, visit the pottery artisans in El Cercado (p193).

Day Two

Today, you're off to northern La Gomera, one of the most fertile places in the Canaries. Start among the banana groves of Hermigua (p187), visiting its monastery and ethnography museum, before taking the coastal GM1 to pretty Agulo (p189), above which the Mirador de Abrante (p190) opens up spectacular panoramas across to Tenerife. Continue on to beautiful Vallehermoso (p190) and stroll down to the beach, then make your way back to Hermigua for dinner at El Faro (p188). Alternatively, spend the day tackling the hike (p196) down (or up!) the Hermigua valley via El Cedro.

Day Three

For many people the Valle Gran Rey (p193) is La Gomera's most gorgeous spot. Begin with a tasty breakfast overlooking the beach, perhaps at La Ñamera (p195), then hop on a whale- and dolphin-watching trip (p194). Sleep it all off on the town's beaches and wrap up with dinner at La Salsa (p195).

LA GOMERA FOR CHILDREN

La Gomera doesn't have any of the theme parks, water slides and other family-oriented activities that make the bigger Canary Islands such magnets for children, but there's still plenty of fun to be had in the island's natural thrills.

The first stop for holidaying families is usually the **beach**, with good, often calm options in Valle Gran Rey, Alojera, Playa Santiago and San Sebastián. For tots who aren't strong swimmers, pools like the one in Vallehermoso (p190) or hotels are a safer bet.

Short **boat trips** are guaranteed to brighten children's days. Trips to the spectacular natural formation of Los Órganos (p189) sail from Valle Gran Rey, as do half-day whale-and dolphin-watching cruises (p194), which also run from Playa Santiago. Older kids can also go kayaking, cycling, snorkelling, paddleboarding and even diving here.

Kids of all ages should also enjoy the Parque Nacional de Garajonay (p186), which has a few short, easy, flat routes through forests that feel plucked from a fairy tale.

BUS

Guagua Gomera (☑ 922 14 11 01; www.guagua gomera.com; Estación de Guaguas, Avenida Vía de Ronda, San Sebastián) Runs a comprehensive network of buses throughout the island.

CAR & MOTORCYCLE

Driving is by far the easiest way to explore the island, though La Gomera has a limited number of rental cars available so book ahead.

Cicar (☑ 928 82 29 00; www.cicar.com; Estación Marítima, Avenida Fred Olsen, San Sebastián de la Gomera)

Oasis Rent a Car (☑ 922 87 28 98; www. oasisrentacar.com; Estación Marítima, Avenida Fred Olsen, San Sebastián de la Gomera; ☉ 9am-1pm & 4-7pm)

Rent-a-Car La Rueda (☑ 922 87 07 09; www. autoslarueda.es; Calle Real 19, San Sebastián de la Gomera; ☉ 8.30am-1pm & 4-7.30pm Mon-Sat, 9am-1pm Sun)

SAN SEBASTIÁN DE LA GOMERA

POP 8950

La Gomera's capital in every way – economically, bureaucratically and historically – seaside San Sebastián centres on a delightful historic core with shaded plazas, sun-bleached pastel-painted buildings and pedestrian-friendly streets sprinkled with shops, cafes and restaurants. Its main claim to fame is that Christopher Columbus stayed here on his way to the New World, and the explorer's every footstep (real or imagined) in the town has been well documented for visitors. If you've just hopped off the boat from Tenerife's Los Cristianos, shift down a gear or two: slow-paced San Sebastián feels a world away from its neighbour across the water.

History

When Columbus lingered on the island in 1492, San Sebastián had barely been founded. Four years earlier, in 1488, there had been a terrible massacre in the wake of the failed uprising against Hernán Peraza (p187), the island's governor. When it was all over, what had been Villa de las Palmas, on a spot known to the Guanches as Hipalán, was renamed San Sebastián.

The boom in transatlantic trade following Columbus' journeys helped boost the fortunes of the town, whose sheltered harbour was one of the Canaries' best ports. Nevertheless, its population passed the 1000 mark only at the beginning of the 19th century. The good times also brought dangers, as, like other Canarian capitals, San Sebastián was regularly subjected to pirate attack from the English, French and Portuguese, and it declined from the 16th century onwards. The town's fortunes rose with the cochineal (a scale insect that produces a red dye) boom in the 19th century, but that industry collapsed with the emergence of synthetic dyes. Many *gomeros* emigrated to the Americas or elsewhere in the Canaries in the 19th and 20th centuries.

⊙ Sights & Activities

San Sebastián's colourful streets, compact town centre, ancient nobles' homes and other scattered sights offer an intriguing wander through the island's history. Most attractions are somehow related to Columbus (in either real or contrived ways). Begin at **Plaza de las Américas**, with its buzzy terrace bars and 2018 Columbus statue, and cross **Plaza de la Constitución**, shaded by enormous Indian laurel trees, before strolling up **Calle Real**.

THE ISLE WHERE COLUMBUS DALLIED

A Genoese sailor of modest means, Christopher Columbus (Cristoforo Colombo in his native Italy) was born in 1451. Fascinated by Marco Polo's travels in the Orient, he decided early on that it must be possible to reach the east by heading west into the sunset. After years of doors being slammed in his face, Spain's Reyes Católicos, Fernando and Isabel, finally gave him their patronage in 1492.

On 3 August 1492, at the head of three small caravels – the *Santa María*, the *Pinta* and the *Niña* – Columbus weighed anchor in Palos de la Frontera, Huelva (Andalucía), on the Spanish mainland. But before heading across the Atlantic, he stopped off at La Gomera for last-minute provisions, unwittingly giving the island its biggest claim to fame.

Columbus set sail on 6 September, a day now celebrated in San Sebastián with the Fiestas Colombinas (p185). His ships didn't see land until 12 October, just as provisions and the sailors' patience were nearing their ends. The expedition 'discovered' several Caribbean islands on this trip and returned to Spain in March 1493.

Columbus made three later voyages, but died alone in Valladolid, Spain, in 1506, still convinced he'd found a new route to the Orient rather than America.

The tourist office (p185) provides leaflets for self-guided walking tours.

Iglesia de la Virgen de la Asunción CHURCH

(Calle Real; ⊘ 8am-6.30pm Mon-Sat, 11am-8pm Sun) Columbus and his men supposedly prayed at this ancient church before setting off for the New World. The original chapel was begun in 1450 but destroyed by a fire; original-period features include the pointed arch between the altar and the nave, while the facade is a prime example of Gothic Atlantic architecture (influenced by Portuguese Manueline). The 18th-century triple-nave church here today mixes Mudéjar, Gothic and baroque architectural styles. The floral-carved wooden entrance lobby is stunning.

Casa de Colón MUSEUM, ARCHITECTURE

(www.museoslagomera.es; Calle Real 56; ⊘ 9.30am-1.30pm & 3-5.30pm Mon-Fri) FREE In the style of its 17th-century predecessor, this simple cream-coloured house with handsome wooden galleries and floors is built on the site where Columbus supposedly stayed while on the island. Today it hosts a small museum; the highlight is the gallery of stunning pottery crafted by the South American Chimú tribes, who lived in the region between Ecuador and Lima during the 11th to 15th centuries.

Museo Arqueológico de La Gomera MUSEUM

(⊘ 922 24 25 86; www.museoslagomera.es; Calle Torres Padilla 8; adult/child €2.50/free; ⊘ 9am-2pm & 3-5pm Mon-Fri) Occupying part of the mid-18th-century Casa de los Echeverría (you'll spot the noble/military family's crest on the facade), this worthwhile museum explores both the island's Guanche past and its present-day culture. Displays reveal Guanche day-to-day life and their social, political and religious structures, with information in Spanish and English.

Casa de la Aduana HISTORIC BUILDING

(Casa de la Aguada; www.museoslagomera.es; Plaza de la Constitución) FREE Just off Plaza Constitución, this yellow-walled 16th-century building served as both San Sebastián's customs house and the count's residence. According to folklore, Columbus drew water from the well that sits in the central patio here and used it to 'baptise America'. Sadly, these days you can only admire the building's exterior.

Playa San Sebastián BEACH

The town's sandy volcanic beach is perfect for relaxing and taking a swim. Unlike on many beaches in the Canaries, the waters here are almost always calm and smooth, making it great for children.

Torre del Conde TOWER

(Torre de los Peraza; www.museoslagomera.es; Parque Torre del Conde) Set in a grassy subtropical park, the distinctive, 1477 stone-and-whitewash Torre del Conde is considered the Canary Islands' most important example of military architecture. It was here that Beatriz de Bobadilla, the wife of the cruel and ill-fated Hernán Peraza (p187), had to barricade herself in 1488 until help arrived.

Ermita de San Sebastián CHURCH

(Calle Real; ⊘ dawn-dusk) With its origins in the 15th century but rebuilt in 1850, the fine whitewashed chapel of San Sebastián retains a few original elements, despite being damaged by pirate attacks and storms over the centuries.

Dehesa de Majona Walk
HIKING

North of town, at Km 7.1 on the GM1 (opposite a lookout), a 24km trail leads into the Parque Natural de Majona, a largely uninhabited pastureland. Take the signposted path (not the drivable track) to the left 100m off the GM1; you'll eventually join the long-distance GR132, then end up on sealed roads near Hermigua. Allow five to six hours (one-way).

✦ Festivals & Events

Día de San Juan
RELIGIOUS, FIESTA

(⊙23-24 Jun) St John's Day fills **Playa de la Cueva** with bonfires, music performances and DJ sets to celebrate the summer solstice.

Fiestas Colombinas
FIESTA

(⊙early Sep) A week of street parties, music and cultural events in San Sebastián celebrating Christopher Columbus' first voyage to the Americas.

Bajada de la Virgen de Guadalupe
RELIGIOUS

(⊙Oct) Every five years (2023, 2028 etc) the island celebrates its patron saint with a flotilla of fishing boats escorting a statue of the Virgin Mary southwards from the chapel at Puntallana to San Sebastián's Iglesia de la Virgen de la Asunción (p184). There's plenty of music, drumming, castanets and dancing, and the Virgin then continues on around La Gomera.

🍴 Eating & Drinking

Most restaurants are dotted around Plaza de las Américas, Plaza de la Constitución and Calle Real, and serve typical Canarian fare.

Las Carabelas
CANARIAN €

(☑922 87 07 00; Plaza de la Constitución; snacks €2-6; ⊙8am-11.30pm) Handy for breakfast, this long-running down-to-earth cafe-bar does coffees, fresh orange juice, *bocadillos* of La Gomera goat's cheese and no-fuss tapas such as *patatas bravas* and tortilla, beneath the lovely Indian laurel trees on one of San Sebastián's main plazas.

La Tasca
INTERNATIONAL, CANARIAN €€

(☑922 14 15 98; Calle Ruiz de Padrón 57; mains €5-14; ⊙12.30-3.30pm & 7.30-11.30pm Mon-Sat) Spread over two traditional cottages with four dining rooms and run by the family of trail-running champion Cristofer Clemente (whose trophies adorn every wall), this intimate tavern is hugely popular with both *gomeros* and visitors. On the expansive, unpretentious menu, pizzas, risottos, pastas and mainland-style tapas mingle with Canarian dishes like *potaje de berros* and grilled cheese with palm honey.

Tasca La Salamandra
GASTROPUB €€

(www.facebook.com/tascalasalamandra; Calle Real 16; mains €10-16; ⊙7.30-11pm Mon, 12.30-4pm & 7.30-11pm Tue-Sat) San Sebastián's most creative recipes are plated up in a rustic-chic dining room, where you might try smartly presented, Canarian-inspired avocado-and-artichoke salad with *ibérico* ham, bite-sized goat's-cheese 'chocolates' or beef sirloin in a port sauce.

Restaurante La Hila
CANARIAN €€

(Calle Virgen de Guadalupe 2; mains €9-15; ⊙noon-11pm) Choose one of the daily-changing *a la plancha* fresh fish dishes, add a squeeze of lemon, throw in chips and salad and you have a dish fit for Neptune himself. The hardworking team also rustles up homemade croquettes, grilled cheese drizzled with *mojo* and surprises like prawns in Roquefort sauce, delivered at terrace tables.

Parador de La Gomera
CANARIAN €€€

(☑922 87 11 00; www.parador.es; Calle Lomo de la Horca; mains €19-22; ⊙7.30-10.30am, 1.30-3.30pm & 7-10pm; 🅿🛜) Amid wood-beamed ceilings, white-cloth tables and beautiful subtropical gardens, the Parador's (p189) elegant restaurant is San Sebastián's most refined dining spot, specialising in imaginative updates of Canarian favourites – from smoked goat's cheese to grouper with *patatas arrugadas*. Though perhaps not quite as wowing as prices suggest, it's still worth the diversion.

🛍 Shopping

Mercado Municipal
MARKET

(Avenida de Colón; ⊙7.30am-2pm Mon-Sat) Next to the bus station, San Sebastián's market stocks fruit and veg plus local delicacies such as honey (considered some of the finest in Spain), *miel de palma* (palm honey; made from the sap of palm trees), *almogrote* (a spicy pâté of soft cheese, pepper and tomato, usually spread on bread) and *queso gomero* (La Gomera's mild, smooth goat's cheese).

ℹ Information

Oficina de Turismo (☑922 14 15 12; www.lagomera.travel; Calle Real 34; ⊙9am-1pm & 3.30-6pm Mon-Sat, 10am-1pm Sun) Housed in the 19th-century Casa Bencomo, this helpful tourist office has hiking maps and tips, leaflets for self-guided Columbus-themed tours of San Sebastián and an exhibition on the island's mountainous terrain.

ℹ️ Getting There & Away

BOAT

The Fred Olsen (p182) Benchi Express water taxi links San Sebastián with Valle Gran Rey (€8, 40 minutes) via Playa Santiago (€8, 30 minutes), three times daily in each direction.

BUS

From the **Estación de Guaguas** (Avenida Vía de Ronda), on the west side of town, Guagua Gomera (p183) bus 1 runs to Valle Gran Rey (€5, 1¾ hours, two to five daily); bus 2 to Vallehermoso (€4.50, 1½ hours, two to five daily); bus 3 to Playa Santiago (€4, one hour, two to six daily); and bus 7 to the airport (€4, 1¼ hours), coinciding with flights.

TAXI

Taxis (📞 922 87 05 24; taxisssgomera@gmail.com; Avenida de los Descubridores) charge €25 to Hermigua, €35 to Playa Santiago, €40 to the airport, €28 to Pajarito (for the Parque Nacional de Garajonay) and €55 to Valle Gran Rey.

ℹ️ Getting Around

Bike Hire Marina La Gomera (📞 922 14 17 69; Puerto Deportivo Marina La Gomera, Avenida Fred Olsen; bike hire per day €10; ⊗ 8.30am-1.30pm & 4-6pm Mon-Fri, 9am-1pm Sat & Sun)

PARQUE NACIONAL DE GARAJONAY

An enchanting green jungle of nearly impenetrable ancestral *laurisilva* forest, the 40-sq-km **Parque Nacional de Garajonay** (📞 922 80 09 92; www.miteco.gob.es) is La Gomera's essential drawcard, covering 10%

of its surface and unveiling its finest hiking and cycling. Up here, on the roof of the island, cool Atlantic trade winds clash with warmer breezes, creating a constant ebb and flow of mist through the dense, damp forest, something called 'horizontal rain'. The last Ice Age didn't make it as far as the Canaries, so this landscape was common across much of the Mediterranean millions of years ago.

Garajonay was declared a national park in 1981 and a Unesco World Heritage Site in 1986. In 2012 a massive fire destroyed 7.5 sq km of *laurisilva*, leaving large areas of stark blackened trees, which will take an estimated 30 years to recover – fortunately, there's still plenty of green left.

A universe of organisms has forged out a life in this dark forest. The tangle of trees here is absolutely vital to the health of the island: trees act like sponges, catching moisture on their leaves and allowing it to drip down into the soil, thus feeding them and the springs of the island itself. Relatively little light penetrates the canopy, providing an ideal landscape for moss and lichen to spread over everything. As many as 400 species of flora, including Canary willows and holly, flourish, and nearly 1000 species of invertebrates make their home in the park. Vertebrates here include mainly birds and lizards.

Lighting fires is banned, except in a few designated areas; free camping is also prohibited. Bring walking boots and warm rainproof garments.

ℹ️ Information

Juego de Bolas Visitor Centre (📞 922 80 09 92; www.miteco.gob.es; Carretera La Palmita–Agulo; ⊗ 9.30am-3pm & 3.20-4.30pm) Well outside the national park, 7.5km southwest of Agulo in the north of the island, this visitor centre provides basic hiking maps and route details, and also hosts a small museum on the park's geology and climate.

La Laguna Grande (www.miteco.gob.es; GM2; ⊗ 8.30am-2pm & 2.20-4.30pm) Around 4km northwest of the Pajarito junction on the GM2, this handy visitor centre has hiking-route information as well as a small exhibition about the park's birds.

ℹ️ Getting There & Away

Bus 1 between San Sebastián (€2, 30 minutes, two to five daily) and Valle Gran Rey (€4, 1¼ hours, two to five daily) via El Cercado and Las Hayas stops at the Pajarito junction in the heart of the national park, 4km southeast of La Laguna Grande visitor centre.

MAPS & GUIDES

The park's Juego de Bolas and La Laguna Grande visitor centres hand out decent hiking maps outlining the main possibilities. The 1:35,000 *La Gomera Tour and Trail* (Discovery Walking Guides) is a good walking map with 34 island-wide routes described in its accompanying guide. Other good maps include the 1:35,000 *Gomera* by Freytag & Berndt. Maps and hiking guides are usually available in bookshops in San Sebastián and Valle Gran Rey.

STRIDING OUT IN GARAJONAY

Many of the trails that criss-cross the Parque Nacional de Garajonay have been used by the *gomeros* for hundreds of years as a means of getting around the island. Experienced walkers will generally find most hikes in the Garajonay area fairly easy (but nonetheless rewarding), though there are a few challenging routes.

Although several guiding companies lead convenient, transport-included hikes in and around the national park, the many and varied access points make it simple to explore independently, and most routes are decently way-marked. Walks described on the basic hiking maps available from the Juego de Bolas and La Laguna Grande visitor centres correspond to park way-marking.

Several popular walks begin at La Laguna Grande, at **El Contadero** (a car park 3km southeast of La Laguna Grande), at **Pajarito** (the GM2–CV13 junction/bus stop, 4km southeast of La Laguna Grande) and at various other points along the GM2.

A highlight is the ascent to the **Alto de Garajonay**, the island's tallest peak at 1487m; you can hike here from Pajarito (1km, around 30 minutes one-way), from El Contadero (2km, around 30 minutes one-way) or from La Laguna Grande (5.5km, two hours one way), though this last trail runs through largely fire-damaged areas. From the Alto, cloud permitting, you'll enjoy jaw-dropping, 360-degree views around the island and perhaps even spot Tenerife, La Palma and El Hierro. You can follow any of the three paths to descend, including returning to La Laguna Grande via El Contadero (so you aren't backtracking).

From El Contadero, a signposted trail leads northeast down through a beautiful valley forest to the hamlet of El Cedro (p189) – 5.6km, 2¼ hours – via the Ermita de Nuestra Señora de Lourdes (p189); from El Cedro, it's possible to continue downhill to Hermigua (3km, two hours), or you could return to Pajarito via the Mirador de Tajaqué (around 7km, three hours). The Pajarito–Alto de Garajonay–El Cedro–Pajarito loop (16km, around six hours) is known as the **Gran Ruta Circular Garajonay** (Route 18), with around 680 metres elevation loss followed by 600 metres elevation gain and part of the route along a sealed forest road.

One of La Gomera's standout walks (p196) combines the climb from Pajarito to the Alto de Garajonay with the descent down through El Contadero and El Cedro to Hermigua; it's a challenging 10.5km, four- to five-hour hike, and is popular in the upwards direction too.

The oldest parts of the *laurisilva* forest lie towards the western end of the park, where there are several good walks, including the 2.2km, one-hour (return) Raso de la Bruma hike (p197), which meanders through misty, moss-adorned fairy-tale-like woodlands and can be linked up with other routes.

Finally, the GR131 traverses the southern and western reaches of the park on its cross-island journey from San Sebastián to Vallehermoso. The park authorities offer free three-hour, Spanish-language **guided walks** on Friday year-round and on Wednesday July to September, starting from La Laguna Grande; book ahead online.

The GM2 cuts east–west through the park until it meets the GM1 at the park's western extremity. A minor sealed road connects the Juego de Bolas visitor centre in the north of the island to La Laguna Grande.

banana-growing Hermigua, beyond which the GM1 meanders past colourful little Agulo to reach agricultural Vallehermoso in the northwest.

NORTHERN LA GOMERA

In La Gomera's verdant north, dense banana plantations and swaying palm trees fill deep valleys, cultivated terraces transform hillsides into works of art and white-washed houses lend a bygone-era charm to scattered villages. The north's main hub is

Hermigua

POP 340

A popular base for walkers, the go-slow agricultural town of Hermigua, 20km northwest of San Sebastián, straggles a long way down a lusciously green valley thick with banana groves and other subtropical flora to a volcanic beach that feels a little forgotten about. Often dripping with water, this is one of the dampest parts of the island – and all the more beautiful for it. Hermigua thrived on sugar-cane production in the 16th century, and you'll spot a few elegant baroque merchants' homes around town; now, tourism and the banana trade are its economic mainstays.

◉ Sights & Activities

An excellent 10.5km (four to five hours) hike (p196) meanders along the steep, beautiful valley between Hermigua and the Alto de Garajonay, via El Cedro (4.6km); look for signs opposite Plaza Victoriano Darias Montesinos.

Museo Etnográfico de La Gomera   MUSEUM
(☑922 88 19 60; www.museoslagomera.es; Carretera General (GM1) 99, Las Hoyetas; adult/child €2.50/free; ◷10am-6pm Mon-Fri, to 2pm Sat & Sun) Housed in a handsome 20th-century building with maroon trim, this two-storey ethnographic museum explores the island's natural resources and ecosystems through topics such as fishing, forestry, agriculture and architecture, with info in English and Spanish. Sections on crafts include pottery, weaving and basketry, and there are displays on wine-making, Silbo (p191) and the extraction of *guarapo* (palm honey).

Parque Etnográfico Los Telares   MUSEUM
(www.lostelaresgomera.com; Carretera General (GM1); adult/child €4.50/free; ◷9.30am-4.30pm Mon-Sat; P) A reconstructed 19th-century *gofio* (roasted Canarian grain) mill sits at the heart of this multifaceted ethnographic centre, which also takes in a traditional, self-sufficient organic orchard and a gallery showcasing the local rural lifestyle, typical crafts, Silbo Gomero (p191) and the island's history. Visits are with multilingual audio guides. There's also a gift shop and a cosy **cafe** (snacks €3-6; ◷9.30am-5.30pm Mon-Sat; ☎).

Convento de Santo Domingo   CHURCH
(Plaza de Armas; ◷dawn-dusk) At the heart of Hermigua's original village, just off Plaza Victoriano Darias Montesinos, this 16th-century church and monastery contains an intricately carved Mudéjar ceiling and is topped by a stone bell tower.

Playa de la Caleta   BEACH
(P) The best beach in the Hermigua area, 5km northeast of town, Playa de la Caleta is one of northern La Gomera's prettiest

black-pebble beaches. Framed by rocky headlands, it has fabulous views across the water to Tenerife's Mt Teide, along with picnic space, a tiny chapel, a seasonal beach bar and a colony of friendly cats. It's signposted from the seafront at Hermigua.

✕ Eating

★El Faro   SEAFOOD €€
(☑922 88 00 62; Carretera Playa de Santa Catalina 15; mains €7-16; ◷1-10pm; ✎) Perched above banana plantations near the beach, with tables on a breezy rooftop and a sleek whitewashed dining room, this warm standout restaurant delivers Canarian classics, punchy pastas, crispy salads and some of Hermigua's most deliciously fresh seafood. Pick from the *pescados del día*, try the tasty vegetarian pasta and goat's cheese salad, or preorder paella for two (€44).

Las Chácaras   CANARIAN €€
(☑922 88 10 39; www.laschacaras.com; Calle El Cabo 2; mains €8-13; ◷12.30-3.30pm & 6.30-9.30pm Mon-Sat) Elegantly prepped traditional dishes like *berros* (watercress) soup, tuna with *mojo*, and grilled cheese with lashings of palm honey make this smart yellow-washed restaurant a perennial hit. Old-Hermigua photos hang from the walls; tables are decorated with candles and fresh flowers; and the owners take pride in their homemade desserts, including *quesillo* (a creamy custard). Bar open 9am to 1am.

Tasca Telémaco   CANARIAN €€
(☑922 88 08 12; www.tascatelemaco.com; Plaza de la Encarnación 2; mains €9-16; ◷1-4pm & 6-11pm; ☎) Mismatched chairs, Moroccan lamps, a mural of musicians and a sprawling terrace paint a lightly stylish picture for sipping Lanzarote and La Gomera wines over uncomplicated Canarian meals with the odd Asian twist. Classics of aubergine with palm honey, grilled king's prawns and baked cheese jostle with veggie stir-fries, Thai-inspired omelettes and pork sirloin with dates and bacon.

❶ Information

Oficina de Turismo (☑922 88 09 90; www. hermigua.es; Carretera General (GM1); ◷9am-9pm Mon-Fri, to 7pm Sat) Opposite the health centre; has basic hiking maps.

❶ Getting There & Away

Bus 2 between San Sebastián and Vallehermoso stops in Hermigua (€3, 45 minutes, two to five daily).

El Cedro

POP 17

The bucolic hamlet of El Cedro is tucked between farmed terraces and laurel thickets, 14km southwest and uphill from Hermigua, on the northeastern border of the Parque Nacional de Garajonay. The Boca del Chorro (also called Boca del Cedro) ravine runs roughly north–south through the village, emptying into the Hermigua valley as a waterfall just to the northeast. Though there's little more to El Cedro than a handful of houses, a campsite and a chapel, several exciting walks pass through here.

A popular, steep hiking route (p196) runs from El Cedro to Hermigua (4.6km, two hours), with the option of starting all the way up (southwest) at the Alto de Garajonay (6km from El Cedro, 2½ to three hours) and descending via El Contadero and the Barranco de El Cedro – it's equally appealing in reverse, from Hermigua up to El Cedro then on to the Alto. The Gran Ruta Circular Garajonay (p187) loops through El Cedro, too.

Ermita de Nuestra Señora de Lourdes CHURCH
A 1.7km walk (signposted) southwest from El Cedro along the official national-park Route 2, this small, white forest chapel was founded in 1935 by Englishwoman Florence Stephen Parry.

Bar La Vista CANARIAN €
(dishes €3.50-10; ☺9am-7pm) With bench-style tables overlooking El Cedro's green basin, this traditional bar-restaurant is popular for its heart-warming local food, like *papas arrugadas* (wrinkly potatoes), tangy red *mojo*, goat's cheese *bocadillos* and the famous *potaje de berros* (watercress stew), delivered in wooden bowls accompanied by *gofio* to stir in.

Agulo

POP 625

A pretty scrabble of cobbled lanes and tenderly restored white and pastel buildings, founded early in the 17th century, Agulo rests on a low platform 5km north of Hermigua. Behind looms the steep, rugged hinterland stretching back towards Parque Nacional de Garajonay.

Mirador de Abrante VIEWPOINT
(www.fredolsen.es; ☺11am-7pm Jun-Sep, 10am-6pm Oct-May; P) FREE High above little Agulo, enjoying sprawling panoramas across the ocean to Tenerife, this Fred-Olsen-owned lookout

---

FIVE FAB LA GOMERA HOTELS

Parador de La Gomera (☎922 87 11 00; www.parador.es; Calle Lomo de la Horca; r €120-225; P❄☎≋) Styled like a grand 15th-century Canarian mansion, high above town, San Sebastián's sumptuous Parador is arguably the island's top hotel. Rooms combine elegant furnishings with traditional flair, most gazing on subtropical gardens and an Atlantic-view pool. There's a smart modern-Canarian restaurant (p185).

Hotel Jardín Tecina (☎922 24 51 01; www.jardin-tecina.com; Lomada de Tecina; s/d incl breakfast €97/150; P❄☎≋) ✔ Sprawled along a cliff above Playa Santiago, La Gomera's only proper resort is a delightful jumble of whitewashed bungalows, exquisite tropical gardens, five restaurants (ingredients straight from the organic orchard) and a beach club.

Los Telares (☎922 88 07 81; www.lagomera.apartments; Carretera General (GM1), El Convento; apt €46-70; ☎≋) ✔ Ecoconscious Los Telares' bright, superbly equipped modern-rustic apartments are excellent value: stone floors, colourful furnishings, open-stone walls, kitchenettes and balconies or windows overlooking Hermigua's banana groves.

Apartamentos Tapahuga (☎922 89 51 59; www.tapahuga.es; Avenida Marítima; apt €80-100; ☎≋) Opposite Playa Santiago's harbour, elegant marble staircases and tile-covered corridors lead to a rooftop pool and spacious, light-flooded, modern-rustic apartments boasting beautiful wooden balconies, well-equipped kitchens and calming cream, beige or grey decor.

Playa Calera (☎922 80 57 79; www.hotelplayacalera.com; Calle Punta Calera 2, La Playa; r incl breakfast €114-132; P❄☎≋) Crisp contemporary style, cream walls, warm woods and La Gomera photos set the scene for a roof-terrace infinity pool and spacious open-plan rooms with lounges, kitchenettes, balconies and capsule-coffee kits at this sleek aparthotel in Valle Gran Rey.

point revolves around a spine-tingling glass box jutting out into thin air. There's also a Canarian cafe-restaurant (set menu €14.50) where Silbo demonstrations happen daily sometime between 12.30pm and 3pm. It's a 10km drive southwest of Agulo, via Las Rosas, and a popular stop with visitors.

Pared de Agulo Walk
HIKING

Starting at a 'Mirador de Abrante' signpost on the GM1, next to Agulo's pharmacy, this vertiginous, challenging path climbs the sheer wall behind Agulo, passing below the Mirador de Abrante to reach the national park's Centro de Visitantes Juego de Bolas (p186). From here, loop back down to Agulo via Hermigua (total 12.5km, four hours) or Las Rosas (total 10km, three hours).

La Vieja Escuela
CANARIAN €

(📝 922 14 60 04; www.restaurantelaviejaescuela. es; Calle Trujillo Armas 2; mains €7-12; ⊙ 11am-9pm Mon-Sat) On a ridge in the Las Casas *barrio* (district) of town, near the church, husband-and-wife-owned La Vieja Escuela was a schoolhouse until 1968. Grab a red-bench table on the street and settle in for lovingly cooked fresh fish of the day, *tortilla de patatas* and meaty mains like *carne fiesta* (grilled meats, peppers and potatoes). Service can be slow.

ℹ Getting There & Away

Bus 2 from San Sebastián (€3, 55 minutes, two to five daily) to Vallehermoso (€2.50, 30 minutes) via Hermigua stops in Agulo.

Vallehermoso
POP 800

Living up to its 'beautiful valley' moniker, the sleepy agricultural town of Vallehermoso

---

LA GOMERA COOKING

La Gomera's cuisine is classic, simple Canarian, starring fresh seafood, meaty mains, hearty stews such as *potaje de berros* (watercress stew) and, of course, *patatas arrugadas* (wrinkly potatoes) with lashings of *mojo* (spicy sauce made from coriander, basil or red chilli peppers). The island's international community has introduced a few other flavours too, especially in Valle Gran Rey, which hosts some good fusion and vegetarian restaurants.

---

makes a great base for exploring the secluded northwest of the island. Small mountain peaks rise on either side of the deep gorge that runs through town to meet a volcanic beach; admire the green terraced hillsides peppered with palm trees, in the shadow of the 650m-tall iconic volcanic monolith of Roque Cano.

The heart of town is **Plaza de la Constitución**, where you'll find most bars, restaurants and services.

Playa de Vallehermoso
BEACH

(🅿) A beautiful strip of rocky black beach pounded by waves and hemmed in by tall cliffs, 3km northeast of town. Two seasonal **pools** (⊙ 11am-7pm Tue-Sun approx Jun-Sep) and a summer-only seafood-fuelled **restaurant** (📝 922 80 15 61; mains €7-9; ⊙ noon-4pm Tue-Sun May-Sep; 🅿) overlook the shore.

ℹ Getting There & Away

Bus 2 runs to/from San Sebastián (€4.50, 1½ hours, two to five daily).

Alojera
POP 390

Languid little Alojera unravels just inland from a jet-black volcanic beach on La Gomera's northwest coastline, amid a fertile palm-studded valley that stands out as an oasis of green amid a sea of dry hills. It's reached by a seemingly endless series of hairpin bends off the GM1 from Epina and is popular with self-catering visitors looking for a quiet, rural escape.

Playa de Alojera
BEACH

Jagged cliffs, rock formations and natural pools offshore lend a sense of drama to Alojera's sweeping, rarely crowded silty black beach, 1.5km west of town. Though no secret, it's ideal for swimming when there's no swell (but if a big swell is running, keep well away from the water). It's backed by a cluster of white houses and apartments.

ℹ Getting There & Away

Bus 5 runs between Vallehermoso and Alojera (€4, one hour, two daily Monday to Friday).

Los Órganos

Something like a great sculpted basalt church organ rising from the ocean's depths, the utterly extraordinary cliffscape of Los

SILBO: LA GOMERA'S WHISTLING LANGUAGE

Alternately chirpy and melodic, shrill and deeply resonating, the ancient Silbo Gomero whistling language really is as lovely as birdsong. Silbo, once a dying art, but now being brought back to life, is steeped in history and boasts a complex vocabulary of more than 4000 whistled words that can be heard from miles away.

In pre-Hispanic La Gomera, Silbo developed as the perfect tool for sending messages back and forth across the island's rugged terrain. In ideal conditions, it could be heard up to 4km away. At first, it was probably used as an emergency signal, but over time a full language developed. While other forms of whistled communications have existed in pockets of Greece, Turkey, China and Mexico, none is as developed as Silbo Gomero. Its sounds replace Spanish language with two whistled vowels and four consonants and were traditionally learnt in a family environment, resulting in different accents between various areas.

Modern conveniences and emigration from the island had all but killed the language, but in the past few years Silbo has gone from being La Gomera's near-forgotten heritage to being its prime cultural selling point. Silbo has been a mandatory school subject on the island since 1999, and in 2009 it was inscribed on the Unesco List of Intangible Cultural Heritage. This inclusion is a big morale boost for *silbadores*, though some have expressed concern that Silbo could eventually end up becoming a tourism cliché.

Órganos clings to La Gomera's northernmost coastline and has been battered into its present shape by the Atlantic. Though it's just a few kilometres north of Vallehermoso, to visit, you'll need to head out to sea with a boat-tour company, such as Tina (p194), from Valle Gran Rey or Playa Santiago in the island's south.

SOUTHERN LA GOMERA

The sunniest part of La Gomera, the south is endlessly changing, from dry sunburnt peaks to lush banana-filled valleys, and from stern rocky coasts to silty black-sand beaches. This is where you'll find the island's two resort areas – modest Playa Santiago and sprawling Valle Gran Rey, each overlooking the Atlantic at the mouth of a plunging green valley. Inland, quiet villages such as Alajeró, Imada, El Cercado and Las Hayas pepper the terraced hillsides.

Playa Santiago

POP 1140

Curled into La Gomera's sunny southeastern coast, Playa Santiago is a small, oceanside resort where a sleepy village centre and soothing seafront promenade give way to a few undulating banana plantations and a long cobblestone **beach** washed by calm waters.

Until the 1960s this area was the busiest centre on the island, with factories, a shipyard and a port for exporting local bananas and tomatoes. But the farming crisis hit hard, and by the 1970s the town had all but shut down, its inhabitants having fled to Tenerife or South America. In recent years, tourism has breathed new life into Playa Santiago, particularly in the form of the huge, luxurious Hotel Jardín Tecina (p189) owned by Fred Olsen, and several excellent restaurants.

◉ Sights & Activities

Several appealing walks thread through the hills north of Playa Santiago around the villages of Alajeró (p192), Imada and Benchijigua. The steep Route 23 links the **Mirador Roque de Agando** (GM2, Km 18.4), with Playa Santiago (12.4km, around four hours) via the tiny settlement of Benchijigua. Circular Route 24 tracks between Playa Santiago, Benchijigua and the hamlet of Imada through the Barranco de Santiago (15km, five hours).

The long-distance GR132 passes through Playa Santiago; you can follow it to/from San Sebastián (20km, around 6½ hours, with some challenging climbs and descents) via the hamlet of El Cabrito, or northwest to/from Alajeró (10.5km, 2½ hours).

Playas de Tapahuga, del Medio & de Chinguarime   BEACH

This trio of secluded hippy-hang-out beaches, with sparkling volcanic sand mixed in among the pebbles, extends around 1km to 3km northeast of the landmark Hotel Jardín Tecina (follow signposts), and is known for being something of a nudist spot.

LA GOMERA PLAYA SANTIAGO

DON'T MISS

CASA EFIGENIA

On the Parque Nacional de Garajonay's southern border, **Casa Efigenia** (La Montaña; ☎922 80 42 48, 659 807458; www.efigenialagomera.com; Carretera General, Las Hayas; menú €10; ⊗8am-8pm; ✍) is the island's must-try for La Gomera cuisine in all its simple deliciousness. Efigenia started cooking for local road engineers in 1960. The communal tables and set family-style vegetarian menu are still here: *puchero gofio* (vegetable-based stew), mixed salad, *almogrote* and almond flan, plus homemade cakes, juices and lemonade.

Doña Efigenia is a gracious hostess who makes a point of talking to all her guests. These days her family helps out with the business, which has expanded to encompass a bodega and **accommodation** (r €45-65, apt €75-80; P✱ 🛜 🐕).

Splash Gomera WATER SPORTS
(☎626 658901, 922 14 58 87; www.splashgomera.es; Club Laurel, Hotel Jardín Tecina; ⊗10-11am & 4-5pm) This water sports specialist hires out kayaks and paddleboards (€15 per hour) and runs dive trips (single dive €39), PADI courses (Open Water €460), snorkelling trips (€35) and two-hour kayaking jaunts (€30).

Gomera Cycling & Walking CYCLING, HIKING
(☎922 89 51 45, 636 897512; www.gomeracycling.com; Avenida Marítima; ⊗9am-8pm) A well-organised bike-hire operator (mountain/road per day €20/30) that also arranges customised guided (from €40) or self-guided hikes, with transport at either end.

✖ Eating

The top-end Hotel Jardín Tecina (p189) has some excellent eateries.

La Chalana SEAFOOD €
(☎922 89 59 69; Barranco Colón; mains €6-9; ⊗noon-4pm & 7pm-late Thu-Tue) This buzzy blue-washed shack, tucked away at the eastern end of town, is part laid-back beach-bar and part friendly restaurant starring the fruits of the sea, which twinkles beyond. Dig into crunchy salads, fresh fish of the day and *queso frito* (fried cheese) topped with *mojo*, or call ahead for paella.

★ Junonia INTERNATIONAL €€
(☎922 89 57 61; www.facebook.com/resjunonia; Avenida Marítima 58; mains €12-17; ⊗12.30-3pm &

6.30-10pm Fri-Sun, 6.30-10pm Mon, Wed & Thu) A local favourite overlooking the harbour, with an elegant dining room full of contemporary artwork Internationally trained chef Fran Mora fuses ambitious creativity with classic La Gomera cuisine. Highlights include a sophisticated take on Italian dishes like black pasta with salmon in lobster-vodka-and-prawn sauce and exquisitely prepared fish such as grilled *dorada* (sea bream). Book ahead.

La Cuevita SEAFOOD €€
(☎922 89 55 68, 619 765969; www.facebook.com/lacuevitaplayasantiago; Avenida Marítima; mains €10-14; ⊗noon-4pm & 6.30-10.30pm Mon-Sat) Folded into a natural cave beside a small chapel at the west end of town, with leafy dangling plants, low lighting and earthy-red tablecloths, well-established La Cuevita serves Canarian wines alongside fine fresh local seafood – tuna, *vieja* (parrot fish), *chocos* (cuttlefish) – and grilled meats, all plated up with *patatas arrugadas* and tangy red *mojo*.

ⓘ Information

Oficina de Turismo (☎922 89 56 50; www.lagomera.travel; Avenida Marítima, Edificio Las Vistas; ⊗9am-1.30pm & 3.30-5.30pm Mon-Wed, 9am-3pm Thu & Fri, 9am-12.30pm Sat)

ⓘ Getting There & Away

The Fred Olsen (p182) Benchi Express water taxi runs between Valle Gran Rey and San Sebastián (€8, 40 minutes) via Playa Santiago (€8, 30 minutes), three times daily in each direction.

Bus 3 links Playa Santiago with San Sebastián (€4, one hour, two to six daily) and Alajeró (€2, 30 minutes, two to six daily).

Alajeró & Around

POP 500

A peaceful oasis centred on a 16th-century church and clinging to a ridge high above the ocean, 12km northwest of Playa Santiago, Alajeró is the starting point for several good hikes. The tiny hillside hamlet of Imada, 4km north of Alajeró, makes a blissfully quiet base or rest point for hikers.

⊙ Sights & Activities

The long-distance GR132 trail passes through Alajeró, linking the town with Playa Santiago (10.5km, 2½ to three hours). You can also hike north to the Drago de Agalán along Route 21 (2.4km, 45 minutes) and to Imada along several paths including Route 20 (4.7km, 1½ to two hours); look for signs in the main car park opposite the church. Various other paths link Alajeró, Imada, Playa Santiago and the Barranco de Santiago.

Drago de Agalán   NATURAL FEATURE
The island's oldest *drago* (dragon tree) rests in a palm-sprinkled valley, 2km north of Alajeró. Take the signposted road 300m west (downhill) from the Imada junction on the CV13, which leads to an old farmhouse; from here, a signed trail drops steeply for around 10 minutes to reach a lookout point with views down to the *drago,* a further five-to 10-minute walk below. For hikers, from the Imada junction, a signposted stone path leads 0.9km directly to the *drago.*

Iglesia del Salvador   CHURCH
(Calle Fagundo; ☉dawn-dusk) Alajeró's modest 16th-century church contains a beautifully carved late-16th- or early-17th-century wooden Christ.

✖ Eating

Mesón de Clemente   CANARIAN €€
(☑922 89 57 21; Carretera General Las Cruces 6; mains €8-17; ☉noon-10pm Thu-Tue) In a fabulous hillside position with sea views sprawling all around and tables on a sunny terrace, Mesón de Clemente specialises in succulent grilled and roast meats, including the signature *cochinillo* (suckling pig) and *cordero* (barbecued lamb).

❶ Getting There & Away

Bus 3 links Alajeró with San Sebastián (€4, 1½ hours, two to six daily) via Playa Santiago.

El Cercado

POP 190
Clinging to green slopes amid tidy terraces and stone houses, on the southern fringes of the Parque Nacional de Garajonay, the village of El Cercado is the last refuge for La Gomera's ancient pottery tradition, known for its sturdy pieces with a distinctive ochre tinge. A handful of artisans keep traditional, centuries-old techniques alive: three *talleres* (workshops) along the main road – María, María del Mar and Rufina – are usually open to visitors daily from around 10am to 6pm.

**Centro de Interpretación
Las Loceras**   MUSEUM
(☑922 80 41 04; CV18; ☉11am-3pm Tue-Sun) FREE El Cercado's small but fascinating earthenware museum explores the history of the island's pottery tradition through multilingual panels and collections of local pieces. Vessels were traditionally made by women from clay, sand and water, with almagre (red ochre) added in later stages to produce the characteristic red-brown colour.

❶ Getting There & Away

Bus 1 between San Sebastián (€3, 50 minutes, two to five daily) and Valle Gran Rey (€3, 50 minutes, two to five daily) passes through El Cercado.

Valle Gran Rey

POP 4480
A deep, brilliant-green gorge running down to meet the island's most popular beaches, the naturally spectacular Valle Gran Rey (Valley of the Great King) is La Gomera's tourist epicentre. Dramatic bare-rock cliffs line the valley and coast, creating a large part of the scenery's grandeur, and when the rest of the island is soaking in drizzle, the Valle Gran Rey is often happily working on its suntan. Most services here are geared towards the many German visitors in search of sunshine and nature (there are some good walks), plenty of whom are long-stay. Come sunset, people congregate along the seafront promenade, where fire dancers and other performers set up.

Valle Gran Rey proper is the low-key resort strip along the beachfront, with the *barrios* of La Playa and Vueltas at its northern and southern ends respectively and La Puntilla between, though the Valle Gran Rey district extends up the valley.

◉ Sights

The beaches here are among La Gomera's prettiest, with calm waters and lapping waves, though Valle Gran Rey is often very windy.

OFF THE BEATEN TRACK

ERMITA DE GUARÁ
• •
Dedicated to the island's patron saint, the Virgen de Guadalupe, **Ermita de Guará** is a tiny white 1960s chapel perched on a spectacularly scenic crag 6km southwest of El Cercado, engulfed in sweeping panoramas across the Barranco de Argaga to the ocean and, beyond, the distant island of El Hierro. A gentle walking trail leads here from El Cercado (around 1½ hours).

La Playa   BEACH
Towards the northern end of town, the beach at La Playa is long, volcanic and sandy, with bars and a waterfront promenade. People gather here in the evenings to watch the sun sink into the ocean.

Charco del Conde   NATURAL POOL
(La Puntilla) A natural saltwater pool fringed by a grey-sand beach and tucked into the heart of Valle Gran Rey's seafront.

Playa de Vueltas   BEACH
(Vueltas) Right beside the port and its low-key bars, Vueltas' soft black-sand strand is the most wind-sheltered of the town beaches and usually busy with sun-soakers, yogis and families. The water here is as calm and current-free as a pond.

Ermita del Santo   CHURCH
(Arure) At the top of the valley, in the village of Arure, this tiny stone chapel is built into the rock face, surrounded by a lookout showing off the southern landscape. It's signposted from Calle del Santo.

🏃 Activities

Dolphin- & Whale-Watching
Local operators offer whale- and dolphin-watching boat trips (on which you might spot some of 23 species of cetaceans, including bottlenose dolphins, pilot whales, sperm whales and rough-toothed dolphins), plus excursions to Los Órganos (p189) on the north coast. The best months for cetacean sightings are March to June, though chances are high year-round.

Oceano   WILDLIFE
(☑ 922 80 57 17; www.whalewatching-gomera. com; Calle Quema 7, Vueltas; adult/child €40/26; ⊙ 9.30am-1pm & 5-7pm Mon-Fri, 9am-1pm Sat) 🔝 One of the island's most responsible whale-watching outfits, Oceano runs two daily (excluding Sunday) three- to four-hour tours, with a focus on research, and works with environmental and animal-welfare organisations.

Tina   BOATING, WILDLIFE
(☑ 922 80 58 85, 629 990643; www.excursiones-tina.com; Camino Lagarto Gigante 16, Vueltas; adult €35-43, child €23; ⊙ 9.30am-1.30pm & 5-7pm) A long-running multilingual boating outfit offering excursions to Los Órganos (p189), as well as half-day dolphin- and whale-watching trips, all rounded off with

tapas, sangría and/or a swim, from Valle Gran Rey or Playa Santiago.

Excursiones Pura Vida   BOATING, WILDLIFE
(☑ 686 023194, 661 703491; www.lagomerapura vida.com; Puerto de Vueltas; adult/child €43/26) Twice-daily three- to four-hour trips aboard a traditional 10-person boat, on which you'll enjoy local snacks and have good chances of spotting whales, dolphins and even turtles, courtesy of an on-the-ball team.

Hiking
Valle Gran Rey is the starting point for an endless array of hiking routes, though most are quite challenging. The GR132 swings through town, linking Valle Gran Rey with Arure (7km, three hours) and Alojera (15km, six hours), while the popular official 3.5km Route 14 (1½ hours) heads into the Barranco de Arure to meet several waterfalls. There are also good walks up/down the valley to Las Hayas (7.5km, two to three hours) and El Cercado (7.5km, two to three hours).

Timah   HIKING
(☑ 922 80 70 84, 616 472250; www.timah.net; La Puntilla; per person €30; ⊙ 10am-1pm & 5-8pm Mon-Fri, 6-8pm Sun) This experienced, multilingual operator runs day hikes from Valle Gran Rey and Playa Santiago and organises multiday hiking holidays.

Yoga & Meditation
Drop-in yoga (€5), meditation (€3) and Pilates (€5) are offered at Finca Argayall (☑ 922 69 70 08; www.argayall.com; Playa de Argaga) 1km east of Valle Gran Rey's harbour; check schedules online..

Other Activities

Bike Station Gomera   CYCLING
(☑ 922 80 50 82; www.bike-station-gomera.com; La Puntilla 7; ⊙ 9am-1pm & 5-8pm Mon-Sat) Island-wide bike tours (from €45) and mountain and road bike hire (per day from €12).

Gomeractiva   WATER SPORTS
(☑ 638 239854; www.gomeractiva.com; Calle Las Vueltas 3, Vueltas; ⊙ 10am-5pm Mon & Wed-Sat, to 2pm Sun) Offers kayak trips and SUP trips and rental (one hour €12), as well as e-bike tours (per person €60).

🍴 Eating & Drinking

Some of La Gomera's most creative dishes are served in Valle Gran Rey, with a range of cuisines reflecting the international community here. Restaurants are huddled together in Vueltas and La Playa.

The beach is the place to be at sunset, when fire dancers and musicians get going.

Abisinia
CANARIAN €

(☑922 80 58 93; Cuesta de Abisinia 7, Vueltas; mains €8-12; ⏰6-11pm Mon-Sat) You'll have to book ahead or queue for a table at this cosy, traditional-style place beneath beamed ceilings. Tenerife and La Gomera wines accompany lovingly prepared classic island cuisine, with choices dancing from *potaje de berros*, homemade fish croquettes and goat's-cheese salad to seafood spaghetti and pork tenderloin in a world of styles.

La Ñamera
INTERNATIONAL €

(☑922 80 58 84; Paseo Las Palmeras 8, La Playa; snacks €3-8; ⏰9am-6.30pm; 🔊) A cheerful, German-owned, yellow-and-blue-themed cafe tucked into La Playa's buzzing stretch of restaurants and bars, always-busy La Ñamera sells luscious home-baked breads and cakes, and throws together tasty breakfasts (yoghurt-and-fruit bowls, *bocadillos*, eggs and bacon), fresh juices and tapas.

La Salsa
FUSION €€

(☑922 80 52 32; Calle Telémaco, Vueltas; mains €9-17; ⏰6-10pm Mon-Sat; 🖊) Abstract artwork hangs from bright-orange walls above just a handful of tables at La Salsa, one of Valle Gran Rey's most loved restaurants. The punchy, inspired menu turns out such seductive fusion creations as veggie tempura, courgette-and-carrot rolls dipped in yoghurt sauce and spinach-ricotta pasta in mushroom sauce, with lots of vegetarian/vegan choice. Wines include excellent Canarian picks. Book ahead.

Colorado
INTERNATIONAL €€

(☑922 80 62 17; Calle Punta de la Calera, La Playa; mains €13-17; ⏰6-9.30pm Thu-Tue) Down a little alley just back from the beach, this cosily elegant restaurant with peach-pink walls and blankets at terrace tables entices with its lightly creative Spanish-Canarian menu. Artily presented tapas include goat's-cheese *bombones* (chocolates), *patatas bravas* and bacon-wrapped dates, while mains turn to white-wine *dorada* (bream) or tagliatelle with truffle oil and goat's cheese.

El Puerto
SEAFOOD €€

(☑922 80 52 24; Puerto de Vueltas, Vueltas; mains €8-15; ⏰1-11pm) Specialising in fresh fish, this traditional bar-restaurant by the port is one of the best spots in town to try fresh local delicacies such as grilled *peto* and *medregal* (both local fish), and it also does paellas and meaty mains. The atmosphere is informal and friendly; you may have to wait for a table on weekends.

Tuyo
ASIAN €€

(☑922 80 60 20; www.tuyo-lagomera.com; Calle Vueltas 5, Vueltas; mains €10-18; ⏰6-10pm Tue-Sun; 🖊) Delivering a touch of Asian creativity amid the harbour's shoal of seafood restaurants, tempting Tuyo has an excellent menu of mainly Thai dishes, including yellow and green curries, tom yum (spicy-sour shrimp soup), wok stir-fries and tofu Buddha bowls, along with the odd Indian special. The decor is suitably soothing: all warm ochre and yellow and scattered lamps and statues.

Gomera Lounge
BAR

(www.gomeralounge.de; Calle Punta de la Calera 1, La Playa; ⏰8.30pm-1am Mon-Sat) A fun-filled La Playa club/piano bar hosting a great regular line-up of live music and events – from flamenco performances to tango workshops to DJ parties. Also has a boho boutique, colourful apartments (€60 to €90) and a spa offering massages (€60), Ayurveda and a hot tub.

🛍 Shopping

Mercadillo de Valle Gran Rey
MARKET

(Plaza Lomo Riego; ⏰9am-3pm Sun) Locally based artisans sell handcrafted jewellery, original cards, tye-dye clothes and fabrics brought from India at Valle Gran Rey's small Sunday market, next to the bus station.

ℹ Information

Oficina Municipal de Información Turística (☑922 80 54 17; GM1, La Calera; ⏰8am-3pm Mon-Fri)

Oficina de Turismo (☑922 80 54 58; www. lagomera.travel; Calle Lepanto, La Playa; ⏰9am-1.30pm & 3.30-5.30pm Mon-Sat, 10am-1pm Sun)

ℹ Getting There & Away

The Fred Olsen (p182) Benchi Express water taxi links Valle Gran Rey with San Sebastián (€8, 40 minutes) via Playa Santiago (€8, 30 minutes), three times daily in each direction.

From the **Estación de Guaguas** (Calle Lomo Riego), just off the main roundabout at the entrance to La Playa, bus 1 connects with San Sebastián (€5, 1¾ hours, two to five daily) via Las Hayas and El Cercado.

Taxis (☑922 80 50 58; GM1, La Calera) stop just north of the roundabout.

LA GOMERA VALLE GRAN REY

HIKING ON LA GOMERA

Raso de la Bruma–
Risquillos de Corgo–
Las Creces

Epina

Convento de
Santo Domingo
Hermigua

Mirador Risquillos
de Corgo

**Rasa de
la Bruma
Car Park**

Boca del Chorro

Embalse de
los Tiles

Las Creces

Bar La Vista

El Cedro

Parque Nacional
de Garajonay

Barranco de
El Cedro

Casa
Efigenia

Las Hayas

El Cercado

Ermita de Nuestra
Señora de Lourdes

Alto de
Garajonay
(1487m)

El Contadero Car Park

Chipude

Pajarito

Igualero

Alto de Garajonay–Hermigua

THE BASICS

Most people come to La Gomera to hike its beautiful trails, which range from scenic coastal walks to cross-island marathons.

Hiking maps are provided by tourist offices and, for the national park, by its **Juego de Bolas** (p186) and **La Laguna Grande** (p186) visitor centres. Path signage corresponds with numeration on the tourist office or national park maps (rather than the 'PR' route numbers usually used across Spain). Helpful guides include Discovery Walking Guides' *Walk! La Gomera* and accompanying map, and the 1:35,000 Gomera map by Freytag & Berndt. Bookshops in San Sebastián and Valle Gran Rey stock maps and guides. La Gomera's **tourism body** (p185) also offers hiking information online and by downloadable app.

Many of the best routes thread through the Parque Nacional de Garajonay (p187) at the heart of the island, but there are excellent walks all across the island, especially around Playa Santiago (p191) in the south

and Hermigua (p188) in the north. The 120km to 130km GR132 loops around the island's coastline, with two variations (one through Vallehermoso), taking six to eight days. The 37km GR131 tracks right across the centre of island, through the national park, between San Sebastián and Valle-hermoso (two to three days). Bear in mind that, given the island's sharp natural terrain, many routes have quite vertiginous sections.

ALTO DE GARAJONAY–HERMIGUA

START PAJARITO
END HERMIGUA
LENGTH 10.5KM; FOUR TO FIVE HOURS
DIFFICULTY DIFFICULT

This demanding downhill **hike** is one of the island's finest, running from its highest point to Hermigua through eerily evocative national-park *laurisilva* forest and the pastoral Barranco de El Cedro. It can also be tackled uphill (a popular alternative), though Hermigua's restaurants are perfect

Tackle the island's tallest, view-laden peak then descend through a lush, precipitous ravine to the sleepy town of Hermigua, or meander through the forested mist-cloaked reaches of the pristine Parque Nacional de Garajonay.

for a post-hike rest, whereas Pajarito has no facilities.

On the west side of the **Pajarito roundabout** (at the GM2–CV13 junction, 4km southeast of La Laguna Grande visitor centre), a signposted 'Alto de Garajonay' trail heads uphill, with views of Tenerife emerging beyond La Gomera's greenery. After 1km (30 minutes), past trees damaged by the 2012 fire, you reach the **Alto de Garajonay**, at 1487m the tallest peak on La Gomera; on a clear day Tenerife's El Teide stands snow-bound in the distance, and below you the tangled web of La Gomera's forests fall away. The Alto was a sacred spot for the Guanches, and archaeological excavations have unearthed remains of sacrificial offerings here.

From the Alto, head downhill following signs for Ruta 18 (the Gran Ruta Circular de Garajonay) to reach the **El Contadero** car park after 2km. The path descends northeast into the **Barranco de El Cedro** through shaded *laurisilva* woodlands. At the Y junction, follow 'Arroyo de El Cedro' signs and the trail soon criss-crosses a stream to emerge at Las Mimbreras clearing, 2.8km from El Contadero. Around 400m further on is the whitewashed, 20th-century **Ermita de Nuestra Señora de Lourdes** (p189) amid the trees.

Following signs to the hamlet of El Cedro (1.7km away), you come to the national park's north boundary before passing a few *casas rurales* to arrive in **El Cedro** via a paved road. El Cedro's bar-and-campsite **La Vista** (p189) is ideal for a Canarian-lunch break.

Leave El Cedro below the campsite following signs to Hermigua (3km). A steep stepped path heads downhill along a sheer cliff to a viewpoint over El Cedro's **Boca del Chorro waterfall**, then zigzags down the valley to the Embalse de los Tiles reservoir. From here, the easily followed trail continues amid views of cascading palms, the Roque Pedro, Hermigua's colourful houses and the sea beyond, then arrives into **Hermigua** itself, emerging (and signposted) opposite Plaza Victoriano Darias Montesinos and the **Convento de Santo Domingo** (p188).

RASO DE LA BRUMA–RISQUILLOS DE CORGO–LAS CRECES

START RASO DE LA BRUMA CAR PARK
END RASO DE LA BRUMA CAR PARK
LENGTH 4KM; ONE HOUR
DIFFICULTY EASY

A scenic introduction to the *laurisilva* forest that the Parque Nacional de Garajonay is famed for, the gentle official national-park **Route 12** weaves along a north-facing ridge thick with *laurisilva* forest and often cloaked in mist. Though it parallels the GM2 in parts, it's a rewarding trail and, as such, popular, with easy extensions southeastwards.

Begin in the **Raso de la Bruma car park**, around 5km northwest of La Laguna Grande on the north side of the GM2, where a board details the route. Following signs, you're engulfed in a fairy-tale forest where moss and lichen wrap green branches and rain sporadically floats through. The path wanders downhill through the forest, with views across the Vallehermoso valley opening up here and there, and emerges after around 1.2km at the **Mirador Risquillos de Corgo**, where you can peer down the valley to Vallehermoso town and the sea and, on clear days, even spot Tenerife looming behind La Gomera's mountains.

From the lookout, it's possible to loop directly back to the car park on an alternative signposted path, or join the long-distance GR131 southeastwards briefly to meet the GM2 then continue on through the forest. Crossing to the south side of the GM2, you reach the **car park for national-park Route 5**, from where signs lead along a wide path into a tranquil, drier *fayal-brezal* (Canarian heath forest) typical of the park's southern slopes. After 0.7km, the trail emerges at **Las Creces**, a clearing with a couple of picnic tables.

From here, double back to the car park and recross the GM2 to pick up the signposted return trail to the **Raso de la Bruma car park**. Or, if you're keen to extend the walk, Route 5 carries on from Las Creces in a 3.8km loop through the forest to return to the Route 5 car park, or, from Las Creces, you can walk 2.6km to the village of Las Hayas, where restaurant **Casa Efigenia** (p193) awaits.

1. Hiking through Parque Nacional de Garajonay (p194)
La Gomera's biggest draw is its beautiful hiking trails, from scenic coastal walks to cross-island marathons.

2. San Sebastián de la Gomera (p183)
Christopher Columbus is rumoured to have stayed in La Gomera's capital on his way to the New World.

3. Mirador Roque de Agando (p191)
Linked with Playa Santiago by the steep hiking Route 23.

4. Mirador de Abrante (p189)
Lookout high above Agulo, designed by architect José Luis Bermejo Martín.

La Palma

✆ 922 / POP 82,000

Best Places to Eat

➡ Enriclai (p207)

➡ La Casa del Volcán (p213)

➡ Restaurante Chipi-Chipi (p207)

➡ Tapas Trekking (p214)

➡ Casa Goyo (p214)

Best Beaches

➡ Puerto Naos (p219)

➡ Piscinas de la Fajana (p221)

➡ Los Cancajos (p213)

Why Go?

La Palma, the greenest of the Canarian islands, offers the chance to experience real, unspoiled nature – from the verdant forests of the north, where lush vegetation drips from the rainforest canopy; to the desertscapes of the south, where volcanic craters and twisted rock formations define the views; to the serene pine forests of the Parque Nacional de la Caldera de Taburiente. No wonder the entire island has been declared a Unesco biosphere reserve.

The absence of golden beaches has diverted many travellers' attention and tourism (aside from walkers and cruise liners) has yet to make a major mark on the island. The capital is also an architectural gem, its 16th-century centre lined with beautiful balconied mansions and houses.

In fact it is hard to find an unattractive corner on La Isla Bonita (the Pretty Island) and, provided unchecked development stays at bay, it is likely to remain that way.

When to Go

➡ Spring and autumn offer the most pleasant conditions for hiking, with generally clear skies and warm temperatures.

➡ As the most northwesterly island, La Palma catches more Atlantic cloud and rain than any other island and winters (November to February) in the north can be quite wet.

➡ Carnaval (March/April) in Santa Cruz is an unmissable spectacle of costumes, floats and locals caked in talcum powder.

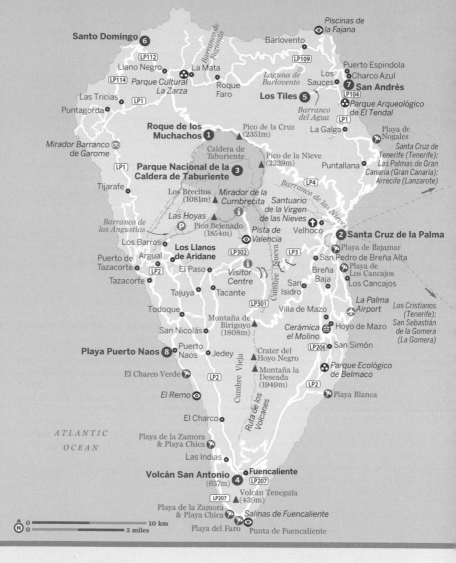

La Palma Highlights

1 **Roque de los Muchachos** (p217) Gazing deep into the Milky Way from this world-class stargazing spot.

2 **Santa Cruz de la Palma** (p202) Taking an evening stroll through the historic streets of this picturesque city.

3 **Parque Nacional de la Caldera de Taburiente** (p215) Hiking into a natural wonderland.

4 **Volcán San Antonio** (p212) Walking along the crater rim, before hiking down to the sea.

5 **Los Tiles** (p221) Grabbing a rain jacket and hiking boots for a trek through this lush, enchanted forest.

6 **Santo Domingo** (p226) Driving the winding road to the mirador for knockout views.

7 **San Andrés** (p220) Wandering slowly down the cobbled streets of the delightful village to its small cove.

8 **Playa Puerto Naos** (p219) Basking in the sun on the black-sand beach.

History

Long before Castilla (Spain) conquered the island in the 15th century, this rugged land was known as Benahoare. The first inhabitants are thought to have arrived as early as the 5th century BC, setting up an orderly society that eventually divided into 12 cantons, each with its own chief.

The island officially became part of the Spanish empire in 1493, after Alonso Fernández de Lugo (a conquistador and, later, island governor) used a tribesman-turned-Christian to trick the Benahoaritas into coming down from their mountain stronghold for 'peace talks'. They were ambushed on the way at the spot now known as El Riachuelo. Their leader, Tanausú, was shipped to Spain as a slave, but went on a hunger strike on board the boat and never saw the Spanish mainland.

The next century saw an important period of development and prosperity for the island. Sugar, honey and sweet *malvasía* (Malmsey wine) became the major exports and abundant and durable Canarian pine provided timber for burgeoning shipyards. By the late 16th century, as transatlantic trade flourished, Santa Cruz de la Palma was considered the third most important port in the Spanish empire after Seville and Antwerp, and the city's grand heritage that can be seen today is testament to that status.

The sugar, shipbuilding and cochineal (a beetle used to make red dye) industries kept the island economy afloat for the next several centuries, but the island's fortunes eventually took a downward turn, and the 20th century was one of poverty and mass emigration, mainly to Venezuela, Uruguay and Cuba. These days around 40% of the island's workforce depends on the banana crop, but tourism is another crucial ingredient.

❶ Getting There & Away

AIR

La Palma's airport (p209) is 7km south of Santa Cruz, with good connections to the rest of the archipelago and a range of European destinations.

BOAT

Santa Cruz has ferry connections (p209) to Tenerife, La Gomera, Gran Canaria and Cádiz.

❶ Getting Around

BUS

Transportes Insular La Palma (TILP; ☑ 922 41 19 24; www.tilp.es) buses keep Santa Cruz well connected with the rest of the island. The bus stops are near Plaza Constitución and along Avenida Marítima. Routes include bus 300 to Los Llanos de Aridane (€2.40, 45 minutes) every half-hour or so.

The island-wide bus ticket system has been revamped with just three tariffs depending on distance: €1.50 (0–10km), €2.40 (10–20km) and €2.60 (over 20km).

CAR & MOTORCYCLE

Having your own car is the best way to explore the island.

Avis (☑ 928 09 23 30; www.avis.es; La Palma Airport; ☉ 8am-9pm)

Cicar (☑ 922 42 80 48; www.cicar.com; La Palma Airport; per day/week €31/99)

Oasis (☑ 922 43 44 09; www.autosoasisla palma.com; Centro Cancajos, Local 301; per day/week from €30/100)

SANTA CRUZ DE LA PALMA

POP 15,700

One of the prettiest towns in the Canary Islands, the historic capital of the island, Santa Cruz de la Palma is a compact city strung out along the shore and flanked by beautiful, fertile green hills. The city centre is breathtakingly picturesque, while the beach and kilometre-long promenade have considerably boosted the city's summer-in-the-sun appeal. Wandering the historic streets around and uphill above Plaza España, either during the day or at night (when they are even more sublime), is a joy. With its location midway down the east coast, bus connections across La Palma and proximity to the airport, the city makes for a very good-looking base for getting pretty much everywhere.

History

In the 16th century the dockyards of Santa Cruz earned a reputation as the best in all the Canary Islands. Ships were made with Canarian pine, a sap-filled wood that was nearly impervious to termites, making the ships constructed here some of the most reliable and longest-lasting in the world. The town became so important that King Felipe II had the first Juzgado de Indias (Court of the Indias) installed here in 1558, and every single vessel trading with the Americas from mainland Spain was obliged to register.

The boom brought economic security, but it led to problems as well. Santa Cruz was frequently besieged and occasionally sacked

THREE DAYS ON LA PALMA

Day One

Drive from Santa Cruz to Los Tiles biosphere reserve (p221) and out under the shadows of giant trees. Continue the short distance on to San Andrés (p220) for an Asian-inspired lunch at La Placita and a stroll around the pretty cobbled streets. Drive towards Barlovento (p221) but veer off down the steep hillside cloaked in banana plants to the soaring cliffs around the Piscinas de la Fajana (p221) and La Gaviota (p221) restaurant for a sunset meal at the end of the day.

Day Two

Start your day exploring the picturesque streets of Santa Cruz (p202) then drive south for a superb seafood lunch under the roar of aeroplanes at Casa Goyo (p214). Continue on via quaint Villa de Mazo (p210) to the barren, volcanic terrain around Fuencaliente (p211) to walk around part of the rim of Volcán San Antonio (p212). If time allows, hike south to the tip of the island and the Salinas de Fuencaliente (p212). Otherwise, push on up the west coast to the seaside resort of Puerto Naos (p218) and your stop for the night.

Day Three

From Puerto Naos, take the winding road upward to the Parque Nacional de la Caldera de Taburiente (p215); lace up your boots for a half-day hike. If you've time, the 2 1/2-hour clamber up to Pico Bejenado (p223) is well worth it. Restore burned-off calories by driving the short hop to El Paso (p214) for some excellent food at Tapas & Trekking.

---

by a succession of pirates, including those under the command of Sir Francis Drake.

⊙ Sights

Wander down to the waterfront to stroll alongside a series of wonderful **old houses** with traditional Canarian balconies overflowing with flowers. Many of the houses date from the 16th century and have been converted into upscale restaurants. The islanders' penchant for balconies came with Andalucian migrants and was modified by Portuguese influences.

After a stroll along the inviting new beachside promenade, head for **Calle O'Daly**, the city's main street. Named after an Irish banana merchant who made La Palma his home, the street is full of shops, bars and some of the town's most impressive architecture and sights, including the grand spectacle of Plaza de España. Don't overlook exploring the streets higher up the steep hills as the whole area is infused with history and charm.

★ Museo Insular   MUSEUM

(Plaza San Francisco 3; adult/child €4/free; ⊙9.30am-7pm Mon-Fri, 10am-1pm Sat) This excellent museum is housed in a former 16th-century monastery with diverse exhibits ranging from Guanche skulls to cupboards of sad stuffed birds, pickled reptiles and an impressive shell and coral collection. There are also galleries dedicated to

20th-century Spanish paintings, as well as contemporary art.

★ Iglesia del Salvador   CHURCH

(☑922 41 32 50; www.parroquiadeelsalvador. com; Calle Adolfo Cabrera Pinto 1, Plaza de España; ⊙10am-8.30pm) The interior of this magnificent church boasts a glittering baroque pulpit dating back to 1750 and a stunningly intricate and coloured 16th-century wooden ceiling considered to be one of the best Mudéjar (Islamic-style architecture) works in all the Canaries. There are also several fine sculptures, dazzling stained-glass windows and a huge portrait of St Christopher and another portraying St Michael. The church overlooks and dominates Plaza de España.

Plaza de España   SQUARE

(Calle Real) This delightful, irregularly shaped square hosts buildings that are considered the most perfect exemplars of Renaissance architecture in the Canary Islands. The square is particularly beautiful and tranquil at night.

Iglesia de San Francisco   CHURCH

(Plaza San Francisco; ⊙9am-1pm & 5-8pm) This Renaissance church is decorated with a magnificent coffered ceiling.

Ermita de San José   CHURCH

(Calle San José; ⊙hours vary) A simple whitewashed 17th-century chapel that gives the name to the street on which it stands.

LA PALMA SANTA CRUZ DE LA PALMA

Santa Cruz de la Palma

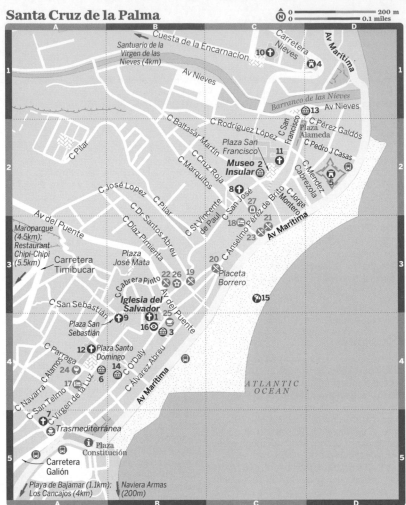

Ermita de San Sebastián CHURCH
(Calle San Sebastián; ⊙ hours vary) This small and tranquil chapel, centrally located in the Plaza de San Sebastián behind the Iglesia de San Salvador, is generally closed to the public.

Ayuntamiento HISTORIC BUILDING
(Town Hall; ☎ 922 42 65 00; Plaza de España 6; ⊙ 9am-2pm Mon-Fri) Wander north along Calle O'Daly and you'll come to the irregularly shaped, palm-shaded Plaza de España, to the south of which sits the grand and imposing *ayuntamiento,* built in 1559 after the original was destroyed by French pirates.

Playa de Santa Cruz de La Palma BEACH
(Avenida Marítima) With boardwalks to protect your feet from the scorching sand, this superb, huge and very deep black-sand beach is quite a sight, stretching along much of Avenida Marítima and luring beach-seekers from far and wide.

Iglesia de Santo Domingo CHURCH
(Plaza Santo Domingo; ⊙ hours vary) If you follow the steps heading up out of Plaza de España to the upper town, you will find the shady Plaza Santo Domingo. The substantial Iglesia de Santo Domingo here boasts an important collection of Flemish paintings and

Santa Cruz de la Palma

dates to 1530. Note that the church is often shut; the adjacent building, which looks like it is part of the church, is actually a school (it has maroon doors, while the church has green doors) which you should not enter.

Centro de Interpretación de La Bajada
MUSEUM

(La Bajada: Centro de Interpretación Fiestas Lustrales de La Palma; Calle Virgen de la Luz 13; adult/child €4.50/free; ⊙10am-2pm Mon-Fri) This excellent museum is dedicated to the history, events and parades of the Fiesta de Nuestra Señora de las Nieves (p206), including the Dance of the Dwarves, by way of an entertaining virtual tour. A combined ticket (€7) includes admission to the Naval Museum.

Ermita de Nuestra Señora de la Luz
CHURCH

(⊙hours vary) Head southwest on Calle Virgen de la Luz for a look at the simple 17th-century facade of the modest Ermita de Nuestra Señora de la Luz, one of several small 16th- and 17th-century chapels in town. Notice that the church has a front door and a side door, a common Canarian church motif.

Palacio de Salazar
HISTORIC BUILDING

(☎922 411957; Calle O'Daly 22; ⊙10am-8pm Mon-Fri, to 2pm Sat) FREE This handsome 17th-century, late-Renaissance palace is on your left soon after you enter the street from Plaza Constitución. It's home to a government-run cultural centre.

Iglesia de la Encarnación
CHURCH

(⊙hours vary) This lovely church dates to around the 15th century and was the first to be built in Santa Cruz after the Spanish conquest. One way to reach it is to cross the footbridge over the Barranco de las Nieves by the Museo Naval, turn left and walk to the end of the road and then climb the steps up the hill which will take you to the church.

Museo Naval
MUSEUM

(Avenida las Nieves, Plaza de la Alameda; adult/child €3/1.50; ⊙10am-6pm Mon-Fri, to 2pm Sat & Sun) Gaze north across leafy Plaza de la Alameda and you may think Christopher Columbus' ship, the *Santa María,* became stranded here. This is actually the city's painted concrete naval museum where you can peruse magnificent model ships, marine-related exhibits and other maritime displays and snippets of seafaring history. A combined ticket (€7) with the Centro de Interpretación de La Bajada is available.

Castillo de la Virgen
CASTLE

This modest 17th-century castle is more like a simple fortress that was built as a defence against piracy. The castle looks out over lovely views of the town and the sea.

★ Santuario de la Virgen de las Nieves
CHURCH

(Avenida las Nieves; ⊙8.30am-8pm; P) For splendid views down the valley to Santa Cruz, put aside time to tackle the 4km uphill hike north of town to La Palma's main object of pilgrimage, the 17th-century Santuario de la Virgen de las Nieves with its fabulously ornate interior. The wooden Mudéjar-carved ceiling, sculptures and sparkling crystal chandeliers are the precursor to the 82cm-tall Virgin Mary herself, surrounded by a glittering altar. The 14th-century sculpture is the oldest religious statue in the Canary Islands and the object of deep veneration.

The sculpture was believed to have been brought by merchants before the arrival of the Spaniards; every five years she is carried down to Santa Cruz in a grand procession.

The church sits in a peaceful spot in the hills surrounded by trees and greenery, all in typical Canarian colonial style with balconies and simple facades. The walk up is quite steep going, so take some water. By car, follow signs from Avenida Marítima where it crosses the *barranco,* then turn right on the Carretera de las Nieves (LP-101) and continue winding up the hillside until you see signs for the sanctuary; the curve-filled 5km trip takes nearly 15 minutes. Bus 10 (€2, approximately 20 minutes) comes up hourly from the town centre from 6.45am until 8.45pm, less frequently on weekends.

There's a bar-restaurant in the square right by the church. If you take the steep path to the right (as you face it) of the souvenir shop opposite the church, it takes you to a higher position to photograph the mountains and also to find a track that leads to excellent views over the city below. Other stunning views across the *barranco* (river gorge) valley to Santa Cruz await down the road away from the church to just before the first bend.

Maroparque   ZOO
(www.maroparque.com; Calle Cuesta 28; adult/child under 12 yr €11/5.50; ☉11am-5pm Mon-Fri, to 6pm Sat & Sun; Ⓟ) Children will love Maroparque,

a small zoo and animal rescue centre where marmosets, meerkats, toucans, Siamese fighting fish, African porcupines, pythons and other reptiles crawl, clamber, swim, flap and slide around their (thankfully) spacious living quarters. The zoo is set in pleasantly landscaped gardens. Refreshments are available. You can get here by car or on buses 302, 303 and 300 from Santa Cruz.

Castillo de Santa Catalina   CASTLE
(St Catherine's Castle; ☉10am-2pm Mon-Fri) At the northern end of the seafront, the Castillo de Santa Catalina was one of several forts built in the 17th century to fend off pirate raids. Named after a hermitage nearby dedicated to Santa Catalina, it was the main castle in a series of defences protecting the city.

🎉 Festivals & Events

Carnaval   CARNIVAL
(☉Feb, dates vary) This is a riotous two-week celebration with music, dancing and drinking, including that infamous crazy night of talcum-powder-throwing mayhem, known as Día de Los Indianos.

Semana Santa   RELIGIOUS
(☉late Mar-early Apr) Members of lay brotherhoods parade down Calle O'Daly in their blood-red robes and tall, pointy hoods.

Fiesta de Nuestra Señora
de las Nieves   SAINT'S DAY
(☉Jul-Aug) The Feast Day of Our Lady of the Snows is the island's principal fiesta. The highlight in Santa Cruz is the parade of giants and 'fat heads' (fanciful, squat characters with exceptionally large heads), and the **Dance of the Dwarves**, which has been performed here since the early 19th century. The fiesta is celebrated every five years: 2020, 2025 etc.

WORTH A TRIP

HIKING TO THE SANTUARIO DE LA VIRGEN DE LAS NIEVES

The 4km hike up into the hills to the Santuario de la Virgen de las Nieves (p205) is a spectacular and not-too-demanding hike. Trekking up first thing in the morning or towards later afternoon sees the best light and also avoids the midday heat. To set off from Plaza de la Alameda, cross the footbridge near the Museo Naval to the far side of the Barranco de las Nieves and turn left; follow the road to its conclusion where you will see some narrow steps and a sign that says 'Pico de la Nieve 14.2km'. Head up the steps which will take you shortly to the Iglesia de la Encarnación (p205). Facing the church, turn left and head up Cuesta la Encarnación; take the first left after around 500m and walk down Avenida José Pérez Vidal for around 350m and then take the first right and walk up this road which becomes Barranco de las Nieves, following the *barranco* (river gorge). It will take around 45 minutes to an hour to walk up, but coming back is faster.

DON'T MISS

DÍA DE LOS INDIANOS

Tenerife and Gran Canaria are known for their, ahem, lively celebrations of Carnaval (p206), but unassuming Santa Cruz de la Palma also has a wild side. For two weeks in February (dates vary) there's music, dancing, drinking and talcum powder. On Carnaval Monday, known here as Día de Los Indianos, the good citizens of La Palma bring buckets of white, fragrant powder down to the centre of Santa Cruz and prepare to do battle with their neighbours. After loosening up with a few drinks and a little music, the snowy spectacle begins. Anyone is a target and the town ends the night coughing and blinking furiously, covered head to toe with talcum powder. The tradition began to mock *los indios,* Canarian emigrants who became wealthy in the Americas and returned to the island decked in white suits and Panama hats. Now it's just another excuse for a fiesta.

The full name of the festival is the **Fiestas Lustrales de la Bajada de la Virgen de las Nieves** (The Lustral Festivals of the Bringing Down of the Virgin of the Snows), which refers to a religious procession where the islanders take the Virgin from the Santuario de la Virgen de las Nieves (p205) around the island throughout the months July and August, celebrating her arrival in each important town with a big party. The word *bajada* means 'bringing down', in reference to the statue of the Virgin coming down from her church; the festival is fully explained at the Centro de Interpretación de La Bajada (p205).

✖ Eating

★**Habana**　　　　　　　　　　CANARIAN €
(Calle Anselmo Pérez de Brito 27; mains €7.50-9; ⊗8.30am-11pm) This delightful pink-and-white wedding cake of a building has its terrace on a picturesque plaza overlooking a fountain and surrounded by flower-filled balconies. The coffee is superb, the staff are busy but all smiles and the menu won't disappoint with risottos, bruschettas and fried cheese with *mojo* (Canarian spicy salsa). It's Cuban-run, so the music should get you foot-tapping as well.

Mercado Municipal　　　　　　MARKET €
(Avenida del Puente; ⊗7am-2pm Mon-Sat) Situated on the site of a 16th-century house-hospital dedicated to Nuestra Señora de los Dolores (Our Lady of Sorrows), this excellent market is the place for fresh produce and deli items. Try a sugar-cane juice with rum, mint and lemon (€4), sold at a stand here – or possibly without the rum if it's 7am in the morning!

Tasca Luis　　　　　　　　　CANARIAN €
(Taburiente; ☑680 47 68 31; https://tasca-luis. negocio.site; Calle Pedro Poggio 7; mains €7-8.50, menú €10; ⊗noon-11pm Tue-Sat, to 4pm Sun) Look for the barn-like doors at this locals' place

fittingly decorated with faded B&W photos of Santa Cruz in yesteryear. Portions are huge, but don't bother asking for a menu; it's whatever struck the owner's fancy that day. One thing's for sure though – it will be traditional Canarian cuisine through and through.

Pizzeria Piccolo　　　　　　　ITALIAN €
(Avenida Marítima 53; pizzas €6-9.50, pastas €11-13; ⊗noon-4pm & 7pm-11pm) Trade is good at this pizzeria on Avenida Marítima. A slice above the pizza norm, these have crisp thin bases and generous toppings. The homemade pastas are al dente delicious, plus there are risottos and lighter bites like focaccias and salads. The building is historic with beams, original tiles and loads of creaky atmosphere, with tables out front for alfresco dining.

★**Enriclai**　　　　　　　　　　CANARIAN €€
(☑680 20 32 90; Calle Dr Santos Abreu 2; mains €13-15; ⊗12.30-3.30pm & 7.30-10.30pm Tue-Sat, 7-10.30pm Mon; ☑) Just four tables, a 200-year-old building, cool jazz on the soundtrack, a choice of dishes that alters daily according to what is fresh in season and universal acclaim from diners. Plus Carmen, an owner-cum-chef who is such a delight you want to adopt her. The food includes vegetarian options. You'll need to reserve way ahead.

★**Restaurante Chipi-Chipi**　　CANARIAN €€
(☑922 41 10 24; www.chipichipi.es; Calle Juan Mayor 42, Velhoco; mains €10-15; ⊗noon-5pm & 7-11.30pm Mon, Tue & Thu-Sat; ℗ 🚼) Despite the name, this is no greasy diner, but a famous local restaurant that specialises in a variety of grilled meats, all served with loads of *papas arrugadas* (wrinkly potatoes) and *mojo,* with individual dining areas in rambling gardens as well as a central terrace.

Find it located off the LP-101 a few kilometres west of Santa Cruz, in the hills on the southern outskirts of the town of Velhoco.

La Lonja
SPANISH **€€**

(📋922 415266; www.lalonjarestaurante.com; Avenida Marítima 55; mains €12-18; ◷noon-4pm & 7-11pm Wed-Sun) Occupying an old Canary house on the seafront with balconies bursting with colourful flowers, La Lonja is one of the most popular restaurants in town, with a mix of Canarian, Castillian and Mediterranean fare, like paella, suckling pig and roasted cheese with *mojo*. There's also fish on the menu and classic Canarian *postres* (desserts) such as *bienmesabe* and the house dessert.

 Drinking & Entertainment

In town head to Calle Álvarez Abreu for the closest thing you'll find to a nightlife scene. Plaza José Mata, off Avenida Puente, also has a few late-night bars. Avenida Marítima is lined with cafes and *zumerías* (juice bars).

★ El Cafe de Don Manuel
CAFE

(www.elcafededonmanuel.com; Calle Anselmo Pérez de Brito 2; ◷8am-8.30pm Mon-Fri, 9am-2pm Sat & Sun) In the refined setting of Casa Cabrera (dating to 1864), the atrium-capped, light-filled courtyard here is delightful, with an abundance of hanging greenery and jazz piano wafting through the air. Soak up the ambience and sip a *cortado* (espresso with a dribble of milk) for just €1 – Don Manuel is famed for its coffee. It's tricky to find though; look for the advertising bicycle parked right outside.

Cinnamon Bar
BAR

(📋922 41 02 24; Calle San Telmo 2; cocktails €4.50, tablas €7-8; ◷12.30-4pm & 7.30-11pm; 📶) Cinnamon Bar has a choice position right on the corner of Plaza Santo Domingo, one of the most elegant squares in the city. Its interior is all sharp lines and dazzling white contrasting with red and black, while the tables outside sit beneath the gracious Iglesia de Santo Domingo. A bar primarily, but gastrobar too, serving *tablas* (platters) to share.

★ Teatro Chico
CINEMA

(📋922 416 045; www.cineteatrochico.com; Calle Díaz Pimienta 1; tickets €5.50) Once located on the site of an old house-hospital founded in 1514, this magnificent but very petite former theatre originally opened in 1866 and reopened in 2014 as a cinema. Ask staff if you can pop inside to admire the interior with its painted ceiling above the stage and elegant old galleries. Even better, go see a film.

TOP FESTIVALS & EVENTS

Like any Spaniards worth their heritage, the *palmeros* love a good party, and the year is packed with festivals and celebrations.

Each town has feast days celebrating its patron saint with several days of parades, parties and other activities. The following are some of the best events:

Breña Alta (◷late Jun)

Breña Baja (◷25 Jul) ·

Barlovento (◷12–13 Aug)

San Andrés y Los Sauces (◷early Sep)

Tazacorte (◷late Sep)

Other festivals worthy of note the following:

Fiesta del Almendro en Flor (Fiesta of the Almond Blossom; ◷Jan-Feb) A celebration of the beauty of the almond blossom in Puntagorda and of the town's patron saint, San Mauro Abad.

Fiesta de las Cruces (◷3 May) The island's crosses are bedecked in jewellery, flowers and rich clothes – truly a sight to see.

San Juan (◷23 Jun) Marks the summer solstice, and is celebrated in Puntallana with bonfires and firecrackers galore.

El Diablo (◷8 Sep) Fireworks, parades of devils and grim music in Tijarafe provide a graphic show of the triumph of good over evil. About 30kg of gunpowder is used in the 20-minute show honouring Nuestra Señora de Candelaria.

Castanets (◷24 Dec) After Midnight Mass in Breña Alta and throughout the island, *palmero* men perform skits accompanied by the noisy music of castanets.

LA PALMA TIPPLES

Since the early 16th century, when Spanish conquerors planted the first vines on the island, La Palma has been known for its sweet *malvasía* (Malmsey wine). Thanks to the merchants and colonists who came in and out of La Palma's ports, the wine acquired fame throughout Europe, and some referred to the tasty stuff as 'the nectar of the gods'. Even Shakespeare wrote about sweet Canary wine, making it Falstaff's favourite in *Henry IV* and calling it a 'marvellous searching wine' that 'perfumes the blood'. You can also find dry *malvasía* as well as a variety of reds, whites and rosé, especially in the areas around Fuencaliente. For an alcohol-filled journey embark on the **Wine Route** (📞922 44 44 04; www.vinoslapalma.com/vino-y-ocio/enoturismo.html), which includes wineries you can visit; details are available at the tourist office in Santa Cruz de la Palma.

Although the sugar plantations have all but gone, what remains is put to good use in the production of *ron* (rum) by the last producer on the island, Ron Aldea.

Shopping

★Vinatería Albillo　　FOOD & DRINKS
(📞922 41 08 95; Calle Anselmo Pérez de Brito 59; ⏰10am-4pm Mon-Wed, 10am-3pm & 6.30-8.30pm Thu & Fri, 10am-3pm Sat) An excellent deli which specialises in local and national Spanish cheese, gourmet olives, preserves, coffee and other goodies like anchovies and smoked salmon as well as wines. You can also take a pew outside for a coffee and chug a large cup of *gofio con leche* (ground roasted grain with milk) or whatever else takes your fancy.

ℹ️ Information

Tourist Office (📞922 41 21 06; www.lapalmacit.com; Plaza Constitución; ⏰9am-6.30pm Mon-Sat, to 6pm Sun)

ℹ️ Getting There & Away

AIR

La Palma Airport (📞922 41 15 40, 902 404704; www.aena.es) is 7km south of Santa Cruz. Within the Canary Islands, **Air Europa Express** (www.aireuropa.com) and Binter Canarias (p269) link the island with Tenerife and Gran Canaria. For Fuerteventura and Lanzarote, you usually need to go via Tenerife or Gran Canaria, though sometimes there are direct flights. A growing number of international flights include Gatwick (London), Manchester, Frankfurt, Paris, Madrid, Amsterdam, Brussels and Barcelona.

BOAT

Naviera Armas (📞902 45 65 00; www.navieraarmas.com; Estación Marítima) Connects La Palma with San Sebastián de la Gomera (€24, 2¼ hours, one daily Tuesday to Sunday), La Gomera; Los Cristianos (€41, 3½ hours, one daily Tuesday to Sunday), Tenerife; and Las Palmas de Gran Canaria (€72, 14½ hours, one daily Tuesday to Sunday), Gran Canaria, with stops at La Gomera and Tenerife.

Fred Olsen (p269) Ferries run to Los Cristianos (€42, two hours), Tenerife. From Tenerife, you can then continue to El Hierro.

Trasmediterránea (📞902 45 46 45; www.trasmediterranea.es; Plaza de la Constitución) Sails for Santa Cruz de la Tenerife (€22, 5½ hours, 4pm Friday), Tenerife. The same boat continues on to Las Palmas de Gran Canaria, Gran Canaria, and Cádiz, Andalucía, in one and three days respectively.

BUS

TILP (p202) buses arriving from north, south and west of the city stop at bus stops on Avenida Los Indianos, one on the northern side, the other on the southern side of the road; there is also a bus stop on Avenida Marítima, and another further north along the same road. Destinations include Fuencaliente (€2.60, one hour, up to nine daily), El Paso (€2.40, 35 minutes, regular), Los Llanos de Aridane (€1.50, 55 minutes, regular), Los Cancajos (€1.50, 10 minutes, every 30 minutes) and Barlovento (€2.60, 55 minutes, regular).

ℹ️ Getting Around

TO/FROM THE AIRPORT

Bus 500 makes the journey between Santa Cruz and the airport (€1.50, 35 minutes, every 30 minutes) from 7.15am to 10.45pm, stopping in Los Cancajos on the way. At weekends, the service runs at least hourly. A taxi to the airport costs about €17.

IN TOWN

The best way to get around Santa Cruz is on foot. If you come in by car, try to find a parking spot by the waterfront; parking in the old streets uphill behind the centre can be particularly tricky. Buses run up and down Avenida Marítima (€1.35), or you can hop in a **taxi** (📞922 18 13 96).

SOUTHERN LA PALMA

A mind-bogglingly diverse mix of lush vegetation, pine forests, banana plantations, agricultural land and barren volcanic wastelands characterises southern La Palma.

The Fuencaliente area, at the southern tip of the island, is home to the most recent volcanic activity in the archipelago with several volcanic eruptions recorded in the 20th century, the last being the explosion of Volcán Teneguía in 1971, which increased the size of the island by pouring lava into the sea. The surrounding volcanic Llanos Negros (black plains) support the viticulture of the south and can be seen fanning out below the Volcán San Antonio. Trekkers will delight in the opportunity to hike here.

Villa de Mazo

POP 4821

This quiet and sleepy village tucked away in the hills 13km south of Santa Cruz is surrounded by green, dormant volcanoes. The town is known for its cigars and handicrafts and is also home to several absorbing museums, one squirrelled away within a particularly noble building.

Villa de Mazo is also a highlight of La Palma's wine route (p209), an island-wide series of driving routes that take in the best of the island by way of the pleasure of the grape. Leaflets detailing the routes can be picked up at tourist offices or downloaded from the website.

⊙ Sights

★ Museo Casa Roja   MUSEUM
(☑922 42 85 87; www.villademazo.com/museos; Calle Maximiliano Pérez Díaz; adult/child €2/free; ⊙10am-2pm Mon-Sat) This handsome ochre-red mansion (built in 1911), located down one of the steep streets from the main road, has downstairs exhibits on Corpus Christi – a festival Villa de Mazo celebrates with particular gusto: streets are decorated with elegant 'carpets' made of flower petals, seeds and soil. Upstairs are displays of linen and embroidery; don't miss the fabulous tiled bathroom with the painted toilet. The house also has an impressive imperial staircase, further ornate tiled floors and a lovely, small landscaped front garden with another garden behind.

Escuela Insular de Artesanía   MUSEUM
(☑922 44 00 52; Vía Enlace Dr Morera Bravo 1; adult/child €2/free; ⊙10am-2pm Mon-Fri) This former handicrafts school still has a weaving studio (which you can peek into), but otherwise has been transformed into a museum focusing on crafts and handicrafts on the island. There is a short multilingual film and a shop where you can buy embroidery, ceramics, baskets and other locally produced crafts.

Templo de San Blas   CHURCH
(Calle Caridad Salazar 24; ⊙hours vary; ℗) Down a steep hill from the centre of town is this lovely whitewashed church dating from 1512, dedicated to St Blaise and overlooking the ocean. Inside the cool interior, the church boasts a baroque altarpiece (wrapped in a shroud when we last visited) beneath a magnificent ceiling; the church is also home to several intriguing pieces of baroque art.

Cerámica el Molino   MUSEUM
(☑922 44 02 13; Carretera Hoyo de Mazo; ⊙9am-1pm & 3-7pm Mon-Sat; ℗) Well signposted from the town is this meticulously restored mill that houses a ceramics museum (including a short film) and workshop where artisans

---

ADVENTURE SPORTS

If just plain walking seems too tame, try rock climbing or caving. Ékalis (p222) offers a variety of climbing and rappelling experiences as well as a two-hour spelunking expedition. It also offers bike rental and guided mountain-biking trips, another popular activity on the island. If you're in shape, La Palma's endless climbs and dips will be thrilling, but if trudging uphill isn't your thing, guide services like those offered by Bike'n'Fun (p218) offer transport to the top of a peak followed by a mostly downhill ride. Other recommended cycling outfits include Atlantic Cycling (p219) and Bike Station (p219), both in Puerto Naos. All operators can pick you up at your hotel or a central meeting point.

In recent years, paragliding has really taken off and the island is now considered one of the world's best places to glide. Try it in Puerto Naos with Palmaclub (p219).

For those wanting to get out on the water, diving outfitters in Puerto Naos and Los Cancajos will hook you up with tanks, wetsuits and fins. Sea-kayaking expeditions are also available at both locations; contact Ékalis for more information.

SCENIC DRIVE: THE SOUTHWESTERN COAST

The road up the west coast from the bottom tip of the island is full of open curves that swoop past green hills dotted with cacti and low shrubs. The highway runs along a ridge, leaving the glittering ocean a blue haze to the left. Other than the view, there's not much here, unless you count the small bar at the mirador 6km out of Fuencaliente in the tiny town of **El Charco**, but even so it all makes for a great detour from either Fuencaliente or even Puerto Naos and the drive only takes around half an hour.

Keep heading north and you'll travel through a series of tiny, almost uninhabited villages. Stop in San Nicolás for a while (it's 1km past the village of Jedey) to eat at **Bodegón Tamanca** (☑922 49 41 55; www.facebook.com/bodegas.tamanca; Carretera General Las Mancha-Fuencaliente; mains €10-18; ☺11am-11pm Tue-Sat, to 5pm Sun; P), a very popular and atmospheric restaurant located in a huge natural cave.

make attractive reproductions of brown Benahoare pottery; you can watch them at work. There's also a large and popular souvenir shop as well with everything from small vessels to vast bowls. You can also get here from the LP-132 highway.

 Eating

San Blas CANARIAN €
(Calle Maria del Carmen Martínez Jerez 4; mains €8-10; ☺7am-3pm & 5.30-10.30pm Tue-Thu, to 11pm Fri, 9am-11pm Sat, to 3pm Sun; 🚻) This handy place in the centre of town serves simple fare such as pasta, salad, *chocos* (cuttlefish) with *mojo verde* (coriander-based sauce) or goat with potatoes. Sit on the pretty outdoor terrace surrounded by stout palms and a dazzle of flowers. It's also a cafe if all you want is a *cortado*.

❶ Getting There & Away

Villa de Mazo is sandwiched between the LP-1 and LP-132 highways. Get here on bus 201 from Santa Cruz (€2.40, 10 daily, 20 minutes), which continues to Fuencaliente (€2.60).

Parque Ecológico de Belmaco

**Parque Ecológico
de Belmaco** ARCHAEOLOGICAL SITE
(☑922 44 00 90; Carretera a Fuencaliente, Km 7; adult/child €2/free; ☺10am-3pm Mon-Sat; P) The first ancient petroglyphs found on the archipelago were discovered at this site in 1752. A 300m trail that winds around various cave dwellings (complete with animal sound effects!) once inhabited by Benahoare tribespeople is the heart of this archaeological park; the highlight is the squiggling etchings, which date back to AD 150. There's also a two-room

museum with reproductions and information regarding the history of the discovery.

There are four sets of engravings, and experts remain perplexed about their meaning, though they speculate that the etchings could have been religious symbols. You can't actually enter the caves but at the entrance to one of them the engraved stones are clearly visible. You can climb up beyond this on the path for a short hike, at one point through a very narrow fissure in the rock.

Bus 201 from Santa Cruz (€2.40, 25 minutes) to Fuencaliente runs down this way nine times daily Monday to Friday, with four buses on Saturday and Sunday. The nearest bus stop is about 400m south of the Belmaco archaeological site.

Fuencaliente

POP 1705

Fuencaliente (Hot Fountain) is the best tourist base in the south of the island and offers a mix of marine and volcanic attractions. The area gets its name from hot springs that were once believed to treat leprosy, but were buried by a fiery volcano in the 17th century. Don't think that the volcanoes have gone sleepy and tame since then though – the last eruption was in 1971, when Volcán Teneguía's lava flow added a few hectares to the island's size.

◎ Sights

Creating a stark, at times lunar-like, landscape, the volcanoes in this area are the newest in the archipelago and are the main draw of Fuencaliente. The beauty of their low, ruddy cones belies the violence with which they erupted while the dark and hard fields of lava form a severe and largely barren landscape that contrasts with the soft blue of the sea.

WORTH A TRIP

SCENIC DRIVE: TO THE END OF THE ISLAND

If you're in the mood for some scenic driving, and possibly some scenic swimming, take the winding LP-209 west from Fuencaliente, which then becomes the LP-207 before heading down past the Princess resort complex to the very southern tip of the island (a birdwatchers paradise). Located here is the **Playa del Faro** (Lighthouse Beach; Carretera la Costa el Faro; P) and Salinas de Fuencaliente (p212), some 3.5 hectares of salt flats; the salt produced here, under the brand name Teneguia, is sold across the island. The nearby Volcán Teneguía (p212) almost destroyed the lighthouse during its eruption and formation in 1971.

On the coast, the black-lava rock and crystal-blue ocean are perfect contrasts to one another, but if you do choose to swim off one of the beaches here, be wary of heavy undertows and dangerous dumping waves. Return by following the LP-207 north to complete the loop, taking you back to Fuencaliente.

If you've spent too long behind the wheel, you can also hike from here up to Volcán San Antonio past Volcán Teneguía as the lighthouse marks the end of the trek down from the visitor centre. Buses from Fuencaliente (€2.40, 30 minutes) run to the lighthouse at a quarter past the hour.

★ **Volcán San Antonio Visitor Centre & Volcán San Antonio** VISITOR CENTRE
(www.lapalmacit.com; adult/child €5/free; ⊙9am-6pm; P♿) The visitor centre is your first stop if you want to explore the volcanoes. Displays are well-captioned and informative, but the layout is not very imaginative and rather dated. It's far more interesting to head out and walk along a section of the rim of Volcán San Antonio, a yawning chasm of this great black cone, which last blew in 1949 and has now been repopulated by hardy Canarian pines. The crater is also a superb stargazing viewpoint.

The views down into the crater are excellent as are the panoramas of the endless sea beyond, to the islands of La Gomera and El Hierro. You can also see the Volcán Teneguía below and the small lighthouse just beyond that. Note that it can get pretty windy on the rim of the volcano, so watch your footing. Back at the visitor centre, a cafe is at hand for refreshments. Just beyond the gate is the start of the signposted path downhill for the terrific one- to two-hour hike to the Volcán Teneguía and the lighthouse.

Volcán Teneguía VOLCANO
Volcán Teneguía's 1971 eruption was the most recent in the archipelago. A signposted trail from Volcán San Antonio, near the visitor centre, leads you here on a downhill hike over scrunchy volcanic gravel (wear sturdy shoes). The easy to moderate walk to the volcano and back takes about two hours. If that's not far enough, you can continue onwards for a further hour (one way) down to

the coast at the Faro (Lighthouse) de Fuencaliente near the southern tip of La Palma.

Buses (€2.40, 30 minutes) run from the lighthouse back to Fuencaliente at a quarter to the hour between 9.45am and 5.45pm, via the settlement of Las Indias.

Bodegas Teneguía WINERY
(☎922 444078; www.bodegasteneguia.com; Calle Antonio Francisco Hernández Santos 10; ⊙10am-6pm Mon-Fri, to 1pm Sat & Sun, tours 12.30pm Mon-Fri; P) Fuencaliente is famous for the wines made from the grapes that flourish in its volcanic soil. Founded in 1947, Bodegas Teneguía is well known for its white and red wines, as well as its famous sweet *malvasía*, sold all over the island and beyond. Note that the restaurant here is exclusively for tour groups. There is a wine shop where you can also taste (or rather drink) the wines (you pay per glass from €0.50).

If you would like a tour, advance reservations are essential; the price varies according to how many are in your group.

Salinas de Fuencaliente SALT PANS
(☎922 411 523; www.salinasdefuencaliente.es; Carretera la Costa el Faro 5; ⊙10am-7pm) FREE Beyond the lighthouse at the south of the island are the Salinas de Fuencaliente, which you can explore along a self-guided path; explanations on boards tell you all about the processes of salt extraction from seawater. The pans cover a huge area, totalling 3.5 hectares.

Beaches

The volcanic coast around Fuencaliente is largely inaccessible, much of it lined with banana plantations, rocky outcrops and steep cliffs. Two pleasant exceptions are **Playa de la Zamora** and **Playa Chica**, black-sand beaches tucked side by side in neighbouring coves. They're no secret but are rarely crowded, so you may find them quiet.

✖ Eating

Panadería Zulay BAKERY €
(☑711 74 19 17; www.facebook.com/zulayline; Carretera General 84; ☺8.30am-8pm Mon-Sat, 9am-8pm Sun) Perfect for cakes, baked goodies, breakfast, a *bocadillo* or a very decent coffee. Take a seat outside at this relaxing and good-looking *panadería* not far from the bus station.

★La Casa del Volcán CANARIAN €€
(☑922 44 44 27; www.lacasadelvolcan.es; Calle Los Volcanes 23; mains €9-14; ☺1-4pm & 6-9.30pm Tue-Sat, 1-4pm Sun; 🅿🕏) This bodega's sophisticated restaurant is one of the best places on the island to enjoy innovative and exquisitely prepared Canarian dishes. The atmosphere is rustic yet refined, with an intimate dining room fronted by a wood-clad bar with barrel seating. Dishes include rabbit with red *mojo* (Canarian spicy sauce) with potatoes, goatmeat goulash or fresh fish of the day.

Tasca La Era CANARIAN €€
(☑628 02 11 22; Carretera Antonio Paz y Paz 6; mains €9-13; ☺noon-10pm Thu-Tue; 🅿🖐) This farmhouse-style restaurant has a terrace overlooking a pretty garden studded with palms. It's a charming spot for fish and meat dishes. *Solomillo* (fillet steak) is the speciality with a choice of eight accompanying sauces while the homemade fish croquettes and watercress soup are also recommended.

❶ Getting There & Away

Buses 200 and 201 head between Fuencaliente and Santa Cruz (€2.60, one hour, up to nine daily). Jump on bus 210 for Los Llanos (€2.60, 50 minutes).

CENTRAL LA PALMA

Central La Palma is where the majority of visitors will spend their days exploring, and with very good reason. The bowl-shaped Caldera de Taburiente, and the national park named after it, dramatically dominates the centre of the island, with jutting peaks, deep ravines and lush pine forests blanketing its slopes. This spectacular region offers some of the most breathtaking hiking in all

of the Canary Islands, topped with some its most unparalleled views.

Two of La Palma's important commercial centres, El Paso and Los Llanos (the island's largest town), are in this area, making it the island's economic engine. As you near the west coast, huge banana plantations fill the valleys, while the coast itself is home to some of the island's longest, prettiest beaches.

Los Cancajos

The appealing promenade and small volcanic beach of Los Cancajos are the main attractions of this cluster of hotels, apartments and restaurants 4km south of Santa Cruz. Los Cancajos has none of the charm or history of Santa Cruz or other authentic, lived-in towns, but it nevertheless makes a good home base thanks to its abundance of quality lodging options and agreeable beach, which is one of the best on the island.

🏃 Activities

Los Cancajos is a popular spot for diving. A gentle 20-minute stroll along the seafront promenade takes you past tiny coves and contorted lava flows that have been colonised by hardy plants that seem almost luminous in comparison to the dramatic black rocks on which they live.

Buceo Sub DIVING
(☑922 18 11 13; www.4dive.org; Calle Las Gaviotas 24A; dive incl equipment from €32; ☺9am-5pm Mon-Sat) This reputable and well-respected diving operator located next to the Spar supermarket offers a number of diving packages and courses, from newbie to instructor level, as well as canoeing courses.

La Palma Diving Center DIVING
(☑922 18 13 93; www.la-palma-diving.com; Centro Comercial Los Cancajos, Local 227; dive incl equipment from €41, courses from €69; ☺10am-6pm Mon-Sat) Located in the main Los Cancajos

LA PALMA LOS CANCAJOS

---

❶ LOS CANARIOS

If you are scratching your head, perplexed, searching on your map for the town Los Canarios (which is often signposted), don't fret. This is just a short version of Los Canarios de Fuencaliente, although the town is rarely referred to by its full name.

shopping centre and aimed mainly at a German clientele, although instructors do speak English. A large range of diving courses are offered from beginner to instructor level. Snorkelling tours are also offered.

✖ Eating

★ Casa Goyo   SEAFOOD €€
(☑922 44 06 03; www.facebook.com/casagoyola palma; Carretera General Lodero 120; mains €10-15; ⊘1-4.30pm & 7-11pm Tue-Sun; ℗) This simple palm-roofed shack by the airport has become one of the most well-known seafood restaurants on the island. Hear the roar of the planes as you savour *vieja à la plancha* (pan-grilled parrot fish) and *papas* (potatoes). The fish here really *is* as fresh as that day's catch.

El Pulpo   SEAFOOD €€
(☑922 43 49 14; Playa de Los Cancajos; mains €10-15; ⊘12.30-4pm & 6-9pm Thu-Tue) This simple beach restaurant started out as a rough-and-ready shack back in 1971 and is still renowned by locals as one of the best places to enjoy fried fish. With chairs sprawled on a terrace on the sand, it's justifiably popular for families with bucket-and-spade-aged toddlers.

ⓘ Information

Tourist Office (☑922 18 13 54; www.lapalma cit.com; Calle de la Arena, Playa de Los Cancajos; ⊘9am-1.30pm & 3-6pm Mon-Fri, 9am-1pm & 4-6pm Sat, 9.30am-2pm Sun)

ⓘ Getting There & Away

Bus 500 (€1.50, 10 minutes, every 30 minutes) runs from the airport to Santa Cruz de la Palma, stopping at Los Cancajos en route. Buses 35, 200, 201 and 300 (€1.50, 10 minutes) regularly pass through Los Cancajos from Santa Cruz de la Palma, stopping at Cruce Cancajos.

El Paso

POP 7457

The gateway to the amazing Parque Nacional de la Caldera de Taburiente – the park's visitor centre is just outside town – El Paso is the island's largest municipality, with sprawling forests and around 8 sq km of cultivated land. The very colourful, pretty and historic town centre and its stone streets make it well worth a leisurely amble. If you're driving into town, turn right at the 'Casco Histórico' sign to reach the main attractions, including the gorgeous little church.

◉ Sights & Activities

★ Museo de la Seda   MUSEUM
(Silk Museum; ☑922 48 56 31; Calle Manuel Taño 6; adult/child €2.50/free; ⊘10am-2pm Mon-Fri) Learn the secrets of the caterpillars that spin dresses fit for a marriage. The silk produced here is made according to traditions that have barely changed since the industry arrived on the island in the 16th century. There is an upstairs museum with some magnificent silk garments on display from as far afield as China and India, plus a short film about silk production. End your visit at the downstairs workshop where you can see the weaving in action.

Ermita de la Virgen de la Concepción de la Bonanza   CHURCH
(Calle General Mola; ⊘hours vary) This beautifully restored 18th-century *ermita* (chapel) has some elegant painted patterns on the white-painted exterior. Renovations mercifully left intact the splendid Mudéjar ceiling above the altar. The Virgen de la Concepción de la Bonanza herself is venerated in the form of a fully clothed effigy behind the altar.

Mercado   MARKET
(El Mercadillo del Agricultor y Artesanal de El Paso; Calle Antonio Pino Pérez; ⊘3-7pm Fri, 9am-2pm Sat) This popular farmers market also sells some arts and crafts. It's in the same building as the tourist office.

★ Ruta de los Volcanes   HIKING
(LP-301) The demanding, but breathtaking, Ruta de los Volcanes is a 19km hiking trail that meanders through ever-changing volcanic scenery, providing stunning views of both coasts as it heads south along a mountain ridge across the heart of volcanic territory and towards Fuencaliente. This trail is part of the long-distance GR131. Allow six to seven hours for the trek – it's demanding and is best undertaken on cool, cloudy days, as there is not much shade or fresh water along the way.

The trailhead is the Refugio del Pilar, an expansive park with a picnic area, on the LP-301 highway. The walk finishes in Fuencaliente, from where you will probably have to arrange homeward-bound transport.

✖ Eating

★ Tapas & Trekking   TAPAS €
(https://tapastrekking.negocio.site/; Calle Sagrado Corazón 4; tapas €4-5.50, tablas €4-8; ⊘9am-4pm Sun & Mon, to 11pm Wed-Sat; ☎) Situated in the

---

FOUR PERFECT LA PALMA HOTELS

Hotel La Palma Romántica (☑ 922 18 62 21; www.hotellapalmaromantica.com; Las Llanadas, Barlovento; r incl breakfast €80; P 🛜 🛋) This excellent-value rural Barlovento hotel has 40 elegant rooms, a classy restaurant, sweeping views of the valley, professional service and a small spa. If it's sunny, take a dip in the outdoor pool; if it's grey, slip into the heated indoor pool.

Hotel San Telmo (☑ 922 41 53 85; www.hotel-santelmo.com; Calle San Telmo 5; s/d from €80/90; 🛜) Just eight rooms at this wonderful Santa Cruz boutique hotel: two in the original building with beamed ceilings, wooden shutters and balconies overlooking the delightful flower-filled terrace. The other rooms are more contemporarily decorated in tasteful muted earth colours.

Apartamentos Playa Delphin (☑ 922 40 81 94; www.playadelphin.com; Avenida José Guzman Pérez 1; studio €62, 2-/3-person apt €69/75; P 🛜) Hard to miss in Puerto Naos, this family-run apartment complex is in an imposing semi-circular building close enough to the beach to ensure you're lulled to sleep by the Atlantic waves. Rooms have balconies with sunloungers and are well-kitted out, with little extras such as toasters and fruit bowls.

La Fuente (☑ 922 41 56 36; www.la-fuente.com; Calle Anselmo Pérez de Brito 49; apt €41-65; 🛜) The nine apartments at German-owned Santa Cruz address La Fuente are all different. The most expensive have large rooms, plus balconies and amazing sea and town views. A roof terrace is at hand for sun-catching.

---

shadow of the evocative 18th-century *ermita*, this place keeps it simple with a superb menu of tapas and *tablas* (platters) to share. Offerings range from homemade fish and chorizo *croquetas* to scrambled eggs with cod, Italian sweet peppers, grilled goat's-milk cheese, stuffed cuttlefish and *papas arrugadas* (wrinkly potatoes).

ℹ Information

Tourist Office (☑ 922 48 57 33; www.lapalma-cit.com; Calle Antonio Pino Pérez; ⊙10am-6pm Mon-Fri, to 2pm Sat & Sun)

ℹ Getting There & Away

Bus 300 runs between Santa Cruz de la Palma (€2.40, 35 minutes) and El Paso every half hour from Monday to Friday and every hour at weekends, before continuing to Los Llanos de Aridane (€1.50, 20 minutes).

Parque Nacional de la Caldera de Taburiente

The **Parque Nacional de la Caldera de Taburiente** (☑ 922 92 22 80; www.reservasparquesnacionales.es) FREE is glorious hiking territory and home to the best views La Isla Bonita ('the pretty island') can muster. It's an unmissable destination even for those with little time on their hands.

The heart of the astonishing park is the **Caldera de Taburiente** itself (literally, the Taburiente 'Stewpot' or 'Cauldron'). A massive depression 8km wide and surrounded by soaring rock walls, it was first given the name in 1825 by German geologist Leopold von Buch, who took it to be a massive volcanic crater. The word 'caldera' stuck, and was used as a standard term for such volcanic craters the world over. This caldera, however, is no crater, although volcanic activity was key in its creation. Scientists now agree that this was a majestically tall volcanic mountain, and that it collapsed on itself. Through the millennia, erosion excavated this tall-walled amphitheatre.

The LP-2 highway, which links Santa Cruz with Los Llanos, skirts the southern rim of the park, and from the road you can sometimes see the characteristic cloud blanket that fills the interior of the caldera and spills over its sides like a pot boiling over. At other times you may see fantastical clouds form, hanging over the peaks and ravines, before diffusing into the air. You may also see rainbows come and go during the day as sunlight and water vapour interplay in a regular exchange.

🏃 Activities

Many trails traverse the park, but unless you plan to spend several days exploring, you'll probably stick to the better-known paths (p222). Most are in good shape, though the trail from La Cumbrecita to the campsite is notoriously slippery and should be avoided by novice hikers, and the trail running down the Barranco de las Angustias can be dangerous in rainy weather. Keep an eye on the weather forecasts and plan accordingly.

Signposting is generally quite clear. Although you're unlikely to get really lost (and there are usually groups of hikers out on the trail to help you if necessary), you're best off buying a detailed map, like the 1:25,000 *Caldera de Taburiente Parque Nacional*, for sale at the visitor centre (p217). See also the excellent website www.senderos delapalma.com for route descriptions and news on trail closures.

🏃 The Southern End

Most people access the park from either El Paso or Los Llanos. You'll need a car, taxi or guide to cart you up to one of the miradors that serve as trailheads.

To get an overview of the park, there's no better walk than the PR LP 13 trail, which begins at **Los Brecitos** (1081m). Get there from Los Llanos by following the signs first to Los Barros and then on to Los Brecitos. The path leads through a quiet Canarian pine forest, past the park campsite, across a babbling brook and down the **Barranco de las Angustias**, crossing countless small streams along the way. Watch out for fascinating sights like brightly coloured mineral water that flows orange and green, intriguing shapes made by pillow lava and rock formations such as the phallic **Roque Idafe**, an important spiritual site for the Benahoaritas. This six-hour (22km) hike is popular and is suitable for anyone in average-to-good physical shape. Be careful if it has rained recently or if a storm seems

imminent; the 'Gorge of Fear' can quickly become a raging torrent, and people caught in its fast-rising waters have died.

When the trail is fully open, the best way to tackle it is to park at Las Hoyas, at the base of the Barranco de las Angustias. From here, 4WD **taxi shuttle services** (☑922 40 35 40; per person €10; ☺8am-noon) whisk you up to Los Brecitos and allow you to enjoy the descent back to your car without backtracking.

Another option is to drive from the visitor centre up the LP-302 and then the Carretera Caldera Taburiente to the **Mirador de la Cumbrecita** (1287m), where there is a small **information office** (☺9am-6pm). The 7km drive passes turn-offs for the Pista de Valencia and the Ermita del Pino, leading you through a peaceful pine forest to sweeping views of the valley. From the car park here, you can make a round-trip hike up to the panoramic views from Pico Bejenado (p223); allow 2½ hours for the trek. Those with less time can take a 3km circuit trail to both the **Mirador de los Roques** and the **Mirador Lomo de las Chozas**; the final part of the loop is a flat, wheelchair- and stroller-friendly 1km trail between Lomo de las Chozas and the car park.

Take note that the trails leading off from the Mirador de la Cumbrecita are by far the most popular in the park and, due to overcrowding and limited space in the car park, park authorities have enforced a strict traffic quota. If you want to drive up to the mirador, you have to register online with the visitor centre (p217) just past El Paso three days before your visit and wait for your turn to drive up. Sometimes the wait might only be a few minutes but at weekends and in high season it can be over an hour.

An excellent, moderately difficult walk is the PR LP 13.3 (p222) from the Pista de

---

THE SWEET TASTE OF LA PALMA

La Palma's main dishes, like those on other islands, are simple. What the island is really known for is its indulgent desserts. Honey is an important food here, and historically La Palma was an important sugar producer. Most of the sugar cane is gone, but the islanders' sweet tooth remains; head to the mercado municipal (p207) in Santa Cruz to taste sugar-cane juice, which you can have combined with lemon, mint and rum if you're feeling racy. The honey-and-almond desserts, *rapaduras*, are justifiably popular, as well as the *almendrados* (almond, sugar and egg cakes baked with cinnamon), *bienmesabe* (a paste of almonds and sugar) and *Príncipe Alberto* (mousse of chocolate and almonds).

Local cheeses, most made with unpasteurised goat's milk and many smoked, are worth trying. Get more information online at www.quesopalmero.es. For an excellent selection of locally produced cheese, as well as wines and deli items, visit Vinatería Albillo (p209) in Santa Cruz.

STARRY SKIES

The huge telescopes on the peak of Roque de los Muchachos belong to the **Observatorio del Roque de Los Muchachos** (www.iac.es), one of the world's best places to study the night sky and in 2012 deemed the world's first Unesco-certified Starlight Reserve. The mammoth Grantecan (Gran Telescopio Canarias; GTC) is the largest single-aperture optical telescope on the planet. The observatory can be visited by booking a tour.

Guides who are authorised to conduct visits to the observatory can be found through Cielos-La Palma (www.cielos-lapalma.es).

The observatory allows scientists to study the formation and evolution of the galaxies throughout the history of the universe as well as investigate the stars and observe the rings of spatial material that give birth to new planets. Far from urban centres and city lights, La Palma is an ideal place to stargaze. More than 75% of the nights here on El Roque are clear, a statistic that's hard to beat.

La Palma's observatory is linked with the Observatorio del Teide (p164) on Tenerife, and together they form the Instituto de Astrofisica de Canarias (IAC).

Ad Astra La Palma (www.adastralapalma.com; tour €9) is a private company offering morning tours to the observatory, but it is essential to book in advance (minimum age six). Tours are held daily except on Monday and Wednesday; take along a coat as it can be cold. Night-time tours of the observatory are not permitted, but other stargazing tours are also provided – see the website for details.

Valencia parking area to the 1854m Pico Bejenado. This four- to five-hour (11.4km) return hike climbs up through some wonderful old pine forest before popping out on the caldera ridge for terrific views. The trail is easy to follow and it's a good choice for any reasonably fit walker who wants something less trodden and more challenging than the routes around the Mirador de la Cumbrecita, but not as demanding as the Los Brecitos trails. Along the route up the mountain you can take a fork for the Mirador de la Cumbrecita.

🏃 The Northern End

A string of rocky peaks soaring nearly 2500m high surrounds the caldera, and the trail running along these rock walls affords a thrilling vantage point from which to observe the park and the rest of the island. A narrow dirt trail, part of the long-distance GR131, skims the entire northern border of the park, and shorter trails branch off it and venture down deeper into the park.

One of the most spectacular sections runs between the **Roque de los Muchachos** and the **Pico de la Nieve**, which is off the LP-4, a winding highway that branches off the LP-1 highway 3km north of Santa Cruz and snakes its way across the island, skirting the rim of the park and its northern peaks. Avoid backtracking by taking two cars and leaving one at the *pico* (the parking area is a 20-minute walk from the trail itself). Then

drive (or get a ride) up to the Roque de los Muchachos, the highest point on the island at 2426m and the location of the Observatorio Roque de Los Muchachos. The walk back down to the Pico de la Nieve should take four to five hours (approximately 9km).

Numerous miradors dot the LP-4 highway around the Roque de los Muchachos; even if you don't hike the rim, the views from up here are worth seeking out. At night, this area offers unbeatable stargazing.

ℹ️ Information

Visitor Centre (📞 922 49 72 77; www.reservas parquesnacionales.es; Carretera General de Padrón 47; ⊙9am-6pm) This helpful centre is 5km east of El Paso on the LP-3 highway and offers free general information (pick up the English *Caldera de Taburiente Paths* map), detailed maps (including a geological map) as well as guides, an exhibition centre and a botanical garden.

ℹ️ Getting There & Away

No roads run through the park, and there are only three ways to access it: via the LP-202 near the visitor centre, via the track that goes from Los Llanos to Los Brecitos, or via the LP-1032 highway in the north. There are no buses into the park.

Bus 300 (€1.50 from El Paso, 10 minutes) between Santa Cruz de la Palma and Los Llanos stops by the visitor centre twice hourly from Monday to Friday and hourly at weekends.

THE CANARIAN PINE

One of the most visible features of a hike through the stunning landscape of the Caldera de Taburiente is the ever-present Canarian Pine (*pinus canariensis*), a towering green subtropical coniferous tree that is endemic to the Canary Islands and which is the source of the dense carpet of needles underfoot in any hike in the hills.

A highly drought-tolerant species of tree, the pine can climb to over 40m in height, the tallest tree variety in the Canary Islands. Although you will see the tree all around you in forests at elevation on La Palma and in forests on Gran Canaria and Tenerife, it's barely visible on Fuerteventura or Lanzarote and is present in smaller numbers on the other islands. The tree is among the most fire-resistant trees on the planet, partly due to its very thick bark, and capable of continued growth after forest fires.

The largest example you will probably see is Pino Gordo (Fat Pine), outside Vilaflor up in the hills towards El Teide on Tenerife, which reaches a heady 45.12m in height and an amazing 9m circumference!

Los Llanos de Aridane

POP 20, 043

The economic centre of the island and a true-blue working town, Los Llanos lacks the obvious charm of the capital or some of the smaller villages, but the shady plazas and pedestrian streets of the historic centre are attractive and worth exploring.

Set in a fertile valley, this has historically been one of the island's richest areas, with a long tradition of cultivating sugar cane, bananas and, more recently, avocados. These days it's home to many of the island's businesses and services, and many young *palmeros* are moving here to find jobs. Colourful murals and modern sculptures are dotted throughout the centre, making the city an open-air museum.

Plaza España   PLAZA

Relaxing and good-looking Plaza España is the heart of the historic town. Majestic, ancient and sizeable Indian laurel trees provide a much-welcome leafy canopy on even the sunniest days, making this the perfect spot to picnic, people-watch or relax in a cafe. The Iglesia de Nuestra Señora de los Remedios dominates the northern flank of the square. Have a coffee in one of the cafes bordering the square and afterwards wander the surrounding streets and plazas, which preserve considerable traditional character.

Bike'n'Fun   CYCLING

(☑922 40 19 27; www.bikenfun.de; Calle Calvo Sotelo 20; guide service per person €55, bike rental per day from €14; ☺10am-1pm) This reputable outfit organises a wide range of biking excursions throughout La Palma, including a tour around Los Llanos. Offers mountain bike and e-bike rental too.

La Vitamina   INTERNATIONAL €

(www.facebook.com/lavitaminalosllanos; Calle Real 29; mains €8.50-10; ☺noon-9.30pm Mon-Wed & Fri; ☑) This laid-back, slightly bohemian, slightly disorganised choice with painted chairs and mismatched furniture is often busy, supplying diners with largely but not exclusively vegetarian and vegan meals that pull together flavours of Africa, Asia and Spain into highly unexpected combinations. Portions are ample.

ⓘ Information

Tourist Office (☑922 40 25 83; Avenida Dr Fleming; ☺9.30am-2.30pm & 4-7pm Mon-Fri, 9.30am-3.30pm Sat & Sun)

ⓘ Getting There & Away

Services from the **bus station** (Calle Luis Felipe Gómez Wanguemert) include bus 300, which runs from Santa Cruz de la Palma (€2.40, 45 minutes) every half an hour from Monday to Friday and every hour at weekends, passing through El Paso (€1.50, 20 minutes). Bus 210 runs to Fuencaliente (€2.60, 40 minutes, up to six daily) and bus 24 links with Puerto Naos (€2.40, 20 minutes, up to 21 daily).

Puerto Naos

One of La Palma's two tourism centres (Los Cancajos, on the east coast, is the other), Puerto Naos is a town that exists almost solely for tourists. Set to a backdrop of a huge and dramatic rock face, huddled around a long, rounded bay and protected on either side by tall cliffs, the town makes a fine base for sun-worshippers and beach-lovers who want easy access to the north and interior.

The town is not unattractive, but has no real sights beyond its black-sand beach, though there are activities you can sign up for if you want to get the heart pumping, including paragliding which is increasingly popular.

Sights & Activities

Playa Puerto Naos
BEACH

(P) The black-sand beach at Puerto Naos is the longest on the island, measuring around 1km. Backed by towering palm trees, the excellent facilities here include showers, changing rooms and toilets, plus sunbeds and umbrellas for hire. A bustling promenade of bars, restaurants and shops backs the sweep of sand and includes several places to stay. At the northern end is the smaller black-sand cove of Playa Chica.

El Charco Verde
BEACH

(LP-213; P) With boardwalks on the sands, this small black volcanic beach beyond Puerto Naos is a fun stop on the way to El Remo. Note the rock jutting into the sea, which is the site of a small shrine. There's parking at either end of the beach and a small kiosk on the sand, serving coffee, beer and tapas. Bus 24 (€2.40) runs here from from Los Llanos, travelling via Puerto Naos.

El Remo
VILLAGE

(LP-213; P) Just a short way down to the very end of the road beyond Puerto Naos, past the banana greenhouses, is this small village right by the sea, composed of a gathering of low-build houses, cafeterias and restaurants. It's a fun place to scramble over the rocks looking for crabs (plentiful) and watching the waves crash ashore. A black-sand *playa* runs largely the length of Calle Remo; sunsets are terrific.

Bus 24 (€2.40, 30 minutes) runs here from Los Llanos, travelling via Puerto Naos.

Atlantic Cycling
CYCLING

(www.atlantic-cycling.de; Calle Mauricio Duque Camacho 27; bike rental per day €23, e-bikes per day €55) Sells all manner of bikes, rents bikes and e-bikes and arranges racing bike tours. If you rent a bike for more than three days, the daily rate drops by €3. It's best to organise bike rental a few days in advance if possible.

Tauchpartner
DIVING

(922 40 81 39; www.tauchpartner-lapalma.de; Edificio Playa Delfín 1; dive incl equipment €41; 9.30-11am & 5-7pm Mon-Sat) Offers an extensive range of PADI and CMAS scuba-diving courses as well as single dives.

Palmaclub
PARAGLIDING

(610 69 57 50; www.palmaclub.com; Calle Juana Tabares 3; tandem glide €100-150; 10am-6pm) Paragliding has seriously gained momentum here and aficionados come from throughout Europe to take advantage of the island's ideal conditions and easy take-off and landing sites. Swiss-run Palmaclub can arrange tandem glides, though you will need a licence. Prices depend on the length of flight, either seven minutes from the huge cliffs behind Puerto Naos or 15 from a more distant peak.

Bike Station
CYCLING

(922 40 83 55; www.bike-station.de; Avenida Cruz Roja 3; bike rental per day €6-24, guided trip from €50; 9am-noon & 5-7pm Mon-Sat) Offers rentals and a range of challenging guided mountain-bike rides. Also sells secondhand bikes.

Eating

Orinoco
SEAFOOD €

(www.islalapalma.com/orinoco; Calle Manuel Rodriguez Quintero 1; tapas €2.50-7, mains €6-10; 1-11pm Thu-Tue) It's not the kind of place that charms by looks alone, but this homey spot up a side street from the main promenade is the favourite of locals for fish soup, seafood tapas, fresh fish and traditional *palmero* desserts like *bienmesabe* and *quesillo* (flan).

LA PALMA PUERTO NAOS

LA PALMA FOR CHILDREN

Building sandcastles on the black-sand beaches of Puerto Naos and Los Cancajos (p213), hunting for crabs at El Remo or splashing in the saltwater pools in the Piscinas de la Fajana (p221) and Charco Azul (p220) are givens, but what to do after the beach and the brine? Older children may enjoy striding out on suitable hikes including the Mirador de los Roques and the Mirador Lomo de las Chozas, both in the Parque Nacional de la Caldera de Taburiente (p215). Kids will also enjoy the volcanic thrill of walking along the rim of the Volcán San Antonio (p212) and you can throw in some history by taking the 1.5km walk around the Parque Cultural La Zarza (p221) or set them exploring the model ships at the Museo Naval (p205) in La Palma. The younger crowd will also get a kick out of the animals at Maroparque (p206).

Restaurante Playa Chica
SEAFOOD €€

(☑922 40 84 52; Avenida Marítima 2, Playa Chica; mains €15-20; ⊙noon-11pm Wed-Mon) Overlooking the delightful and small namesake cove at the northern end of the beach, this appealing seafood restaurant with its jaunty blue decor enjoys one of the best locations in town – hence its popularity. Dishes are well executed – even the salads, something of a rarity in a Spanish seafood restaurant. The seafood soup is good value at €3.

❶ Getting There & Away

Bus 24 makes the trip to and from Los Llanos (€2.40, 20 minutes, up to 21 daily), continuing on to El Remo, 5.5km south of Puerto Naos.

NORTHERN LA PALMA

The dense tropical forests, fertile hills and pines that create such a blanket of green over the northern half of the island couldn't be further away from the lava-encrusted, sun-baked south. The winding roads make this the least-accessible, but many say most beautiful, part of the island, with rocky cliffs plunging into sapphire waters and deserted black beaches surrounded by palm trees.

San Andrés

POP 4473

San Andrés is like something from a story-book, with hilly, cobblestone streets that steeply lead down past low, whitewashed houses to a small cove. A delightful place by the sea, the sleepy village is ideal for a slow wander and exploration of its idyllic, picturesque shades. The short hike along the coast to the pools at Charco Azul makes for a very pleasant and breezy diversion.

The nearby Los Tiles biosphere reserve (p221) is one of the top sights of the island and is a short journey from San Andrés.

◎ Sights

Iglesia de San Andrés
CHURCH

(Calle Plaza) Sitting at the quiet heart of San Andrés, this church has its origins in 1515 and was one of the first churches the Spanish conquerors built on the island, though most of what you see today was built in the 17th century. Inside, take a look at the lavish baroque altarpieces and the coffered ceiling. The small Ermita de El Pilar is just down the road.

★ Charco Azul
SALTWATER POOL

Creatively designed Charco Azul is a blending of moulded concrete with natural volcanic rocks. The effect is stunning, especially when the waves are whipping up: a series of natural-looking saltwater pools with sunbathing platforms and a walkway between them. Bus 100 (€2.40) regularly runs from Santa Cruz de la Palma to Los Sauces where you can change to bus 104 from Los Sauces to Charco Azul (€1.50, 10 minutes, three daily).

If going by car, Charco Azul is located 6km northwest of San Andrés on the LP-104 highway. You can walk between Charco Azul and San Andrés along the **coastal path**; from San Andrés walk down the steep slope of Calle Abajo to the cove, cross the bridge and keep heading north. Bus 4 runs from Los Sauces to Charco Azul via San Andrés.

**Parque Arqueológico
de El Tendal**
ARCHAEOLOGICAL SITE

(El Tendal Archaeological Park; ☑639 98 38 79; Camino San Juan; ⊙10am-5pm Tue-Sat, to 3pm Sun & Mon) With a new and very informative exhibition centre with touchscreen displays, this museum and cave complex at the side of the LP-1 road to Los Sauces was still opening up when we visited. The centre faces a series of caves used by Benahoarita people in the *barranco* below, some of which should be accessible by the time you read this. The exhibition centre has a video on the history of the caves and their importance to the early people who settled here.

Also on display in the exhibition hall are pottery pieces, tools and other fragments discovered here.

✗ Eating

La Cantina
SEAFOOD €

(Charco Azul; mains €8-10; ⊙11am-7pm) This bar-restaurant is the natural choice for all-comers, overlooking the frolicking going on in the pools below, and beyond them, the endlessly sapphire sea. There's a lovely terrace slung out beneath bamboo roofing for those all-important views and a good-value, tempting seafood menu.

La Placita
THAI, CANARIAN €€

(☑922 10 63 34; www.facebook.com/laplacitafoodandcoffee; Calle La Plaza 5; mains €10-14; ⊙noon-9pm Tue-Thu, to 10.30pm Fri & Sat) You may not expect to find a Thai restaurant in the middle of a sleepy village like San Andrés – but here it is. Run by a German-Thai couple, it has a palm-shaded terrace overlooking the church and a menu predominantly Thai but also including some innovative Canarian dishes. The word is out so don't expect too many empty tables, especially on Saturday.

ℹ Getting There & Away

Bus 100 connects Santa Cruz (€4, 35 minutes, up to 19 daily) with the centre of the nearby town of Los Sauces; for San Andrés, change to bus 4 (€1.50, 15 minutes). If driving, San Andrés is 3km off the main LP-1 highway along the LP-104, which forks off the LP-1.

Los Tiles

A biosphere reserve since 1983, the nearly 140 sq km of Los Tiles are covered with a beautiful, lush rainforest that's bursting with life. This moist, cool, natural wonderland is one of the most magical spots on the island, a must-explore place where you can wander among the diverse flora and fauna and the largest *laurisilva* (laurel) forest on the island. The nearest town is Los Sauces, around 4km to the northeast of the visitor centre.

Mirador Topo de las Barandas   HIKING

The shortest and most popular of the hiking trails in Los Tiles is the steep climb up to the Mirador Topo de las Barandas (1.5km; allow one hour for the round trip), which leads to a pavilion at the top and spectacular views on two sides, one into the valley and the hills layered upon each other, the other down to the sea. The climb up is quite exerting but the trail – full of birdsong – is easy to follow.

Marcos & Cordero Springs   HIKING

The long, ravine-side trail to the Marcos and Cordero Springs (8.1km) passes through a dozen damp tunnels (bring a flashlight and rain jacket) and winds past waterfalls, through forest and alongside volcanic dikes. It's not incredibly steep (except in short stretches), but it can be slick; wear hiking boots and exercise caution.

A popular approach to tackling this trail is to get a taxi (€15 per person) from Los Tiles car park up to Casa del Monte, from where the hike to the springs and back should take about four hours.

ℹ Information

Visitor Centre (☑ 922 45 12 46; ⊙ 9am-2pm & 2.30-6.30pm) At the helpful visitor centre you'll find literature (but no maps when we last visited) and detailed exhibitions, and staff can suggest hiking routes.

ℹ Getting There & Away

Coming from Santa Cruz, follow the signs to Los Tiles off the LP-1 highway. The visitor centre is 3km up the LP-105, which runs alongside the lush Barranco del Agua. No buses venture up here, so you'll need either your own wheels or strong legs.

Barlovento

POP 2360

You may want to skip the town itself in favour of the natural attractions that lie near the coast, especially the lovely saltwater pools of the Piscinas de la Fajana, just east of Barlovento.

Piscinas de la Fajana   SALTWATER POOL

(P) At these calm – and calming – saltwater pools, frothy sea waves pound just beyond the concrete barriers. About 5km east of Barlovento, on the LP-1 highway, you'll turn off towards this beautiful coastal spot, where dramatic dark rocks and a savage ocean forge a sublime panorama.

La Gaviota   SEAFOOD €€

(☑ 922 18 69 14; Piscinas de la Fajana; mains €10-16; ⊙ 8am-10pm; P) This suitably marine-themed blue-on-blue restaurant has a vast terrace right on the water and overlooking the pools; the menu includes all the fishy favourites served with a generous portion of potatoes with *mojo* (Canarian spicy sauce).

ℹ Getting There & Away

Bus 100 from Santa Cruz (€2.60, 55 minutes) runs to Barlovento (the last stop), with 18 services daily Monday to Friday and nine services daily Saturday and Sunday.

Parque Cultural La Zarza

Parque Cultural La Zarza   ARCHAEOLOGICAL SITE

(La Mata; adult/child €2/1; ⊙ 10am-6pm Mon-Sat, to 3pm Sun; P) Two Benahoare petroglyphs are the main attraction at the Parque Cultural La Zarza. The geometric-shaped etchings lie along a 1.5km circuit within the park itself. Back at the visitor centre, you can watch an informative 20-minute video about the life of the original inhabitants and take a tour around the interactive museum. To reach the park, head west along the LP-1; it's on a curve and easy to miss – keep an eye out for the signpost

HIKING ON LA PALMA

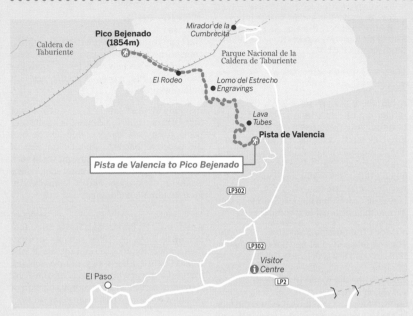

THE BASICS

Don't come to La Palma without allowing a generous chunk of time to explore its wondrous landscapes on foot. La Palma is said to be the world's steepest island and while this may not be strictly true, expect lots of healthy gradients, aching calf muscles and long, long views. And with 850km of trails, this is the ideal place for a walking holiday – you'll see a lot of hikers exploring the island on foot.

Several companies offer guided hikes; the best is **Natour** (☑ 922 43 30 01; www.natour-trekking.com; guided hikes from €32; ⊙ 9am-1pm & 4-8pm Mon-Fri, 4-7pm Sat & Sun), a company operating island-wide. Popular routes include the walk around the **Parque Nacional de la Caldera de Taburiente** (p215), the **Ruta de los Volcanes** (p214) and the 'Enchanted Forest' walk through forest land in the north. The company will pick you up at your hotel or a central meeting point.

Another reputable guide service is **Ékalis** (☑ 922 44 45 17; www.ekalis.com; Calle la Molina 9, Tijarafe; per day €38), which also offers hotel pick-ups.

However, it's not necessary to hike with a guide; La Palma offers safe walking conditions for anyone who's prepared and carries a good map. The beauty of having a guide, other than the history and anecdotes they can share, is enjoying a long one-way trek with transport arranged at either end.

PISTA DE VALENCIA TO PICO BEJENADO

START PISTA DE VALENCIA
END PICO BEJENADO
LENGTH 5.4KM OR 6.4KM; 2 1/2 OR 3 HOURS
DIFFICULTY MODERATE

This trail runs from Pista de Valencia up a moderately steep path through the pine trees to a superb lookout point with views

Clamber past petroglyphs wrapped in mystery and eerie lava tubes to the 1854m-high Pico Bejenado.

in all directions from Pico Bejenado. On the climb, you may encounter mist and low cloud while at other times you may find yourself in full sun; although the pine trees afford considerable shade, there are stretches that are unshaded. Often all you can hear is the wind in the pines and birdsong. Take water and snacks for the climb and wear hiking boots. As the information board at Pista de Valencia says, do not attempt the hike on very windy days or when there is a dust haze, as you could get caught in a forest fire.

After driving your car up from the **visitor centre** (p217) along the LP-302 (which becomes a rough dirt road sprinkled with stones for the last few kilometres), leave it at **Pista de Valencia** (Estacionamento Valencia; Ⓟ), which marks the start of the climb. The information board has a map describing the trail and marking the various altitude changes and distances involved from the start to the end of the hike.

Set off along the marked trail up through the pines and remember you should not leave the designated trail (which is marked here and there by two rectangles, one white, one yellow). After around 10 minutes' hiking, you will come to a **sign** welcoming you to the national park; look back to views of El Paso in the valley below. You then reach a fork with a choice of two routes up to the peak: either the shorter 4.9km path via *petroglifos* (petroglyphs), or the longer route via Roque de los Cuervos (6.2km).

Our route follows the path via the petroglyphs. After 10 minutes you pass a sign pointing to El Paso (6.7km away) and Bejenado (4.5km away); then the road widens and you will soon reach some **lava tubes** in the rock face. Originally, these were conduits in the rock through which lava would pass, formed when slow-moving lava cooled enough for a tube to form. Note there's a QR code on a post here that your smartphone

can read to take you to an online audioguide (if you can get a signal) for more explanations about the tubes.

After a further five minutes, you reach a gap in the pines and an astonishing view. Keep following the signposts dotted along the way before the path narrows through the pine trees before you reach a sign pointing to the **Lomo del Estrecho Engravings**, 150m along a path to your right. The carving – housed within a metal cage – was discovered in 1988. It is quite hard to make out the pattern on the rock if the sun is shining directly onto it, but you can discern the curved lines. It possibly served the purpose of marking out pasture fields or former shepherding roads, but its precise purpose is unknown.

Backtrack to rejoin the path to Pico Bejenado, 3km uphill. On your way up, note the plentiful evidence of fire on the carbonised bark of the pine trees around you; the Canarian pine (p218) is one of the most fire-resistant trees on the planet.

After another 20 minutes or so you reach another, with the right fork to Cumbrecita (2.7km away) and the **left fork to Bejenado** (1.6km away). The views get quite stunning at this point, with panoramas to jagged mountain ridges and solitary pines on rocky outcrops, before you arrive at an exposed area signposted **El Rodeo**. You may really start to feel the wind here. Keep your eyes on the path from here on; it can be easy to lose it and a couple of places below are steep, so watch your footing.

After another 30 minutes you'll reach the summit: **Pico Bejenado**. Plunging views drop down either side to the sea and over El Paso and Los Llanos as well as to the mountain peaks. Note the visitor's book in the metal box chained to one of the rocks – there is a pen for you to leave your thoughts. Don't build stone cairns: they can topple and send stones falling down the mountainside.

El Hierro

POP 10,800

Best Places to Eat

➡ Joapira (p236)

➡ El Refugio (p233)

➡ Casa Juan (p233)

➡ La Higuera de Abuela (p228)

➡ Restaurante Mirador de la Peña (p229)

➡ Casa Carlos (p229)

Best Natural Pools

➡ La Maceta (p234)

➡ Cala de Tacorón (p233)

➡ Charco Azul (p237)

➡ Charco de los Sargos (p234)

➡ Charco Manso (p228)

➡ Tamaduste (p229)

Why Go?

Impassable cliff-lined shores and a far-flung Atlantic location make the Unesco Geopark island of El Hierro remote in every sense – which is exactly what is so alluring about the Canaries' second-smallest isle. El Hierro was even considered the end of the world until Columbus sailed off to the Americas from here in 1492.

It's impossible not to be entranced by the island's slow pace and simple soulfulness; by its craggy coast, where waves hurl themselves against lava-sculpted rock and shimmering natural pools; by the eerily beautiful juniper groves and serene pine forests; by the peaceful walking trails and flower meadows; and by the volcanic southern moonscapes. Then there's the protected Mar de las Calmas, off the south coast, with its ethereal underwater wonders.

Several worlds away from the rest of the Canarian archipelago, El Hierro is entirely unique – so much so that it's planning to become the globe's first energy-self-sufficient island.

When to Go

➡ The best months for hiking are September and October, with reliably warm, dry weather; in spring (March/April) the highland meadows are ablaze with wildflowers, though there may be some rain.

➡ July, August and September, plus Easter, make up high season, when Spanish holidaymakers arrive; book cars and accommodation ahead.

➡ June to early July and September, with temperatures around 25°C, are also perfect for lazing around at natural swimming pools or diving into La Restinga's underwater paradise (though October is the top diving month).

➡ If you're on El Hierro in April, don't miss the Fiesta de los Pastores, in honour of the Virgen de los Reyes.

ATLANTIC

OCEAN

Charco Manso

Pozo de las Calcosas
Roques de Salmor
Punta de Salmor
El Mocanal
Echedo
Tamaduste 🔟
HI5
HI10
Mirador de la Peña 3️⃣
Guarazoca
Valverde
Aeropuerto de El Hierro
HI115
Risco de Tibataje
Punta Grande
Las Montañetas
HI2 HI3
El Golfo
Punta Grande
Las Puntas
Árbol Garoé
HI2
La Caleta
La Maceta 2️⃣
HI120 HI10
HI1
Charco de los Sargos
HI550
Ecomuseo de Guinea & Lagartario
HI55 9️⃣
Puerto de la Estaca
Playa de las Arenas Blancas
Charco Azul
Los Mocanse
San Andrés
Bahía de Timijiraque
Pozo de la Salud
HI500
El Sabinar 7️⃣
Bodega Soterana
Tigaday
La Frontera 6️⃣
Mirador de Jinama
1️⃣ **Camino de Jinama**
Timijiraque
Los Cristianos (Tenerife)
Playa de Verodal
La Dehesa
HI50
Sabinosa
Los Llanillos
HI1
Bodega Uwe Urbach
Isora
HI35
HI30
Malpaso (1501m)▲
Mirador de la Llanía
HI1
HI4
Mirador de Isora
HI506
Ermita de Nuestra Señora de los Reyes
HI500
HI503
Camino de la Virgen
HI45
HI40
Mirador de Las Playas
Roque de la Bonanza
Camino de Isora
8️⃣
Faro de Orchilla
HI400
Parque Cultural de El Julan
Hoya del Morcillo
Las Casas
Las Playas
El Pinar 5️⃣
Bodega Elysar
Taibique
Mar de las Calmas
HI4
Cala de Tacorón
HI410
Centro de Interpretación del Geoparque
4️⃣ **La Restinga**

El Hierro Highlights

1️⃣ Camino de Jinama (p238) Tackling one of the island's top hikes.

2️⃣ La Maceta (p234) Taking a dip at this Atlantic-washed natural pool then wandering the coastal cliffs.

3️⃣ Mirador de la Peña (p229) Soaking up the spectacular gulf panorama.

4️⃣ La Restinga (p232) Plunging into warm waters from El Hierro's diving hub.

5️⃣ El Pinar (p232) Strolling in a pristine forest.

6️⃣ La Frontera (p236) Tasting El Hierro wines at volcanic gulf vineyards.

7️⃣ El Sabinar (p240) Strolling among juniper trees.

8️⃣ Faro de Orchilla (p240) Making a pilgrimage to Spain's rugged southwestern tip.

9️⃣ Ecomuseo de Guinea & Lagartario (p236) Meeting the endangered El Hierro lizard.

🔟 Tamaduste (p229) Relaxing in a protected emerald bay

History

Geographically speaking, El Hierro is the youngest island in the archipelago, born a mere 1.2 million years ago. Through the millennia, volcanic activity built up a steep island with a towering 2000m-high peak at its centre. But about 50,000 years ago, the area was hit by an earthquake so massive that one-third of the island was ripped off the northern side. The peak and the surrounding land slipped away beneath the waves, creating the amphitheatre-like coast of El Golfo.

The island's original inhabitants, the Bimbaches, arrived from northern Africa and created a peaceful, cave-dwelling society that depended on agriculture, fishing, hunting and gathering. They may have called the island Hero or Esero, possibly the origin of its modern name. The Bimbaches left interesting petroglyphs (geometrical etchings) on rocks and cave walls across the island; the most interesting is at El Julan (p232).

French explorer Jean IV de Béthencourt arrived on the island in the early 15th century, and it was swiftly incorporated into the Crown of Castilla. After the Spanish conquest, a form of feudalism was introduced and Spanish farmers gradually assimilated with those locals who had not been sold into slavery or died of disease.

It wasn't until 1912 that the island became self-governing. Throughout the 20th century many *herreños* were forced to emigrate to find work, mostly to Cuba after a severe 1911 drought and to Venezuela in the 1940s. The island's economy has since recovered and is now based on cheese, fishing, fruit-growing, livestock and, increasingly, tourism, and many emigrants have returned. The struggle now is balancing the preservation of the island's unique, Unesco-protected natural beauty with the need for economic growth.

Although El Hierro's last major volcanic eruption was 200 years ago, between October 2011 and March 2012 major underwater volcanic eruptions took place off the coast at La Restinga, leading to a precautionary evacuation of the town (fortunately, there were no casualties).

ⓘ Getting There & Away

AIR

El Hierro's tiny **airport** (☑ 913 21 10 00; www.aena.es; ☺ 6am-7pm), 10km east of Valverde on the northeast coast, has just a few flights with Binter Canarias (p269) and Canary Fly (p269) to/from Tenerife Norte and Gran Canaria, where you can take onward transport to the rest of the archipelago.

BOAT

Naviera Armas (☑ 922 55 45 60; www.naviera-armas.com; Puerto de la Estaca; ☺ 6am-3pm Mon, 9am-3pm Tue, Thu & Fri, 3.30-5am & 9am-5pm Wed, noon-4pm Sun) has one daily return sailing Sunday to Friday between El Hierro's Puerto de la Estaca, and Tenerife's Los Cristianos (€49.50, 2¾ hours). Departure times vary by day; check online.

ⓘ Getting Around

TO/FROM THE AIRPORT

Buses travel between the airport and Valverde (€1.20, 15 minutes, five to six daily), usually coinciding with flights. Taxis charge €15 to/from Valverde.

BICYCLE

MTB-Active (☑ 669 157567, 620 005998; www.mtb-active.com; Calle de la Corredera 9, Tigaday; bicycle hire per day €20-33)

Velohierro (☑ 674 736565; www.velohierro.com; Calle El Paseo 6B, Echedo; bicycle hire per day €20; ☺ 10am-6pm Mon-Fri)

Yahé Aventuras (☑ 639 039946; www.yahe aventuras.es; Calle Santiago 19, Valverde; mountain bike per day €20; ☺ 9am-9pm)

BUS

TransHierro (☑ 922 55 11 75; www.transhierro.es; Calle El Molino 14, Valverde; ☺ 7am-7pm) buses run to most places across the island several times daily.

CAR & MOTORCYCLE

There are just a few car-rental firms on El Hierro and the number of cars is limited, so book ahead. Car-hire companies will usually deliver your car on arrival at the airport or port. **Cicar** (☑ 928 82 29 00; www.cicar.com; Aeropuerto de El Hierro; ☺ 8am-7pm) is a reliable Canaries-wide choice.

There are only three petrol stations on the island: in Valverde, in La Frontera and on the HI4 to La Restinga.

NORTHERN & EASTERN EL HIERRO

The island's northern and eastern coasts are lined with ruggedly beautiful (though often inaccessible) cliffs, interspersed with strings of delightful little coves, natural volcanic rock pools and, high above, spectacular lookout points. Inland, grassy fields extend over much of the landscape, with a few farming villages and hardy vineyards dotted between.

THREE DAYS ON EL HIERRO

Day One

El Golfo (p233) is arguably the most spectacular part of El Hierro (you'll want more than a day here!). Admire the volcanic coastal scenery by walking (p236) between Las Puntas and La Maceta (p234) natural pool. Meet El Hierro's giant lizards at the Ecomuseo de Guinea & Lagartario (p236), before a meal at Joapira (p236) in La Frontera. Then choose between lazing at quiet Charco Azul (p237), visiting a winery (p236), heading into wild La Dehesa (p240) or tackling the Camino de Jinama (p238).

Day Two

Drive north to the Mirador de la Peña (p229) for unforgettable views of El Golfo, then spin on to the incredible Mirador de Isora (p231), near San Andrés, before continuing to the majestic El Pinar forest (p232). Zigzag downhill through increasingly barren, volcanic mountainscapes to coastal La Restinga (p232) and the best diving in the Canaries. Dine at El Refugio (p233) or Casa Juan (p233), and don't miss sparkling Cala de Tacorón (p233).

Day Three

Many people ignore El Hierro's east coast – a shame! Head south to windswept Las Playas (p230), a long stretch of cobblestone beach perfect for a stroll. Lunch at the swish Parador (p230), then retrace your steps north to Tamaduste (p229), with its calm cove, or La Caleta (p230), with its family-friendly saltwater pools. Then check out pint-sized capital Valverde.

EL HIERRO VALVERDE

Valverde

POP 4950

The only landlocked capital in the Canaries, Valverde sits atop a windy mountain ridge overlooking the Atlantic. Having emerged in the 16th century, today it's El Hierro's unremarkable centre of commerce, transport and services. Much of the town's original architecture was destroyed in a devastating 1899 fire, and the low white houses here aren't as scenic as the balconied mansions of the other Canarian capitals, but, when clouds don't interfere, there are pretty valley views across rooftops, steep streets and agricultural terraces. On rare clear days you can see La Gomera and Tenerife's El Teide perfectly from the unassuming town centre. Even if you don't stay in Valverde, you'll probably end up passing through.

Though Jean de Béthencourt conquered El Hierro in 1405, Valverde only established itself as the island's leading town in the 16th century. Many islanders fled to this small inland hamlet seeking shelter during a disastrous 1610 hurricane, beginning a relative boom that would eventually see the town become the seat of the *municipio* (town council) that covered the whole island. The island's first town council was established here in the early 20th century.

◉ Sights

Start on pedestrian-friendly **Calle Dr Quintero**, with a few shops and bars, before ducking down to attractive **Plaza Quintero Nuñez** (Plaza Cabildo), home to the church.

Iglesia de Nuestra Señora de la Concepción   CHURCH

(Plaza Quintero Núñez; ⊙dawn-dusk) Valverde's church is a simple three-nave, late-18th-century structure crowned by a bell tower with a railed-off upper level that serves as a lookout. Beyond the neo-baroque façade, you'll find a magnificent wooden coffered and vaulted *artesonado* (ceiling of interlaced beams with decorative insertions), while the polychrome altar is the town's most prized piece of artwork.

Casa de las Quinteras   MUSEUM

(☑922 55 20 26; Calle Armas Martel; adult/child €4/free; ⊙10am-6pm Mon-Sat) At this cluster of small yellow-washed stone houses turned ethnographic museum, multilanguage exhibits on rural island life take in traditional clothing and ceramics, horse-riding equipment, a blacksmith's forge and a loom. There's a video on El Hierro's cultural heritage, and the excellent craft shop stocks locally made baskets, blankets, pottery and more.

✳️ Festivals & Events

Fiestas de la Concepción   FIESTA

Concerts, fireworks and cultural acts build over a couple of weeks into Valverde's major festival on 8 December, which honours the Virgen de la Inmaculada Concepción with religious celebrations and a big town party.

✖️ Eating & Drinking

There are some good *tascas* (tapas bars) along the main Calle Dr Quintero and overlooking Plaza Quintero Núñez.

Tasca El Charquete   CANARIAN €

(☑️ 922 55 06 04; www.facebook.com/tascael charquete; Calle de la Constitución 4; dishes €5-9; ⊘ 1pm-late Tue-Sat) Cram into this snug, locally loved *tasca*, where peach-orange walls, cheery service and a short-but-sweet chalkboard menu set the tone for heart-warming island cooking with just a touch of contemporary flair: *huevos rotos* (fried eggs, chorizo and chips), *tomates aliñados* (dressed tomatoes), vegetable fajitas, cheese-stuffed *tortilla de patatas*. Homemade desserts include a luscious chocolate mousse.

La Mirada Profunda   BISTRO €€

(☑️ 922 55 17 87; Calle Santiago 25; mains from €10; ⊘ 1-4pm & 8-11pm; ☑️) Don't expect anything as pedestrian as a menu at this elegant, purple-walled, bistro-style pick. Instead, chef Antonio García Corujo pops over to your table to share what he's prepared for the day – soups, salads, fresh fish and jazzed-up local favourites, such as roast *cochinillo* or octopus with *papas arrugadas*. Veggie-friendly options might include broccoli soup or avocado-and-Roquefort salad.

La Taberna de la Villa   CANARIAN €€

(Calle General Rodriguez y Sánchez Espinosa 10; mains €8-14; ⊘ 1-4.30pm & 7.30pm-midnight Mon-Sat; ☎️) Good, simple food, a welcoming atmosphere and a warm ochre-washed space collide in one of the most popular dining spots in town, just off the main plaza. Choose from, say, grilled *herreño* cheese with honey, *papas arrugadas* dipped in *mojo* and meaty mains like pork tenderloin in pepper sauce, and wash it all down with El Hierro wines.

ℹ️ Information

Oficina de Turismo (☑️ 922 55 41 09; www. elhierro.travel; Calle Dr Quintero 11; ⊘ 10am-6pm Mon-Fri, 9am-3pm Sat) Also has an **airport branch** (www.elhierro.travel; Aeropuerto de El Hierro).

ℹ️ Getting There & Away

From Valverde's **bus station** (Calle El Molino), at the southern end of town, TransHierro (p226) buses run to destinations across the island. Bus 3 serves Frontera (€1.20, 30 minutes, six daily); bus 6 Tamaduste (€1.20, 15 minutes, six daily); buses 3 and 5 El Mocanal (€1.20, 15 minutes, 11 or 12 daily); and bus 8 El Pinar (€1.20, 30 minutes, five to six daily). Bus 10 travels to/from the airport (€1.20, 15 minutes, five to six daily) and buses 7 and 11 to Puerto de la Estaca (€1.20, 15 minutes, five to seven daily), usually coinciding with flights and ferries.

Taxis charge €15 to/from the airport or port; there's a **taxi stand** (☑️ 922 55 07 29; www. transhierro.com; Calle San Francisco; ⊘ 24hr) in the town centre.

Echedo

POP 250

Echedo, 4km north of Valverde, sits at the heart of El Hierro's northern wine-growing region, whose minimalist vineyards are planted behind stout dry stone walls to block the wind that often swirls through. At the time of writing, however, the area's bodegas weren't open to the public.

Charco Manso   NATURAL POOL

(🅿️) The narrow HI151 meanders 4km north from Echedo, past shrubs and volcanic rock, to these natural saltwater pools dotted with spectacular lava arches. On a fine day the clear turquoise waters are heavenly, though at high tide or when the ocean is stirred there can be strong currents. Be especially careful around the caves dug into the shore; peek into them on a calm day, but never swim here. There's an erratically open kiosk for light bites by the water.

La Higuera de Abuela   CANARIAN €€

(☑️ 922 55 10 26; Calle Tajaniscaba 10; mains €9-15; ⊘ noon-4pm & 7.30-10.30pm Wed-Mon Jun-Nov) For a delightful dining experience in a tranquil rustic setting, head to this popular leafy patio restaurant, where traditional dishes like fried rabbit or goat, grilled shellfish and fresh island fish are served in all their hearty deliciousness. The name 'Higuera' recalls the enormous fig tree that once stood here. Only opens in season.

EL HIERRO FOR CHILDREN

Although El Hierro lacks the theme parks and myriad organised activities of the larger Canary Islands, there's still plenty of good, clean, healthy outdoors fun for children here. Several of the natural pools dotted around the island offer safe swimming, including La Maceta (p234), La Caleta (p230) and wildly beautiful Charco Azul (p237). Older children will enjoy the snorkelling and diving (p232) around La Restinga, and everyone likes learning about giant lizards at La Frontera's Ecomuseo de Guinea & Lagartorio (p236). Up on the inland plateau there are plenty of chances for youngsters to burn off excess energy on fairly gentle hiking trails and at fantastic lookout points.

🛈 Getting There & Away

Bus 9 links Valverde and Echedo (€1.20, 10 minutes, two to four daily) with an hour's advance request (922 55 07 29), continuing to Pozo de las Calcosas.

El Mocanal

POP 830

Perched on a green-clad hillside with views sprawling down to the cliff-edged north coast, El Mocanal is the largest of several farming villages in the island's north, with accommodation, a couple of supermarkets and restaurants, and a 17th-century stone-and-whitewash **church** (HI5; ☉ dawn-dusk) built in typical Canarian style.

Pozo de las Calcosas   VILLAGE

(🅿) Clustered around a natural north-coast pool, this 18th-century summer village of traditional generations-old small houses made of lava rock (called *pajeros*) lies 5km north of El Mocanal. The homes are owned by local villagers, who move here in July and August, together with their animals (which graze in the precipitous fields above). A steep stone path ambles down to the village; above the waterfront there are a couple of restaurants, a lookout and a tiny stone chapel.

Casa Carlos   SEAFOOD €

(Restaurante Las Calcosas; ☑ 690 227360, 620 111589; Calle El Letime 3, Pozo de las Calcosas; dishes €5-9; ☉ 11am-9pm) Decked with potted plants and red-check tablecloths, this cosy old-fashioned dining room clings to the hillside, affording fabulous views of the extraordinary ancient beach houses below. Owner Julia whips up wonderfully simple seafood, including grilled tuna, fish soup, *vieja* (parrot fish), paella and mussels, plus home-style coffee and platters of *herreño* cheese. Also has two- to four-person apartments (€40).

🛈 Getting There & Away

Bus 3 runs to/from Valverde (€1.20, 15 minutes, six daily) and Frontera (€1.20, 15 minutes, six daily). Bus 5 also serves Valverde (€1.20, 15 minutes, five to six daily).

Mirador de la Peña

Designed by famous Lanzarote-born artist César Manrique in 1989, the clifftop **Mirador de la Peña** (☑ 922 55 03 00; Guarazoca; ☉ 11am-10.30pm; 🅿) **FREE**, just a kilometre west of agricultural hamlet Guarazoca, is one of El Hierro's most mesmerising attractions. Mist permitting, this stone-walled lookout affords sweeping views across El Golfo, its coastline and the Roques de Salmor. Wander the pathways fringed by wild lavender, palms and dragon trees, to several vantage points, then dine at the elegant **restaurant** (☑ 922 55 03 00; Guarazoca; mains €13-19; ☉ 11am-10.30pm; 🅿 🛜), one of the island's smartest. The glass-fronted interior is all whitewashed walls and overflowing greenery.

Tamaduste & La Caleta

POP 320 (TAMADUSTE), 270 (LA CALETA)

Strung around a pretty, protected bay, framed by low-lying cliffs and a scenic boardwalk dotted with wooden beach umbrellas, the tiny and charming resort village of Tamaduste is the perfect place to escape the outside world for swimming, sunbathing and seaside relaxing. Together with La Caleta, just south, it's Valverde's summer playground. At high tide the cove fills with water, and people dive head first into the Atlantic from platforms, steps and ladders; at low tide, the rough waves disappear, leaving nothing more than still pools.

Piscinas de La Caleta
NATURAL POOL

At the south end of town, huddled against expansive coast-and-cliff panoramas, La Caleta's turquoise salt-water pools are well maintained and ideal for children (though it can get a little windy here).

Harina y Tomate
PIZZA €

(☑ 922 10 90 76; Calle Tabaiba; pizza €5-8; ⊘ 1-3.30pm & 7-11pm Thu-Tue) Just back from the north side of Tamaduste's bay and one of only a couple of places here to grab a bite, this low-key pizza specialist has tables on a sunny back terrace or doughy deliciousness to go. Pick from classic toppings or go for local flavour (prawns, Iberian ham).

❶ Getting There & Away

Bus 6 runs between Valverde and Tamaduste (€1.20, 15 minutes, six daily), then continues to La Caleta (€1.20, 40 minutes).

Timijiraque & Las Playas
POP 190

South from sleepy Puerto de la Estaca (p226), the island's only ferry port, the HI30 curves 3km around the coast to the little town of Timijiraque, home to a pretty black-pebble beach (watch the undertow!), a couple of good restaurants and a handful of colourfully painted houses. Another 8km southwest, slicing through a no man's land of rocky shores and rockier hillsides, you reach the majestic 4km-long pebbly black bay of **Las Playas** (𝖯), home to El Hierro's top-end Parador (p235). Just off Las Playas' northern shore is the famous **Roque de la Bonanza**, a distinctive 200m-tall rock formation jutting out of the ocean.

From Las Playas, a popular 3.8km (three hours) hike (p238) climbs to the Mirador de Isora (p231).

Restaurante Bahía
CANARIAN €

(☑ 646 691361; HI30; mains €8-12; ⊘ 12.30-5pm & 7-11pm Mon & Wed-Fri, noon-11pm Sat & Sun) Baby-blue walls, check-print tablecloths and chalkboard menus create a laid-back atmosphere for tucking into lovingly prepared local classics such as *carne fiesta* (grilled meats, peppers and potatoes), *tablas* of Canarian meats and cheeses, or *salpicón* (seafood salad). Handily positioned right opposite Timijiraque's beach.

Parador de El Hierro
CANARIAN €€

(☑ 922 55 80 36; www.parador.es; Las Playas; mains €17-20; ⊘ 7.30-10.30am, 1.30-3.30pm & 7.30-10pm; 🐾) One of El Hierro's finest restaurants is hidden away in Las Playas' luxurious seafront Parador (p235). Creative contemporary flair is breathed into local specialities in a smart dining room dressed in graceful whites and blues – from platters of *herreño* and other Canarian cheeses to baked tuna or seafood paella. Or pop in for a coffee or Frontera wines on the beach-facing terrace.

❶ Getting There & Away

Bus 7 travels between Valverde and the Parador de El Hierro (€1.20, 30 minutes, five to six daily) via Timijiraque.

San Andrés
POP 220

A huddle of buildings either side of the HI1, 9km southwest of Valverde, San Andrés is the agricultural hub of central-north El Hierro. For travellers, the draw here is the smattering of intriguing sights and viewpoints sprinkled around nearby. From San Andrés, the HI10 continues northwest on its narrow, curvy path towards the Mirador de la Peña (p229).

Árbol Garoé
HISTORIC SITE

(PREH11 Km 8.4; adult/child €2.50/free; ⊘ 10am-6pm; 𝖯) According to legend, the Bimbaches' ancient holy tree, the Garoé, miraculously spouted water, providing for the islanders and their animals. Today we know it's really no miracle – mist in the air condenses on the tree's leaves and produces fresh water. The original tree was felled by a hurricane in 1610 and wasn't replaced with the current lime tree until 1949. It's 2.6km down a signposted track off the HI10 (800m north of San Andrés), with some steep, rocky sections.

Mirador de la Llanía
VIEWPOINT

(𝖯) Soak up the beauty of El Golfo's rambling agricultural expanses from this windswept lookout high above. It's a five-minute (signposted) walk north from the La Llanía fountain car park on the HI1, 7km southwest of San Andrés.

From the viewpoint, the fairly easy but immensely rewarding 4.2km (1½ hours) Camino de la Llanía (p239) loops through the pristine surrounding *laurisilva* and fern forest and volcanic hills.

Mirador de Jinama   VIEWPOINT

(P) About 3.5km southwest of San Andrés, the 1230m-high Mirador de Jinama opens up soul-stirring views over the mammoth amphitheatre that is El Golfo (of course, depending on the day, you could be looking at a big pot of cloud soup). Also here are a scenic (if windy) picnic spot and a small mango-yellow chapel.

This breezy lookout marks the top end of the ancient and popular Camino de Jinama (p238).

Casa Goyo   CANARIAN €

(☑ 922 55 12 63; www.facebook.com/restaurante casagoyo; Carretera General San Andrés 11; mains €9-11; ☉ 10.30am-10pm Tue-Sun) Spread across a typical village house with four small dining rooms and fronted by an earthy local bar, deservedly popular Casa Goyo is all about no-fuss traditional cooking like roast beef, *garbanzas* (chickpeas with chorizo), *solomillo al ajillo* (tenderloin in garlic) or smoked El Hierro cheese dipped in palm honey and blueberry jam, plus wines from nearby Frontera.

❶ Getting There & Away

Buses 2 and 5 link San Andrés with Valverde (€1.20, 20 to 30 minutes, five to six daily each); bus 2 continues to El Pinar, while bus 5 runs via El Mocanal then continues to Isora.

Isora

POP 400

Famous for its *herreño* cheese (produced from a combination of goat, sheep and cow's milk), the charming agricultural and farming village of Isora sits 4km south of San Andrés. Vegetable gardens and houses crafted from volcanic stone flank its slender streets, and there are good hikes into the surrounding countryside (including the 3km to/from San Andrés using the PREH4.1 and PREH3.3 – about 40 minutes).

Mirador de Isora   VIEWPOINT

(P) From the 800m-high Mirador de Isora, perched on the Risco de los Herreños cliffs, the mountain falls away at your feet to reveal the smooth volcanic coast of Las Playas. It's 1km south of Isora; bus 5 (Valverde–Isora, €1.20) continues on to the mirador from Isora.

You can hike (p238) all the way down to Las Playas along the PREH3 (3.8km, around two hours).

Food on El Hierro might be unpretentious, but it's delicious, much of it produced on the island or off its coasts. The lack of tourist traffic ensures restaurants are catering mainly to a local clientele, which means higher standards. Specialities include *queso herreño* (island cheese), *quesadillas* (three-cheese cakes) and dried figs, along with Canarian favourites like *potaje de berros, patatas arrugadas* and fresh seafood. El Hierro wines (p236) are gaining popularity.

Centro de Interpretación
de la Reserva de la Biosfera   MUSEUM

(Antiguo Casino de Isora, Calle Ferinto 32; adult/child €3/free; ☉ 10am-6pm Tue-Sat) Housed in a 1970s social club (known as a *casino*), originally built by a returned emigrant from Venezuela, this environment and ecology interpretation centre focuses on the island's well-known commitment for a sustainable future (58% of El Hierro is a protected space).

Cooperativa de Ganaderos
Central Quesera   CHEESE

(☑ 922 55 03 27; gerencia@cooperativa ganaderos.com; Polígono El Majano; ☉ 8am-2.30pm Mon-Fri) Farmers from all over the island deliver milk to this cooperative, 2km north of Isora, where delicious *herreño* cheese is produced. Pop in to buy varieties from *queso fresco* (fresh cheese) to *ahumado* (smoked), as well as local honey, or contact the cooperative ahead to arrange a free tour of its cheese-making facilities.

❶ Getting There & Away

Bus 5 travels between Isora and Valverde (€1.20, 40 minutes, five to six daily), via San Andrés and El Mocanal.

SOUTHERN EL HIERRO

Lush and green, with an idyllic year-round climate and gently undulating landscapes, southern El Hierro is for many people the most beautiful part of the island.

El Pinar

The serene, electric-green El Pinar pine forest cloaks a long swathe of the southern half of the island, casting cool shade over the hardy volcanic terrain. With walking trails meandering off into the trees, several dramatic viewpoints and the odd traditional vineyard, this area lures hikers, cyclists and anyone looking for a scenic drive. El Pinar municipality's two small pleasant agricultural and farming towns, **Las Casas** and **Taibique**, strung along the steeply descending HI4, are often jointly talked about as 'El Pinar' (it's near impossible to tell where one ends and the other begins).

⊙ Sights

Bodega Elysar   WINERY
(☑ 662 509381, 609 270479; www.facebook.com/bodegaelysar; Taibique; ℗) Under the watch of self-trained viticulturist Ambrosio Martín, family-run, 2015-founded Bodega Elysar works with traditional island grapes (negramoll, baboso negro) to craft such delicious drops as its prize-winning Tinto Lajiales Herreños, with plans for organic wines also in the pipeline.

Mirador de Las Playas   VIEWPOINT
(off HI4; ℗) Around 2km north of Las Casas and well signed off the HI4, the Mirador de Las Playas reveals a spectacular show of bottle-green pines tumbling down the hillside to meet the volcanic Atlantic coastline below.

Parque Cultural de El Julan   HISTORIC SITE
(☑ 922 55 84 23; HI400; ⊙ 10am-6pm Tue-Sun; ℗) Closed indefinitely for renovations at research time, this modern exhibition centre highlights one of the island's most important cultural sights, Los Letreros, where a scattering of indecipherable petroglyphs was scratched into a lava flow by the Bimbaches. The signposted centre is 7km west of the **Hoya del Morcillo** (HI400; ℗) recreation area, but the actual site is an 11km round trip away on the seafront and can only be visited with a guide either on foot or by jeep.

❶ Getting There & Away

Bus 2 travels to/from Valverde (€1.20, 30 minutes, five to six daily), while bus 8 links El Pinar and La Restinga (€1.20, 30 minutes, five to six daily).

La Restinga

Tucked into El Hierro's southernmost point, the once-sleepy fishing village of La Restinga is slowly morphing into a seaside resort thanks to its dozens of scuba-diving outfitters, which spotlight the underwater marvels of the **Mar de las Calmas** (Sea of Calm) – the warm, still waters that surround the island's southwestern shore. Centred on a sunny port with two volcanic beaches, backed by a jumble of apartment blocks, La Restinga itself is a fairly modern, characterless town and still feels like it's being built.

The HI4 road down to La Restinga rambles through majestic volcanic badlands. Part of the glassy Mar de las Calmas is a marine reserve (at the time of research there were plans to turn it into a 200-sq-km national park).

⊙ Sights & Activities

Most dive companies offer similar dives and courses (PADI or SSI). Prices are around €25 to €30 for a single dive around the Mar de las Calmas, where you can expect to encounter colourful coral, majestic rock formations and a wide variety of marine life (dolphins, turtles and several species of whales roam these waters). October is considered the best month for diving, though dives run year-round (weather permitting).

Centro de Interpretación del Geoparque   MUSEUM
(HI4; adult/child €5/free; ⊙ 10am-6pm Tue-Sat; ℗) Set amid glorious volcanic landscapes, 6km north of La Restinga, this insightful multilingual centre details the original creation of the Canary Islands and studies what exactly causes a volcanic eruption through computerised screens, special effects and a suitably evocative soundtrack. Then you wander through lava fields to a second building, where the 2011 volcanic eruption that took place just off El Hierro is brought to life by giant screens.

Green Shark   DIVING
(☑ 662 921370, 687 966160; www.thegreenshark.com; Calle El Lajial 7; 2-/4-dive trip €54/104; ⊙ 8am-8pm) 🐾 This professional, ecoconscious Spanish-Swiss dive centre works with researching biologists and oceanographers. Options range from two-dive trips to Discover Scuba (€80) and PADI Open Water courses (€340), in the Mar de las Calmas but also

at sites all around the island. There's accommodation available, too.

Arrecifal
DIVING

(☑ 696 617201, 922 55 71 71; www.arrecifal.com; Calle La Orchilla 30; 1-dive trip €28; ⊙ 8.40am-3pm) Under efficient Irish management, Arrecifal offers day and night dives, gear rental (€9), accommodation (€45 to €60) and a variety of PADI courses, from Discover Scuba (€50) to Open Water (€343) to Divemaster (€650).

El Hierro Taxi Diver
DIVING

(☑ 626 789205; www.clhicrrotaxidiver.net; Avenida Marítima 4; 1-dive trip €25-32; ⊙ 8am-8pm) Based right on the seafront, one of La Restinga's longest-established operators does PADI courses (Open Water €329) as well as baptisms and night dives (€32), at sites all over El Hierro, with various accommodation packages also on offer.

🗡 Eating

★ El Refugio
SEAFOOD €€

(☑ 675 830886; Calle La Lapa 1; mains €9-13; ⊙ 1-4.30pm & 6-10pm Tue-Sun) A cheerful team welcomes you with their own day's catch at seafood-tastic favourite El Refugio, hidden down a narrow alley in the town centre. Fish is fried, grilled or oven-baked and plated up with *papas arrugadas,* perhaps with a side of El Hierro cheese dressed in Canarian honey. Go with the recommendation of the day, or a seafood feast for two.

★ Casa Juan
SEAFOOD €€

(☑ 922 55 71 02; www.facebook.com/casajuanla restinga; Calle Juan Gutiérrez Monteverde 23; mains €12-16; ⊙ 1.30-4.15pm & 7-10.30pm Thu-Tue) A stylish white-and-dove-grey makeover has put husband-and-wife-run Casa Juan on the map as one of El Hierro's most creative restaurants. Prize-winning chef Arabisén Quintero works local produce into imaginative, originally presented island-inspired creations – fried shrimp, tuna samosas with *mojo,* delectable seafood *arroces* (rice dishes) and elegantly prepped fresh fish of the day. *Peto* fishballs in curry sauce are a speciality.

ℹ Information

Oficina de Turismo (☑ 922 55 71 37; www.elhierro.travel; Calle El Carmen 4; ⊙ 8.30am-1.30pm & 4-6.15pm Wed-Sun)

CALA DE TACORÓN

Baking in a near-ceaseless sun, the stark yet tranquil volcanic coves of Cala de Tacorón (P) abut a sapphire sea and are loved by swimmers, sunsoakers, kayakers and divers (many of the La Restinga–based companies come here). A rustic log-and-branch picnic area overlooks twinkling natural pools accessed by little ladders, behind which rises a sweep of rust-and-black coastline, all 9km northwest of La Restinga (signed off the HI4).

ℹ Getting There & Away

Bus 8 runs to/from El Pinar (€1.20, 30 minutes, five to six daily), where you can change for Valverde.

EL GOLFO

An amphitheatre-shaped depression dominating El Hierro's northwestern flank, the gloriously green Golfo is, like the rest of the island, largely rural, with banana plantations dominating its low-lying coastal areas. A string of quiet hamlets are laid out just inland from the coast, where tempting natural swimming pools sparkle against a desolate yet peculiarly beautiful volcanic wasteland.

Inland, the growing commercial centres of Tigaday and, to a lesser extent, La Frontera serve as the economic engines of the western half of the island. To the south, a rugged mountain ridge looms like a 1000m-high wall hiding the rest of the island.

Tigaday
POP 1270

The commercial hub (by El Hierro standards) of La Frontera municipality, workaday Tigaday flanks the main HI50 3km inland from El Golfo's coast. Apart from a pretty avenue dotted with laurel trees, there isn't much to see in its centre, but as El Hierro's second town, Tigaday is the only place with shops, restaurants and services to rival the capital (and it has one of the island's three petrol stations!). Though technically independent from neighbouring La Frontera (p235), the two towns now blend together.

THE EL HIERRO GIANT LIZARD & ITS CANARIAN COUSINS

Imagine the Spaniards' surprise when they began to explore El Hierro and, among the native birds, juniper trees and unusual volcanic rock, they discovered enormous greyish-brown lizards – weighing around 700g, growing up to 60cm in length and living up to 20 years in the wild. By the 1940s, however, these giant lizards (neither venomous nor harmful) were almost extinct, their populations decimated by human encroachment on their habitat, introduced predators (particularly cats) and climatological factors. A few survived on the Roques de Salmor rock outcrop off El Golfo's coast (giving the species its name, 'Lizard of Salmor'), but before long, those too had disappeared.

Then, in the 1970s, herdsmen began reporting sightings of large, unidentified animal droppings and carcasses of extra-long lizards that had been killed by dogs. To the delight of conservationists, a small colony of giant lizards had survived on a practically inaccessible mountain crag above El Golfo, the Fuga de Gorreta.

In 1985 the Giant Lizard of El Hierro Recovery Plan was put into place. These days you can see it in action at the Ecomuseo de Guinea & Lagartario (p236), where lizards are bred in captivity then released into supervised wild areas. There are now thought to be around 400 giant lizards in the wild across El Hierro.

Giant lizards were once found on all the islands in the Canaries (each island had its own individual species), but almost all went into the dustbin of extinction once humans, cats and dogs got their hands (or claws) on them. Or did they? Just as the El Hierro Giant Lizard was rediscovered in the 1970s, the Tenerife Giant Lizard reappeared in 1996; scientists discovered a population of 10 La Gomera Giant Lizards in 1999; and then, in 2007, along came the La Palma Giant Lizard. These three populations are only just on the brink of survival and are classed as critically endangered (as are the El Hierro lizards), though things are looking slightly brighter for La Gomera's lizards, which now number an estimated 580 (250 of them in the wild). The Gran Canaria Giant Lizard, which can reach up to 80cm in length, is the only reptile of its kind not currently in danger of extinction.

◉ Sights & Activities

★ La Maceta   NATURAL POOL

(P) Taking a refreshing dip is a dream at La Maceta, arguably top pick among El Hierro's beautiful natural coastal pools and just as popular with *herreños* as with visitors. There are several different pools of varying depth and wave shelter, including one ideal for children (though at high tide the ocean swallows the pools, making swimming dangerous). La Maceta is 4km north of Tigaday, signposted off the HI550.

The great little down-to-earth beach bar here, **Kiosco Los Arroyos** (mains €6-12; ⊙10am-9pm), rustles up fresh seafood, and a lovely coastal path (p236) winds 2.5km north to Las Puntas. Bus 4 to/from Tigaday (€1.20, 15 minutes, up to six daily) serves La Maceta.

Charco de los Sargos   NATURAL POOL

(P) Calm west-coast pools reached by a small web of trails and boardwalks buffer the crashing waves at gorgeous all-natural Los Sargos, 4km north of Tigaday. At the top of the cliff, there's a little *kiosko* that keeps erratic hours. Look for signs off the HI550.

Bus 4 to/from Tigaday (€1.20, 15 minutes, up to six daily) stops nearby on the HI550.

Fly El Hierro   ADVENTURE SPORTS

(✆684 297672; www.flyelhierro.com; 10-/25-/45min flight €80/100/130) An experienced, prize-winning paraglider leads morning and afternoon tandem flights above El Golfo. Book a couple of days ahead.

✖ Eating & Drinking

Quesadillas La Herreña   PASTRIES €

(www.facebook.com/quesadillaslaherrena; Calle Las Lajas; quesadillas €3; ⊙9am-2pm & 4-9pm) Pop into a cheerful roadside bakery with just a few terrace tables to sample the flower-shaped, three-cheese delights of El Hierro's divine *quesadilla,* a much-loved cake-like dessert infused with aniseed and lemon.

Las Flores del Mar   ITALIAN, SEAFOOD €€

(✆632 692430; Calle Las Lajas 4B; mains €9-13; ⊙6-11pm Mon, Tue & Thu-Sat, 1-6pm Sun) It's all cheerful service and a laid-back atmosphere at Italian-owned Las Flores del Mar, a sweet indoor-outdoor roadside restaurant awash with fairy lights, dangling plants and pale-blue walls. The creative menu has fun fusing authentically good Italian cuisine and local seafood favourites: artistically presented pastas include tortelli with prawns, spinach and *almogrote* sauce, served up in a frying pan.

Casa Pucho
CANARIAN €€

(Restaurante Don Din 2; ☑ 922 55 53 27; Calle de la Corredera 5; mains €9-14; ⊗ 8am-11pm; 🛜🍽️) All your favourite El Hierro staples are well prepared without fanfare at this supercentral address. Specialities roam from roast lamb, Canarian cheeseboards and fish soup to *vieja* (parrot fish) in a world of styles, while vegan/vegetarian options include grilled-vegetable platters. Sit under laurel trees on the roadside terrace, in the small dining room or the simple bar.

🛍️ Shopping

Mercadillo La Frontera
MARKET

(www.facebook.com/mercadillolafrontera; Plaza Vieja; ⊗ 8am-1pm Sun) Tigaday's small craft and food market, stocked with local produce, takes over Plaza Vieja each Sunday.

ℹ️ Getting There & Away

From Tigaday's **Terminal de Guaguas** (Estación de Frontera; Calle de la Corredera), bus 3 runs to Valverde (€1.20, 30 minutes, six daily), bus 12 to Pozo de la Salud (€1.20, 30 minutes, five to six daily) and bus 4 (€1.20, 30 minutes, up to six daily) loops around Frontera via Las Puntas and La Maceta.

The central **taxi stand** (☑ 922 55 29 91; www.transhierro.com) is at Tigaday's bus station.

La Frontera

POP 1520

Although La Frontera is the large municipality that extends across El Golfo, it's also the name of a small, very peaceful village perched on the hillside above Tigaday and centred on charming **Plaza de la Candelaria**. The popular Camino de Jinama (p238) begins (or ends, depending on your route) opposite its plaza.

Iglesia de la Candelaria
CHURCH

(Plaza de la Candelaria; ⊗ dawn-dusk) The most important sight in La Frontera, this 19th-century church is built on the site of a 17th-century chapel. The three-nave interior reveals two rows of pretty stone columns and an ornate golden 19th-century altar, while out the back, a short but steep climb leads up to a late-20th-century hilltop bell tower.

Consejo Regulador Denominación de Origen El Hierro
WINERY

(☑ 616 517962, 922 44 89 37; www.doelhierro.es; Calle El Hoyo 1; tasting per person €5; ⊗ 8am-1pm Mon-Fri) The El Hierro Denominación de Origen (DO) organisation offers local-wine tastings at its headquarters in a beautiful 19th-century firewater bodega painted canary-yellow; book two days ahead. You can also pick up info on other island wineries here.

EL HIERRO LA FRONTERA

FOUR PERFECT EL HIERRO HOTELS

El Sitio (☑ 922 55 98 43; www.elsitio-elhierro.com; Calle La Carrera 26; r €41-56; 🛜) 🍴 Just outside La Frontera's centre, this reimagined bodega is an utterly charming, ecoconscious hideaway, with a soothing boho-rustic look.

Hotel Puntagrande (☑ 922 69 16 93, 611 285983; www.hotelpuntagrande.com; Las Puntas; r incl breakfast €120-170; 🅿️🛜) An old stone port building perched on a spectacular rocky outcrop in Las Puntas; the five snug boutiquey rooms complement a smart **restaurant** (☑ 922 69 16 93, 611 285983; mains €13-19; ⊗ 1-11pm Thu-Tue; 🍽️) 🍴.

Parador de El Hierro (☑ 922 55 80 36; www.parador.es; Las Playas; r €100-120; 🅿️❄️🛜🏊) Resting right on a pebbly cliff-flanked beach, the island's top hotel delights with its elegant green- or blue-clad rooms; the pool overlooks crashing waves and an excellent restaurant (p230).

Hotel Balneario Pozo de la Salud (☑ 922 55 59 46, 922 55 95 61; hotelbalneariopozodela salud@gmail.com; Pozo de la Salud; s/d incl breakfast €67/82; 🅿️🛜🏊) Right next to the famous Pozo de la Salud (p237), Spain's westernmost hotel has an impressive choice of therapies and bright, uncluttered, contemporary rooms.

DON'T MISS

EL HIERRO DROPS: WINES & WINERIES

Traditionally stemming from mineral-rich volcanic soils, El Hierro's unique wines are growing in popularity and recognition, with young reds, delicate rosés and a wide range of whites (both dry and sweet) produced at its usually small-scale bodegas. Grape varieties here – such as *listán*, *baboso* and *verijadiego* – are unusual and often acidic, many of them grown since several centuries ago. The island's main wine-producing areas are Echedo in the north, La Frontera in the west and El Pinar in the southeast.

Wine tourism on El Hierro is (slowly) blossoming: several local bodegas have now thrown open their doors to visitors for multilanguage tours and tastings, though you'll still need to call ahead to arrange a visit. An excellent place to start is La Frontera's Consejo Regulador Denominación de Origen El Hierro (p235), where you'll get tips on visiting wineries across the island and try a wine or two in a sun-yellow 19th-century firewater bodega. Other standout vineyards open to the public include Los Llanillos' Bodega Soterana (p237), La Frontera's Bodega Uwe Urbach (p236) and El Pinar's Bodega Elysar (p232).

Bodega Uwe Urbach   WINERY
(📞603 180950, 619 015087; uweurbach@hotmail.com; Pico de Brezo; tour & tasting per person €25; 🅿) 🍴 With its origins in the 19th century, the well-established Uwe Urbach vineyard specialises in organic wines, produced with a mix of traditional and innovative techniques. Four-hour guided tour-and-tasting sessions with expert owner Uwe, in a range of languages, include local-produce tapas and at least four wines. Book ahead, by phone or at the Uwe Urbach stand at Tigaday's weekly Mercadillo La Frontera (p235).

★ **Joapira**   CANARIAN €
(📞922 55 98 03; Plaza Candelaria 8; mains €9-13; ⏰8am-11pm Mon-Sat; 🍴) Joapira's friendly team takes great pride in its cooking, which shows in such specials as Venezuelan *cachapas* (stuffed corn pancakes) and *carne fiesta* (grilled meats, peppers and potatoes). Lightly creative dishes like veg-stuffed peppers, perhaps with *herreño* cheese, are a godsend for vegetarians and vegans. Fresh flowers dot the tables and the front veranda gazes out on La Frontera's church.

ⓘ Getting There & Away

Bus 4 (€1.20, 30 minutes, up to six daily), which loops around the entire La Frontera municipality, stops on Plaza de la Candelaria.

Las Puntas

POP 300

Sitting right on the water (though offering no access to it), 5km northeast of Tigaday at the foot of the Risco de Tibataje cliff, the peaceful little hamlet Las Puntas exists almost purely for tourism. Its main attractions are the volcanic-coast views and the sound of roaring waves.

**Ecomuseo de Guinea
& Lagartario**   MUSEUM
(📞922 55 50 56; HI55; adult/child €9/free; ⏰10am-6pm, tours 10.30am, 11.30am, 12.30pm, 1.30pm & 4pm; 🅿) 🍴 El Hierro's premier cultural site, this open-air museum combines two in one. The fascinating **Casas de Guinea** encompasses a volcanic cave and 20 traditional houses dating from the 17th to 20th centuries – previously home to the Bimbaches, it's one of the island's original post-Spanish-conquest settlements. The attached **Lagartario** is a sanctuary, reproduction and reintroduction centre for the endangered El Hierro giant lizard (p234); you'll learn all about these 60cm-long creatures and see 11 lizards lolling about (visit after 11am for maximum activity).

The Ecomuseo is signposted off the HI55, 3km south of Las Puntas. All visits are guided and run at specific times, in Spanish, English and/or German according to demand.

Las Puntas–La Maceta Walk   WALKING
Part of the PREH8.1, this boardwalk-and-stone path meanders through 2.5km of red-black volcanic coastline battered by Atlantic waves and backed by the towering Risco de Tibataje cliff, between Las Puntas and La Maceta. Signposted from the southern end of Las Puntas, it's an easy route dotted with lookout points, taking around 45 minutes (one-way) and unveiling sublime ocean views.

Garañones
SEAFOOD €

(☑649 509696, 699 160854; www.restaurante
garanones.es; Calle Cascadas del Mar 3; mains
€7.50-12; ☺12.30-4pm & 7-10pm Tue-Sat, 12.30-
4pm Sun) Look for the jaunty blue window
trim and tiny terrace: welcoming and relaxed Garañones is one of just a couple of
spots to eat and drink in Las Puntas. Feast
on tapas of *herreño* cheese, crunchy spinach
croquettes, hearty pumpkin soup and gloriously fresh seafood, often delivered on enormous sharing platters with salad, *mojo* and
papas arrugadas.

❶ Getting There & Away

Bus 3 between Valverde and Tigaday (€1.20, 30
minutes, six daily) stops in Las Puntas, as does
bus 4 to/from Tigaday (€1.20, 15 minutes, up to
six daily).

Los Llanillos & Sabinosa

POP 500

Dotted with traditional flat-roofed stone-
trim houses, little **Los Llanillos** hugs the
HI50 2.5km west of Tigaday. The road grows
steeper as it meanders 6.5km west from
Los Llanillos to small and remote **Sabinosa**, Spain's westernmost village. There's
not much to see in town (apart from an
18th-century chapel), but the surrounding
volcanic scenery is breathtaking.

Pozo de la Salud
HISTORIC SITE

(Calle Pozo de la Salud; ℗) El Hierro's famed
Pozo de la Salud (Well of Health) was long
known for miraculously healing local cattle,
but has been recognised for its mineral-rich
healing properties since the 18th century (in
the mid 19th-century its water was even exported to New York and Cuba). You can walk
down to the small seaside well, whose waters are said to cure a variety of ills, though
it's generally closed up. It's 3.5km northwest
of Sabinosa off the HI500.

If you fancy taking the waters, book in
for a stay or treatment at the adjacent Hotel
Balneario Pozo de la Salud (p235).

Bodega Soterana
WINERY

(☑626 295453; bodegasoterana@gmail.com; Los
Llanillos; tasting per person €25-45; ☺5-8pm
Mon-Fri, 10am-8pm Sat & Sun; ℗) While this
expertly run bodega on the western edge of
Los Llanillos may be a newcomer on El Hierro's blossoming wine scene, its volcanic-soil
vines date back centuries. The enthusiastic
owner Carmelo Padrón single-handedly
makes wines using traditional age-old techniques, and hosts detailed tours and three-
wine tastings (minimum two people; in
Spanish, English, French or German). Book
ahead by email or via the Facebook page.

Continued on p240

THE ECOLOGICAL ISLAND

Dry, rocky El Hierro might not immediately strike you as the most beautiful of the Canary
Islands, but clamber up onto the central plateau, relax at a natural pool or head down to
El Golfo and first impressions are quickly overturned. Not only is the island enveloped in
a gentle pastoral beauty, it's also home to some of the most unusual plant and animal
life in the eastern Atlantic – a distinction that earned it the label of a Unesco Geopark in
2014 (the first in the Canary Islands, followed in 2015 by the Lanzarote and Chinijo Archipelago Geopark).

Environmentalists' attention is mainly focused on protecting the marine reserve in
the Mar de las Calmas (slated to become a *parque nacional* – national park – at the
time of research), the otherworldly juniper trees of El Sabinar (p240) and the quiet El
Pinar (p232) pine forest, but the whole island benefits from its Unesco listing, with funds
going towards using unique natural local resources in sustainable ways. Find out more
by visiting La Restinga's Centro de Interpretación del Geoparque (p232) or at www.
elhierrogeoparque.es.

In 2014 the island took its conservationist leanings to a whole new level by becoming
the world's first island to initiate projects that will allow it to eventually rely entirely on
renewable sources for its energy needs. This ecological mindset is seen in other ways as
well, such as the island-wide plan to promote and support organic farming and a scheme
to use only electric cars by 2020. In 2018, El Hierro succeeded in running entirely on
renewable energy for 18 days in a row. Learn all about these and other eco-initiatives at
the Centro de Interpretación de la Reserva de la Biosfera (p231) in Isora.

EL HIERRO LOS LLANILLOS & SABINOSA

HIKING ON EL HIERRO

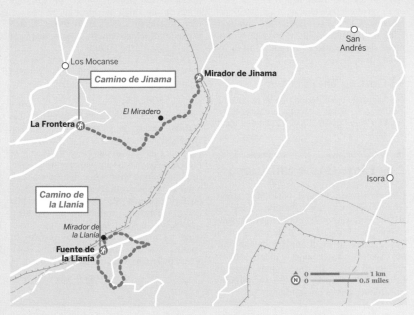

La Frontera · Los Mocanse · Camino de Jinama · Mirador de Jinama · El Miradero · San Andrés · Isora · Camino de la Llanía · Mirador de la Llanía · Fuente de la Llanía

0 — 1 km
0 — 0.5 miles

THE BASICS

Valverde's **tourist office** (p228) offers hiking tips and basic maps, though it's best to come armed with a detailed guide such as *Walking on La Gomera & El Hierro* (Cicerone; 2016). The island's best-known path is the ancient 27km **Camino de la Virgen**, stretching from the **Ermita de Nuestra Señora de los Reyes** (p240) to Valverde (eight hours). Other challenging walks include the thigh-burning 3.8km **Camino de Isora** between the Mirador de Isora and Las Playas (two hours); the 4.4km, 2½-hour cliff-traversing **Camino de Jinama** (p238); and the climb up to the **Fuente de Mencáfete** (a branch of the PREH1, in the island's west). Among the gentler worthwhile trails are the 4.2km, 1½ hour **Camino de la Llanía** (p239) and El Golfo's 2.5km, 45-minute coastal **Las Puntas–La Maceta walk** (p236).

CAMINO DE JINAMA

START LA FRONTERA
END MIRADOR DE JINAMA
LENGTH 4.4KM; 2½ HOURS
DIFFICULTY DIFFICULT

Both spectacular and challenging, the locally famous Camino de Jinama (part of the PREH8) follows an ancient donkey trail up the sheer mountainside behind La Frontera. Once the only link between El Golfo and northern El Hierro, it's now of the island's most rewarding hiking routes. It can be done in either direction, but climbing up is less jarring on the knees – and you'll wrap up with seriously thrilling clifftop views.

Start on La Frontera's **Plaza de la Candelaria** (p235). The **Camino** begins directly opposite the square, next to the excellent cafe-restaurant **Joapira** (p236); follow the 'Jinama' sign, then almost immediately, the wooden '4.4km' sign and yellow-and-white markers to branch left at the fork. You

El Hierro bursts with scenic hiking trails, both gentle and demanding (and rewarding). Two of our top choices: a spectacular climb above El Golfo, and a forested ramble between awe-inspiring lookouts.

head southeast uphill on a paved road, past houses that give way to volcanic vineyards. The route becomes a signposted stone path and crosses the main road as it continues climbing.

After 1km the trail levels out and heads into the **laurisilva forest**, then reaches a clearing with a wooden cross perched atop a rock, known as the **Cruz del Fraile**. From here, you're tracking steeply uphill in switchbacks, passing fine *mocán* trees.

The path leaves the trees at 2.5km and continues along the side of a rocky cliff; shortly afterwards you come to awe-inspiring lookout point **El Miradero**. Back into the forest to the **Descansadero de la Virgen**, a stone bench amid the *laurisilva*.

At around 3.5km, the track opens out again, with a sheer drop, and ridgetop pines appear beyond a **picnic area**. Finally, the Camino emerges through a wooden archway beside a yellow-washed chapel and the 1230m-high **Mirador de Jinama** (p231), from where a vertical wall sweeps down almost to your starting point.

From the Mirador, you could continue another 4.7km (signposted) through pastoral fields to San Andrés (p230); alternatively, a taxi back down to La Frontera costs €25 (book ahead!).

CAMINO DE LA LLANÍA
START FUENTE DE LA LLANÍA
END FUENTE DE LA LLANÍA
LENGTH 4.2KM; 1½ HOURS
DIFFICULTY EASY

This gentle, popular circular hiking route (SLEH1) weaves through the forested centre of the island, linking classic El Hierro landscapes of *laurisilva,* pine forest and volcanic

hills. Following the trail anticlockwise means you save the most majestic viewpoints for last.

Begin in the car park at the stone **Fuente de la Llanía**, 7km southwest of San Andrés, and cross the HI1 eastwards to find signposts to 'El Brezal' (a Canarian heath forest) and a board outlining several variations of this walk. Our route follows the 4.2km **green trail** (SLEH1), but if you like, can be extended at the northeastern and/or southwestern ends (5.6km or 7.4km/two or three hours total).

Plunge south into the fairy-tale-like forest along a shady path that soon passes a **picnic table** then a couple of sky-reaching pine trees whose needles carpet the floor. After less than a kilometre, the trail doubles back on itself before crossing the HI40 into heathland, with wooden 'Sendero La Llanía' signposts keeping you on track.

Around 2.5km into the route, you re-cross the HI1 via an underpass, then follow signs north uphill to the 1330m-high **Hoya de Fireba** – a 450m-wide, 160m-deep crater on El Golfo's escarpment. The long-distance GR131 also passes through here. Back on the path, head west downhill for a few hundred metres to a pine-studded clearing: this is the **Bailadero de las Brujas**, a mythical meeting point for witches.

The trail wanders briefly uphill and northwest through a bare volcanic mountainscape, ducks into the moss-covered woods and finally emerges (at approximately 3.5km) at the wowing **Mirador de la Llanía** (p230), with El Golfo laid out far, far below. From here, follow the path down through a final patch of enchanting forest to the **car park** where your adventure began.

Continued from p237

Charco Azul   NATURAL POOL

(**P**) Worked into its distinctive form by ancient lava flows and the pounding Atlantic waves, the 'Blue Pond' is a pristine natural cove with calm natural turquoise pools for swimming, 1.5km north of Los Llanillos. One of the pools sits beneath a natural stone arch.

Playa de las Arenas Blancas   BEACH

Curled into the isolated western end of El Golfo, just off the HI500 6.5km northwest of Sabinosa, this spectacularly positioned swathe of blonde sand melts into volcanic rock at the water's edge. It's a fantastic spot – wild and beautiful and with views sprawling all across El Golfo – but take care with the dangerous currents if you're swimming.

ℹ Getting There & Away

Bus 12 runs between Tigaday's bus station (p235) and Pozo de la Salud (€1.20, 30 minutes, five to six daily) via Los Llanillos and Sabinosa.

LA DEHESA

Across the practically uninhabited westernmost part of El Hierro, wild volcanic landscapes dominated by fierce-looking rock formations, hardy shrubs, wind-sculpted juniper trees and the odd volcanic beach are the main attractions. Known as La Dehesa (the Pasture), this protected area is only accessible via the arching (paved) HI500 road.

This is a lovely part of the island to explore by hiking, with the long-distance GR131 linking the Faro de Orchilla (p240) and the Ermita de Nuestra Señora de los Reyes (p240) – 5.7km – before heading northeast through the hills to Valverde.

THE DESCENT OF THE VIRGIN

El Hierro's fiesta par excellence, the **Bajada de la Virgen de los Reyes** (www.bajadaelhierro.com; ☉ early Jul) or 'Descent of the Virgin' has been held every four years since 1745 (next in 2021, 2025 etc). Most of the island's population gathers to witness or join a procession parading a statue of the Virgin, seated in a sedan chair, from the Ermita de Nuestra Señora de los Reyes in the west all the way across to Valverde.

Playa del Verodal   BEACH

(**P**) At the far western end of the island, this curious volcanic red-sand beach, 1km off the HI500 (and signposted), backs up to a majestic rock cliff. It's often deserted, leaving you with your own private paradise, though strong currents make it dangerous for swimming.

Ermita de Nuestra Señora de los Reyes   CHURCH

(HI506; ☉10.45am-5.30pm Tue-Sun) Made all the more intriguing by the long history and strong tradition behind it, this whitewashed, rust-roofed, pine-fringed 18th-century chapel conceals the image of the island's patron saint, Nuestra Señora de los Reyes (Our Lady of the Kings; local shepherds bought her from foreign sailors on Three Kings Day, 6 January, in 1545 or 1546). The *herreños* attribute several miracles to the Virgin, including ending droughts. From the chapel, which gazes downhill to sea, walking routes weave into the hills.

Every four years (2021, 2025 etc) the Virgin is paraded around the island on an animated procession, the Bajada de la Virgen de Los Reyes. If you can't be here for this extravaganza, the late-April **Fiesta de los Pastores** sees the Virgin carried from her chapel to the Cueva del Caracol, where she was originally kept.

El Sabinar   FOREST

(**P**) Sculpted by nature into wild shapes that look frozen in time, the beautiful and surreal wind-twisted *sabinas* (juniper trees) that grow across the hillside at El Sabinar have become the island's symbol. Undoubtedly some of the most unusual trees you'll ever see, the wonderfully weird *sabinas* are part of the reason that Unesco declared the entire island a biosphere reserve. You'll find them 3.5km north of the Ermita de Nuestra Señora de los Reyes along a signposted dirt track.

Faro de Orchilla   LIGHTHOUSE

(**P**) Though robbed of its status as Meridiano Cero by the UK's Greenwich in 1885, the concrete lighthouse that marks the most southwesterly point in Spain remains an island icon. With an astonishing seaside cliff perch, surrounded by lava-flow hills, it's an evocative spot. It's an 8.5km drive southwest of the Ermita de Nuestra Señora de los Reyes on the HI503, signed off the HI500.

Understand Canary Islands

The Canary Islands Today

Many visitors to the Canary Islands may be too overawed by the scenery and dazzled by sunlight to examine any frays in the social fabric. The islands bring in a vast amount of wealth, but this capital remains unevenly distributed through communities. High unemployment and a shaky welfare system are realities for many locals, and you can add in a mood of uncertainty generated by Brexit. A host of positive environmental measures, including huge investment in wind power, however, are beginning to have a beneficial impact.

Best on Film

Broken Embraces (Pedro Almodóvar; 2009) Romantic thriller starring Penelope Cruz shot in Lanzarote, featuring Famara and El Golfo.

The Dictator (Sacha Baron Cohen; 2012) Satirical political drama extensively filmed in Fuerteventura.

Wild Oats (Andy Tennant; 2016) Action drama with Demi Moore and Billy Connolly shot largely in Gran Canaria.

Guarapo (Santiago Ríos and Teodoro Ríos; 1987) The first film shot in La Gomera, about emigration to Venezuela after the Spanish Civil War.

Fifty Shades of Grey (Sam Taylor-Johnson; 2015) Infamous honeymoon scenes shot at La Tejita in Granadilla de Abona, Tenerife.

Best in Print

More Ketchup than Salsa (Joe Cawley; 2006) Witty account of running a bar in Tenerife.

Canary Island Song (Robin Jones Gunn; 2011) Touching tale by the author of the popular Christy Miller series.

Walk! Lanzarote (Jan Kostura, David Brawn, Ros Brawn; Discovery Walking Guides; 4th edition; 2017) The ins and outs of Lanzarote's hiking trails.

The Wind off the Small Isles (Mary Stewart; 1968) Romantic thriller set in Lanzarote.

Tourism

The classic double-edged sword, tourism continues to represent an essential pillar of the economy of the Canary Islands, with over 32% of Canarian economic activity linked to it. More than 14 million visitors passed through the islands in 2017, with the majority heading to a single island: Tenerife. But with almost 40% of visitors to the Canary Islands in 2016 arriving from the UK, Brexit storm clouds have been darkening economic predictions, especially as the slumping British pound took the wind from British travellers' sails in 2018. The fear of British holidaymakers saying *adiós* to the Canary Islands prompted the local government to consider sweeteners such as exempting British holidaymakers from paying IGIC (Canary Indirect General Tax). It is estimated the move – if it comes into effect – could cost around €100 million a year, but is considered to be money well spent. Elsewhere, however, there are signs that overtourism could be becoming a problem. A sustainable tourism tax could be in the offing too, similar to the tax recently introduced by the Balearic Islands to help control visitor numbers and provide money for environmental protection and heritage conservation.

The Land of Black Skies

With their blustery trade winds keeping clouds on the go, the Canary Islands are home to some of the clearest night skies in Europe. Indeed, with Fuerteventura recently added to the list, there are now three Unesco-protected Starlight Reserves on the Canary Islands (the other two are La Palma and the highlands of Tenerife). Stargazers and astrophotographers will find themselves in seventh heaven, beneath skies of exceptional clarity, so if you ever wanted that time-lapse shot of the Milky Way doing its thing, now's your chance. To meet the increasing demand, a growing number of astronomy tours (some provided by hotels) are available for anyone keen to observe the night skies. The world's third-largest solar telescope is on Tenerife, and the Roque de los Muchachos Observatory on La Palma is located in one of the best positions for optical and infrared astronomy in the Northern Hemisphere.

Politics & the Economy
The main force in Canary Islands politics since its first regional election victory in 1993 has been the Coalición Canaria (CC). A large source of social discontent is unemployment, which is highly visible on some of the islands. The number of people out of work spiralled to a shocking 33.2% in 2013, but by 2018 this rate had fallen to 20% (albeit 5% to 6% above the national rate for Spain). Ironically, one of the causes of small businesses failing is directly related to tourism as, increasingly, hotels are offering all-inclusive deals, which means many visitors rarely venture beyond their resorts.

Migration from Africa had stabilised for several years; however, immigration figures for 2018 showed a four-fold increase on the previous year, partly due to the EU spending huge amounts of money severing land routes in North Africa. With over 1200 migrants arriving between January and November 2018, the figures remain a fraction of the 32,000 arrivals in 2006, when on some days several hundred Africans would reach the islands in rickety wooden boats, but they may presage the return of a contentious issue.

Environmental Issues
The huge megaport of Granadilla in Tenerife opened in 2017, after the European commission pledged €67 million for its construction. This was despite more than 5000 official complaints, mainly from ecological groups concerned about the port's impact on the fauna and flora of the Los Sebadales area, as well as on nearby beaches and the local fishing industry. Allegations surfaced in 2017 that a resort in Gran Canaria had imported sand, in defiance of international law, from Western Sahara.

On the flipside, the islands are investing massively in wind farms, with wind power growing by almost 140% between 2015 and 2018. In addition to its onshore wind energy infrastructure, the Canary Islands aims to achieve 300MW of offshore wind capacity by 2025, a target date for increasing the proportion of renewable energy in its energy mix to 45%.

El Hierro continues to flaunt its evergreen credentials: it was recently designated a Unesco geopark in recognition of the island's noteworthy progress in promoting sustainable development, and it aims to become the world's first energy-self-sufficient island via a combination of solar, wind and water power.

GDP: **€44 BILLION**

INFLATION: **1.6% (2018)**

UNEMPLOYMENT: **20%**

POPULATION: **2.1 MILLION**

if Canary Islands were 100 people

73 would be Canarian
13 would be European
12 would be Mainland Spanish
2 would be African

belief systems
(% of population)

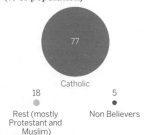

77
Catholic

18
Rest (mostly Protestant and Muslim)

5
Non Believers

population per sq mile

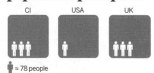

CI   USA   UK

≈ 78 people

History

There is a delightful whiff of mystery concerning both the Canary Islands' origins and the first inhabitants, the indigenous Guanches, subsequently banished by waves of marauding invaders. In 1821 the islands were declared a province of Spain, but the economic fallout from the Spanish Civil War and WWII plunged them into deep economic misery. It wasn't until the 1960s that the economy began to pick up with the onset of mass tourism. The rest is history, as they say.

And in the Beginning

There's a whimsical theory that the Canary Islands are the remains of the legendary sunken continent of Atlantis. The less romantic and more scientific explanation attests that the Macaronesian archipelago represents the tiniest part of massive volcanoes beneath the sea. El Teide on Tenerife is not only the highest mountain in Spain but, if measured from the ocean floor, is the third tallest volcano on the planet.

According to carbon dating of the islands' sparse archaeological finds, the earliest settlement found here dates to around 2000 BC, although earlier occupation is conceivable – and goat bones found in Fuerteventura have been dated back to 3000 BC. It is possible that early reconnaissance of the North African Atlantic coast by the Phoenicians and their successors, the Carthaginians, took a look at the easternmost islands of the archipelago. Some historians believe a Phoenician expedition landed on the islands in the 12th century BC, and that the Carthaginian Hanno turned up in 470 BC.

What is certain is that the expanding Roman Empire defeated Carthage in the Third Punic War in 146 BC. However, the Romans appear not to have been overly keen to investigate the fabled islands, which they knew as the *Insulae Fortunatae* (Fortunate Isles). A century and a half later, shortly after the birth of Christ, the Romans received vaguely reliable reports on the isles, penned by Pliny the Elder and based upon accounts of an expedition carried out around 40 BC by Juba II, a client king in Roman North Africa. In AD 150, Egyptian geographer Ptolemy fairly accurately located the islands' position with a little dead reckoning, tracing an imaginary meridian line marking the end of the known world through El Hierro.

TIMELINE	2000 BC	40 BC	AD 150
	Carbon dating of archaeological discoveries indicate that Cro-Magnon were the first settlers on the Canary Islands, possibly arriving from North Africa.	An expedition lands on the islands, led by King Juba II, Emperor Augustus' protégé, who used Mogador in present-day western Morocco as a base.	The famous Egyptian geographer Ptolemy fairly accurately locates the islands' position, tracing an imaginary meridian line marking the end of the known world through El Hierro.

Early (Known) Inhabitants

Tall, blond and good looking; how the Guanches actually arrived on the islands has been a question that's baffled historians for centuries. Could they be a result of lost Nordic adventurers? Or Celtic immigrants from mainland Iberia, possibly related to the Basques?

Recent analysis of DNA extracted from Guanche skulls on Gran Canaria and Tenerife instead identified the people's origins in North Africa, establishing that the Guanches were most closely related to North Africans of Berber ancestry. Similarities in Guanche place names, burial practices and rock carvings had also suggested a link with North Africa. What little is known of the extinct Guanche tongue furthermore suggests a Berber language, while the occasional instance of blue eyes and blondish hair occurs among Berbers.

As far as numbers are concerned, before the 15th-century conquest it is believed that the Guanche population numbered approximately 30,000 in Gran Canaria and Tenerife, over 4000 in La Palma, over 1000 in El Hierro and a few hundred in Lanzarote and Fuerteventura.

Early Conquests

After the fall of the Roman Empire and with Europe falling into the shadows of the Dark Ages, the Canary Islands slipped off the radar for an astonishing 1000-plus years, with virtually no written record of visits here until the early 14th century, when the Genoese captain Lanzarotto (or Lancelotto) Malocello bumped into the island that would later bear his name: Lanzarote.

The conquest of the islands began in earnest in 1402 when Norman noble and adventurer Jean de Béthencourt set out from La Rochelle with a small and ill-equipped party bound for the Canary Islands. So commenced a lengthy and inglorious chapter of invasion, treachery and bungling. Many Guanches would lose their lives or be sold into slavery in the coming century, with the remainder swallowed up by the invading society.

De Béthencourt's motley crew landed first in Lanzarote, at that stage governed by *mencey* (king) Guardafía. There was no resistance and de Béthencourt went on to establish a fort on Fuerteventura.

That was as far as he got. Having run out of supplies, and with too few men for the enterprise, he headed for Spain to gain the backing of the Castilian crown. Fuerteventura, El Hierro and La Gomera then quickly fell under Spanish control. Appointed lord of the four islands by the Spanish king, Enrique III, de Béthencourt encouraged the settlement of farmers from his Norman homeland and began to pull in the profits. In 1406 he returned for good to Normandy, leaving his nephew Maciot in charge of his Atlantic possessions.

Guanches were considered elderly at age 35. They ate lots of sun-dried dates and figs that were concentrated with sugar, and this, combined with the use of mill stones to grind (gritty) grain, meant that people were toothless by their mid-20s, leading to infection and early death.

1312	1402	1464	1479
The Genoese explorer and seafarer Lanzarotto Malocello lands on the farthest northeast island of the archipelago, which is how it subsequently became named Lanzarote.	On 1 May, Jean de Béthencourt, from Normandy (France) and something of an adventurer, sets out from La Rochelle with a small and ill-equipped party bound for the Canary Islands.	On learning of the Portuguese interest in the islands, Spain's Catholic Monarchs grant Diego de Herrera, the appointed lord of La Gomera, the right to attack the remaining islands.	Portugal recognises Spanish control of the Canaries under the Treaty of Alcáçovas.

GUANCHE SOCIETY

Guanche society was essentially tribal in nature, with a chieftain or king at its head who enjoyed almost absolute rule. They lived in natural caves or simple low stone houses, while smaller grottoes and caverns were used for storing grain and as places of worship. A system of matrilineal descent existed on La Gomera and other islands of the archipelago, with inheritance passed down the mother's side of the family. Today little remains of the Guanche culture, aside from the Silbo (whistling language) of La Gomera and a number of place names and monuments.

Economy

The Guanches relied on farming, herding, hunting and gathering, and their diet was based on protein (goat and fish) and *gofio,* made of toasted and ground barley. These remain dietary staples in the Canaries even today.

Religion

The Guanches worshipped a god known as Alcorac in Gran Canaria, Achaman in Tenerife and Abora in La Palma. It appears the god was identified strongly with Magec (the sun). Tenerife islanders commonly held that Hades (hell) was in the Teide volcano and was directed by the god of evil, Guayota.

The Role of Women

Although living in an essentially patriarchal society, women did have some power. On Gran Canaria, in particular, succession rights were passed through the mother rather than the father. But when times got tough, they got tougher still for women. Infanticide was practised throughout the islands in periods of famine, and it was girls who were sacrificed, never boys.

Clothes & Weapons

Goat-skin leather was the basis of most garments, while jewellery and ornaments were largely restricted to earthenware bead-and-shell necklaces. Implements and weapons were fashioned roughly from wood, stone and bone.

Power Struggle

The island clans were not averse to squabbling, and by the time the European conquest of the islands got under way in the 15th century, the islands were divided into some 25 fiefdoms (La Palma alone boasted an astonishing 12 cantons).

Squabbles & Stagnation

What followed hardly ranks as one of the world's noblest colonial endeavours. Characterised by squabbling and occasional revolt among the colonists, the European presence did nothing for the increasingly oppressed islanders in the years following de Béthencourt's departure.

1493	1501–85	1599	1666
Tenerife provides the toughest resistance to Spanish conquest. In May, Alonso Fernández de Lugo lands on the island, with 1000 infantry soldiers and a cavalry of 150.	The islands' wealth leads to attacks by pirates and privateers: Ottoman admiral Kemal Reis ventures into the Canaries, while Murat Reis the Elder captures Lanzarote in 1585.	A major offensive takes place against Las Palma de Gran Canaria during the Dutch War of Independence, with 12,000 men attacking the Castillo de la Luz, which guards the harbour.	Tenerife's Garachico winemakers revolt against the emergence of a British monopoly of the wine trade, created by recent settlers, by destroying their cellars and wine.

The islanders were heavily taxed and Maciot also recruited them for abortive raids on the remaining three independent islands. He then capped this all off by selling his rights to the four islands (inherited from his uncle) to Portugal. Portugal only recognised Spanish control of the Canaries in 1479 under the Treaty of Alcáçovas. (In return, Spain agreed that Portugal could have the Azores, Cape Verde and Madeira.)

Maciot died in self-imposed exile in Madeira in 1452. A string of minor Spanish nobles proceeded to run the show in the Canaries with extraordinarily little success.

The Christian Campaign Continues

In 1478 a new commander arrived with fresh forces and orders from the Spanish Reyes Católicos (Catholic Monarchs), Fernando and Isabel, to finish the Canaries campaign once and for all. Despite being immediately attacked by a force of 2000 men at the site of modern-day Las Palmas de Gran Canaria, they carried the day and went after the *guanarteme* (island chief), Tenesor Semidan, in a naval attack on Galdar. Semidan was sent to Spain, converted to Christianity and returned in 1483 to convince his countrymen to give up the fight. This they did, although 20 years of battles followed which included a failed attempt to deport hundreds of islanders from Las Palmas de Gran Canaria to be sold as slaves in Spain. Fortunately, locals learned of the dastardly scheme and forced the ships transporting the men to dock at Lanzarote instead.

The Final Campaigns

In May 1493, the Spanish commander Alonso Fernández de Lugo landed on Tenerife together with 1000 infantry soldiers and a cavalry of 150, among them Guanches from Gran Canaria and La Gomera. In what was known as the first battle of Acentejo, Lugo suffered defeat by Guanche forces who had the advantage of being familiar with the mountainous terrain.

On 25 December 1494, 5000 Guanches, under the *mencey* Bencomo, were routed in the second battle of the Acentejo. The spot, only a few kilometres south of La Matanza, is still called La Victoria (Victory) today. By the following July, when de Lugo marched into the Valle de la Orotava to confront Bencomo's successor, Bentor, the diseased and demoralised Guanches were in no state to resist. Bentor surrendered and the conquest was complete. Pockets of resistance took two years to mop up, and Bentor eventually committed suicide.

Four years after the fall of Granada and the reunification of Christian Spain, the Catholic Monarchs could now celebrate one of the country's first imperial exploits – the subjugation of a small Atlantic archipelago defended by primitive tribes. The contrast between this conquest and that on the mainland was that the Catholic Monarchs were not dealing

---

Top Historic Churches

Iglesia de Nuestra Señora de Regla (Pájara, Fuerteventura)

Nuestra Señora de Antigua (Antigua, Fuerteventura)

Catedral de Santa Ana (Las Palmas de Gran Canaria)

Iglesia de Nuestra Señora de la Concepción (Valverde, El Hierro)

Iglesia del Salvador (Santa Cruz de la Palma)

Iglesia de Nuestra Señora de la Concepción (La Laguna, Tenerife)

1730–37	1821	1850–90	1923
Massive volcanic eruptions of Timanfaya in Lanzarote. The lava flow was devastating in many ways, but created fertile ground for many crops, in particular grapes.	The Canaries are declared a province of Spain, with Santa Cruz de Tenerife as the capital; Las Palmas de Gran Canaria demands that the province be split in two.	The continuing lack of employment and food leads to emigration figures peaking, with up to 40,000 islanders heading to Venezuela and elsewhere in Latin America.	General Miguel Primo de Rivera rises to power in Spain via a military coup and improves the infrastructure in the Canaries, including roads and water supplies.

with their traditional enemy, Islam, which boasted a culture far richer and more sophisticated than their own, but with a primitive native people who they proceeded to mercilessly exploit. This could be viewed as the world's first example of true colonialism and a subsequent blueprint for similar conquest in the Americas and elsewhere in the world.

Economic & Foreign Challenges

From the early 16th century, Gran Canaria and Tenerife in particular attracted a steady stream of settlers from Spain, Portugal, France, Italy and even Britain. Each island had its own local authority, and sugar cane became the Canaries' main export.

The 'discovery' of the New World in 1492 by Christopher Columbus, who called in to the archipelago several times en route to the Americas, proved a mixed blessing. It brought much passing transatlantic trade but also led to sugar production being diverted to the cheaper Americas. The local economy was rescued only by the growing export demand for wine, particularly in Britain, which was produced mainly in Tenerife.

Poorer islands, especially Lanzarote and Fuerteventura, remained backwaters, their impoverished inhabitants making a living from smuggling and piracy off the Moroccan coast – the latter activity part of a tit-for-tat game played out with the Moroccans for centuries.

Spain's control of the islands did not go completely unchallenged. The most spectacular success went to Admiral Robert Blake, one of Oliver Cromwell's three 'generals at sea'. In 1657, Blake annihilated a Spanish treasure fleet (at the cost of only one ship) at Santa Cruz de Tenerife.

British harassment culminated in 1797 with Admiral Horatio Nelson's attack on Santa Cruz. Sent there to intercept yet another treasure shipment, he not only failed to storm the town but lost his right arm in the fighting.

On a more bucolic note, in 1799 the illustrious explorer and botanist Alexander von Humboldt stopped briefly in Tenerife en route to Latin America. Apparently when he spied the Orotava Valley, he famously declared it as "the most enchanting view that eyes have ever seen". This comment and his overall praise of the islands certainly contributed to their ensuing popularity and launch as a tourist resort initially reserved for the truly elite. However, it was not until around a century later that tourism became a viable part of the local economy.

Island Divisions

Within the Canary Islands, a bitter feud developed between Gran Canaria and Tenerife over supremacy of the archipelago.

When the Canaries were declared a province of Spain in 1821, Santa Cruz de Tenerife was made the capital. Bickering between the two main islands remained heated and Las Palmas frequently demanded that the

Capturing the spirit and excitement surrounding Admiral Nelson, *1797: Nelson's Year of Destiny* (Colin White; 2006) covers the battle of Cape St Vincent and the fateful attack on Santa Cruz de Tenerife where Nelson lost his arm.

1927	1936	1940s	1950s
Madrid finally decides to split the Canaries into two provinces: Tenerife, La Gomera, La Palma and El Hierro to the west; Fuerteventura, Gran Canaria and Lanzarote in the east.	In March the government decides to transfer General Franco, a veteran of Spain's wars in Morocco and sympathetic to the ruthless Spanish Foreign Legion, to the Canary Islands.	The damaging effect of the Spanish Civil War on the Canary Islands is considerable, with rationing, food shortages and overall poverty. The black market thrives.	The postwar fallout continues, with economic misery throughout Spain and the Canaries. Once again, this is a time of mass emigration, including 16,000 *canarios* who head for Venezuela.

province be split in two. The idea was briefly, but unsuccessfully, put into practice in the 1840s.

In 1927 Madrid finally decided to split the Canaries into two provinces: Tenerife, La Gomera, La Palma and El Hierro in the west; Fuerteventura, Gran Canaria and Lanzarote in the east, with land being distributed between the local farmers. The main crops of bananas and tomatoes were cultivated and, even today, remain a major agricultural export. More unusually, cochineal farming was introduced and became one of the most important industries, particularly in Lanzarote. This parasitic beetle feeds on the prickly pear cacti and is cultivated for its crimson dye, although the industry reduced drastically with the subsequent emergence of synthetic dyes.

The island of La Gomera was the last place Christopher Columbus touched dry land before setting sail to the New World.

Decades of Emigration

Emigration to the Americas was rife throughout the latter part of the 19th and 20th centuries, and it was not uncommon for villages to be left with virtually no young male population. The exodus continued even after the Spanish-American War (1898), when Cuba and Puerto Rico were no longer Spanish territories. Cuba was initially the most popular country, followed by Venezuela, a trend which increased considerably after the Spanish Civil War, a time of considerable economic misery with rationing, food shortages and a thriving black market. In the 1950s the situation was so desperate that 16,000 migrated clandestinely, mainly to Venezuela, even though by then that country had closed its doors to further immigration. One-third of those who attempted to flee perished in the ocean crossings.

Cuba was a particularly welcoming destination for many *canarios* fleeing the effects of the Civil War, and there remain strong links between the Canary Islands and Cuba, at both governmental and personal levels.

Franco's Spain

In the 1930s, as the left and the right in mainland Spain became increasingly militant, fears of a coup grew. In March 1936 the government decided to 'transfer' General Franco, a veteran of Spain's wars in Morocco and beloved of the tough Spanish Foreign Legion, to the Canary Islands.

Suspicions that he was involved in a plot to overthrow the government were well founded. When the pro-coup garrisons of Melilla (Spanish North Africa) rose prematurely on 17 July, Franco was ready. Having seized control of the islands virtually without a struggle (the pro-Republican commander of the Las Palmas garrison died in mysterious circumstances on 14 July), Franco flew to Morocco on 19 July. Although there was virtually no fighting on the islands, the Nationalists wasted no time in rounding up anyone vaguely suspected of harbouring Republican sympathies, including writers, artists, teachers and politicians, who all mysteriously disappeared.

The postwar economic misery of mainland Spain was shared by the islands, and many *canarios* continued to emigrate. During WWII, Winston

1960s	1983	1986	1993
Fortunes are reversed as jobs are created in response to the onset of tourism to the islands, particularly from the UK and Germany. Immigration concurrently increases.	The new constitution that was introduced in Madrid in 1978 impacts the Canary Islands by deeming that they become a *comunidad autónoma* (autonomous region) in August of this year.	The Canary Islands join the EU as a special member state and outside of the EU VAT area.	The Coalición Canaria (CC) is formed, working in conjunction with the Spanish government.

Churchill developed (but never activated) a plan to invade the Canary Islands to use as a naval base in the event of Gibraltar being invaded by the Spanish mainland. At the same time exports to Europe, aside from Spain, ceased.

Tourism, 'Nationalism' & Shifting Demographics

When Franco decided to open up Spain's doors to Northern European tourists by abolishing tourist visas in 1959, the Canaries benefited as much as the mainland. The scene was set for huge numbers of holiday-makers to begin pouring into the islands year-round.

Always a fringe phenomenon, Canaries nationalism started to resurface in opposition to Franco. MPAIC (*Movimiento para la Autodeterminación e Independencia del Archipiélago Canario*), founded in 1963 by Antonio Cubillo to promote secession from Spain, embarked on a terrorist campaign in the late 1970s, including the bombing of a shopping mall in Las Palmas de Gran Canaria in 1976. There were also bomb threats, and a bomb explosion at Gran Canaria International Airport contributed to the worst aviation disaster in history in March 1977 when two Boeing 747 airlines (one KLM and one Pan Am) were diverted to now congested Los Rodeos Airport (today's Tenerife North Airport) and collided on the runway, killing 583 people. Dodging Spanish authorities, Cubillo fled to Algeria in the 1960s, but in 1985 he was allowed to return to Spain.

In 1978 a new constitution was passed in Madrid with devolution as one of its central pillars. Thus the Canary Islands became a *comunidad autónoma* (autonomous region) in August 1982, yet they remained divided into two provinces.

The main force in Canary Islands politics since its first regional election victory in 1993 has been the *Coalición Canaria* (CC). Although not bent on independence from Spain (which would be unlikely), the CC nevertheless puts the interests of the islands before national considerations.

Immigration from Africa and other parts of the world has changed the Canaries' population landscape drastically over the past two decades and has forced the islands to reassess their relationship with the African continent. The EU has also encouraged a growing relationship between the Canary Islands and Africa to help form a bridge between the European trading block and Africa. Since the 1990s, the Canary Islands have made co-operation with Africa a major priority, with bilateral agreements with several African nations, including Morocco, Mauritania, Cape Verde and Senegal.

Top History Museums

Casa-Museo de Colón, Gran Canaria

Museo de la Piratería, Lanzarote

Museo de la Historia de Tenerife

Museo Arqueológico de Lanzarote

Museo Arqueológico de Betancuria, Fuerteventura

Museo de la Naturaleza y el Hombre, Tenerife

2007	2011	2015	2018
The world's largest telescope starts monitoring the stars at La Palma's Observatorio del Roque de los Muchachos, one of the top astronomical sites in the northern hemisphere.	El Hierro residents are evacuated after over 8000 minor earthquake tremors are recorded, leading to fears of a volcanic eruption.	Repsol cancels controversial oil drilling some 50km off the shores of Fuerteventura and Lanzarote.	The seven-island archipelago gains a new sibling to make it eight: Isla Graciosa is officially declared a Canary Island.

Canarian Arts & Culture

Although the Canary Islands are Spanish, their architecture, art and overall culture are subtly distinctive from those of the mainland, with more than a glimmer of Latin American influence. Overall, the Canarians are a warm and friendly people, deeply devoted to tradition, the family and having fun. Fiestas here are wonderfully exuberant affairs: try to attend one if you can.

The Arts

Architecture

The majority of pre-Hispanic architecture on the islands is either a reconstruction or heavily restored. The Guanches lived mainly in caves, and very little of the rudimentary houses they built remains; however, there are a couple of fascinating sites of archaeological value in Gran Canaria and Fuerteventura, though what you will find there are ruins or the foundations of buildings. They can give you a good idea of the kind of habitations constructed in pre-Hispanic times. One example can be found on the way to Pozo Negro in Fuerteventura, the Poblado de La Atalayita (p99), the remains of a settlement positioned in a suitably lunar landscape.

People may refer to 'typical Canarian architecture', but there have been so many different influences over the centuries, it is problematical to specify exactly what this is. It is also not uncommon for a building to reflect more than one architectural style.

Colonial Period

Colonial-era architecture is a good example of the potpourri of influences, including elements from the Spanish, Portuguese, French, Flemish, Italian and English architectural schools.

By the time the conquest of the islands was completed at the end of the 15th century, the Gothic and Mudéjar (a distinctive Islamic-style architecture) influences already belonged more to the past than the present. The interior of the Catedral de Santa Ana in Las Palmas is nevertheless a fine example of what some art historians have termed Atlantic Gothic. Only a few scraps of the fascinating Mudéjar influence made it to the islands, most in evidence in magnificent wooden ceilings known as *artesonado*.

You can get the merest whiff of plateresque (meaning silversmith-like, so called because it was reminiscent of intricate metalwork) energy at the Catedral de Santa Ana in Las Palmas and the Iglesia de Nuestra Señora de la Concepción in La Laguna – the latter a veritable reference work of styles from Gothic through Mudéjar to plateresque. Baroque, the trademark of the 17th century, left several traces across the archipelago and is best preserved in the parish church of Betancuria, Fuerteventura.

Some of the most distinctive aspects of architecture from this period are the internal courtyards and beautiful carved wooden balconies. Las Palmas de Gran Canaria's historic Vegueta *barrio* has some superb examples, as does the Avenida Marítima in Santa Cruz de la Palma and La Orotava.

César Manrique Architecture

Jameos del Agua, Malpaís de la Corona, Lanzarote

Parque Marítimo, Santa Cruz de Tenerife

Casa Museo César Manrique, Haría, Lanzarote

Fundación César Manrique, Tahíche, Lanzarote

Mirador del Río, Lanzarote

LagOmar, Lanzarote

Modern Architecture

A large number of Modernist buildings can be seen along the Calle Mayor de Triana and in the private houses and villas of the Triana district of Las Palmas de Gran Canaria. Some further superb examples are in the streets around Parque San Telmo, not far away.

Canary architecture's greatest genius is the late César Manrique. His ecologically sensitive creations, often using volcanic stones and other Canary materials, are found throughout the islands, but especially on Lanzarote, where he was born. His designs are so compelling that some people base an entire trip around visiting them all.

Contemporary Architecture

Tenerife boasts two icons of contemporary Canary architecture: Santiago Calatrava's 'wave', the multifunction Auditorio de Tenerife dominating the waterfront of Santa Cruz de Tenerife with its unmistakable profile of a wave crashing onto shore, and the powerful lines and sympathetic vision of the Tenerife Espacio de las Artes (TEA). The latter is an architecturally stunning and innovative art space with a showstopping library (open 24 hours) downstairs.

Las Palmas de Gran Canaria is another architectural hotspot; interesting architectural spaces include the interior of the Atlantic Modern Art Centre by Sáenz de Oiza, the Auditorio Alfredo Kraus by Òscar Tusquets and the Woermann Tower by Iñaki Ábalos and Juan Herreros.

Painting & Sculpture

The Guanches

The islands' art traditions and timeline date back to the Guanches; some fine examples of Guanche cave drawings can be discovered at various sites, including the Cueva Pintada in Gáldar, Gran Canaria.

Normally geometric in design, ancient Guanche drawings have served to inspire some of the most famous local artists, including Manolo Millares (1926–72), a native of Las Palmas de Gran Canaria, as well as more accessible and widely seen souvenir T-shirts and ceramic designs. The best-loved sculpture from these times is the *Ídolo de Tara* from Gran Canaria – a curvaceous female terracotta figure, fertility symbol and Guanche icon which you will see stamped on textiles and in pottery replicas.

17th- to 19th-Century Artists

Gaspar de Quevedo from Tenerife was the first major painter to emerge from the Canary Islands in the 17th century. Quevedo was succeeded in the 18th century by Cristóbal Hernández de Quintana (1659–1725), whose paintings still decorate the Catedral in La Laguna in Tenerife. More important was Juan de Miranda (1723–1805), among whose outstanding works is *La adoración de los pastores* (The Adoration of the Shepherds) in the Iglesia de Nuestra Señora de la Concepción in Santa Cruz de Tenerife.

MARTÍN CHIRINO

Martín Chirino is widely considered to be one of the most significant Spanish sculptors of the 20th century. Born in Las Palmas de Gran Canaria in 1925, he spent time in Africa as a young man, including Morocco and Senegal, and this influence can be seen especially in some of his earlier pieces. Chirino's giant, mainly bronze sculptures are on view throughout the islands. They include *Espiral* (1999) in Santa Cruz de Tenerife; *El pensador* (2002), gracing the grounds of the University of Las Palmas de Gran Canaria; and perhaps most easily viewed of all, *Lady harimaguada* (1999), on Avenida Maritima in Las Palmas de Gran Canaria. For more information and images of his artwork, see www.martinchirino.com.

In the 19th century, Valentín Sanz Carta (1849–98) was among the first Canarians to produce landscapes. Other painters of his ilk included Lorenzo Pastor and Lillier y Thruillé, whose work can be seen in the Museo de Bellas Artes in Santa Cruz de Tenerife.

The Canaries' main exponent of impressionism was Manuel González Méndez (1843–1909), whose *La verdad venciendo el error* (Truth Overcoming Error) hangs in the *ayuntamiento* (town hall) of Santa Cruz de Tenerife.

20th-Century Artists

The Cuban-Canario José Aguiar García (1895–1976), born of Gomero parents, has works spread across the islands. His *Friso isleño* (Island Frieze) hangs in the casino in Santa Cruz de Tenerife.

All the great currents of European art filtered through to the Canary Islands. Of the so-called Coloristas, names worth mentioning include Francisco Miranda Bonnin (1911–63) and Jesús Arencibia (1911–93), who created the impressive large mural in the Iglesia de San Antonio Abad in Las Palmas de Gran Canaria.

The first surrealist exhibition in Spain was held on 11 May 1935 in Santa Cruz de Tenerife. The greatest local exponent of surrealism, *tinerfeño* Óscar Domínguez (1906–57), ended up in Paris in 1927 and was much influenced by Picasso. Others include cubist Antonio Padrón (1920–68), who has a superb museum displaying his work in his former Gran Canaria studio.

Leading the field of abstract artists is Manolo Millares (1926–72), while Alberto Manrique (1926–) from Gran Canaria enjoys altering perspective to dramatic, surreal effect. You can see a permanent exhibition of his work at the Centro de Arte Canario in La Oliva, Fuerteventura.

Crafts

A deep-rooted tradition of craftwork exists, with different islands specialising in particular crafts. Fine lacework and embroidered tablecloths, napkins and table linen can be found all over the archipelago, with Ingenio (Gran Canaria), Mazo (La Palma) and La Orotava (Tenerife) particularly famous for their embroidered works of art. Be wary of Chinese imports being passed off as local products, particularly at the street markets. One way to identify the real item (aside from the quality) is cost: original embroidery does not come cheap, reflecting the skill and time taken in its creation. Prices are dropping, however, as there is less demand for these items today.

Simple woven carpets and rugs – usually striped and brightly coloured – have a more timeless quality and are still made painstakingly with a handloom. Other popular items to weigh down your luggage with are woven baskets, Guanche-style pottery, ceramic pots and straw hats of all sizes and shapes.

Music

The symbol of Canarian musical heritage is the *timple,* a ukulele-style instrument of obscure origin, possibly introduced to the islands by Berber slaves in the 15th century. It's a small five- or four-stringed instrument with a rounded back and a sharp tone.

Whenever you see local traditional fiestas, the *timple* will be there accompanying such dances as the *isa* and *folía* or, if you're lucky, the *tajaraste* – the only dance said to have been passed down from the ancient Guanches, and still popular in La Gomera.

Culture

Regional Identity

It's tricky to sum up the peoples and traditions spread across an archipelago of seven islands. Mannerisms, expressions, food, architecture and music vary significantly from island to island, and rivalries (especially

---

Each island of the archipelago was settled by people of Berber origin from North Africa, and each tribe has a different name depending on the island they made their home. Tenerife: Guanche; Gran Canaria: Canarians; Fuerteventura and Lanzarote: Majos; La Palma: Benahoarites; La Gomera: Gomeritas; and El Hierro: Bimbaches.

People of the Islands

····················

*Gran Canaria:
grancanarios or
canariones*

····················

Tenerife: tinerfeños

····················

*Lanzarote:
conejeros*

····················

*Fuerteventura:
majoreros*

····················

*La Gomera:
gomeros*

····················

*La Palma:
palmeros*

····················

El Hierro: herreños

between heavyweights Tenerife and Gran Canaria) are pronounced. Yet all inhabitants share a fierce pride in being Canarian, and a belief that their unique history and culture set them apart from the rest of Spain. While most of the Canary Island locals have the classic Mediterranean looks of the Spaniards – dark hair and eyes and an olive complexion – you might find that they don't consider themselves very Spanish.

Soon after the socialists' 1982 electoral victory, the Canary Islands were declared a *comunidad autónoma,* one of 17 autonomous regions across Spain. A few vocal *canarios* would like to see their islands become completely autonomous, and indeed you may see graffiti declaring '*Canarias no es España*' (the Canaries are not Spain), '*Viva Canarias Libre*' (Long Live the Free Canaries) or '*Godos fuera*' (Spaniards go home).

The archipelago's division into two provinces, Santa Cruz and Las Palmas, remains intact, as does the rivalry between the two provinces – so much so that the regional government has offices in both provincial capitals, which alternate as lead city of the region every four years.

Macaronesia is the name given to a collection of four archipelagos in the Atlantic Ocean, namely (from north to south): the Azores, Madeira, the Canary Islands and Cape Verde. Only Cape Verde is a country; the other archipelagos belong to Portugal (the Azores and Madeira) and Spain (Canary Islands).

Lifestyle

The greatest lifestyle change that has come to the Canary Islands has been as a result of the tourism industry. From the 1960s, the primarily agricultural society evolved into a society largely dependent on the service industry within just a few decades. Traditional lifestyles on small *fincas* (farms) or in fishing villages have been supplanted by employment in the tourism sector.

As the islands close the gap between their traditional, rural lifestyles and the fast-paced, modern lifestyle of the rest of Spain, some problems are inevitable. The cost of living has skyrocketed, forcing those who have kept traditional agriculture jobs to supplement their income with positions in the tourism industry. Education is another issue; since the small islands have no universities, young people have to study in Tenerife or Gran Canaria, and this can deplete a family's already over-stretched budget. After school, many college-educated islanders end up leaving the island of their birth to look for better jobs on Tenerife, Gran Canaria or the mainland. By necessity, many Canarian families are separated.

Nevertheless, family remains at the heart of Canary culture. Big island festivities are often celebrated with family, and islanders come from as far away as the Americas to reunite with family and friends. Most religious and cultural celebrations are also family-focused. Although families are now smaller than they used to be – one or two children is the norm – they're still an important social unit. As elsewhere in Europe, couples are waiting longer to get married and have children, proving that Canarian society is not as traditional as it once was.

Sport

The Canary Islands are a sport-friendly destination, as they have a balmy, sunny climate, plenty of coastline and a laid-back, outdoor lifestyle that rewards activity. As part of Spain, the top sport here is, of course, football (soccer). Although there is a regional football team for the Canary

LOS SABANDEÑOS

The Canaries' best-loved folk group, Los Sabandeños, has been singing and strumming since 1966, when these *tinerfeños* banded together in an effort to recover and popularise Canary culture across the islands. It's impossible to quantify the effect this group of nearly 25 men (including a few new recruits) has had on the islands. Suffice to say, they have a statue in their honour in Punta de Hidalgo, Tenerife, and (at last count) seven streets named after them. Their collections of light, melodic music are widely available; look for their greatest hits compilation *60 Canciones de Oro* (2012).

LOCAL HEROES

Famous people from the Canary Islands include:

➤ César Manrique – artist, sculptor and architect, born in Lanzarote.

➤ David Silva – international footballer who has won major honours with Manchester City and Spain.

➤ Carmen Laforet – 20th-century writer and author of *Nada* (1945). Laforet was actually born in Barcelona, but moved to the Canary Islands at two and grew up there.

➤ Javier Bardem – film actor, with parts in *No Country for Old Men, Skyfall* and *Jamón, Jamón,* among other films; born in Las Palmas de Gran Canaria.

➤ Juan Carlos Fresnadillo – film director, producer and writer; director of apocalyptic zombie horror *28 Weeks Later* and *Intacto.*

Islands, they are not affiliated with FIFA, UEFA or CAF, because the islands are represented internationally by the Spanish national team. The team only plays friendly matches.

Far more unusual is *lucha canaria* (Canarian wrestling), which is said to date back to the Guanches, a particularly robust and warlike crowd who loved a trial of strength: jumping over ravines, diving into oceans from dizzying heights...and this distinctive style of wrestling. One member of each team faces off against an adversary in the ring and, after a formal greeting and other signs of goodwill, they set about trying to dump each other into the dust. No part of the body except the soles of the feet may touch the ground, and whoever fails first in this department loses.

If you want to find out if any matches are due to be held locally, ask at the nearest tourist office or check out www.fedluchacanaria.com/federacioncanaria.

Multiculturalism

The Canary Islands today, for so long a region of net emigration, admit more people than they export. Workers in the hotel, restaurant and construction industries, and migrants from Northern Europe seeking a place in the near-perpetual sun, all bolster the islands' population figures. With more than half a million tourist beds in hotels, apartments and houses across the islands, there is a steady influx of visitors from across the world, mainly Europe, some of whom decide to stay and make a life here.

A newer phenomenon are the immigrants from the Americas, many of them family members of Canarians who emigrated to Venezuela or other South American countries and are now returning to the islands of their ancestors.

In the past, the Canary Islands have faced serious problems with illegal migrants arriving from African shores in droves. In recent years, the number of boats carrying illegal migrants has significantly dropped, though locals are still wary of the situation. Prejudice is hard to gauge, but some tourists of African origin have reported discrimination, mainly in shops and restaurants, and particularly in the southern resorts of Tenerife.

Religion

The Catholic church plays an important role in people's lives. Most *canarios* are baptised and confirmed, have church weddings and funerals, and many attend church for important feast days – although fewer than half regularly turn up for Sunday Mass. Many of the colourful and often wild fiestas that take place throughout the year have some religious context or origin.

One of the most famous shoe designers in the world, Manolo Blahnik, was born in 1943 in Santa Cruz de La Palma. The son of a Czech father and Spanish mother, he spent his childhood among banana plants on his mother's plantation – a perhaps unlikely beginning for a world-famous fashion designer!

If you want to catch some traditional Canarian tunes, check out Tenderete, a TV show that's been running for almost 50 years. Watch it on Sunday evenings on TVE1.

Life on a Volcano

Many people think of the Canary Islands as consisting of little but flat, featureless semi-idesert, and while there are areas like this, anyone who knows the islands well will speak with great excitement and passion about the sheer variety of landscapes, the huge range of microclimates and flora and fauna contained within this unique archipelago. Yes, large swathes of Fuerteventura may resemble Mars, but other islands such as Gran Canaria and La Palma have deeply lush and verdant regions that are not dissimilar from cooler parts of continental Europe. Expect to be surprised.

Volcanic Landscape

Formation of the Islands

The seven islands and six islets that make up the Canary Islands archipelago are little more than the tallest tips of a vast volcanic mountain range that lies below the Atlantic Ocean. Just babies in geological terms, the islands were thrown up 30 million years ago when tectonic plates collided, crumpling the land into mammoth mountains both on land, as in the case of Morocco's Atlas range, and on the ocean floor, as in the case of the Cape Verde islands, the Azores and the Canaries (Atlantic islands that are collectively referred to as Macronesia). After the initial creation, a series of volcanic eruptions put the final touches on the islands' forms. Volcanic eruptions continue to shape the islands to this day, though more rarely and less dramatically.

The Islands Today

The seven main islands have a total area of 7447 sq km. Their collective size may not be great, but packed into this area is just about every imaginable kind of landscape, from the long, sandy beaches of Fuerteventura and dunes of Gran Canaria to the majestic Atlantic cliffs of Tenerife and mist-enveloped woods of La Gomera. The easternmost islands have an almost Saharan desertscape, while corners and pockets of La Palma and La Gomera are downright lush. At higher altitudes on La Palma and Gran Canaria, pine forests swathe the mountainsides and carpet the soil in needles. The highest mountain in Spain is Pico del Teide (3718m), which dominates the entire island of Tenerife.

La Palma is the steepest island in the world, relative to its height and overall area.

El Teide & Others

El Teide, that huge pyramid that stands at the very centre of life on Tenerife, is, at 3718m, both the highest mountain in Spain and – if measured from its true base on the ocean floor – the third-largest volcano in the world. Teide is what's known as a shield volcano: it's huge and rises in a broad, gently angled cone to a summit that holds a steep-walled, flat-based crater. Although seemingly quiet, Teide is by no means finished.

Wisps of hot air can sometimes be seen around Teide's peak, and seismic activity is quite common. Where the lava is fairly fluid, steam pressure can build up to the point of ejecting lava and ash or both in an

CUMBRE VIEJA & THE MEGA-TSUNAMI
• •

On the island of La Palma is the Cumbre Vieja (Old Ridge). In 1949 a series of volcanic eruptions here caused a fissure about 2.5km long to open up, which sent the western side of the Cumbre Vieja slipping downwards, and westwards, by around 2m.

Experts believe that it's only a matter of time before Cumbre Vieja erupts again. When it does, some people fear that it could send up to 1.5 trillion metric tons of rock cascading down into the Atlantic. The resulting tsunami could measure up to 600m and, travelling at a speed of around 1000km an hour, would reach the east coast of the US within six hours (and the coastlines of Africa and Europe much sooner). By this time the tsunami waves would be around 30m to 60m high, though on reaching shallower water they could grow to a several hundred metres. Surprisingly, perhaps, Hollywood has yet to make a film about the threat, which could see the waves travelling around 25km inland, devastating the Caribbean and the eastern shores of the US.

With some experts playing down fears as others ramp up the doomsday scenarios, the jury remains out on the likely size and destructive power of such a tsunami, while the timescale before the next eruption is simply not known. Some research has suggested the western side of the Cumbre Vieja is unlikely to collapse into the sea within the next 10,000 years.

eruption through the narrow vent. The vent can simply be blown off if there is sufficient pressure.

Other volcanoes on the islands have been known to sometimes literally blow their top. Massive explosions can cause an entire summit to cave in, blasting away an enormous crater. The result is known as a caldera, within which it is not unusual for new cones to emerge, creating volcanoes within volcanoes. There are several impressive calderas on Gran Canaria, most notably Caldera de Bandama. Oddly enough, massive Caldera de Taburiente on La Palma does not belong to this group of geological phenomena, although it was long thought to.

These days in the Canary Islands, you can best get a feel for the rumblings below the surface on Lanzarote, where the Montañas del Fuego still bubble with vigour, although the last eruptions took place way back in 1824. Of the remaining islands, not an eruptive burp has been heard from Fuerteventura, Gran Canaria, La Gomera or El Hierro for centuries; Tenerife's most recent display was a fairly innocuous affair in 1909; and it was La Palma that hosted the most recent spectacle – a fiery outburst by Volcán Teneguía in 1971, with rivers of lava flowing into the sea, which added to the size of the island.

Nature Trek (www.nature-trek.co.uk) is a British-based wildlife-watching tour company that runs an eight-day tour in search of the native wildlife and plants of the Canary Islands.

Wild Things
Canaries, Whales & Other Animals

There is wildlife out there, but it tends to be small, shy and largely undetectable to the untrained eye. Lizards and birds are the biggest things you'll see – and in some cases they can be quite big, like the endemic giant lizard (*Gallotia simonyi*) of El Hierro, which measures around 60cm in length. There are around 200 species of birds on the islands, though many are imports from Africa and Europe. Five endemics are found in the Canaries: Bolle's Pigeon, Laurel Pigeon, Blue Chaffinch, Canary Islands Chiff-Chaff and Canary Islands Chat. And yes, before you ask, this is where canaries come from, but the wild cousins are of a much duller colour than the popular cage birds.

If it's big animals you want, you need to get off land and turn to the ocean. The stretch of water between Tenerife and La Gomera is a traditional feeding ground for as many as 26 species of whales, and others

Look out for books by David Bramwell, the curator of Gran Canaria's Jardín Botánico Canario, who is an authority on the flora of the islands and has penned numerous books on the subject.

LAND OF GIANTS

The best-known native animals in the Canaries today are the giant lizards (p234), which still survive in a number of spots. Impressive as some of these are, they're smaller than a species of now-extinct lizard that once scampered and hissed among the hills. Hailing from Tenerife and other islands, fossils and bones of *Gallotia goliath* reveal that this colossal lizard measured a good metre in length and died out some time in the 15th century. Today skeletons and casts of the lizards can be seen in Tenerife's Museo de la Naturaleza y el Hombre (p143).

Living alongside these lizards was a nightmarish creature: the Tenerife Giant Rat (*Canariomys bravoi*). This outsize rodent was around a metre long (including the tail) and weighed possibly 1kg when fully grown. The rat still inhabited Tenerife when the Guanches first arrived, but people, and possibly domestic cats, quickly put an end to the monster. Gran Canaria had its own type of giant rat, but this was a comparative minnow at just 25cm in length.

It's also thought that a type of giant tortoise (*Geochelone burchardi*) once lived on Tenerife, with other species of tortoise inhabiting the other islands.

pass through during migration. The most common are pilot whales, sperm whales and bottlenose dolphins.

Whale-watching is big business around here, and 800,000 people a year head out on boats to get a look. A law regulates observation of sea mammals, prohibiting boats from getting closer than 60m to an animal and limiting the number of boats following pods at any one time. The law also tries to curb practices such as using sonar and other devices to attract whales' attention. Four small patrol boats attempt to keep a watchful eye on these activities. If you decide to take a whale-watching tour, join up with a reputable company.

Aside from the majestic marine mammals, the ocean waters teem with other life forms, including over 500 species of fish. The best way to see fish in their habitat is on a dive.

Plants

The islands' rich volcanic soil, varied rainfall and dramatic changes in altitude support a great diversity of plant life, both indigenous and introduced.

The Canary Islands are home to about 2000 species of plants, around 700 of which are endemic to the islands. The only brake on an even more abundant range of flora in this largely subtropical environment is a shortage of water. Even so, botanists will be amply rewarded, and numerous botanical gardens are scattered around the islands for the observation of a whole range of local plant-life.

Possibly the most important floral ecosystem in the Canaries is La Gomera's Parque Nacional de Garajonay, host to one of the world's last remaining Tertiary-era forests and a Unesco World Heritage Site. Known as *laurisilva*, the beautiful forest here is made up of laurels, holly, linden and giant heather, clad in lichen and moss and often swathed in swirling mist.

Up in the great volcanic basin of the Parque Nacional del Teide on Tenerife, the star botanical attraction is the flamboyant *tajinaste rojo*, or Teide viper's bugloss *(Echium wildpretii)*, which can grow to more than 3m in height. Every other spring it sprouts an extraordinary conical spike of striking red blooms like a great red poker. After its brief, spectacular moment of glory, all that remains is a thin, desiccated, spear-shaped skeleton, like a well-picked-over fish. Leave well alone; each fishbone has thousands of tiny strands that are as itchy as horsehair.

The Bardino (Perro Bardino), or Majorero, is indigenous to Fuerteventura. A muscular and quite hefty breed of dog, it is thought to have been brought to the island by the first settlers but possibly by later Hispanic arrivals. Historically a shepherding dog, it can weigh more than 40kg and survives only in very small and decreasing numbers.

Environmental Issues

The Problems

As in mainland Spain, the 1960s saw the first waves of mass sea-and-sun tourism crash over the tranquil shores of the Canary Islands. The government of the day anticipated filling up the state coffers with easy tourist dollars, and local entrepreneurs enthusiastically leapt aboard the gravy train. Few, however, gave a thought to what impact the tourists and mushrooming coastal resorts might have on the environment.

The near-unregulated building and expansion of resorts well into the 1980s created some shocking eyesores, particularly on the southern side of Tenerife and Gran Canaria. Great scabs of holiday villas, hotels and condominiums spread across much of these two islands' southern coasts. And the problem is not restricted to the resorts – hasty cement extensions to towns and villages mean that parts of the islands' interiors are being increasingly spoiled by property developers and speculators.

The massive influx of visitors to the islands over recent decades has brought or exacerbated other problems. Littering of beaches, dunes and other areas of natural beauty, both by outsiders and locals, remains a burning issue. Occasionally, ecological societies organise massive rubbish cleanups along beaches and the like – worthy gestures but also damning evidence of the extent to which the problem persists.

One of the islands' greatest and most persistent problems is water, or rather the lack thereof. Limited rainfall and the lack of natural springs have always restricted agriculture, and water is a commodity still in short supply. Desalination appears the only solution for the Canaries; pretty much all potable water on Lanzarote and Fuerteventura is desalinated sea water.

In summer, the corollary of perennial water shortages is the forest fire. With almost clockwork regularity, hundreds of hectares of forest are ravaged every summer on all the islands except the already-bare Lanzarote and Fuerteventura. The Canarian pine bears the brunt of much of the inferno, but is an astonishingly fire-resistant tree and regenerates speedily after the flames have swept through.

Wild Books

Whales and Dolphins of the Canary Islands (Volker Boehlke; 2006)

Native Flora of the Canary Islands (Miguel Ángel Cabrera Pérez; 1999)

The Geology of the Canary Islands (Juan Carlos Carracedo & Valentin Troll; 2014)

A Field Guide to the Birds of the Atlantic Islands (Tony Clarke; 2006)

LIFE ON A VOLCANO ENVIRONMENTAL ISSUES

DRAGON TREES: A LONG, SHADY PAST

Among the more curious trees you will see in the Canary Islands is the *drago* (dragon tree; *Dracaena draco*), which can reach a height of 18m and live for centuries.

Having survived the last ice age, the tree looks prehistoric and unique. Its shape resembles a giant posy of flowers, its trunk and branches being the stems, which break into bunches of long, narrow, silvery-green leaves higher up. As the plant (technically it is not a tree, though it's always referred to as one) grows, it becomes more and more top-heavy. To stabilise itself, the *drago* ingeniously grows roots on the outside of its trunk, eventually creating a second, wider trunk. What makes the *drago* stranger still is its red sap or resin – known, of course, as 'dragon's blood' – which was traditionally used in medicine.

The plant once played an important role in Canary Island life, for it was beneath the ancient branches of a *drago* that the Guanche Council of Nobles would gather to administer justice.

The *drago* is one of a family of up to 40 species (*Dracaena*) that survived the ice age in tropical and subtropical zones of the Old World, and is one of the last representatives of Tertiary-era flora.

If you would like to cultivate a *drago,* look out for small potted saplings of the plant to take back home; you can even find them at the airport (but will pay a premium there).

Roque Cinchado, Parque Nacional del Teide (p162)

Arguments

For the islands' administrators, it's a conundrum. Tourism has come to represent an essential pillar of the Canaries' economy, which they quite simply cannot do without. They argue that profits from the tourist trade are ploughed back into the community. However, this is still fairly haphazard, and there have long been calls for more regional planning – and, every year more insistently, for a total moratorium on further tourism development. Short-term moratoriums are at times established on an island-by-island basis. Some of the damage done over the years, especially to the coastline, is irreversible.

The new Puerto Industrial de Granadilla in southeastern Tenerife has created concern about the adverse effects the huge commercial port will have on the environment. The contentious plan to drill for gas and oil off the coasts of Fuerteventura and Lanzarote was fortunately laid to rest after exploratory probes deemed the project unworthy.

One island that has taken giant steps towards conservation is El Hierro, where, after years of planning, the government was about to achieve its goal to become the world's first island able to meet all its energy needs with renewable sources (wind, water and solar) alone. Next on the agenda: El Hierro is planning to run all its vehicles on electricity by 2020 as well as operating an island-wide policy of promoting organic farming.

Wind power has also been hugely developed in the Canary Islands, growing by a vast 137% over the three years to 2018. You will observe large wind farms on Tenerife, Gran Canaria and other islands, part of the archipelago's ambition to meet a staggering 45% of its energy needs from renewable sources by 2025.

For the latest updates on ecological issues on the islands, check the Facebook page of the Asociación Tinerfeña Amigos de la Naturaleza, which contains a resourceful list of posts and links regarding ecological issues on Tenerife.

Survival Guide

Directory A–Z

Accessible Travel

The Canary Islands are not especially well geared towards smooth travel for people with disabilities. Most restaurants, shops and tourist sights are not equipped to handle wheelchairs, although the more expensive hotels and resorts will have rooms with appropriate facilities. Naturally, check before booking. Restaurants, bars and shops in commercial centres will have access ramps for wheelchair users, however.

Transport is quite complicated, although you should be able to organise a specially modified hire car from one of the international hire companies (with advance warning). In fact, advance warning is always a good idea; start with your travel agent and see what it can offer in terms of information and assistance. In the archipelago's cities, such as Las Palmas and Santa Cruz, some buildings (eg museums or government offices) provide Braille in the lifts, and specially textured floors before stairs, but not much else. Few concessions are made in the public infrastructure for people who are deaf. Mobility scooter hire is straightforward in Los Cristianos on Tenerife, and you will see a lot of people using them.

The **tourist office** (☑928 51 05 42; www.puertodelcarmen. com; Avenida de las Playas; ☺10am-6pm) in Puerto del Carmen in Lanzarote can advise on arranging amphibious chairs for anyone with mobility issues wanting to use the beach.

Mobility Equipment Hire

Mobility Abroad (www.mobility abroad.com) A long-standing company with outlets in Gran Canaria and Lanzarote.

Orange Badge (☑922 79 73 55; www.orangebadge.eu; Avenida Amsterdam, Los Cristianos; ☺10am-5pm Mon-Fri, to 1pm Sat & Sun) Wheelchair and mobility-scooter hire in Tenerife.

Organisations

Can Be Done (☑0044 208 907 2400; www.canbedone.co.uk) UK-based travel agency specialising in travel for people with disabilities.

Society for Accessible Travel & Hospitality (☑0212 447 7284; www.sath.org) This non-profit organisation aims to raise awareness of the needs of all travellers with disabilities and can provide general information.

PRACTICALITIES

Newspapers & Magazines Local newspapers include *Diario de Avisos, Canarias 7, La Provincia* and the English-language *Island Connections*. You can also get Spanish newspapers *El País* and *El Mundo* and the foreign *International Herald Tribune, Hello!* and – in the resorts – all the British and German tabloids.

Radio Radio Nacional de España has four stations. Local FM stations abound on the islands. The BBC World Service (www.bbc.co.uk/worldserviceradio) can be found mainly on 6195kHz, 9410kHz, 12095kHz, 15485kHz and 15105 kHz. You can also listen to the 24-hour European program stream live online via the Radio Player link on the BBC World Service home page.

TV The Canaries receive the mainland's big TV channels (TVE1, La 2, Antena 3, Cuatro, Tele 5, La Sexta) and have a few local stations that are of very limited interest.

Smoking Laws prohibit smoking in all bars and restaurants, as well as near hospitals, in school playgrounds and even on TV broadcasts.

Weights & Measures The metric system is used.

Customs Regulations

Although the Canary Islands are part of Spain, for customs purposes they are not considered part of the EU. For this reason, allowances are much less generous than for goods bought within EU countries. You are allowed to bring in or take out, duty free, a maximum of the following items:

➡ 4L of still wine

➡ 1L of spirits (or 2L of sparkling wine)

➡ 16L of beer

➡ 200 cigarettes

➡ €300 worth of other goods and gifts

Discount Cards

To receive any available discounts, photo ID is essential.

➡ Seniors get reduced prices at some museums and attractions and occasionally on transport. Minimum age varies between 60 and 65.

➡ Students receive discounts of usually half the normal fee, though student cards are not accepted everywhere.

Electricity

Type C
230V/50Hz

Embassies & Consulates

Countries have their main diplomatic representation in Madrid but also consular representation in Las Palmas de Gran Canaria.

German Consulate (📞928 49 18 80; www.spanien.diplo.de; Calle Albareda 3, 2nd fl)

Irish Consulate (📞928 29 77 28; www.embassyofireland.es; Calle León y Castillo 195)

UK Consulate (📞928 26 25 08; www.gov.uk; Calle Luis Morote 6, 3rd fl)

US Consulate (📞928 27 12 59; https://es.usembassy.gov; Calle Los Martínez de Escobar 3)

There is a small number of consulates in Santa Cruz de Tenerife.

French Consulate (📞922 53 35 36; www.ambafrance-es.org; Calle Robayna 25)

Irish Consulate (📞922 24 56 71; www.embassyofireland.es; Calle Villalba Hervás 9, 9th fl)

UK Consulate (📞in Gran Canaria 928 26 25 08; www.gov.uk/world/organisations/british-consulate-santa-cruz-de-tenerife; Plaza General Weyler 8, 1st fl)

Health

Health Insurance

For EU citizens, the European Health Insurance Card (EHIC), which you apply for online, by phone or by post, entitles you to medical care at the same cost that a local would pay – sometimes for free. It doesn't cover emergency repatriation home and isn't meant as a substitution for travel insurance.

Depending on the eventual outcome of the UK's departure from the EU, British citizens may find their EHIC card invalidated and will need to make alternative health insurance preparations before travelling to the Canary Islands.

Citizens from other countries should find out whether there is a reciprocal arrangement for free medical care between their country and Spain. If you need health insurance, strongly consider a policy that covers the worst possible scenario, such as an accident requiring an emergency flight home. Find out in advance if your insurance plan will make direct payments to providers or reimburse you later for overseas health expenditures.

Recommended Vaccinations

No jabs are required to travel to Spain. The World Health Organization (WHO), however, recommends that all travellers should be covered for diphtheria, tetanus, measles, mumps, rubella and polio, regardless of their destination. Since most vaccines don't provide immunity until at least two weeks after they're given, visit a physician at least six weeks before departure.

Availability of Healthcare

Spain has an excellent healthcare system that extends to the Canary Islands. If you need an ambulance, call 112 (the pan-European emergency telephone number that can be called for urgent medical assistance). An alternative medical emergency number is 061. Alternatively, go straight to the *urgencias* (casualty) section of the nearest hospital.

Indicated with a green cross, *farmacias* (pharmacies) offer valuable advice and sell over-the-counter medication. Throughout the Canaries, a system of *farmacias de guardia* (duty pharmacies) operates so that each district has one open all the time. When a pharmacy is closed, it posts the name of the nearest open one on the door.

Altitude Sickness

If you are hiking at elevations above 2500m (such as at El Teide in Tenerife), altitude sickness may be a risk. Lack of oxygen at high altitudes affects most people to some extent. Symptoms of acute mountain sickness (AMS) usually develop during the first 24 hours at altitude, but may be delayed up to three weeks. Mild symptoms include headache, lethargy, dizziness, difficulty sleeping and loss of appetite. AMS may become more severe without warning and can be fatal. Severe symptoms include breathlessness, a dry irritating cough, severe headache and lack of balance.

Treat mild symptoms by resting at the same altitude until you recover, usually for a day or two. Paracetamol or aspirin can be taken for headaches. If symptoms worsen, immediate descent is necessary: even 500m can help.

Heat Exhaustion

Heat exhaustion occurs following excessive fluid loss with inadequate replacement of fluids and salt. Symptoms include headache, dizziness and tiredness. Dehydration is already happening by the time you feel thirsty – aim to drink sufficient water to produce pale, diluted urine. To treat heat exhaustion, replace fluids through water and/or fruit juice, and cool the body with cold water and fans.

Tap Water

Much of the tap water found throughout the Canary Islands is desalinated sea water. It is safe to drink, though doesn't taste particularly good and most locals buy bottled water, which is cheap and readily available. If you are in any doubt, ask ¿Es potable el agua (de grifo)? (Is the (tap) water drinkable?). Do not drink from lakes as they may contain bacteria or viruses that can cause diarrhoea or vomiting.

Insurance

A travel-insurance policy to cover theft, loss and medical problems and cancellation or delays to your travel arrangements is a good idea. Paying for your ticket with a credit card can often provide limited travel-accident insurance, and you may be able to reclaim the payment if the operator doesn't deliver. Worldwide travel insurance is available at www.lonely planet.com/travel-insurance. You can buy, extend and claim online anytime – even if you're already on the road.

Internet Access

Wi-fi is available at airports and pretty much all hotels, and most but not all cafes and restaurants; generally, but not always, free. Connection speed often varies from room to room in hotels, so always ask when you check in.

Language Courses

Tenerife is particularly noted for its Spanish-language courses. There are also several schools in Las Palmas de Gran Canaria. Accommodation can be arranged at a number of schools, some offering the chance to live with a Spanish family. Some activities schools such as **Magma Kitesurf School** (626 200345; www.magma-kiteschool.com; Calle Central 1; 1-day surfing course €50, 2-day kitesurfing course €255) in Lajares on Fuerteventura can tie in Spanish language courses with kitesurfing.

Canarias Cultural (Map p142; 922 21 21 86; www.canarias cultural.es; Avenida de Buenos Aires 54, Santa Cruz de Tenerife; 1-week intensive course €150) A range of part- and full-time courses, with a standalone one-week intensive course costing €150. Accommodation can be arranged.

Don Quijote (Map p154; 922 36 88 07; www.donquijote.org; Avenida Colón 14, Puerto de la Cruz, Tenerife; 1-week intensive course €185, enrolment €55, textbook €35) Nationwide organisation offering private or group classes, plus a two-week course for the over 50s. Accommodation can be arranged.

Gran Canaria School of Languages (Map p60; 928 26 79 71; www.grancanariaschool. com; Calle Dr Grau Bassas 27; 1-week intensive course €170) Has been in business for more than 50 years and has an excellent reputation. Lodging can also be arranged.

Study Abroad International (www.studyabroadinternational. com) A variety of study-abroad programmes in Gran Canaria and Tenerife.

Legal Matters

Should you be arrested, you will be allotted the free services of an *abogado de oficio* (duty solicitor), who may speak only Spanish. You are also entitled to make a phone call. If you use this call to contact your embassy or consulate, it will probably be able to do no more than refer you to a lawyer who speaks your language. If you end up in court, the authorities are obliged to provide a translator if you have to testify.

In theory, you are supposed to have your national ID card or passport with you at all times. If asked for it by the police, you are supposed to be able to produce it on the spot. In practice it is rarely an issue, and many people choose to leave passports in hotel safes.

There are three main types of *policía*: the Policía Local, the Policía Nacional and the Guardia Civil. Should you need to contact the police, don't agonise over which kind to approach: any of them will do, but you may find that the Policía Local is the most helpful. The Canary Islands government provides a toll-free telephone number (☎112), which ensures that any emergency situation can be attended to by the nearest police available.

Spanish law defines any individual under the age of 18 to be a minor.

LGBT+ Travellers

Same-sex marriages are legal in Spain and hence on the Canary Islands. Playa del Inglés and Maspalomas, on the southern end of Gran Canaria, are where the bulk of Europe's gay crowd heads when holidaying in the Canaries, and the night-life here bumps and grinds year-round. By day, nudist beaches are popular spots to hang out.

Spanish people generally adopt a live-and-let-live attitude to sexuality, so you shouldn't have any hassles in the Canary Islands. That said, some small rural towns may not quite know how to deal with overt displays of affection between same-sex couples.

Resources

Canarias Gay (www.canariasgay. com) Search engine for gay friendly holidays in the islands.

Gamá (www.colectivogama.com) Gay and lesbian association covering the entire archipelago.

Gay Homestays (www. gayhomestays.com) LGBT accommodation listings options on Tenerife, Gran Canaria and Lanzarote (and the rest of the world).

Gay Welcome (www.gay welcome.com) Resourceful website for Europe-wide travel, including the Canary Islands.

Money

The most convenient way to bring your money is in the form of a debit or credit card, with some extra cash for use in case of an emergency.

ATMs

The Canary Islands has a surfeit of banks, and virtually each one has a multilingual *cajero automático* (ATM). There is usually a charge of between 2% and 3% on ATM cash withdrawals abroad.

Cash

Even if you're using a credit card you'll still need to carry some cash – bus drivers and some smaller restaurants and shops don't accept cards.

Credit Cards

All major *tarjetas de crédito* (credit cards) and debit cards are widely accepted. They can be used for many purchases (including at petrol stations and larger supermarkets, which sometimes ask to see some form of ID) and in hotels and restaurants (although smaller establishments tend to accept cash only). Contactless payment by credit and debit cards is also widely available.

Moneychangers

Exchange facilities can be found at most air and seaports on the islands. In resorts and cities that attract large numbers of foreigners, you'll find them easily – they're usually indicated by the word *cambio* (exchange). Most of the time, they offer longer opening hours and quicker service than banks, and in many cases they offer better rates. Shop around and always ask from the outset about commission, the terms of which differ from place to place, and confirm that exchange rates are as posted. A typical commission is 3%. Places that advertise 'no commission' usually make up the difference by offering poorer exchange rates.

Tipping

Not obligatory but most people at least leave some small change if they're satisfied; 5% is normally fine and 10% considered generous. Porters

will generally be happy with €1. Taxi drivers don't have to be tipped but a little rounding up won't go amiss.

Opening Hours

The following standard opening hours are for high season only; hours tend to decrease outside that time:

Banks 8.30am to 2pm Monday to Friday

Bars 7pm to midnight

Post offices 8.30am to 8.30pm Monday to Friday, 9.30am to 1pm Saturday (large cities); 8.30am to 2.30pm Monday to Friday, 9.30am–1pm Saturday (elsewhere)

Restaurants meals served 1pm to 4pm and 7pm to late

Shops 10am to 2pm and 5pm to 9pm Monday to Friday, 10am to 2pm Saturday

Supermarkets 9am to 9pm Monday to Saturday

Post

Correos (www.correos.es), the Spanish postal system operating on the Canary Islands, is generally efficient, if sometimes a bit slow. Post-boxes are bright yellow and labelled 'Correos'.

Public Holidays

There are at least 14 official holidays a year in the Canary Islands. When a holiday falls close to a weekend, locals like to make a *puente* (bridge) – meaning they also take the intervening day off. On occasion, when a couple of holidays fall close to the same weekend, the *puente* becomes an *acueducto* (aqueduct)!

Following are the major national holidays, observed throughout the islands and the rest of Spain:

Año Nuevo (New Year's Day) 1 January

Día de los Reyes Magos (Three Kings Day) 6 January

Viernes Santo (Good Friday) March/April

Fiesta del Trabajo (Labour Day) 1 May

La Asunción de la Virgen (Feast of the Assumption) 15 August

Día de la Hispanidad (National Day) 12 October

Todos los Santos (All Saint's Day) 1 November. Gets particular attention on Tenerife.

La Inmaculada Concepción (Feast of the Immaculate Conception) 8 December

Navidad (Christmas) 25 December

In addition, the regional government sets a further five holidays, while local councils allocate another two. Common holidays include the following:

Martes de Carnival (Carnival Tuesday) February/March

Jueves Santo (Maundy Thursday) March/April

Día de las Islas Canarias (Canary Islands Day) 30 May

Día de San Juan (St John's Day) 24 June

Día de Santiago Apóstol (Feast of St James the Apostle, Spain's patron saint) 25 July. In Santa Cruz de Tenerife the day also marks the commemoration of the defence of the city against Horatio Nelson.

Día del Pino (Pine Tree Day) 8 September. This is particularly important on Gran Canaria.

Día de la Constitución (Constitution Day) 6 December

Safe Travel

In terms of personal security, the Canary Islands generally feel safe and nonthreatening. The main thing to be wary of is petty theft.

➡ Keep valuables concealed or locked in your hotel room and don't leave anything on display in your car.

➡ Be wary of pickpockets in areas with plenty of other tourists.

➡ Women travellers may encounter sexual harassment; this is often nothing more sinister than catcalling or staring, but it is enough to be intimidating.

➡ Watch out for rip tides when swimming on all the islands.

Rip Tides

If caught in a rip tide in deep water, do not fight against it as you may rapidly, and dangerously, tire. It is more advisable to try to call for help and to go with the flow to conserve energy; the rip tide will take you further out to sea, but you should be able to swim back. Rip tide channels are quite narrow, so another technique is to gradually swim parallel to the shore when caught in a rip tide and you should escape it.

Telephone
Mobile Phones

Buy a pay-as-you-go mobile with credit from €30. Local SIM cards are widely available and can be used in unlocked GSM phones.

If you have a GSM, dual- or tri-band cellular mobile phone you can buy SIM cards and prepaid time.

All the Spanish phone companies (including Orange, Vodafone and Movistar) offer prepaid accounts for mobiles. You can then top up the cards in their shops or outlets, such as supermarkets and tobacconists.

The Canaries uses GSM 900/1800, which is compatible with the rest of Europe and Australia but not with the North American GSM 1900 or the system used in Japan. From those countries, you will need to travel with a tri-band or quadric-band phone.

Phone Codes

Mobile phone numbers Start with 6

International access code 00

Canary Islands country code 34 (same as Spain)

Island area codes Gran Canaria, Lanzarote and Fuerteventura 928; Tenerife, La Gomera, La Palma and El Hierro 922

National toll-free number 900

Time

The Canary Islands are on Greenwich Mean Time (GMT/UTC), plus an hour in summer for daylight-saving time. The islands keep the same time as the UK, Ireland and Portugal and are always an hour behind mainland Spain and most of Europe. Daylight-saving (summer) time starts on the last Sunday in March, when clocks are put forward one hour. Clocks are put back an hour on the last Sunday in October.

Australia During the Australian winter (Spanish summer), subtract nine hours from Australian Eastern Standard Time to get Canary Islands' time; during the Australian summer, subtract 10 hours.

US Canary Islands' time is US Eastern Time plus five hours and US Pacific Time plus eight hours.

Although the 24-hour clock is used in writing, you'll find people generally use the 12-hour clock in everyday conversations.

Toilets

Public toilets are not common and not always too pleasant. The easiest option is to wander into a bar or cafe and use its facilities. The polite thing to do is to make a small purchase, but you're unlikely to raise too many eyebrows if you don't. That said, some curmudgeonly places in popular tourist areas post notices saying that their toilets are for customers only.

The cautious carry some toilet paper with them when out and about as many toilets don't have it. If there's a bin beside the toilet, put paper and so on in it (there may be a sign in Spanish, English and German telling you to do so) – probably because the local sewage system has trouble coping.

Tourist Information

All major towns in the Canary Islands have a tourist office where you will usually get decent maps and information about sights and activities in the area. Though the Canarian government offers region-wide and island-specific information on its excellent website www.hola islascanarias.com, the tourist offices themselves are run by the *cabildos* (island governments) or *ayuntamientos* (town halls).

The major airports also have tourist offices and can usually assist with last-minute accommodation bookings.

Visas

Spain is one of the 26 member countries of the Schengen Convention, under which 22 EU countries (all but Bulgaria, Croatia, Cyprus, Ireland, Romania and the UK) plus Iceland, Liechtenstein, Norway and Switzerland have abolished checks at common borders.

The visa situation for entering Spain is as follows:

Citizens or residents of EU & Schengen countries No visa required.

Citizens or residents of Australia, Canada, Israel, Japan, NZ and the US No visa required for tourist visits of up to 90 days.

Other countries Check with a Spanish embassy or consulate.

To work or study in Spain A special visa may be required – contact a Spanish embassy or consulate before travel.

Extensions & Residence

Schengen visas are valid for 90 days and cannot be extended. Nationals of EU countries, Iceland, Norway and Switzerland can enter and leave the archipelago at will and don't need to apply for a *tarjeta de residencia* (residence card), although they are supposed to apply for residence papers if they are staying for longer than 90 days.

People of other nationalities who want to stay in Spain longer than 90 days have to get a residence card, and for them it can be a drawn-out process, starting with an appropriate visa issued by a Spanish consulate in their country of residence. Start the process well in advance.

Women Travellers

Harassment is much less frequent than the Spanish stereotypes would have you believe, and though the country has one of the developed world's lowest incidences of reported rape, there have been some high-profile cases of violence against women

in recent years in Spain. Any unpleasantness you might encounter is more likely to come from drunken Northern-European yobs in the big resorts than from the locals.

In towns you may get the occasional unwelcome stare, catcall or unnecessary comment, to which the best (and most galling) response is indifference. Don't get paranoid about what's being called out; the *piropo* – a mildly flirty compliment – is deeply ingrained in Spanish society (even though it will generally make women feel uncomfortable).

Topless bathing and skimpy clothes are generally OK at the coastal resorts, but otherwise a little more modesty is the norm, although lots of Spanish women bathe topless now.

Work

EU, Norway and Iceland nationals are allowed to work anywhere in Spain (including the Canary Islands) without a visa, but if they plan to stay more than three months they are supposed to apply within the first month for a residence card. Virtually everyone else is supposed to obtain (from a Spanish consulate in their country of residence) a work permit and, if they plan to stay more than 90 days, a residence visa. While jobs (especially in tourist resorts) aren't that hard to come by, the procedures necessary to get your paperwork in order can be difficult and time-consuming.

Transport

GETTING THERE & AWAY

Getting to the Canary Islands is a cinch. Low-cost carriers are plentiful from all over Europe, particularly from Germany, the UK and, of course, mainland Spain. Flights, tours and rail tickets can be booked online at www.lonelyplanet.com/bookings.

Entering the Canary Islands

Citizens of most EU member states, as well as Switzerland, can travel to the Canary Islands with just their national identity card. UK nationals – and all other nationalities – must have a full valid passport.

Check that your passport's expiry date is at least six months away, otherwise you may not be granted a visa, should you need one.

By law you are supposed to have your identity card or passport with you at all times in the Canaries, in case the police ask to see it. In practice, this is unlikely to cause trouble. You might want to carry a photocopy of your documentation instead of the real thing. You will need to flash one of these documents (the original, not the photocopy) for registration when you take a hotel room.

Air

All of Spain's airports share the user-friendly website and flight information telephone number of **Aena** (☑91 321 10 00; www.aena.es), the Spanish national airport authority.

Airports & Airlines

All seven major Canary Islands have airports. Tenerife, Gran Canaria, Lanzarote, Fuerteventura and, increasingly, La Palma absorb nearly all the direct international flights and those from mainland Spain, while the others are principally for inter-island hops.

The following main airports handle international flights:

Aeropuerto Tenerife Norte (Los Rodeos; ☑902 40 47 04, 922 63 56 35; www.aena.es; Los Rodeos) Handles just about all inter-island flights and most of those to the Spanish mainland.

Aeropuerto Tenerife Sur (Reina Sofía; ☑922 75 95 10; www.aena.es; Reina Sofía) Handles the remaining scheduled flights, and virtually all charter flights to the island.

Aeropuerto de Gran Canaria (☑913 21 10 00; www.aena.es; off GC-1) Located 16km south of Las Palmas.

Aeropuerto César Manrique–Lanzarote (www.aena.es) Located 6km southwest of the capital, Arrecife.

Aeropuerto de Fuerteventura (☑902 40 47 04; www.aena.es; El Matorral) Located 6km south of the capital, Puerto del Rosario.

Dozens of airlines, many of which you'll have never heard of, fly into the Canary Islands. There are direct flights to cities in Morocco, Senegal, Venezuela, Israel, Madeira and many other destinations; however, there are no nonstop flights from North America to the archipelago. Increasingly, there are flights into La Palma Airport, including flights from Gatwick (easyjet) and Manchester (Tui Airways) in the UK.

Sea

Just about every visitor flies into the Canaries; the only alternative is to take a ferry from mainland Spain.

DEPARTURE TAX

There is no departure tax in the Canary Islands at present. However, a sustainable tourism tax, similar to the tax levied on visitors to the Balearic Islands, was being considered at the time of writing to help finance environmental protection efforts and manage visitor numbers.

CLIMATE CHANGE & TRAVEL

Every form of transport that relies on carbon-based fuel generates CO_2, the main cause of human-induced climate change. Modern travel is dependent on aeroplanes, which might use less fuel per kilometre per person than most cars but travel much greater distances. The altitude at which aircraft emit gases (including CO_2) and particles also contributes to their climate change impact. Many websites offer 'carbon calculators' that allow people to estimate the carbon emissions generated by their journey and, for those who wish to do so, to offset the impact of the greenhouse gases emitted with contributions to portfolios of climate-friendly initiatives throughout the world. Lonely Planet offsets the carbon footprint of all staff and author travel.

Naviera Armas (☑902 45 65 00; www.navieraarmas.com) Runs a weekly service from Huelva on the Spanish mainland stopping at Arrecife (27 hours) on Lanzarote, Las Palmas de Gran Canaria (32 hours) and Santa Cruz de Tenerife (36 hours).

Trasmediterránea (☑902 45 46 45; www.trasmediterranea. com) Runs a weekly ferry service between Cádiz on the Spanish mainland and Santa Cruz de Tenerife (49 hours), with stops at Arrecife in Lanzarote (31 hours), Las Palmas de Gran Canaria (40 hours) and Santa Cruz de La Palma (64 hours).

GETTING AROUND

Air

Seven of the eight islands have airports, making flying the most comprehensive (and quickest) option if you intend to do some island-hopping. Binter Canarias is the long-standing airline, with a comprehensive network of flights and on certain routes (particularly in the western islands) some seriously tiny planes! Canary Fly and Air Europa Express also fly between most of the islands, usually with at least one transfer in Tenerife.

Boat travel from mainland Spain isn't cheap, and if you opt for a simple seat on the ship, you'll spend a similar amount reaching the Canaries as you would if you flew. If you want a cabin, boat travel

will be three to four times the price of a flight – and takes almost 10 times longer!

Air Europa Express (www. aireuropa.com) Flies from Tenerife to Gran Canaria, Fuerteventura, Lanzarote and La Palma.

Binter Canarias (☑902 39 13 92; www.bintercanarias.com) Flights to all islands.

Canary Fly (☑902 80 80 65; www.canaryfly.es) Covers Tenerife, La Palma, Gran Canaria and Lanzarote.

Bicycle

Biking around the islands is an extremely pleasant (and energetic) way to see the sights, and drivers on the whole are tolerant and patient with cyclists on the hilly roads of the Canary Islands (though you will find some impatience too). Sadly, bicycle lanes in the urban environment are minimal, although Las Palmas now has cycle lanes and beachside boulevards are increasingly incorporating space for bike riding.

If you plan to bring your own bike on a flight, check whether there are any extra costs and whether you'll need to disassemble and pack your bike for the journey. Taking your bike on ferries is pretty straightforward, and it's either free or very cheap.

Bicycle Hire

Bike hire is plentiful across all the islands, with a large number of bike shops selling and renting all manner of

bikes, including e-bikes as well as specialist equipment.

You can rent mountain bikes, city bikes and e-bikes at various resorts and in the more tourist-orientated areas of the islands. Expect to pay a minimum of €12 per day, with a standard deposit of around €50. Rental rates will include a helmet and some basic equipment. Some of these rental outfits also arrange guided bike tours as well.

To help tame its sprawling distances, Las Palmas de Gran Canaria has a public bike hire scheme called **Sitycleta** (www.sitycleta.com/es); look for the yellow and blue bikes dotted in stations around the city.

Boat

The islands are connected by ferries, 'fast ferries' and jetfoils.

Schedules and prices – and even routes – can and do change. This isn't so important on major routes, where there's plenty of choice, but it can mean a big delay if you're planning to travel a route that has only a couple of boats running per day, or even per week. If time is tight, flying is a much faster alternative (often with competitive prices).

The three main companies are as follows:

Fred Olsen (☑902 100107; www.fredolsen.es; ☺telephone enquiries 8am-8pm)

Naviera Armas (☑902 45 65 00; www.navieraarmas.com)

Trasmediterránea (☎902 45 46 45; www.trasmediterranea.com)

Bus

A bus in the Canary Islands is called a *guagua*, pronounced 'wa-wa'. If you've bounced around Latin America, you'll be familiar with the term. Still, if you ask about *autobuses*, you'll be understood.

Every island has its own interurban service. One way or another, they can get you to most of the main locations but, in many cases, there are few runs each day (except on the very popular routes) so you will need to plan ahead.

The larger islands of Tenerife and Gran Canaria have an impressive and efficient public-transport system covering the whole island. Frequency, however, varies enormously, from a regular service between major towns to a couple of runs per day for transporting workers and school children to/from the capital.

Check the timetable carefully before you travel on weekends. Even on the larger islands' major runs, a frequent weekday service can trickle off to just a few departures on Saturday and one, or none, on Sunday.

In the larger towns and cities, buses leave from an *estación de guaguas* (bus station). In villages and small towns, they usually terminate on a particular street or plaza. Buy your ticket on the bus.

Global (☎928 25 26 30; www.guaguasglobal.com) Provides Gran Canaria with a comprehensive network of routes, although services between rural areas are infrequent.

Guagua Gomera (☎922 14 11 01; www.guaguagomera.com; Estación de Guaguas, Avenida Vía de Ronda, San Sebastián) La Gomera's limited service operates seven lines across the island.

Intercity Bus Lanzarote (☎928 81 15 22; www.arrecifebus.com) A decent network covering Lanzarote's main points of interest.

Tiadhe (☎928 85 57 26; www.tiadhe.com) Provides a reasonable service, with 18 lines operating around Fuerteventura.

TITSA (Transportes Interurbanos de Tenerife SA; ☎922 53 13 00; www.titsa.com; ☺customer service 8am-8pm) Runs a spider's web of services all over Tenerife.

TransHierro (☎922 55 11 75; www.transhierro.es; Calle El Molino 14, Valverde; ☺7am-7pm) El Hierro's bus service has reasonable coverage throughout the island.

Transportes Insular La Palma (TILP; ☎922 41 19 24; www.tilp.es) Services La Palma with good overall coverage.

Bus Passes

On some of the islands you can buy a bus card that can get you a reduction on the ticket fare, but, although the cards used to net substantial discounts, now the discount is much lower (eg on Fuerteventura, you only receive a 5% discount, on Lanzarote this is 10%). The cards usually cost €2 and can be topped up in increments from a minimum of €5; buy them at bus stations and shops (such as newsagents). Usually you touch the card to the reader on the bus, tell the driver where you are going, and the fare will be deducted from the card. With the 30%-off Ten+ Travel Card on Tenerife, however, you tap in and tap out (remember to tap out or you will pay the full fare for the line). You can usually share a card with a fellow traveller. Las Palmas de Gran Canaria has also issued a **Live bus pass** (www.guaguas.com/tarifas-carnets/tarjeta-turistica) for use on city lines.

Costs

Fares are reasonable and maybe a little bit cheaper if you buy a transport card. Destinations within each island are calculated pro rata according to distance, so ticket fares vary from €1 for a short city hop to €10 or so for journeys of well over an hour (on the larger islands). La Palma

has introduced a standardised fixed bus distance tariff: up to 10km (€1.50), 10km to 20km (€2.40) and over 20km (€2.60).

It pays to have small notes and coins as change, as the bus driver may not be able to break a big note.

Car & Motorcycle

Renting a car in the Canaries is highly recommended, partly – if not largely – because driving may well count among your most memorable experiences on the islands. Bus services are great for journeys between major centres, but if you want to hop between smaller towns you might wait all day for the next bus. Exploring in depth is only really possible with your own wheels – unless you can afford to spend a full day and night in every *pueblo* (village) you happen across. Add to this the huge choice of alluring driving routes across the islands and hiring a car has rarely been more sensible.

Bringing Your Own Car

Unless you're intending to settle on the islands, there's no advantage whatsoever in bringing your own vehicle. Transport costs on the ferry from Cádiz in mainland Spain are high and car-hire rates on the islands are significantly cheaper than in most EU countries. If you're one of the very rare visitors to bring your own vehicle, you will need registration papers and an International Insurance Certificate (or a Green Card). Your insurance company will issue this.

Driving Licences

Although those with a non-EU licence should also have an International Driving Permit, you will find that national licences from countries like Australia, Canada, New Zealand and the USA are usually accepted.

A driving licence is required for any vehicle over 50cc.

Fuel

Gasolina (petrol) is much cheaper in the Canary Islands than elsewhere in Spain because it's not taxed as heavily. *Sin plomo* (lead-free) and *diesel* petrol are available everywhere with generally two grades on offer for each.

Prices vary slightly between petrol stations and fluctuate according to oil tariffs, Organisation of the Petroleum Exporting Countries (OPEC) arm twisting and tax policy. You can pay with major credit cards at most petrol stations.

Note that some petrol stations have attendants who will pump the gas for you while at others you'll have to get out and do it yourself.

Car Hire

All the big international car-rental companies are represented in the Canary Islands and there are also plenty of local operators. To rent a car you need to have a driving licence, be aged 21 or over and, for the major companies at least, have a credit card.

If you intend to stay on one island for any length of time, it might be worth booking a car in advance; for example, in a fly/drive deal. It's also a good idea to reserve in advance during high season or on the smaller islands where hire cars aren't as abundant. Note that the highest rental charges are taken up by the first three or four days and hiring the vehicle for a week instead may not make a huge amount of difference.

Generally, you're not supposed to take a hire car from one island to another without the company's explicit permission. An exception for most companies is the Fuerteventura–Lanzarote sea crossing – most have no problem with you taking your car from one to the other and, in some cases, you can hire on one island and drop the car off on the other.

Avis (☑902 24 88 24, 902 18 08 54; www.avis.es)

Cicar (☑928 82 29 00; www. cicar.com) Well-regarded local company that covers all the islands. Cicar is part of the Cabrera Medina group and offers the same conditions and rates.

Europcar (☑902 50 30 10, 911 50 50 00; www.europcar.es)

Insurance

Third-party motor insurance is a minimum requirement in the Canary Islands (and throughout Europe). Be careful to understand what your liabilities and excess are, and what waivers you are entitled to in case of accident or damage to the hired vehicle. Note that driving on a dirt road may render your policy null and void, so check with the car-hire firm. Larger international car-rental firms such as Avis tend to have a comprehensive vehicle insurance policy built into the quote, so you are pretty well covered for damage to the car, but check when you hire; other firms may give you the choice of leaving a deposit and needing to return the car in the same condition you drove it away in to reclaim that deposit, or comprehensive vehicle cover. If you take out the comprehensive vehicle cover, it may be the case that you end up with a car that has been knocked about more (as car-rental operators are less worried about further damage to it).

Road Rules

The blood-alcohol limit is 0.05% and random breath-testing is carried out. If you are found to be over the limit, you can be fined and deprived of your licence within 24 hours. Nonresident foreigners will be required to pay up on the spot (with a 30% to 50% discount on the full fine). Pleading linguistic ignorance will not help – your traffic cop will produce a list of infringements and fines in as many languages as you like. If you don't pay, or don't have a local resident to act as guarantor for you, your vehicle could be impounded.

Legal driving age for cars 18 years

Legal driving age for motorcycles & scooters 16 (80cc and over) or 15 (50cc and under) years; a licence is required.

Motorcyclists Must use headlights at all times and wear a helmet if riding a bike of 125cc or more.

Roundabouts (traffic circles) Vehicles already in the circle have the right of way.

Side of the road Drive on the right.

Speed limits In built-up areas: 50km/h, which increases to 100km/h on major roads and up to 120km/h on *autovias* (highways).

Hitching

Hitching is never entirely safe, and we don't recommend it. Travellers who hitch should understand that they are taking a small but potentially dangerous risk. People who do choose to hitch will be safer if they travel in pairs and let someone know where they are planning to go.

Hitching is illegal on *autovias*. Choose a spot where cars can safely stop before slipways or use minor roads. The going can be slow on the latter and traffic is often light.

Language

The language of the Canary Islands is Spanish (*español*), which many Spanish people refer to as Castilian (*castellano*) to distinguish it from the other tongues spoken in Spain – Catalan (*català*), Galician (*galego*), and Basque (*euskara*).

Spanish pronunciation is straightforward as there's a clear and consistent relationship between what's written and how it's pronounced. In addition, most Spanish sounds are pronounced the same as their English counterparts. The kh in our pronunciation guides is a guttural sound (like the 'ch' in the Scottish *loch*), ny is pronounced as the 'ni' in 'onion', and r is strongly rolled. Those familiar with Spanish might notice the Andalusian or even Latin American lilt of the Canarian accent – 'lli' is pronounced as y and the 'lisp' you might expect with 'z' and 'c' before vowels sounds more like s while the letter 's' itself is hardly pronounced at all – it sounds more like an 'h' – for example, Las Palmas sounds more like Lah Palmah. If you follow our coloured pronunciation guides (with the stressed syllables in italics) you'll be understood just fine.

Spanish nouns and the adjectives that go with them are marked for gender – feminine nouns generally end with -*a* and masculine ones with -*o*. Where necessary, both forms are given for the words and phrases in this chapter, separated by a slash and with the masculine form first, eg *perdido/a* (m/f).

When talking to people familiar to you or younger than you, use the informal form of 'you', *tú*, rather than the polite form *Usted*. The polite form is used in the phrases provided in this chapter; where both options are given, they are indicated by the abbreviations 'pol' and 'inf'.

BASICS

Hello.	Hola.	o·la
Goodbye.	Adiós.	a·dyos
How are you?	¿Qué tal?	ke tal
Fine, thanks.	Bien, gracias.	byen gra·syas
Excuse me.	Perdón.	per·don
Sorry.	Lo siento.	lo syen·to
Yes./No.	Sí./No.	see/no
Please.	Por favor.	por fa·vor
Thank you.	Gracias.	gra·syas
You're welcome.	De nada.	de na·da

My name is ...
Me llamo ...   me ya·mo ...

What's your name?
¿Cómo se llama Usted?   ko·mo se ya·ma oo·ste (pol)
¿Cómo te llamas?   ko·mo te ya·mas (inf)

Do you speak (English)?
¿Habla (inglés)?   a·bla (een·gles) (pol)
¿Hablas (inglés)?   a·blas (een·gles) (inf)

I (don't) understand.
Yo (no) entiendo.   yo (no) en·tyen·do

ACCOMMODATION

I'd like to book a room.
Quisiera reservar una   kee·sye·ra re·ser·var oo·na
habitación.   a·bee·ta·syon

How much is it per night/person?
¿Cuánto cuesta por   kwan·to kwes·ta por
noche/persona?   no·che/per·so·na

Does it include breakfast?
¿Incluye el desayuno?   een·kloo·ye el de·sa·yoo·no

I'd like a ...	Quisiera una	kee·sye·ra oo·na
room.	habitación ...	a·bee·ta·syon ...

WANT MORE?

For in-depth language information and handy phrases, check out Lonely Planet's *Spanish Phrasebook*. You'll find it at **shop.lonelyplanet.com**, or you can buy Lonely Planet's iPhone phrasebooks at the Apple App Store.

| single | individual | een·dee·vee·*dwal* |
| double | doble | *do*·ble |

campsite	terreno de cámping	te·*re*·no de *kam*·peeng
hotel	hotel	o·*tel*
guesthouse	pensión	pen·*syon*
youth hostel	albergue juvenil	al·*ber*·ge khoo·ve·*neel*

air-con	aire acondicionado	*ai*·re a·kon·dee·syo·*na*·do
bathroom	baño	*ba*·nyo
bed	cama	*ka*·ma
window	ventana	ven·*ta*·na

DIRECTIONS

Where's ...?
¿Dónde está ...? — *don*·de es·*ta* ...

What's the address?
¿Cuál es la dirección? — *kwal* es la dee·rek·*syon*

Could you please write it down?
¿Puede escribirlo, por favor? — *pwe*·de es·kree·*beer*·lo por fa·*vor*

Can you show me (on the map)?
¿Me lo puede indicar (en el mapa)? — me lo *pwe*·de een·dee·*kar* (en el *ma*·pa)

at the corner	en la esquina	en la es·*kee*·na
at the traffic lights	en el semáforo	en el se·*ma*·fo·ro
behind ...	detrás de ...	de·*tras* de ...
far away	lejos	*le*·khos
in front of ...	enfrente de ...	en·*fren*·te de ...
left	izquierda	ees·*kyer*·da
near	cerca	*ser*·ka
next to ...	al lado de ...	al *la*·do de ...
opposite ...	frente a ...	*fren*·te a ...
right	derecha	de·*re*·cha
straight ahead	todo recto	*to*·do *rek*·to

EATING & DRINKING

What would you recommend?
¿Qué recomienda? — ke re·ko·*myen*·da

What's in that dish?
¿Que lleva ese plato? — ke *ye*·va e·se *pla*·to

I don't eat ...
No como ... — no *ko*·mo ...

That was delicious!
¡Estaba buenísimo! — es·*ta*·ba bwe·*nee*·see·mo

To get by in Spanish, mix and match these simple patterns with words of your choice:

When's (the next flight)?
¿Cuándo sale (el próximo vuelo)? — *kwan*·do sa·le (el *prok*·see·mo *vwe*·lo)

Where's (the station)?
¿Dónde está (la estación)? — *don*·de es·*ta* (la es·ta·*syon*)

Where can I (buy a ticket)?
¿Dónde puedo (comprar un billete)? — *don*·de *pwe*·do (kom·*prar* oon bee·*ye*·te)

Do you have (a map)?
¿Tiene (un mapa)? — *tye*·ne (oon *ma*·pa)

Is there (a toilet)?
¿Hay (servicios)? — ai (ser·*vee*·syos)

I'd like (a coffee).
Quisiera (un café). — kee·*sye*·ra (oon ka·fe)

I'd like (to hire a car).
Quisiera (alquilar un coche). — kee·*sye*·ra (al·kee·*lar* oon *ko*·che)

Can I (enter)?
¿Se puede (entrar)? — se *pwe*·de (en·*trar*)

Could you please (help me)?
¿Puede (ayudarme), por favor? — *pwe*·de (a·yoo·*dar*·me) por fa·*vor*

Do I have to (get a visa)?
¿Necesito (obtener un visado)? — ne·se·*see*·to (ob·te·*ner* oon vee·*sa*·do)

Please bring the bill.
Por favor nos trae la cuenta. — por fa·*vor* nos *tra*·e la *kwen*·ta

Cheers!
¡Salud! — sa·*loo*

I'd like to book a table for ...	Quisiera reservar una mesa para ...	kee·*sye*·ra re·ser·*var* oo·na *me*·sa pa·ra ...
(eight) o'clock	las (ocho)	las (o·cho)
(two) people	(dos) personas	(dos) per·*so*·nas

Key Words

appetisers	aperitivos	a·pe·ree·*tee*·vos
bar	bar	bar
bottle	botella	bo·*te*·ya
bowl	bol	bol
breakfast	desayuno	de·sa·*yoo*·no

LANGUAGE EATING & DRINKING

cafe	café	ka·fe
children's menu	menú infantil	me·noo een·fan·teel
(too) cold	(muy) frío	(mooy) free·o
dinner	cena	se·na
food	comida	ko·mee·da
fork	tenedor	te·ne·dor
glass	vaso	va·so
highchair	trona	tro·na
hot (warm)	caliente	ka·lyen·te
knife	cuchillo	koo·chee·yo
lunch	comida	ko·mee·da
main course	segundo plato	se·goon·do pla·to
market	mercado	mer·ka·do
menu (in English)	menú (en inglés)	oon me·noo (en een·gles)
plate	plato	pla·to
restaurant	restaurante	res·tow·ran·te
spoon	cuchara	koo·cha·ra
supermarket	supermercado	soo·per·mer·ka·do
with/without	con/sin	kon/seen
vegetarian food	comida vegetariana	ko·mee·da ve·khe·ta·rya·na

corn	maíz	ma·ees
cucumber	pepino	pe·pee·no
fruit	fruta	froo·ta
grape	uvas	oo·vas
lemon	limón	lee·mon
lentils	lentejas	len·te·khas
lettuce	lechuga	le·choo·ga
mushroom	champiñón	cham·pee·nyon
nuts	nueces	nwe·ses
onion	cebolla	se·bo·ya
orange	naranja	na·ran·kha
peach	melocotón	me·lo·ko·ton
peas	guisantes	gee·san·tes
(red/green) pepper	pimiento (rojo/verde)	pee·myen·to (ro·kho/ver·de)
pineapple	piña	pee·nya
plum	ciruela	seer·we·la
potato	patata	pa·ta·ta
pumpkin	calabaza	ka·la·ba·sa
spinach	espinacas	es·pee·na·kas
strawberry	fresa	fre·sa
tomato	tomate	to·ma·te
vegetable	verdura	ver·doo·ra
watermelon	sandía	san·dee·a

Meat & Fish

beef	carne de vaca	kar·ne de va·ka
chicken	pollo	po·yo
duck	pato	pa·to
fish	pescado	pes·ka·do
lamb	cordero	kor·de·ro
pork	cerdo	ser·do
turkey	pavo	pa·vo
veal	ternera	ter·ne·ra

Fruit & Vegetables

apple	manzana	man·sa·na
apricot	albaricoque	al·ba·ree·ko·ke
artichoke	alcachofa	al·ka·cho·fa
asparagus	espárragos	es·pa·ra·gos
banana	plátano	pla·ta·no
beans	judías	khoo·dee·as
beetroot	remolacha	re·mo·la·cha
cabbage	col	kol
carrot	zanahoria	sa·na·o·rya
celery	apio	a·pyo
cherry	cereza	se·re·sa

Other

bread	pan	pan
butter	mantequilla	man·te·kee·ya
cheese	queso	ke·so
egg	huevo	we·vo
honey	miel	myel
jam	mermelada	mer·me·la·da
oil	aceite	a·sey·te
pasta	pasta	pas·ta
pepper	pimienta	pee·myen·ta
rice	arroz	a·ros
salt	sal	sal
sugar	azúcar	a·soo·kar
vinegar	vinagre	vee·na·gre

QUESTION WORDS

How?	¿Cómo?	ko·mo
What?	¿Qué?	ke
When?	¿Cuándo?	kwan·do
Where?	¿Dónde?	don·de
Who?	¿Quién?	kyen
Why?	¿Por qué?	por ke

Drinks

beer	cerveza	ser·ve·sa
coffee	café	ka·fe
(orange) juice	zumo (de naranja)	soo·mo (de na·ran·kha)
milk	leche	le·che
tea	té	te
(mineral) water	agua (mineral)	a·gwa (mee·ne·ral)
(red) wine	vino (tinto)	vee·no (teen·to)
(white) wine	vino (blanco)	vee·no (blan·ko)

EMERGENCIES

Help!	¡Socorro!	so·ko·ro
Go away!	¡Vete!	ve·te
Call ...!	¡Llame a ...!	ya·me a ...
a doctor	un médico	oon me·dee·ko
the police	la policía	la po·lee·see·a

I'm lost.
Estoy perdido/a. es·toy per·dee·do/a (m/f)

I had an accident.
He tenido un accidente. e te·nee·do oon ak·see·den·te

I'm ill.
Estoy enfermo/a. es·toy en·fer·mo/a (m/f)

It hurts here.
Me duele aquí. me dwe·le a·kee

I'm allergic to (antibiotics).
Soy alérgico/a a (los antibióticos). soy a·ler·khee·ko/a a (los an·tee·byo·tee·kos) (m/f)

SHOPPING & SERVICES

I'd like to buy ...
Quisiera comprar ... kee·sye·ra kom·prar ...

I'm just looking.
Sólo estoy mirando. so·lo es·toy mee·ran·do

May I look at it?
¿Puedo verlo? pwe·do ver·lo

I don't like it.
No me gusta. no me goos·ta

How much is it?
¿Cuánto cuesta? kwan·to kwes·ta

That's too expensive.
Es muy caro. es mooy ka·ro

Can you lower the price?
¿Podría bajar un poco el precio? po·dree·a ba·khar oon po·ko el pre·syo

There's a mistake in the bill.
Hay un error en la cuenta. ai oon e·ror en la kwen·ta

ATM	cajero automático	ka·khe·ro ow·to·ma·tee·ko

NUMBERS

1	uno	oo·no
2	dos	dos
3	tres	tres
4	cuatro	kwa·tro
5	cinco	seen·ko
6	seis	seys
7	siete	sye·te
8	ocho	o·cho
9	nueve	nwe·ve
10	diez	dyes
20	veinte	veyn·te
30	treinta	treyn·ta
40	cuarenta	kwa·ren·ta
50	cincuenta	seen·kwen·ta
60	sesenta	se·sen·ta
70	setenta	se·ten·ta
80	ochenta	o·chen·ta
90	noventa	no·ven·ta
100	cien	syen
1000	mil	meel

credit card	tarjeta de crédito	tar·khe·ta de kre·dee·to
internet cafe	cibercafé	see·ber·ka·fe
post office	correos	ko·re·os
tourist office	oficina de turismo	o·fee·see·na de too·rees·mo

TIME & DATES

What time is it?	¿Qué hora es?	ke o·ra es
It's (10) o'clock.	Son (las diez).	son (las dyes)
Half past (one).	Es (la una) y media.	es (la oo·na) ee me·dya

morning	mañana	ma·nya·na
afternoon	tarde	tar·de
evening	noche	no·che
yesterday	ayer	a·yer
today	hoy	oy
tomorrow	mañana	ma·nya·na

Monday	lunes	loo·nes
Tuesday	martes	mar·tes
Wednesday	miércoles	myer·ko·les
Thursday	jueves	khwe·bes
Friday	viernes	vyer·nes
Saturday	sábado	sa·ba·do
Sunday	domingo	do·meen·go

January	enero	e·ne·ro
February	febrero	fe·bre·ro
March	marzo	mar·so
April	abril	a·breel
May	mayo	ma·yo
June	junio	khoo·nyo
July	julio	khoo·lyo
August	agosto	a·gos·to
September	septiembre	sep·tyem·bre
October	octubre	ok·too·bre
November	noviembre	no·vyem·bre
December	diciembre	dee·syem·bre

TRANSPORT

Public Transport

boat	barco	bar·ko
bus	autobús	ow·to·boos
plane	avión	a·vyon
train	tren	tren
tram	tranvía	tran·vee·a
first	primer	pree·mer
last	último	ool·tee·mo
next	próximo	prok·see·mo

I want to go to ...
Quisiera ir a ... — kee·sye·ra eer a ...

Does it stop at (Vilaflor)?
¿Para en (Vilaflor)? — pa·ra en (vee·la·flor)

What stop is this?
¿Cuál es esta parada? — kwal es es·ta pa·ra·da

What time does it arrive/leave?
¿A qué hora llega/sale? — a ke o·ra ye·ga/sa·le

Please tell me when we get to (Arico Nuevo).
¿Puede avisarme — pwe·de a·vee·sar·me
cuando lleguemos — kwan·do ye·ge·mos
a (Arico Nuevo)? — a (a·ree·ko nwe·vo)

I want to get off here.
Quiero bajarme aquí. — kye·ro ba·khar·me a·kee

a ... ticket	un billete de ...	oon bee·ye·te de ...
1st-class	primera clase	pree·me·ra kla·se
2nd-class	segunda clase	se·goon·da kla·se
one-way	ida	ee·da
return	ida y vuelta	ee·da ee vwel·ta
aisle seat	asiento de pasillo	a·syen·to de pa·see·yo

cancelled	cancelado	kan·se·la·do
delayed	retrasado	re·tra·sa·do
platform	plataforma	pla·ta·for·ma
ticket office	taquilla	ta·kee·ya
timetable	horario	o·ra·ryo
train station	estación de trenes	es·ta·syon de tre·nes
window seat	asiento junto a la ventana	a·syen·to khoon·to a la ven·ta·na

Driving & Cycling

I'd like to hire a ...	Quisiera alquilar ...	kee·sye·ra al·kee·lar ...
4WD	un todo-terreno	oon to·do·te·re·no
bicycle	una bicicleta	oo·na bee·see·kle·ta
car	un coche	oon ko·che
motorcycle	una moto	oo·na mo·to
child seat	asiento de seguridad para niños	a·syen·to de se·goo·ree·da pa·ra nee·nyos
diesel	gasóleo	ga·so·lyo
helmet	casco	kas·ko
mechanic	mecánico	me·ka·nee·ko
petrol/gas	gasolina	ga·so·lee·na
service station	gasolinera	ga·so·lee·ne·ra

Is this the road to ...?
¿Se va a (La Laguna) — se va a (la la·goo·na)
por esta carretera? — por es·ta ka·re·te·ra

(How long) Can I park here?
¿(Por cuánto tiempo) — ¿(por kwan·to tyem·po)
Puedo aparcar aquí? — pwe·do a·par·kar a·kee

The car has broken down (at Masca).
El coche se ha averiado — el ko·che se a a·ve·rya·do
(en Masca). — (en mas·ka)

I have a flat tyre.
Tengo un pinchazo. — ten·go oon peen·cha·so

I've run out of petrol.
Me he quedado sin — me e ke·da·do seen
gasolina. — ga·so·lee·na

SIGNS

Abierto	Open
Cerrado	Closed
Entrada	Entrance
Hombres	Men
Mujeres	Women
Prohibido	Prohibited
Salida	Exit
Servicios/Aseos	Toilets

GLOSSARY

aljibe – water system
artesonado – coffered ceiling
autovía – motorway
ayuntamiento – town hall

barranco – ravine or gorge
barrio – district, quarter (of a town or city)
Bimbaches – indigenous Herreños
bocadillo – sandwich made with baguette bread
bodega – traditional wine bar, or a wine cellar
bote – local variety of shuttle boat developed to service offshore vessels
buceo – scuba diving

cabildo insular – island government
cabra – goat
cabrito – kid (goat)
caldera – cauldron
calle – street
cambio – exchange
cañadas – flatlands
Carnaval – festival celebrating the beginning of Lent, 40 days before Easter
casa rural – a village or country house or farmstead with rooms to let
caserío – traditional farmhouse or hamlet
catedral – cathedral
centro comercial – shopping centre, usually with restaurants, bars and other facilities for tourists
chiringuito – kiosk
churros – fried dough
comida – lunch
Corpus Christi – festival in honour of the Eucharist, held eight weeks after Easter
cruz – cross
cueva – cave

denominación de origen – appellation certifying a high standard and regional origin of wines and certain foods
desayuno – breakfast
drago – dragon tree

ermita – chapel
estación – terminal, station
estación de guaguas – bus terminal/station
estación marítima – ferry terminal

faro – lighthouse
feria – fair
fiesta – festival, public holiday or party
finca – farm

gofio – ground, roasted grain used in place of bread in Canarian cuisine
Gomeros – people from La Gomera
gran – great
guagua – bus
guanarteme – island chief
Guanches – the original inhabitants of the Canaries

Herreños – people from El Hierro
horario – timetable
hostal – commercial establishment providing accommodation in the one- to three-star range; not to be confused with youth hostels (of which there is only one throughout the islands)
hoteles – one- to five-star hotel

IGIC – Impuesto General Indirecto Canario (local version of value-added tax)
iglesia – church

jamón – cured ham

lagarto – lizard
laurisilva – laurel
librería – bookshop
lucha canaria – Canarian wrestling

malpaís – volcanic badlands
malvasía – Malmsey wine
marcha – action, nightlife, 'the scene'
mencey – Guanche king
menú del día – set menu
mercado – market
mesón – old-fashioned restaurant or tavern
mirador – lookout point
mojo – Canarian sauce made with either red chilli peppers, coriander or basil
montaña – mountain
Mudéjar – Islamic-style architecture
muelle – wharf or pier
municipio – town council
museo – museum, gallery

norte – north

Palmeros – people from La Palma
papas arrugadas – wrinkly potatoes
parador – chain of state-owned upmarket hotels
parque nacional – national park
paseo marítimo – seaside promenade
pensión – guesthouse (one-or two-star)
piscina – swimming pool
plateresque – silversmith-like
playa – beach
pozo – well
pueblo – village
puerto – port

GLOSSARY

ración – large tapas

romería – festive pilgrimage or procession

sabina – juniper

Semana Santa – Holy Week, the week leading up to Easter

señorío – island government deputising for the Spanish crown

s/n – *sin numero* (without number); sometimes seen in street addresses

sur – south

taberna – tavern

tapas – bar snacks originally served on a saucer or lid (*tapa*)

taquilla – box office

tasca – pub, bar

terraza – terrace; outdoor cafe tables

thalassotherapy – warm sea-water treatment designed to remove stress and physical aches

timple – type of ukulele and the musical symbol of the Canary Islands

Tinerfeños – people from Tenerife

valle – valley

vega – plain, flatlands

volcán – volcano

zumería – juice bar

Behind the Scenes

SEND US YOUR FEEDBACK

We love to hear from travellers – your comments keep us on our toes and help make our books better. Our well-travelled team reads every word on what you loved or loathed about this book. Although we cannot reply individually to your submissions, we always guarantee that your feedback goes straight to the appropriate authors, in time for the next edition. Each person who sends us information is thanked in the next edition – the most useful submissions are rewarded with a selection of digital PDF chapters.

Visit **lonelyplanet.com/contact** to submit your updates and suggestions or to ask for help. Our award-winning website also features inspirational travel stories, news and discussions.

Note: We may edit, reproduce and incorporate your comments in Lonely Planet products such as guidebooks, websites and digital products, so let us know if you don't want your comments reproduced or your name acknowledged. For a copy of our privacy policy visit lonelyplanet.com/privacy.

OUR READERS

Many thanks to the travellers who used the last edition and wrote to us with helpful hints, useful advice and interesting anecdotes:
Andrew Lelechenko, Charles Citroen, Christian Naenny, David Muir, David Smallwood, Gordon Parfitt, Jan Drenth, Jonathan O' Mahony, Joshua Lumsden, Kim Dorin, Lesley Bradnam, Louis Gempp, Marilú Paz, Neil Milner, Peter Rivers, Phillipa Tinant

AUTHOR THANKS

Isabella Noble

A huge *gracias* to everyone who made this Canarias update such a joy to work on. In Lanzarote, thanks to Tila, Michelle, Richard, Caroline, María, Gaspare, José and team, Faye, Andrew and all the other helpful conejeros. For La Gomera, thanks to Barbara, Christa, Thomas, Sandra, Adelaida, Isabel and, especially, Papi (for the great hikes). In El Hierro, *muchísimas gracias* to Idaira, Eva, Raico, Ida Inés, Carmelo and the Turismo El Hierro team. Finally, special thanks to my brilliant co-writer Damian Harper.

Damian Harper

Many thanks to Isabella Noble for all her support and good humour, gratitude to the ever-helpful Li Jiani and Arman, cheers also to Juan de la Vega, Damien, Carlos Brito, Olga Aresté, Ellen, Ling, Michele, Tim and Emma and everyone else along the way who made this trip such a fascinating journey of discovery.

ACKNOWLEDGMENTS

Climate map data adapted from Peel MC, Finlayson BL & McMahon TA (2007) 'Updated World Map of the Köppen-Geiger Climate Classification', Hydrology and Earth System Sciences, 11, 1633–44.
Cover photograph: Dragon tree and Teide, Cameris/Getty Images ©.

THIS BOOK

This 7th edition of Lonely Planet's *Canary Islands* guidebook was researched and written by Isabella Noble and Damian Harper. The previous edition was researched and written by Lucy Corne and Josephine Quintero. This guidebook was produced by the following:

Destination Editor
Tom Stainer

Senior Product Editors
Genna Patterson, Jessica Ryan

Product Editor
Amy Lynch

Regional Senior Cartographer
Anthony Phelan

Book Designer
Jessica Rose

Assisting Editors
Janet Austin, Daniel Bolger, Nigel Chin, Gabrielle Innes, Kate James, Lou McGregor, Fergus O'Shea, Gabrielle Stefanos, Sam Wheeler

Cover Researcher
Naomi Parker

Thanks to
Gwen Cotter, Sandie Kestell, Claire Rourke, Angela Tinson

Index

Map Pages **000**
Photo Pages **000**

Map Legend

Sights
- Beach
- Bird Sanctuary
- Buddhist
- Castle/Palace
- Christian
- Confucian
- Hindu
- Islamic
- Jain
- Jewish
- Monument
- Museum/Gallery/Historic Building
- Ruin
- Shinto
- Sikh
- Taoist
- Winery/Vineyard
- Zoo/Wildlife Sanctuary
- Other Sight

Activities, Courses & Tours
- Bodysurfing
- Diving
- Canoeing/Kayaking
- Course/Tour
- Sento Hot Baths/Onsen
- Skiing
- Snorkelling
- Surfing
- Swimming/Pool
- Walking
- Windsurfing
- Other Activity

Sleeping
- Sleeping
- Camping
- Hut/Shelter

Eating
- Eating

Drinking & Nightlife
- Drinking & Nightlife
- Cafe

Entertainment
- Entertainment

Shopping
- Shopping

Information
- Bank
- Embassy/Consulate
- Hospital/Medical
- Internet
- Police
- Post Office
- Telephone
- Toilet
- Tourist Information
- Other Information

Geographic
- Beach
- Gate
- Hut/Shelter
- Lighthouse
- Lookout
- Mountain/Volcano
- Oasis
- Park
- Pass
- Picnic Area
- Waterfall

Population
- Capital (National)
- Capital (State/Province)
- City/Large Town
- Town/Village

Transport
- Airport
- Border crossing
- Bus
- Cable car/Funicular
- Cycling
- Ferry
- Metro station
- Monorail
- Parking
- Petrol station
- S-Bahn/Subway station
- Taxi
- T-bane/Tunnelbana station
- Train station/Railway
- Tram
- U-Bahn/Underground station
- Other Transport

Routes
- Tollway
- Freeway
- Primary
- Secondary
- Tertiary
- Lane
- Unsealed road
- Road under construction
- Plaza/Mall
- Steps
- Tunnel
- Pedestrian overpass
- Walking Tour
- Walking Tour detour
- Path/Walking Trail

Boundaries
- International
- State/Province
- Disputed
- Regional/Suburb
- Marine Park
- Cliff
- Wall

Hydrography
- River, Creek
- Intermittent River
- Canal
- Water
- Dry/Salt/Intermittent Lake
- Reef

Areas
- Airport/Runway
- Beach/Desert
- Cemetery (Christian)
- Cemetery (Other)
- Glacier
- Mudflat
- Park/Forest
- Sight (Building)
- Sportsground
- Swamp/Mangrove

Note: Not all symbols displayed above appear on the maps in this book

OUR STORY

A beat-up old car, a few dollars in the pocket and a sense of adventure. In 1972 that's all Tony and Maureen Wheeler needed for the trip of a lifetime – across Europe and Asia overland to Australia. It took several months, and at the end – broke but inspired – they sat at their kitchen table writing and stapling together their first travel guide, *Across Asia on the Cheap*. Within a week they'd sold 1500 copies. Lonely Planet was born.

Today, Lonely Planet has offices in Franklin, London, Melbourne, Oakland, Dublin, Beijing and Delhi, with more than 600 staff and writers. We share Tony's belief that 'a great guidebook should do three things: inform, educate and amuse'.

OUR WRITERS

Isabella Noble

Lanzarote, El Hierro, La Gomera, Canary Islands Plan Chapters English-Australian on paper but Spanish at heart, Isabella has been wandering the globe since her first round-the-world trip as a one-year-old. Having grown up in a whitewashed Andalucian village, she is a Spain specialist travel journalist, but also writes extensively about India, Thailand, the UK and beyond for Lonely Planet, the *Daily Telegraph* and others. Isabella has co-written Lonely Planet guides to *Spain* and *Andalucía*, and is a *Daily Telegraph* Spain expert. She has also contributed to Lonely Planet *India, South India, Thailand, Thailand's Islands & Beaches, Southeast Asia on a Shoestring* and *Great Britain*, and authored *Pocket Phuket*. Find Isabella on Twitter and Instagram (@isabellamnoble).

Damian Harper

Tenerife, Gran Canaria, Fuerteventura, La Palma, Canary Islands Understand Chapters Born off the Strand within earshot of Bow Bells (favourable wind permitting), Damian grew up in Notting Hill way before it was discovered by Hollywood. A onetime Shakespeare and Company bookseller and radio presenter, Damian has been authoring guidebooks for Lonely Planet since the late 1990s. He lives in South London with his wife and two kids, and frequently returns to China (his second home).

Published by Lonely Planet Global Limited
CRN 554153
7th edition – Jan 2020
ISBN 978 1 78657 498 5
© Lonely Planet 2020   Photographs © as indicated 2020
10 9 8 7 6 5 4 3 2 1
Printed in China